Provincial Headz

Transcultural Music Studies

Series Editors
Simone Krüger Bridge, Liverpool John Moores University
Britta Sweers, University of Bern

Monographs and edited collections on contemporaneous explanations surrounding the nature of music and human beings in a (post-)global world. Books in this series encompass a comprehensively wide selection of subject matters alongside a shared interest in fieldwork—physical, virtual, historical—and its complex challenges and fascinations in a postcolonial age. Topics include music's use in social, collective and psychological life; musical individuals; music in globalization and migration; music education; music, ethnicity and gender; and environmental issues.

Published
Cultural Mapping and Musical Diversity
Edited by Britta Sweers and Sarah Ross

The Lifetime Soundtrack: Music and Autobiographical Memory
Lauren Istvandity

Forthcoming
Bikutsi: A Beti Dance Music on the Rise, 1970–1990
Anja Brunner

Türkü and Halay between Gent and Turkey: Turkish Folk Music in a Transnational Context
Liselotte Sels

Provincial Headz
British Hip Hop and Critical Regionalism

Adam de Paor-Evans

SHEFFIELD UK   BRISTOL CT

Published by Equinox Publishing Ltd.

UK: Office 415, The Workstation, 15 Paternoster Row, Sheffield, South Yorkshire, S1 2BX
USA: ISD, 70 Enterprise Drive, Bristol, CT 06010

www.equinoxpub.com

First published 2020

© Adam de Paor-Evans 2020

All rights reserved. No part of this publication may be reproduced or transmitted in any form or by any means, electronic or mechanical, including photocopying, recording or any information storage or retrieval system, without prior permission in writing from the publishers.

British Library Cataloguing-in-Publication Data
A catalogue record for this book is available from the British Library.

ISBN-13 978 1 78179 644 3 (hardback)
978 1 78179 645 0 (paperback)
978 1 78179 646 7 (ePDF)

Library of Congress Cataloging-in-Publication Data
Names: Paor-Evans, Adam de, author.
Title: Provincial headz : British hip hop and critical regionalism / Adam de Paor-Evans.
Description: South Yorkshire ; Bristol, CT : Equinox Publishing, 2020. | Series: Transcultural music studies | Includes bibliographical references and index.
Identifiers: LCCN 2019021252 (print) | LCCN 2019022244 (ebook) | ISBN 9781781796443 (hb) | ISBN 9781781796450 (pb)
Subjects: LCSH: Rap (Music)--Great Britain--History and criticism. | Hip-hop--Great Britain--History--20th century.
Classification: LCC ML3531 .P37 2020 (print) | LCC ML3531 (ebook) | DDC 782.4216490941--dc23
LC record available at https://lccn.loc.gov/2019021252
LC ebook record available at https://lccn.loc.gov/2019022244

Typeset by S.J.I. Services, New Delhi, India

For Huw

Contents

Acknowledgements	ix
Preface: I Owe Hip Hop	xi
Introduction	1
Chapter 1: The Location of Hip Hop: The Provincial, Spatial, Sonic, Material and Non-material	13
Chapter 2: The Relocation of Hip Hop: The Perfect Beat, Duck Rock and Cultural Acquisition	34
Chapter 3: The Territories of Hip Hop: Domesticity, Occupation and Appropriation	79
Chapter 4: The Consumption of Hip Hop: Commercialization, Distinction and the Subaltern	124
Chapter 5: The Production of Hip Hop: Process, Empowerment and Cultural Repositioning	171
Chapter 6: The Identity of Hip Hop: Reality, Image and a State of Mind	223
Conclusions: Critical De-regionalism, Dispelling the Myth and Revealing the Invisible	272
Notes	290
Bibliography	315
Glossary of Terms	326
Index	331

Acknowledgements

There are a number of important people who have aided, influenced and supported me through the making of this book, and of equal importance are those that have helped me shape not only my research agenda, but helped shape me as a Bboy, a student, a researcher, a teacher and an academic. Without all of these people, the fruits that this book bears would be not so sweet. I am hugely indebted to the headz that gave time, words, artefacts, photographs and insights through the interviews. Thanks to Simon "Specifik" Frankland, Rola, Kilo, Eraze, Remer, GeeSwift, Neil Taylor, Michael "Spider" Hooper, DJ Format, Brent Aquasky, DJ Rumage, Figure of Speech, Whirlwind D, Darren Norris aka Big Tunes D, Dr. Krome, Evil Ed, Matt/Junior Disprol, Ricky Also, Steve Rider, Scott Coombes, Uncle Mic Nitro, MCM/Caveman, Stepchild, Mike Mac, DJ Bex, Dren Throwdown, Parker, Mark Cowan (DJ Science), Remark, DJ Smiz/DJ Krash Slaughta, Si Spex/Barry Beats, MC Squared, Nice One, Uncle Colin—The Funky Diabetic, Cobra P.I. (Agent/Rapid Fire), Craig Ellis Leckie (Mr. Peace Unity Love and Havin' Fun), Richie B, Herbie, ShelltoeMel, Nathan Loynes (Nat Drastic), Chrome of Chrome and Illinspired and DefTex, Kit (YML), Ross Adams, Simon Denny, Tom Dartnell, Sleician Cullen/Slicerman (formerly Dek Masha-Slicer Man of the Headcase Ladz and Goatboy), Ben Hughes aka Dr Syntax, Jackie Chat, DJ Baila, Rawman, Havoc, Requiem89, Krissy Kriss, Benny Bronx, Such, Scarse, AJ and DJ Mada from Hardnoise (respect also to Gemini (RIP), Son, Nyce D (RIP), TLP1), Jon Tansley AKA Johnny Scratch, and DJ Jamez Gant, who collectively gave up hours in conversation, discussion, written correspondence and photographs of all thing hip hop and provided me with countless stories, ideas and acumen. Thanks to Jay Tomkins for pointing me towards certain photographic sources. To Justin A. Williams and Ewa Mazierska for their critical feedback and continued support, thank you. Thanks also to Equinox Publishing Ltd. who have been a pleasure to work with. Many thanks to Ann at The Rope Walk, Bristol, and B-Line Recordings for hosting the legendary ROPE-A-DOPE festivals where academia, practice and pure hip hop truly synergize, in the promotion and pursuit of the fifth core element of hip hop: knowledge. As you will discover through this monograph, it is not possible to separate one's personal life from research when it comes to the hip hop state of mind—so these thanks are both personal and professional: Peace and love to the entire South Side Alliance (SSA my crew from back in the day), and to Blade—thank you for the conversations and the inspirational moments. Deepest appreciation to Ruth Manuva for her relentless transcribing and communication with contributors, to the hip hop folks I have met, worked with, and who have had an impact on my past 37 years of involvement in this beautiful culture—and extended gratitude to my brothers Specifik and Rola—hip hop for me would never have been the same without these two unsung heroes of British hip hop, thank you. Finally, to Fiona for her fabulous support, love and encouragement, I am eternally grateful.

Preface:
I Owe Hip Hop

I had been thinking of writing a book about hip hop for longer than I care to remember. The breadth and depth of this incredible thing called hip hop offered up a challenge when considering what approach I might take, what period I might study, and what value would be gained from writing it—then I remembered the age-old tip "start with what you know". I first discovered hip hop in the summer of 1983, as a 12-year-old about to start "big school" in Devon, a low-populated, very green and coastal county in the South-West corner of the UK. Positioned approximately four hours' drive from London and two from Bristol (the nearest major city with any form of multiculturalism), it may seem an unlikely place for an indoctrination into hip hop culture. I had seen a very short television report at the close of the national news one Saturday lunchtime about this new craze called breakdancing, and the following week I witnessed a couple of my peers at school trying it. At the village youth centre on Tuesday night, one of the older lads was body popping to Kraftwerk's 'The Model' (1981) and Malcolm McLaren and the World's Famous Supreme Team's 'Buffalo Gals' (1982), much to the amusement of the village girl gang. He wore white gloves, baggy jeans with too many zips and elasticated bottoms (they were like the prototype to cargo pants), and black boxing boots with white stripes and white laces. I was mesmerized, and I wanted in.

I began going to this youth club in the village hall every week, as I had this mad crush…on hip hop. I needed to get in with the lads who looked after the club's vinyl and disco equipment (a 1970s double-console with BSR belt-drive decks). After a couple of weeks, I was allowed (by my older peers) to flick through the records and choose some of them for the lads to play. I remember vividly selecting records by Kraftwerk, McLaren, Break Machine, and Grandmaster Flash, and by the summer of 1984 they allowed me to play records. I was the 13-year-old gimmick at the village disco, digging as deep as I could in the chart-generated racks, playing records by Miami Sound

Machine, Harold Faltermeyer, Ollie and Jerry, and my top choice, 'Reckless' by Chris "The Glove" Taylor featuring Ice-T which fortunately had found its way onto the flipside of Carol Lynn Townes' '99½'. I also began buying my own records. The first hip hop record I bought was *Street Sounds Electro 1*, which I still love to this day. I started taking the bus into Exeter (the nearest city, although small at a population of barely 100,000) to buy one record a week with the wages from my newspaper round. Over the next year, I built up a collection of *Street Sounds Electro*, Tommy Boy Records and Jive compilations, and the occasional 12″ single by artists like Fat Boys, West Street Mob, and Kurtis Blow. Pickings were thin; hip hop records were not widely distributed in these greener parts of the country (and those that were stocked in retail outlets existed in sparse numbers), so I had to take my chances. It was in late 1984 that I met Rola and our would-be producer (with whom I would later form Ill Beat Productions and Def Defiance—Rola still produces and engineers hip hop records for a huge number of independent artists), and in early 1987 we connected with the hip hop headz[1] in Exeter.

Hip hop remains a major part of my life—through university, jobs, relocations, and in my career so far as an academic, which is where the story of this book begins. As a cultural theorist, I have taught cultural context across many disciplines, and so for my research path to lead me back to the practices embedded within hip hop was a natural progression. As the work that follows explores, ideas of transdisciplinary and multidisciplinary are located both within hip hop practice and hip hop studies; in turn this book feeds back into discipline areas as an interdisciplinary agent for dialogue that cuts across the fields of architecture, sociology, musicology and ethnomusicology, cultural studies, urban design, fine art and visual communication. When I discovered that hip hop studies was becoming "a thing", I revisited the historic work of Castleman and Toop; later Chang, and absorbed the critical writings of Tricia Rose and Murray Forman, while I was forming my own research questions based on my reading of theorists such as Lefebvre, Bhabha, Bourdieu, Foucault, Virilio, and DeLanda. The organic pool of hip hop gradually funnelled into a small receptacle, and I returned back to my village to write about hip hop in the sticks.

My reasons for writing *Provincial Headz* are threefold. First, I wanted to anchor hip hop's transatlantic journey from New York City to the British provinces, unearth the processes of hip hop's nascent and formative years in Britain, and discover more about its growth during what I consider the opening period of non-urban hip hop in Britain, 1983–1994. Second, I wanted to explore the triad of consumer-practitioner-producer and attempt to locate and reveal the shift from hip hop permeating Britain to British hip hop as a genre-defining culture. Third, I sought to expose the invisibility of processes of hip hop outside the city and exemplify non-urban British hip hop as important genius loci for the continual and critical development of hip hop culture, and confirm its value in supporting hip hop headz in everyday life. The book is not an historic survey, nor is it a complete and chronological account of British hip hop, but rather acts as a kind of benchmark for discussing the non-obvious critical practices in regional hip hop. There are contributions and representations made from such places as Northern Ireland, Scotland, Tyneside, East Anglia, Dorset, Hampshire, Devon, Cornwall, Glamorgan and South Wales, Somerset and Gloucestershire. Although representations from the South-West are denser than others and there are areas not represented in the book, this is not intended to deny the life of hip hop in these other non-urban places. Moreover, it features interviews with lesser-known as much as well-known artists and practitioners, as I wanted to illustrate the inclusiveness of hip hop practice and reach beyond the canon of what is now commonly labelled: "UK hip hop".

Since its first reiterations in the late 1970s, hip hop culture has been incredibly inclusive and diverse. As vehicles for expression, the very malleability of its practices is fundamental to its continual life as a culture that responds to a plethora of contexts. *Provincial Headz* addresses one such set of contexts, and while it challenges conventional urban-rural and commercial-conscious binaries, I wanted to comment on what I consider to be a unique relationship that evolved in the world of provincial British 1980s hip hop. The vehicles that initially brought hip hop to the remote and rural parts of Britain either diverted, cloaked or made invisible the black cultures that created it. Until the television screening of the documentary *Beat This!: A Hip Hop History* in July 1984 (and keeping mindful that not all provincial headz would have watched this), there had been 19 months of nationwide breakdancing frenzy since Malcolm McLaren—the ginger-haired white Englishman with a quintessentially Scottish name—had synergized and popularized hip hop's elements for provincial consumption in December 1982. There had also been the release of *Street Sounds Electro 1, 2, 3, 4, Crucial Electro 1*, and *UK Electro*—six monumental compilation albums that, through their graphic presentation, created a visual diversion from any concrete representations of the histories of hip hop or black culture.[2] Furthermore, the very omission of the term "hip hop" from any of its cultural processes during those significant 19 months removed its sensibilities further from provincial

British consumers.[3] Ultimately, the initial consumption of hip hop culture in the provinces was a consumption of the unknown by the unknowing.

In *Provincial Headz*, I describe the primary record releases that carried the culture through Britain as reifications of hip hop as they represented the key concepts of the elements. Yet rather than to truly reify—that is, to make the intangible heritage of hip hop more concrete—many of these representations generated more abstraction, especially from notions of blackness and the black diasporas. The presence of blackness became evident through publications, such as Clare Muller's photographs in *Break Dancing* by Lucy Alford (1984) which features step-by-step tuition by dancers Colin and Venol, and *The Street Scene* magazine (launched in October 1985) which featured a page focusing on hip hop called "Electro Talk" (still no mention of "hip hop" in the title) and at last contained photographs of black artists such as Sparky D, Fat Boys, and the UK's own Hardrock Soul Movement. As producing albums became more commonplace by hip hop artists, UK labels acquired licences to many of these, and by 1985, albums embellished by artists' photographs including Fat Boys, LL Cool J, Run-D.M.C., Mantronix, Newcleus, and Schoolly D occupied most provincial record shops. Although many European compilations persisted with sleeve designs misrepresenting or devoid of black culture (*Rap Attack 3* [Polarvox Oy/Elephant Records], *We Will Rap You* [Sugar Hill Records], and *Rap Attack* [Jive]), 1985 was a pivotal year for provincial headz to navigate the mimesis of hip hop; more greatly engaged headz were beginning to wake up to the truth about the roots of hip hop.

Paramount to the consumption-driven slow awakening was the navigation, negotiation and contestation of the white majority landscape—for example the foyer of Barclays Bank, in Exeter, Devon, where Bboys used to break on Saturdays (discussed in Chapter 3). It is interesting that Barclays Bank was initiated in 1690 by goldsmith-bankers John Freame and Thomas Gould, during the same era as the invention of the double-ownership concept that remains central to contemporary banking (Kim 2011). I would argue that the double-ownership of capital (represented by paper money invented by goldsmith-bankers) is metaphorically evident in the semi-public spaces of the loggia. Here, a suggested shared ownership of space by both banker and patron expresses the capital and trust of the bank; however it is open enough to imply all are welcome to use the space, illustrating a sense of welcoming generosity. Yet, when this space was invaded by headz on Saturday afternoons, occupation becomes problematic. Is this spatial invasion problematic because of its content: loud hip hop music and breakdancing, or because of its context: the space is being occupied in such a way that it breaks western conventions? I would propose that it is both of these things. The performative content drives a powerful dispute of white majority space; the embedded narratives of hip hop, created in The Bronx and replayed through an amplified sound system, contests the provincial British bank foyer. Concurrently, the headz breakdancing in the foyer brought a sense of spatial immediacy, a challenge to the capitalist fallacy of double-ownership. Hip hop culture subsumed provincial headz, and through their actions provincial headz subsumed white majority space. The commercial cooption of hip hop was not on headz' agenda, claiming territory was. Spatial contestations of this nature fostered a grassroots multiculturalism that took its form from evolving provincial British hip hop and challenged the invisible but institutional, structured racism that we witnessed and experienced as dwellers in a rural remoteness. It is this experience of an underground form of rural-regional multiculturalism and belonging which pushed against the grain of institutional and nation-state structures that hip hop gave me.

We are entering a truly exciting time in the development of hip hop studies. While this relatively new field is becoming more established in the US, academics are only recently entering discussions here in the UK and Europe. Scholars such as Justin A. Williams, James McNally, J. Griffith Rollefson, Laura Speers, Monique Charles, Richard Bramwell, and Alex Stevenson are championing the study of hip hop in Britain, Ireland and further afield, and so too in further parts of Europe by Konstantinos Avramidis, Adriana Helbig and Milosz Miszczynski. Furthermore, practitioners Carpetface, Specifk, Kilo, Krissy Kris, Whirlwind D, Juice Aleem and many others are engaging in discussions as we attempt to unify practice and academia to address the challenges of society; and there should be no demography that the positive practices of hip hop culture cannot reach.

At The Rope Walk, Bristol, 3–4 November 2017, Dorset-based label B-Line Recordings hosted the second of their mini ROPE-A-DOPE hip hop festivals. The aim of these events is to cover all elements of hip hop culture, and B-Line director Specifik had invited Carpetface and I to convene discussion panels, focusing on hip hop supporting hard-to-reach communities and the emergence of British hip hop respectively. This invite was hugely welcomed, and we perceived this not only as a willingness for the world of practice to engage with academia, but also as an opportunity to further represent the fifth element of hip hop: knowledge. Here I met with Justin A. Williams, which was the catalyst for the one-day symposium "On Hip Hop: Criticality, Engagement and Praxis" as part of the third ROPE-A-DOPE festival, held

3–4 March 2018. Following a fruitful day of talks and discussions with many of the people mentioned above, I am hopeful that new projects taking new directions will be carried forward, and we can continue to build the arena of hip hop studies within academia and in broader society with rigour, significance and purpose.

Over the past four decades hip hop culture has offered me friendships, community, support, and an alternative, grounded and broader education; it has helped me question, build my confidence, and keep my mind fresh and inquiring. I hope that this book offers some small contribution and will also be of value to this significant, emerging, interdisciplinary field.

Hip hop does not owe me, I owe hip hop.

Adam de Paor-Evans
Spring 2019

Introduction

It is my intention in this book to detail the ways in which hip hop arrived in Britain from New York, and to argue that the provincial practitioners of British hip hop developed a critically regional and de-regional counter-culture that responded to both American hip hop and ideas of Britishness. By focusing on the provinces, I will also evidence the existence and importance of hip hop practice outside Britain's megalopolises, dispelling the myth that hip hop operates under purely urban conditions. Furthermore, I will attest that the practices in such non-urban places equipped headz with contextual frameworks with which to realize their potential for greater critical engagement in both hip hop practice and in everyday life. Why should the non-urban of British hip hop come under investigation now? What are the future benefits of a study situated in the margins of space and culture some thirty years ago? Why should it be distinct from its inner-city context? In fact, a complete survey of British hip hop is still to be done (and is very much necessary), but to answer these immediate questions, this study is crucial to the future practices of hip hop in order to defend its position as a creative, flexible and sustainable culture, one that can operate in contexts of permanence and transience, stability and instability, economic growth or depression. Hip hop is a rich form of creative practice that is not exclusively contained within the imagined silo of the city that urban epistemology would have us believe. This is a field which until now remains academically uncharted and unexplored, and as such the content of this book aims to change the way in which the spatio-cultural landscape of hip hop is considered, how hip hop history is constructed, and how we think about the humanity of hip hop culture through the everyday. Although the contexts for the analyses that follow are largely located in the geographies of the British provinces, it is my ultimate aim that the lines of inquiry explored throughout this book—which act as an introduction to the idea of provincial British hip hop—are of significant value to be of use within other geographical, demographical, political, cultural and environmental contexts.

In order to frame this study, it is important to locate the beginnings of hip hop culture in New York and provide insight to the four original practice-based elements that became the cornerstones of hip hop—these being graffiti, rap, turntablism and Bboying—and how their praxes interrelate.[1] What are also explored here are the nuances within each element (particularly the differences between rap and hip hop in terms of music), and the dialectics between their representations. The depth of exploration between all elements exist to a lesser degree on an academic stage, which tends to favour a focus on either rap music or graffiti, rather than attempt to explore an entire hip hop context throughout an investigation. However, Tricia Rose provides superbly insightful connections between hip hop's elements under the themes of flow, layering and rupture within the context of postindustrial New York, and attests the styles of hip hop relate strongly to Afrodiasporic cultural expression (see Rose 1994). Murray Forman also offers a rich human geography of the 'hood and the ghetto, and the multi-layered complexities of space and place in hip hop culture (see Forman 2002). Both Rose and Forman's work are taken somewhat as a point of departure for my own investigations in this book. The birth of hip hop has been documented extensively by others (Castleman 1982; Toop 1985; Chang 2007; Gastman and Neelon 2010), and the purpose of this proviso is not purely to chronicle the course of conventional hip hop history, but to introduce the complex non-materiality of hip hop culture which operated with a multitude of values, relationships and tactics. Any tactical approach to hip hop depended greatly on specific situations, and the values embedded in this non-material thinking generated a composite belief system that became the underpinning for hip hop culture. Within the culture, this belief system has become known as "a hip hop state of mind", rooted in black thought, African and Caribbean diasporic history, championed by the Afrofuturist work of Afrika Bambaataa and developed expeditiously but somewhat subconsciously during the decade between 1973 and 1983. This was often ambiguous, at times contradictory yet incredibly multifarious. Hip hop continued to reinvent its parts collaboratively, independently and tangentially yet with all its associated material and non-material production and practice it remained robust and retained a particular identity. Its outputs were variable yet its quality assessable, its actions often spoke louder than words, and concurrently its words often spoke stronger than its actions. In 2019, the culture of hip hop can be read as a palimpsest, the result of 46 years of layering and development, which with the complexity of time has led to somewhat of a hip hop identity crisis, some part of which will attempt to be unpacked in this book.

What is also paramount to state, and despite its celebrated multiculturality, is that hip hop is first and foremost a culture created by the black community. As hip hop culture has morphed, evolved and been reinvented in a multiplicity of contexts worldwide, respect to the 1970s pioneers in New York must be acknowledged for their ingenious approach to music, dance and visual art. Furthermore, respect also needs to be extended to the families, communities and neighbourhoods of our hip hop pioneers, for their resolve in building a robust provincial framework in the face of oppression and destitution. Whatever the various global hip hop communities have become since that decade, they owe these people. It is crucial also to document here that when hip hop arrived in Britain, its context and history was little known, with an almost nil existence in the white majority provinces. At various points through the book, observations, ideas and connections are drawn back to black cultural heritage. The value of this cannot be underestimated, not only in terms of hip hop culture itself but in terms of how black histories, values and cultural practices became embedded within a new form of hip hop in provincial and white majority locations. While the major context is provincial Britain 1983–1994, many of the narratives explored here offer an extended and occasionally alternative position to the histories of New York hip hop culture. The politics of space and community building is critical in understanding the provincial perspective that this book defines, a perspective no more parochial than the young black men and women in the 1970s South Bronx who defined hip hop.

In the introduction to *Black Noise*, Rose states with conviction that her work "which grounds black cultural signs and codes in black culture and examines the polyvocal languages of rap as the 'black noise' of the late twentieth century—will foster the development of more globally focused projects" (1994: xiv). Indeed, *Black Noise* serves as an inspiration and a partial point of departure for *Provincial Headz* (although I would not refer to my book as globally focused), which I hope grounds the syncretic development of the cultural signs and codes of a transatlantic form of hip hop and reveals the previously invisible impact of African-American culture on the remote provinces of 1980s Britain. Here, I also want to disgorge the myth that the demographic of headz in provincial Britain during the 1980s was solely of white origin, and in my experience were also represented by Black British, Indian, Pakistani, Middle Eastern and Asian minorities. Parallel experiences were reflected back to me through many conversations with the headz I spoke to during the writing of this book.[2]

I have not stated the individual ethnic origins of those I interviewed, but all interviewees are from either white, black, or mixed ethnic backgrounds. I wrestled with myself for months about whether I should address this at all, but to deny this fact would suggest colour-blindness. Jason Rodriquez (2006) discusses the ideology of colour-blindness in the terrain of white hip hop fans in Massachusetts and Rhode Island, where he argues that the privilege carried by whites enables them to appropriate hip hop for their own purposes. Believing that race does not matter inflicts harm on minority groups, denying negative racial experiences and invalidating cultural heritages. In rural Britain, headz identified each other through similarity and the strangely familiar, and pulled together to form crews and alliances that would turn out to be the first true multicultural society of the remote British provinces. Spread across wide, remote hip hop terrains, these crews recognized and valued cultural and class difference, and utilized these differences to challenge institutional inequality, albeit on a small scale. Small these interventions may have been, but the latent multiculturalism that was nurtured in provincial British 1980s hip hop resisted the racial and class status quo, and to this end, was a progressive rather than pedestrian form of hip hop. Evolving through landscapes of extremes, it developed its own fluid model across a ten-year period, quite different to that of the metropolises.

Methodology

The research methodology used in this book explores its field through ethnographic and autoethnographic study, artefact, product, interview and personal communication analysis with literature review, and here I would like to expand on some of these methods. The book has as its main concern the emergence of non-urban, British hip hop during the period 1983–1994, and this era is explored as it offers a slice of time when the most transformative practices in provincial British hip hop occurred. Beyond a relatively small number of interviews with artists and even fewer overviews written on the emergence of British hip hop in the music press and magazines from that time, the subject has undergone very limited academic study. Additionally, the only accounts that document provincial British hip hop were limited to short video clips and newspaper reports mainly connected to graffiti vandalism or fashion and trends, occasionally supported by a rudimentary description of hip hop, and offer very little by way of critical inquiry. There are no historical documents that detail the internal, domestic, local or regional practices of hip hop. As this field remains unexplored and undocumented until now, the search for primary research resulted in an alternative collection of sources that include a number of artefacts and products—namely records, cassettes, flyers and posters—which, created during the period of study are an inherent part of hip hop, and remain uncompromised by the passing of time and, as yet, unreferenced by academics. The sounds and lyrics embedded within these recordings were manufactured with realism of the moment and within certain contexts by practising proponents of British hip hop, which provide a solid base for interpretation. Particular artwork from record sleeves, cassette inlay cards, flyers and posters are paramount to the sonics, certainly in the case of lo-fi self-released artefacts, where the artwork was executed by crew members themselves or their peers, often graffiti writers. This provides a platform to explore the intimate relationship between hip hop's elements on a domestic-local scale, with many of these self-releases (mainly cassettes) limited by funds, equipment and time to runs of less than a hundred copies.[3] Much of the visual material incorporates drawings, collage, montage and font (all of which are explored in relation to the core themes of material culture and production), and a further, critical primary source is that of the photograph. These photographs speak a certain language, were not taken by professional photographers, but by advocates, participants and practitioners of hip hop culture, and as such document the actions directly and without artistic framing. In this way, they provide a trustworthy sense of the genuine appropriate for interpretive analysis.

The artefact analyses are interrogated in relation to the ethnographic study which draws upon accounts, semi-structured and unstructured interviews and conversations with headz active in that era, most of whom remain practitioners of one or more hip hop element. I considered it critical to allow the interview sessions to run freely and those in conversations to talk openly, offering as much as they desired, with care of judgement carried out in the editing process to ensure they contribute in addressing the research questions and avoid any misrepresentations that could be construed as historical fact. Some of these conversations have taken place over a period of seven years, and have subsequently been followed up through personal communications since the formal interviews during 2017. Self-image, ideology, ego and knowledge of self are central themes in hip hop culture, and this self-portrayal is often emitted autonomously or consciously, and while this is interesting in itself and deserves exploration, further discernments have been made when analysing and editing interview data to reduce any self-portrayal that might lie outside the remit of this inquiry. Furthermore, of absolute importance is the "wokeness" of the interviewees—which I hope comes through in the following work.[4]

Equally, there are moments in the study where the self-referential is important to the work, and where a notion of ego or ideology of self supports a point of some distinction—these are capitalized upon. A major support mechanism for the inquiry is the inclusion of the autoethnographic. As a young practitioner entering hip hop in 1983 who explored all the elements before choosing emceeing as the practice to pursue, many of the points of inquiry are discussed within a frame of my own reflective process and recollections. Primary sources have been extracts from original notebooks and lyrics, and set in dialogue with the artefact and interview analysis. Together these provide a series of critical discourses of lived hip hop experiences and practices that are then situated within the broader cultural and theoretical inquiry discussed in the following section. I must mention here that as much as the analytic-memory dialectic seeks to work between different modes of research, it also seeks to declare my bias to the inquiry and challenge the idea that work of this nature should be situated with objectivity (Haraway 1991). Furthermore, it is my belief that by working within the different modes described above, clearer judgements can be made about the value and location of provincial British hip hop, for judgement advances through engagement with practice. This occurs here in two complementary ways: firstly, the analysis in the following chapters interrogates the past practices of hip hop carried out some thirty years ago, and secondly, the practices of reflective and contextual inquiry contribute to the practice of writing itself (Hegel 1993). I also feel compelled to emphasize that this book has not been written as a typical chronological work, and while there is a loose time-based trajectory running through the chapters, the themes and concepts explored are inter-produced and as such cross the conventions of chronology. It is important here to affirm that in this book I consider the evolution of provincial British hip hop through a polygonal lens, rather than simply a canonical, objective, vacuumed study.

Contextual and Theoretical Framing

The autoethnographic and ethnographic studies, interviews, artefact and object analyses that I outlined above are positioned within a broader context of critical and cultural theory. The work of six core theorists is central to investigate the questions set out in the book, these being Homi Bhabha, Henri Lefebvre, Pierre Bourdieu, Manuel DeLanda, Paul Virilio and Michel Foucault. Bhabha's postcolonial theories of hybridity, mimicry and third space form a part of my inquiry into the cultural acquisition and spatio-tactics of hip hop identity. The sociolinguistics embedded within Bhabha's work support my attempt to define the status of provincial British hip hop culture through three phases: firstly, across hip hop's transatlantic journey, secondly during its acquisition, understanding and appropriation in Britain, and thirdly (and perhaps with more complexity) within the resistance to capitalist-consumption and processes of underground production within the provinces.

Lefebvre's work on spatial production is critical in understanding ideas about ownership, occupation and the territories associated with the spaces and places of hip hop, and provides an opportunity to read the spatial engagements, actions, practices and positions of hip hop culture as process. By taking the view that hip hop is a lived spatial process and not purely objects of production located in spatial capital, a reconsideration of the development and future potential of hip hop praxis is possible. I would further suggest this supports a different way of looking at hip hop historically and geographically. Bourdieu's theory of the habitus offers insights as to how hip hop headz and crews reframed their domestic structure and positioned their hip hop identity within alternative notions of family, representation and cultural heritage. The class system that Bourdieu explores within his thinking and writing about distinction is a worthy approach to understanding the perceptive socio-cultural position of hip hop culture within broader society, as well as how headz saw themselves within the non-urban and urban exchanges of hip hop culture itself. In connection to Bourdieu's concept of the habitus, DeLanda's reconsidered assemblage theory scaffolds my exploration of hip hop object/artefact within the processes of life and the construct of culture.[5] This is of paramount importance to the initial period of hip hop in Britain when headz were attempting to make sense of an imported, malleable culture, distinct and detached from its New York origins. These early coded assemblages of hip hop culture become further distinguishable within Britain's geography, particularly between the metropolis, the province and the region. Although the focus of this book is on the non-urban, observations are drawn from the urban, the city and the metropolis, which additionally raise the issue of life-speed and distancing between city and country. Virilio's concept of the dromosphere and picnolepsy are critical here to interrogate the themes of immediacy, clarity and distancing which shift between the spaces of urban and rural. Foucault's work on heterotopia is also crucial to the understanding of the power and authority shifts within the constructs of urban and non-urban society and indeed within the social advancements of hip hop. The heterotopias of everyday life that are formed through authoritarian ownership or management of certain spaces and places are challenged, and in extreme situations inverted through the actions and language of hip hop.

These loose sketches of the key theoretical works that underpin the book are not exhaustive but rather help frame the overall critical context, and within this frame, other theorists further anchor my study whose respective work on subcultures (Dick Hebdige) and critical regionalism (Douglas Powell) helps to place my investigation in a critical history. The hub of this further theoretical underpinning relates strongly to representation, and the fulcrums of representational shift are human engagement with hip hop as agency. In this way, the book contains a "fat history"—one which although is specific to a period in time (1983–1994), and a place (provincial Britain), presents the practice of hip hop as a cultural evolution of style produced by a series of responses and shifting contexts through time, space, place and geography.

Chapter Outline

The first chapter offers a historic contextualization of hip hop's New York origins, located through its spatial, sonic, material and non-material phenomena. Here, I pose the position that the origins of hip hop are rooted in provincialism where even the South Bronx may be considered a provincial site, after which I frame the provincial in terms of Britishness and regionalism. Location then turns to relocation, as Chapter 2 discusses in depth the relocation of hip hop by focusing on the catalysts and mechanisms that brought the culture to Britain. These discussions are situated within a broader British cultural context before concentrating on the provincial hip hop experience, which is interrogated to understand how and why hip hop culture exploded in the way it did. In the first section of Chapter 2, "On Relocation", regionalism and socio-cultural geographies are explored in order to situate two relative positions: the position of hip hop between New York and Britain, and the position of hip hop within Britain between the urban and the non-urban. I use this cultural positioning to begin to frame the question of identity and cultural acquisition. In the section "The Perfect Beat", I explore the first transatlantic exchanges, cultural acquisition and production within hip hop to argue the value of various means of appropriation. I further this discussion by unpacking the 'Buffalo Gals' video and song as product and its relationship with the languages of hip hop, production and consumption, and continue to explore these themes through the album *Duck Rock*. Throughout this section and drawing on Gadamer's approach to signs and hermeneutics, the signifiers embodied in *Duck Rock* are evaluated in order to define the signified, in terms of the commodification of hip hop culture to a British audience. At this point, I introduce the idea that a critical regionalism in British hip hop was beginning to develop during the infancy of the culture's consumption. Finally, I consider this type of artefact-product consumption alongside accounts of early British hip hop practice, theories of mimicry, cultural hybridity and style identity, and construct a contextual schism between hip hop and conventional British life, before defining the preliminary differences between urban and non-urban British hip hop culture.

Chapter 3 engages with territories, appropriation, occupation and space, and the idea that the terrain of British hip hop is crucially linked to the shifting landscapes between location and relocation, urban and rural. Here I continue to debate the urban versus non-urban via a spatio-cultural model that explores the relationships between non-urban life and urbanism as British hip hop began to take shape. The opening section "On Territory" draws largely on Bhabha's third space theory, Lefebvre's spatial production and Soja's Thirdspace in order to ground the territory of non-urban graffiti, before directing attention to the domestic. Here, I manoeuvre the context from public and semi-public space to the private spaces of domesticity to make a case for the micro-scale engagements of hip hop as critical to the evolution of its broader, public representations. This inquiry is supported by Heidegger's bridge and a detailed reading of the tools and materials (vernacular and global) of hip hop: turntables, microphones, other audio equipment, linoleum, sketchbooks and pens—the appropriated small-scale and everyday products and the two-way transfer of meanings between their appropriated use and their value within hip hop. This fuels a regional reframing of place and belonging by demonstrating the emergence of non-material and territorial spatial practice, which transcends all elements of hip hop. In the closing section "Occupation and Appropriation" I further this debate by analysing some of the earliest informal and appropriated provincial spaces, and by comparison with those of its American predecessors I introduce the notion of acquired cultural heritage. I discuss the spatio-cultural power shifts that occurred between authority and headz, and propose that although temporal, these power shifts fostered a confidence and resilience to mainstream capitalist culture. It is my suggestion in this chapter that the perceived empowerment and ownership that developed during these counter-actions were paramount to the first cognitions of a hybrid British hip hop culture.

Chapter 4 investigates the consumption of hip hop in respect of the broader nation's consumer culture, artefact/product and identity situated within the commercialization of hip hop and rap music in global terms. This is used to develop an argument that takes DeLanda's presentation on assemblage and Bourdieu's theories of habitus as points of departure to construct a provincial hip hop assemblage theory that I promote as distinctive from both American and British city-centric. This theory is demonstrated by comparing pirate radio shows and independent record shops of the city with mainstream radio shows and high street music shops (the latter often the only contact non-urbanites had to hip hop news), to explore how this assembled habitus of hip hop developed through divergent and limited exposure, connection, and distancing. This interrogation brings forth the questions of material representation, taste, class and society, and themes of distinction are pursued to illustrate that during the mid-1980s the provincial hip hop experience was somewhat at odds with both Britishness and the broader perception of British hip hop. The result was an awkward cultural existence which I argue impacted upon the first creations of lo-fi non-urban British hip hop music, where headz' own interpretations of their demographic and cultural context were both suppressed and exploited in an attempt to produce hip hop. Here, I begin to layer the story of acquired cultural hybridity and anchor the formative cultural values of the established and the subaltern as drivers for knowledge and vision within non-urban hip hop. Establishment is discussed within the arenas of Thatcherism, football hooliganism and regional and local identity politics, while the subaltern engages with headz' desire to dig deeper into underground hip hop as a counter-approach to commercial consumption. The concept to "dig" is central to the idea of "knowledge" of self, past, present and future in hip hop, and has become widely accepted as the fifth core element of hip hop culture, which I expand upon here in order to frame how this element supported the trajectory of the provincial British.[6]

In Chapter 5, I turn from consumption to production and further the preliminary investigation of the primary forms of practice in the provinces. The aim of this chapter is to chart specific practices and productions of provincial British hip hop music which currently remain undiscussed, and also to evaluate the operations and modes of this production within the emerging cultural hybridity explored in the previous chapter. This discussion takes points of departure from DeLanda's casual shadows, Foucault's notions of heterotopia and Virilio's theory of dromology, where I argue that the appropriated technologies, demographic and geographic positioning and limitations of exposure to broader hip hop culture were important conditions that affected the development of provincial hip hop practices. Here I explore several sites and processes of technological, social and cultural production that informed provincial hip hop practice. I then demonstrate the power shifts between conventional establishment structures and the structure of the provincial supercrew, their nodes, networks, practices, processes and outputs. Additionally, the tangible outputs of recorded products and the more intangible and ephemeral processes of writing and language development, rehearsal, recording and performance are unpacked in terms of localism and pauses in time. The evolution of regionalist and de-regionalist styles, critique and reflection are of concern here as I anchor a cultural positioning for provincial British hip hop. I also analyse the associated record sleeve designs from 1988–1993 (by urban artists such as Blade, Hijack and Gunshot, the period that is now known historically as the era of "britcore") in comparison with the lo-fi cassette-only productions of the provinces.[7]

Chapter 6 centres on themes of identity, which by drawing on many of the arguments previously presented, asks: what is the identity of provincial British hip hop, and how does it differ from the conceived, perceived and lived hip hop identity of the British city? I tackle this question through a detailed examination of hip hop's imagery and material expression and explore the embedded and suggested meanings within both non-urban and city-centric British hip hop music sonically and lyrically. In an attempt to unravel the story of britcore and its wider impact in Europe, the theme of reality is tackled within this broader context and by revisiting the notions of cultural diaspora discussed previously. The discussion of reality also draws on Hebdige's discourse about forbidden identity and sources of value vis-à-vis a further examination of lesser known, lo-fi non-urban britcore recordings from this period. Taking issue with the commercialism of hip hop as rap music was a common theme in britcore, and the more hardcore the sound became, the more it was perceived as being real or staying true to British hip hop. To "keep it real" is one of the keenest tropes in hip hop globally, and here I further the investigation of reality, image and identity under the theme of "keeping it real" and attempt to solidify the hip hop state of mind in terms of critical, non-urban British regionalism. This regionalist approach takes issue with the global realness continually referred to within mainstream hip hop culture, while concurrently presenting a theory of mind-state that is rooted in hip hop's origins. Rakim's epitomic lyric in 'I Know You Got Soul'

(1987), "It ain't where you're from, it's where you're at", is pivotal to the critique I offer of the "hip hop state of mind" and "keeping it real", which is presented in the final section of this chapter.

In my concluding chapter I consider the arguments presented in the book and discuss and confirm three critical discoveries that contribute to the growing field of knowledge related to critical regionalism, de-regionalism and the global. Firstly, I dispel the myth that hip hop is solely an urban culture, and charge that consumer-capitalists' continual urbanization of hip hop culture is a parodic and heterotopian position within which the tired urban tropes of hip hop are constantly titivated for consumer-capitalist gain, in turn simplifying the rich and diverse cultural dynamics of hip hop. Secondly, I attest the position that an acquired critically regional hip hop culture existed and advanced in Britain evidenced through a set of hybrid practices and productions, and furthermore this hybrid culture was a counter-approach to the established, expected and normalized ways that one should conduct their life. Moreover, I verify that there were clear contextual differences between the city-centric and provincial positions in British hip hop, which helps us consider the importance of regionalism and its role in the evolutionary practices of hip hop. Thirdly, I conclude that the cultural dynamics of provincial British hip hop culture can act as a frame for its practitioners to realize the potential for greater critical engagement in both hip hop practice and everyday life. For many practitioners, hip hop and daily life are inseparable, and the final section of this concluding chapter reveals the invisible attributes that significantly enhance hip hop practice and life experience as a whole.

Chapter 1

The Location of Hip Hop: The Provincial, Spatial, Sonic, Material and Non-material

When one first considers hip hop, it is usual to conjure up images, sounds and tropes that represent certain moments in the evolution of hip hop culture. From its inception on 11 August 1973 at DJ Kool Herc's party at 1520 Sedgwick Avenue, The Bronx, New York City, through to the golden-era revivalist sounds of Action Bronson in 2017, hip hop is laden with symbols and signs that have become normalized and accepted representations of the culture.[1] Hip hop is the master culture of (re)appropriation, reframing and reimagining; a result of lateral thinking and cultural history. Hip hop praxis "develop[s] a negative into a positive picture",[2] telling the stories which may otherwise be lost—about ourselves, others, and hip hop itself. It is essential at this point to support Rose's position that "hip hop is propelled by Afrodiasporic traditions" (Rose 1994: 25), and "hip hop culture emerged as a source for youth of alternative identity formation and social status in a community whose older local support institutions had been all but demolished" (Rose 1994: 34). A truism is that the culture bore something out of nothing, as if that were possible (see Berman and Berger 2007; Evans 2014), and what that actually transcribes is that hip hop borrowed the most relevant and apposite parts of its pre-hip hop history, other cultures, subcultures and counterparts. Through organic, often subconscious (re)appropriation and reimagining, these parts mutated into the multi-tangential culture of hip hop. It is important also to state that although the birth of hip hop is widely attributed to Kool Herc's party on 11 August 1973, the origins of the culture are not so simple to pinpoint. At its birth, the four main elements had paradoxical relationships and were evolving at dissimilar rates. The first graffiti writers were practising rigorously several years before Kool Herc's party; the most famous historical evidence of this can be seen in the *New York Times* on

21 July 1971 when Taki 183's all-city bombing became front page news.³ The next physical elements to arrive were DJing and Bboying with rap being the last, and in the three subsections that follow I discuss the origins of these four elements—not independently from each other—but thematically by locating them through space, sound, material and the non-material.⁴

The Provinciality of Early Hip Hop

While these hip hop facts are widely established, I would like to introduce the idea that during the first seven years of its life, hip hop was a provincial cultural form. When notions of the provincial are discussed, thoughts turn to small, remote towns, often thinly populated with not much in the way of cultural variety; of countryside estates, ranches, farms, and through-villages whose inhabitants write to the local newspaper to object to or support plans for new flower beds. The provincial and its position in respect of the metropolises in Britain and British hip hop are introduced in Chapter 2 and discussed throughout the book; however what could provincialism be in New York? In response to Norman Denzin, Wendy Griswold suggests a provincial positivism, where "within the discourses of the day—a certain place, a certain time, a certain pattern of local knowledge within and outside of the academy—some concepts or theories, provisionally chosen, can get you farther than others" (1990: 1582). While Griswold's argument sits within the frame of cultural studies and the institution, it sets a clear scenario highlighting the values of such localized and provincial context. If the formative years of hip hop are observed through a similar lens, its actions can certainly be considered provincial despite its geographic existence within the metropolitan area of New York City.

Kool Herc's initial party ticked all the boxes for Griswold's argument. It was held in a certain place, at a certain time, with certain patterns of local knowledge—people knew that Kool Herc would bring the funk. During the remainder of the 1970s, and as the bricolage of hip hop evolved through the assemblage of multiple concrete and intangible artefacts and ideas, hip hop remained a site of provinciality. It triangulated localized community engagement (in the form of block parties) with personalized forms of expression and the concept of family, particularly evident in the structure of crews. Furthermore, it expounded the geographic terrains of named districts through its narratives embedded within its lyrics, and shout-outs and name-drops were common emcee tropes to rock during parties, the call and response notions of "place" triggering pride, confidence and conflict through localization. Hip hop had no choice but to develop within its own districts, as, until the national and global explosion of 'Rapper's Delight' in 1979, the progression of hip hop was detached from the music industry—as much metaphorically as literally—as the communities that built hip hop were cut-off from the metropolitanism of New York City and abandoned by the city's authorities.

Forman talks about the "extreme local" (2002: xvii), where rappers construct a spatial imagery by pulling regional and local associations into their verse. Narratives based on these localisms oscillate between the parochial ('Delancey Street' by Dana Dane, 1986) and the insightful ('Broadway' by Duke Bootee, 1986). Forman continues to attest that "rap has evolved as the dominant cultural voice of black urban youth", and "Rap's urban origins and continued urban orientations (in terms of performance, production, and highest concentration of consumption) provide the primary environment for the music's evolution" (2002: xvii), and develops a compelling discussion where various reiterations of the local and localism are explored through the urban realm. My notion of the South Bronx, parts of Harlem and Queensbridge, or any other named place with a link to pioneering hip hop as a provincial site, is not intended to challenge Forman's astute discussion but act as complementary. Where Forman posits "local" within "urban", my further provincial layer in the spatio-cultural palimpsest of hip hop contains both a narrowness of approach—fuelled by oppression—and a circumvention of the city as a whole thing. I use the term narrowness with some caution: I am not suggesting that this period in hip hop's evolution was unsophisticated, but in fact hip hop gained sophistication through its tenacious and lateral practices, working with all that it could harness—and these operations were very much provincial. These practices were both introspective and proactive as a response to knowledge-of-self, community and culture, and the destitute conditions of living in these parts of New York during the 1970s. This is the site of the origins of hip hop.

It is important at this point to explain and define what I mean by the provincial and in order to do this, it is necessary to briefly explore "urban" and "rural", the two general categories of the western built environment. In conventional urban design and architectural thought, urban areas fall into two clear categories, and are either conceived and built as a spatial solution (such as Milton Keynes) or have evolved through time (such as the conurbation of London) to include civic amenities, housing, recreational and social spaces, businesses and educational facilities.[5] These urban areas are most obviously cities, large towns and suburbs, and as one moves away from the centre of an urban area typically the proportion of the built environment reduces and the proportion of the rural (and/or natural) environment increases, presenting the non-urban. Agrarian production generated the first dynamics of city life through markets, and these one-to-one, everyday exchanges and the transient relationship between agrarian producer and market consumer illustrate that the ephemeral threshold between what is "city" and what is "rural" is not so easily defined.

Hip hop was conceived in the dense, dilapidated urban fabric of The Bronx, its urban debility and decay being a direct result of Robert Moses's cronyism-fuelled agenda to capitalize on strengthening the link between the outer suburbs of New York and the centre of Manhattan (see Ballon and Jackson 2007; Plunz 1990; Flint 2011; Berman and Berger 2007). This build program concurrently expanded that which was urban into New York State, New Jersey and Connecticut forming a framework for conurbation. What was the experience of a commuter who dwelled in rural Newtown, Connecticut and drove to Manhattan, for example? There is interplay of some complexity between the rural, the car, the journey, the periphery, and the core of the city; the experience of this daily rhythm affirming and reaffirming an urbanism of homogeneity (Borden 2013). While hip hop was most definitely an urban condition, the breadth of a new kind of urbanism oozed into the surrounding states. Although this urban pattern is usual, it requires further explanation. Examining Lefebvre's "urban zone" (Lefebvre 2014b), I interpret western urbanism (or the city) as having two distinct representations: firstly, the core of the urban zone is organized and controlled by industrial capitalism, anchored in the traditional centre of the city. Secondly, the space outside the city, the fabric of urban sprawl or suburban growth that extends and invades the rural and agrarian, is also controlled and determined by the defunct industrial core, which, reimagined by consumer-capitalism, cloaks the space of urbanism as an expanding canopy of consumption. The city is, in fact, without an edge.

In traditional geography, rural areas comprise villages, hamlets, farms and agricultural space, and the associated morphology of these areas develop from and complement their rural context and natural environment (see for example Philips and Williams 1985). Early rural geographers sought to define functional characteristics of the rural as different from the urban through empirical study (Woods 2011: 7), although during the 1970s and 1980s a more socially engaged approach was taken to align study of the rural with neo-Marxist theories linked to the manoeuvres of capitalism (Buttel and

Newby 1980). Unlike the positivist studies previously, the conclusions here illustrated a new way of thinking about rurality, suggesting that "rural" and "urban" as spatio-political and spatio-economic concepts operate with some amount of synergy, and that rural socio-space transcended the traditional rural boundaries. I would also assert that the same can be said for urbanism, and that the conventional dialectic of "rural versus urban" is antediluvian. That is not to say that the rural is antiquated, but that investigations of "rural" and "urban" require careful handling in terms of their specific contexts, cultural conditions and spatial positions to one another; these considerations I will briefly sketch out here to culturally position the provincial in relation to hip hop in Britain during the 1980s (for recent spatio-cultural analysis of the rural-urban debate, see Stringer 2018).

If the urban was perceived as the metropolis, the megalopolis and the city, these were the spaces of hip hop. Those areas of dense population, of an emerging 24-hour lifestyle, of the tower block and the concrete jungle, of a perceived isolation from nature, accelerating social mobility, networking, the spontaneous, and the unexpected, became the realm for hip hop culture. Hip hop also manifested in the space of pirate radio, of night clubs, independent record and clothes shops; the places for Bboy battles, shops that stocked DJ equipment, emerging underground record labels, jams, and graffiti halls of fame. Then, the rural was the sprinkling of homes, thatched cottages, stone and slate bus shelters, cattle grids and village greens; it was the sparsely populated, the quiet lane, the mines, the marshes and the thickets, the amble, the predictable, the distant, tradition. It was also the space of nationwide airwaves, of the Gallup top 40 pop chart on a Sunday night, throwing sticks up into horse chestnut trees, drinking farm scrumpy, buying batteries from the village shop for the boombox,[6] tagging stiles and gates,[7] scant TV appearances by rap crews, the mundane, and John Peel.

So, what was provincial? The provincial experience is something in-between as it morphs and slides between urban and rural, transcending from representations of the city's core to the extreme edges of rurality where it meets the natural environment. The provincial signals the multiplicity of the non-city, the varying degrees of liminal space between the city's core and the country's natural edge. It suggests the conditions of the hinterland, the scattering of industrialization, and the invasion of the built environment as it consumes land and trees, from the new towns, the suburban pastiche and the converted barn to the corporate petrol stations in opposition to the village green.

The cultural position of British provincial hip hop is that which did not excel or dwell in urbanism with any permanence, but that which was rooted spatio-culturally in the value system embedded within rural thinking and living. Its practitioners hunted for knowledge through secondary, tertiary and quaternary representations of hip hop via radio broadcasts, records and peer group engagement, all of which had variable limitations compared to the complete urban experience. The challenge and complexity of the non-urban hip hop experience is vital to the exploration of hip hop's critical regionalism, and throughout the book I discuss the complex dichotomies between rural and urban from a range of provincial positions.

Regionalism can be described in several ways—political, artistic, architectural and geographical. Politically, regionalism is an ideology based on localized divisions, the socio-economic and economic interests of a locale or region, which can be loaded with notions of sovereignty and separatism. Fredrik Söderbaum offers an eclectic inquiry into regionalism and states that: "More or less every government in the world is engaged in regionalism" (Söderbaum 2016: 2), and "'Regionalism' represents the body of ideas, values and policies that are aimed at creating a region" (Söderbaum 2016: 3). He continues: "Since regions are not formed in a vacuum, the region in itself cannot be the only unit of theory-building. Rethinking regions in global transformation denotes approaching regions from a 'global' perspective. Somehow, a more 'global' approach to the study of regionalism needs to be built" (Söderbaum 2016: 10). He discusses the concept of "regional actorness" as adding "an additional analytical dimension to the regionness concept that helps us to understand a region's ability to influence the external world and its role in global transformation" (Söderbaum 2016: 171). In *Renegade Regionalists: The Modern Independence of Grant Wood, Thomas Hart Benton, and John Steuart Curry*, James Dennis discusses the thematics of social and political protest and criticism, interrogating the misreadings in regional art which normally interpreted themes of family, community and unsophisticated rural living. Architecturally, regionalism takes a point of departure from vernacular architecture; it is constructed of the place, using local trades, techniques and materials, but conceptually relates to regional ideologies (Dennis 1998). Additionally, Wendell Berry comments:

> The regional motive is false when the myths and abstractions of a place are valued apart from the place itself; that is regionalism as nationalism. It is also false when the region is made the standard of its own experience—when, that is, perspective is narrowed by

condescension or pride so that a man is unable to bring to bear on the life of his place as much as he is able to know (Berry 2007: 38).

In human geography, Doreen Massey discusses the characteristics of the hegemonic conception of space through Modernist thinking, and its relation "between space and society", illustrating a key characteristic in the "isomorphism between space/place on the one hand and society/culture on the other" (Massey 2014: 64). This hegemony was only one way to consider space, representational space and representations of space (considerations that are at the heart of Lefebvre 1991, Soja 1996, and Bhabha 2004); however, and additionally, the understanding of society and culture through regional geography is conventionally mapped to fit regional delineations, as "regional geography's paradigmatic narrative strategy" (Natter and Jones 1993: 178). Critical regionalism (a term first introduced by architectural historian-theorists Kenneth Frampton, Alexander Tzonis and Liane Lefaivre) and the exploration of ideas in this book take points of departure from the various disciplinary regionalist positions above, Frampton's 'Toward a Critical Regionalism: Six Points for an Architecture of Resistance' (1993), and particularly Powell's *Critical Regionalism: Connecting Politics and Culture in the American Landscape* (2007).

R. E. Pahl charges that "any attempt to tie particular patterns of social relationships to specific geographic milieux is a singularly fruitless exercise" (Pahl 1968: 302), which I must take issue with here, because—as this book demonstrates—patterns of assemblage, engagement, discourse, practice, process and output share distinct commonalities across the provincial experience of British hip hop. Finally, in this section, I want to explain my use of terms "region", "locale" and "province", all of which are referred to at various points. "The regional" is used when discussing areas that may form a county, or part of a county, which includes two or more locations under discussion and may also have invisible boundaries, but commonality among other qualities such as language, accent, cultural heritage and material culture. Regions are discussed as both subordinate and dominant, to further the interpretation of Raymond Williams' line of thought (Williams 2014). "Locale" is of a smaller scale and signifies a context that is of importance to some event, ritual or process. In Britain, the term "province" generally denotes an area that lies outside Greater London; however, it is with the following caveat that I use the term "province" throughout the book due to its patronizing usage by others elsewhere. While it can be suggested that the

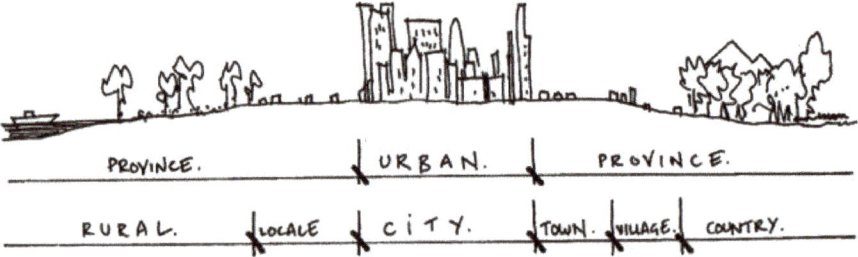

Figure 1.1: Notional section through landscape. Diagram by author.

province suffers a lower level of sophistication and a parochial attitude than that of the capital, it is this province's insularity that is partly responsible for non-urban hip hop practitioners' actions and reactions. Furthermore, it is one's cultural positioning within the province, the province's social positioning to the metropolis, and the perception of the province by both rural and urban headz, that generate some of the key representations and productions discussed in this book. It is for these reasons that although I use the term provincial to describe any space outside the metropolitan borough or area of significant urban density, the terms rural, country(side), non-urban and locale are used interchangeably but not without intent. Figure 1.1 illustrates these terms within the space and cultural distancing from the metropolis. In Chapter 2, I turn attention to the initial infiltration of hip hop in provincial areas of Britain and discuss the major agents for its impact.

Locating the Spatial

In spatial terms, hip hop culture appears most apparent in graffiti; however, mixed and diverse opinions to what extent writing is part of hip hop have existed since the culture's birth.[8] Many headz perceived writing as a critical element while others advocated that graffiti actually *was* hip hop. According to graffiti writer Lee: "Let's face it painting on trains was here way beyond anyone's imagination of hip hop. It was hip hop, before it became hip hop."[9] This is important to the hip hop state of mind (and is taken up later in the book); however, the view that graffiti is a part of hip hop culture is shared by many headz and was expressed extensively through rap records of the 1980s, most notably by KRS-One on 'Nervous'(1988): "You know what, I used to be a graffiti writer, I used to write KRS-One all over the place"; by Rakim on

'I Ain't No Joke' (1987): "write a rhyme in graffiti in every show you see me in"; and also by Rakim on 'My Melody' (1987): "…Or just writin' my name in graffiti on the wall".[10] These cultural reference points trigger my view that graffiti writing is firmly a part of hip hop culture, certainly since the inception of hip hop in Britain, and this position is explored further in Chapters 2 and 3. In "On the Origins of Hip Hop: Appropriation and Territorial Control of Urban Space" (Evans 2014), I argued that graffiti writing is a form of collective and individual spatial practice which evolved as a counter-narrative to the urban condition of the New York City ghettos during the latter half of the twentieth century, and subsequently found empathy with the music and dance elements of hip hop. The origins of hip hop culture are deeply rooted in a sense of cultural exclusion and spatial vacancy inscribed by the built environment of Modernist social housing projects (Evans 2014: 189–91), and a political dialectic ensued which was represented spatially through the language of the authoritarian destitute city fabric and the emergent counter-language of graffiti (Evans 2014: 199–200). My point here is that graffiti did not begin as an art form, but as a spatio-political act that attempted to make sense of an urban condition devoid of opportunity and identity. This urban combat actually manifested into a three-fold dynamic: firstly, the socio-spatial destitution which resulted from Robert Moses' build program and a lack of engagement from Mayors John Lindsay, Abraham Beame and Ed Koch; secondly, the counter-attack on city space by graffiti writers to claim ownership and identity; and thirdly, the narrative within the graffiti environment where writers competed for fame and recognition, using urban space as a grounding for expression.

As graffiti saturated the city fabric, writers began to advance the idea of style. Letters, connections, words, scale, colour, shape, were all attributes that contributed to the early development of style, an idea central to the mindset of hip hop, and the development of style was paramount to the occupation of space. Between 1972 and 1974, three motifs of style arrived—and brought with them a new agenda for graffiti—the cloud, the 3-D (three-dimensional), and the arrow (Figure 1.2). Pioneers including Dead Leg 167, Stay High 149, Dime 2 and Staff 161 incorporated all three of these motifs concurrently into their graffiti to generate impact. The arrow came first and was an efficient way to celebrate one's personal hand style that linked to their letters, and the quality of the arrow could mean the success or failure of the work.[11] The arrow is suggestive of speed and spatial occupation, and through the directional gesture indicated ownership of more surface than the graffiti physically covered. The 3-D achieved something similar in enhancing the letter

Figure 1.2: "Dime 2", circa 1974, illustrating the composite result of the 3-D, cloud and arrow. Photograph courtesy of Jason Clint (Dr. Krome).

style, but also exaggerated the idea of spatial occupation as a well-executed 3-D could suggest the letters project off the wall or train, to invade actual space rather than purely occupy the surface area. Lastly, the cloud: the initial form of background scenery or fill to support the letters could transform a surface adorning letters into a fully-occupied area. When all three motifs were incorporated successfully in the work, a power shift occurred between the owned and the occupied as graffiti consumed entire trains and walls. As graffiti grew physically larger, the authorities became noticeably less in control of public space.[12]

Spatial representations in hip hop culture surpassed engagement with graffiti-only practice. The art of Bboying with its dynamic movement also captured the notion of spatial occupation and ownership instantaneously, although with much more intangibility and bodily scale than the blatancy and macro scale of graffiti. The fluid language of breakdancing first emerged through complete osmosis during the breakdown parts of funk, soul and jazz records (in fact, any records with a powerful beat that the crowd could dance to).[13] By dancing in the "break" of records, these dancers became known as "break boys" as their dancing broke the beat (which was rapidly abbreviated to "Bboys" and "Bgirls"), executing more extreme spatial dance moves during the vibrancy of the drum and rhythm breaks.[14] A sense of urgency was also present, as these breaks were limited in length of time which heightened the drama and energy of Bboying practice. The development of this body language included several pivotal styles and dance moves—robotics, popping, locking, up-rocking and top-rocking—all of which are generally performed in an upright dancing position; and the crazy-legs, caterpillar, back-spin, knee-spin and head-spin, and the turtle and windmill performed when one "throws down" on the floor, usually in a circle comprising one's own crew, rival crews and other Bboys and onlookers. Each of these moves developed greater speed, complexity and fluidity as Bboys became more practised in their agility and ability, evolved their own style and choreographed moves with partners. Nelson George describes a typical breakdance pattern as follows:

> Each person's turn in the ring was very brief—ten to thirty seconds—but packed with action and meaning. It began with an entry, a hesitating walk that allowed him to get in step with the music for several beats and take his place "on stage". Next the dancer "got down" to the floor to do the footwork... Acrobatic transitions such as head spins...served as bridges between the footwork and the freeze (George 1985: 90).

During this formative period of Bboying, pioneering DJ Grandmaster Flash longed to enhance that Bboying frenzy which occurred during the breakdown sections of songs, and developed the backspin—a method of mixing two copies of the same breakdown in order to extend the break in series (Rose 1994: 53). This in turn enhanced the evolution of Bboying, as Flash's extended breaks presented more time on the dancefloor for the dancers.[15] It is important to note here that by extending the break, the dynamism of breakdancing actually increased rather than deflated, which produced an incredibly intense context for the evolution of "the battle", where competing teams, partners or individuals would challenge each other in direct combat. The concept of battling is a strong hip hop value that is rife throughout the elements.[16]

It was not only at block parties where Bboying was practised; further spatial engagement with the environment took place as crews occupied basketball courts, parks and sidewalks to rehearse, busk and battle.[17] By the mid-1970s location and context clearly linked graffiti to Bboying, which were further synergized as these new styles of expression reclaimed fragments and sections of urbanism through constructed representational spaces that challenged the conceived and perceived spatial practices of the built environment (Lefebvre 1991). The practices associated with graffiti in particular resonate greatly with Lefebvre's discussions on spatial production and what he refers to as "the perceived-conceived-lived triad" (Lefebvre 1991: 40), where he presents space in a theoretical model of the perceived (spatial practice), the conceived (representations of space), and the lived (representational space) (Lefebvre 1991: 38–40). I will expand this theoretical frame later through discussion of representational spaces within the provincial British context, but here I want to outline the spatial responsiveness between hip hop's music practitioners, the tenacity of writers, and the drive of Bboys.[18] The actions of DJs and emcees were also incredibly spatial.[19] DJs would take control of the music and the sound set up, and the act of doing so presented opportunity between the sonic and space, where each block party required planning in terms of power, space, enclosure and quality of sound. A very clear practice of re-appropriation is evident here as block parties were held outside in basketball and handball courts and parks, as well as in community rooms and centres within housing projects and schools. In terms of practicality, designing a party depended much on the location; one of the most evident moments of (re)appropriation is the harnessing of electric power from street lighting, as abandoned buildings also became homes for parties, documented extensively but most apparent through the lyrics to 'South Bronx' by Boogie Down Productions (Bboy Records, 1986):

> They tried again outside in Cedar Park
> Power from a street light made the place dark
> But yo, they didn't care they turned it out
> I know a few understand what I'm talking about
> Remember Bronx River rolling thick
> With Kool DJ Red Alert and Chuck Chill Out on the mix

> When Afrika Islam was rocking the jams
> And on the other side of town was a kid named Flash
> Patterson and Millbrook projects
> Casanova all over, ya couldn't stop it

KRS-One's lyrics here document some of the physical actions, intents, locations and key players clearly within the South Bronx context who (following the lead of DJ Kool Herc) constructed their sound systems to operate with flexibility within Afrodiasporic urban spaces. This flexibility enabled the rise of the emcee, and although Coke La Rock as DJ Kool Herc's emcee is widely credited as the first hip hop emcee, the art of emceeing truly developed during the years of the sound system parties between 1977 and 1980. The combination of emcee and DJ provided a testbed for the emcee's lyrics and the DJ's routines as they worked together to develop their shows. Celebrating the idea of identity through turf and territorial references became significant themes in live shows. Call and response dialogue between the emcee and the crowd invited the names of locales and districts to be shouted out, positioning the party between the existing space and an emerging new heterotopic identity of the space.[20] These heterotopias were not purely temporal, and neither did they operate within a cultural vacuum; reflection, rehearsal and designing new routines for the next battle or performance were vital to one's own development, as was a broader understanding of the sociopolitical condition of this time, which I will revisit in Chapter 5.

Locating the Sonic

The term "hip hop music" is often used synonymously and incorrectly with the term "rap music". Hip hop music relates to its broader cultural context and might not necessarily incorporate rap in the music and may also be used to describe certain funk and drum breaks that are mixed or used as rap backing tracks at hip hop parties. Hip hop music is untypical in terms of genre definition; in fact, hip hop music *is* hip hop music due to its cross-cultural and cross-genre attributes. Rap music on the other hand is *associated* with hip hop culture, and is one of several genres of music positioned alongside specific types of funk, soul, reggae and even rock (and, particularly in California, Miami and Europe: electro) that make up the bricolage of hip hop music.[21] The structural mechanics of rap music has moved through a series of progressions over the past 40 years. In its infancy, emcees would rap over certain parts of records that the DJs were spinning at parties, their raps taking a rudimentary form of vocal content, mainly by name-checking, self-promotion and offering basic announcements to the crowd.[22] Often these raps were not yet formed into rhyme structures or bars, but were simple sentences that responded to the pattern of the music and the activities of the party. By the late 1970s, all four hip hop elements were well represented, with rap music being "the last element to emerge in hip hop" (Rose 1994: 51), although clarification here is required as hip hop's earliest DJs Kool Herc and Afrika Bambaataa were working with emcees in 1973–1974. Soulsonic Force's Mr. Biggs confirms:

> I was rapping before the Zulu Nation even started. I started rapping back in about 1974—just me and Bambaataa... Bam had just been given a new DJ set for a graduation present when he got out of high school and he started spinning records. I just picked up a mike one time, just playing around rapping, and I just kept rapping from there (Mr. Biggs in Toop 1985: 60).

Kool Herc's Herculoids (his collective crew) and Bam's Mr. Biggs, G.L.O.B.E., and Pow Wow (Soulsonic Force) were not alone; during the mid-1970s important emcees who were representing hip hop included the Crash Crew, Kurtis Blow, and Lovebug Starski, all of whom continued to become successful rap artists with various degrees of commercial victory.[23] However, Lil Rodney Cee contests that at this point in the mid-1970s emcees were not rapping in terms of structured verses, but were more spoken phrases:

> The way rap is *now*—it isn't the way it was *then*. Whereas then it was just phrases; the MC would say little phrases like, "to the Eastside, make money, to the Westside, make money", or "to the rock, rock, rock, to the rock, rock, rock". In 77–78 I was with The Magnificent Seven. We was playing in the streets. Rap, then, was only a street thing. At that time everything was happening at once. Bboying was happening at the same time as DJing and rapping came out. Everything was strictly competitive (Lil Rodney Cee in Toop 1985: 70).

This form of rap that Lil Rodney Cee speaks about was practised in the street in a cappella fashion, over songs or parts of songs recorded by others, or over a handclap and other chants. The phrases that made up the rap contained time and environment-based contexts and commentary on the immediate situation dynamics, which formed the early concept of freestyle rap—responding and commenting directly on events in the moment.

Some of the nuances with respect to hip hop music are explored at key moments in this book, and of particular concern are the importance of electro and its representation in British hip hop during the early years. While rap in America has become the biggest selling music genre of the past 25 years—as the drivers of consumer-capitalism learned how to frame, package and market rap music—the origins and ethos of hip hop culture could not be further from the literal and projective individualism that commercial rap music promotes (James and Scerri 2012). Through use by the music industry, the term "rap music" has become associated with saleable entities rather than the holistic nature of hip hop culture, and in turn has developed a particular formulaic approach that relates only inconsequentially to the essence of hip hop.[24]

Rap music as an identifiable genre began with the commercial success of 'Rapper's Delight' (1979) by Sugarhill Gang some six years after the first motions of hip hop. Although 'King Tim III' (1979) by Fatback is considered by many to be the first rap record, released on 29 March 1979, and 'Rapper's Delight' some six months later on 16 September 1979, there are cultural differences that extend much further than their respective release dates. 'Rapper's Delight' was, for people outside the immediate Afrodiasporic urban context of New York, their first encounter with hip hop culture despite its manufactured construct. Furthermore, it pinpoints the moment when hip hop ceased being a community-driven provincial practice, yet hip hop as urban representation was not visually evident until Kurtis Blow's 1982 album cover, *Tough*. The popularity of 'Rapper's Delight' lends much to the appealing bassline and backing track which mimics Chic's 'Good Times' (1979), a formula that would generate much success for subsequent rap artists leaning on the disco vibe of the time. The impact of 'Rapper's Delight' has been extensively documented, and here it suffices to state two key facets of this impact—firstly that the record sold several million copies worldwide by 1980 and topped many charts, and "changed everything; most important, it solidified rap's commercial status" (Rose 1994: 56), setting a precedent for a torrent of records that comprised disco-esque vibes with overlaid raps.[25] Following this wave of disco-oriented rap music, a rich period of rap records began which broadened and deepened musical and cultural influences and references, triggered by Afrika Bambaataa & the Soul Sonic Force's 'Planet Rock', discussed through a British lens in the following chapter. If 'Rapper's

Delight' enjoyed such commercial success globally, the second point of impact was in the locale—and was initially not so joyful—forcing emcees to re-evaluate their practice and position. Sugarhill Gang were a construct of Sugar Hill Records, and their rhymes on 'Rapper's Delight' were largely bitten from raps by The Cold Crush Brothers and other esteemed emcees' rap phraseology.[26] Big Bank Hank, one of the rappers from Sugarhill Gang, was The Cold Crush Brothers manager, and in order to pay for their sound system, he was working in Crispy Crust Pizza when Sylvia Robinson of Sugar Hill Records entered, as Grandmaster Caz recounts:

> He used to take a little boombox to work with him, and I used to give him tapes that I used to make at home or our tapes from our shows, and he's in the pizza place lip-syncing… Sylvia Robinson walks into the shop and sees him and says "hey that's kinda, why don't you come outside to the car…we auditioning people to become part of this group I'm putting together." So, what is Hank supposed to tell Sylvia Robinson?…"I don't rap lady, but I manage one of the best emcees in The Bronx." He never said that. He went out to the car, repeated the stuff that was on the tape, they loved it, and they made him part of the Sugar Hill Gang. Right there on the spot (Grandmaster Caz interview, VladTV 2014).

The bomb of 'Rapper's Delight' was initially something that shell-shocked hip hop practitioners who had helped develop the culture as local, contextual and vernacular since its inception, but almost instantaneously emcees and DJs reframed their agendas to make records. Before 'Rapper's Delight', the output of an emcee was to sustain a long party performance, and although in vinyl terms Sugarhill Gang's debut at over 15 minutes long was epic by comparison to others, this was perceived as something of a serious act of consolidation by Chuck D:

> Fuck, how you gon' put hip hop onto a record? 'Cause it was a whole gig, you know? How you gon' put three hours on a record?… Bam! They made 'Rappers' Delight'. And the ironic twist is not how long that record was, but how short it was. I'm thinking, "man they cut that shit down to fifteen minutes?" It was a miracle (Chuck D in Chang 2007: 130).

The response of the community's emcees and DJs to 'Rapper's Delight' triggered substantial progress in terms of hip hop culture's migration outside the ghetto. Jazzy Jay talks about "the great hip hop drought" at the turn of the new decade as emcees and DJs became artists, reaching further out into the fabric of the city's other boroughs and beyond, leaving behind the spaces and places that birthed and supported hip hop's infancy (Chang 2007: 128). They were not physically constructing localized sound systems anymore—but constructing a tangible culture by producing records—consumable products as representations of their views and position in a growing hip hop scene that operated as both entity and network simultaneously. Hip hop had now entered a different mode of cultural production—one that began to lose its provinciality; the organics, dynamics, ephemeral and spontaneous needed somehow to be captured and represented in a physical, industry standard product—the vinyl record. The cultural production of vinyl records aids the distinction that I offer between rap and hip hop music. Before 'Rapper's Delight', the sonics of hip hop were created organically by live performance, influenced by the immediate spatio-cultural context. Spontaneous events and actions as well as rehearsing practice would result in new vernacular and colloquial developments in the craft, and refinements to these practices would come through critical reflection on performances, battles and comments from peers. Until the first rap record, hip hop music was a provincial fusion of emcees' and DJs' actions vis-à-vis the recorded sounds of funk, soul, reggae, disco and jazz, but also rock, metal and even pop music; effectively hip hop music was genre-less: it was about beats, rhythm and style. Afrika Bambaataa would often mix in specific parts of records by Black Sabbath, The Monkees and The Rolling Stones, much to the disbelief of the crowd; by critically evaluating the beats and rhythm, Bam created a holistic sonic collage that was perceived as hip hop music. While these mixes occasionally resulted in tape recordings, hip hop needed the release of 'Rapper's Delight' to generate a seismic paradigm shift for what it would become.

Locating the Material and the Non-material

The first-generation material culture of hip hop can be located within three interrelated categories: the first contains artefacts, products and practices that existed before hip hop, and were appropriated and referenced by hip hop; the second contains artefacts, products and practices that were created by the critical processes within hip hop; and thirdly, the artefacts, products and practices that attempt to *be* hip hop but were produced by those outside hip hop for broader consumption. These categories of first-generation material evolution are critical in understanding the different points of departure and arrival in British hip hop. Earlier, I stated that hip hop is the master culture of (re)appropriation and reimagining, and this is embedded nowhere more clearly than in the original, appropriated tools of the trade. Consider a range of domestic everyday products and objects that began life in the 1970s as record players, spray-cans/spray-paint, sketchbooks, marker pens, linoleum, cardboard sheeting and records—all of which were appropriated (and still are) for the practices of hip hop. What becomes intriguing here is that all of these objects were produced and consumed within other cultural arenas before hip hop existed, yet some, particularly in the cases of the turntable and spray-paint, now serve as material evidence attributable to hip hop culture due to their creative reimagining. Similarly to the spatial sense of territorial ownership felt by writers—DJs, Bboys and emcees felt a sense of material ownership by mastering their practice with these tools. The acts of reimagining and (re)appropriation were amplified (quite literally) as DJs would be knee-deep in materials, such as "Grandmaster Flash trolling vacant lots for components, or a sawdust-encrusted Jazzy Jay building speaker cabinets" (Katz 2012: 64). This sense of ownership became stronger as practitioners revised and adapted these tools to become part of their emerging cultural construct. Furthermore, the significant (re)appropriation of these objects has also had an industry-shifting impact on manufacturing, and the Technics SL-1200 is a prime example.

During the 1980s the Technics SL-1200 (and the later SL-1210 models) arguably became regarded as the only turntable worthy of use by hip hop DJs. Technics became the official sponsors of the DMC (Disco Mix Club) World DJ Championships (initiated in 1985) and celebrated the status of the turntable by offering a pair of gold-plated turntables as the prize in 1989.[27] The Technics SL-1200 was first produced in October 1972 as a top-end home hi-fi product. Aspiring DJs from the ghetto were not able to afford such luxuries, and much can be attributed to the New York City blackout of 1977 when 1,161 stores were looted (including many hi-fi and audio stores). Across the city 3,766 people were arrested in connection with vandalism and looting. As a consequence of this tumult, hip hop was transformed, almost overnight, as DJs acquired the equipment they needed to mix on high quality, direct-drive turntables. The turntable was appropriated from consumer object to production instrument, critical to the development of hip hop music, and in time turntablism became a subculture of its own, overlapping particularly with the UK and European drum 'n' bass movement of the 1990s.[28] The ingenuity of creating music from physically manipulating a record by hand epitomizes the inventive approach to (re)appropriation in hip hop, a practice that greatly influenced turntable design. Many DJs began their careers on much more affordable turntables which were usually belt-drive, had no pitch-control or anti-skate device, and were much less robust and stable than the SL-1200. This made for extreme difficulty in controlling the deck,[29] as records would often skip when manipulated, and the belt-drive system made for slow starts upon release of the vinyl. However frustrating though, learning to DJ on such low technology brought with it a steep learning curve, and techniques, tactics and gadgets were invented and reinvented to successfully mix on such equipment. Plastic carrier bags or the transparent polycarbonate inner bags of 12" records were cut to shape and placed on the platter before a record, providing a layer of material to aid the backspin (and to limit damage to the underside of records). Thin strips of sticky tape (often from blank audio cassette stickers) were threaded through the centre-hole of records to ensure a snug fit around the centre-spindle to reduce jolting, and penny-pieces and lumps of Blu-Tac were placed strategically on top of the stylus head shell in place of a counterweight. Each situation demanded a slightly different assemblage as the weight and width of record grooves differed, needles wore at dissimilar rates, and turntables were positioned at alternative heights and surfaces which all required consideration and appropriate engineering intervention. Other ergonomic factors also contributed to the DJ's assemblage: one's physical movements, body structure, stability of furniture, and floor construction. Once turntablism was mastered on this kind of set-up, moving up to the SL-1200 was effortless.

The SL-1200 truly solidified its place in hip hop culture, and when, throughout the 1980s, the emerging globalization of hip hop fostered a desire to start DJing for youths across the world, other audio equipment manufacturers (as well as Technics) began to realize the potential market hip hop had created for them. Vestax, Stanton, Gemini and Numark were among the first companies to enter the DJ market, with Vestax launching its range of professional turntables, the PDX models in the 1990s. Technics' competitors all based their products on the attributes of the SL-1200 but were often cheaper (certainly in the case of Gemini) and aimed to attract novices to their entry-level products, with their sales pitches aligned to the values and actions of turntablism. Stanton's ST-150's selectable pitch control ranges from +/-8%, +/-25%, +/-50% (compared to the standard +/-8% on the SL-1200), and Vestax's pioneering reverse mode were features introduced in an attempt to draw consumers away from Technics. However, the SL-1200 (and its subsequent models) remains a cultural icon associated with hip hop and is arguably the only piece of mainstream hi-fi equipment to closely retain its price, with only minimal value depreciation.[30] Many of these other turntables are excellent products, but why do they depreciate rapidly while the SL-1200 holds its price? The answer lies in the non-material cultural value embodied within the object.

The SL-1200 is one of many products attributed to hip hop culture; others additional to those referenced above include appropriated items of clothing, including the Kangol Bermuda hat made famous by LL Cool J and MC Shan, the Adidas shelltoes famed by Run-D.M.C., and the name-belt buckle championed by T La Rock which enhanced identity and carried a symbolism associated with bespoke jewelry. These clothing accessories were, however, acquired by hip hop culture before they were made famous by these artists, and it is the search for style, originality and availability that contribute to this reimagining and innovation of fashion. The donning of sports clothes was initially a result of practicality and affordability, and Kangol hats enhanced

Figure 1.3: The Shure SM58 microphone, name-belt buckle, Kangol Bermuda and toweling beer mat (used to shine-up lino and dancefloors, a popular accessory in formative British Bboying). Photograph by author.

the look and dynamics of breaking Bboys (Figure 1.3). As well as Kangol products, other hats were desirable such as deer stalkers and trilbys, which added style but also class and status; plus, they were easy to steal. Again, these are physical representations and components of the assemblage of hip hop but attached to these is the cultural non-materiality of hip hop which is triple-faceted. Firstly, it is a reflective and projective mind state that embraces the search for knowledge of history, self and contextual positioning; secondly, it is the mastering of techniques, skills and the creation of original practice; and thirdly, it is the evolution and celebration of style manifest in the final results and output. Within these three facets, there exists a series of unwritten, organic rules which at times can be construed as paradoxical when observed from outside hip hop culture. These rules include approaches to battling, style, mentorship, crew organization, communication with authority, and attitude to turf and neighbourhoods and ultimately respect to pioneers. The non-materiality of hip hop is complex and increases in complexity when cultural practices and values are imported to a different context. Non-material value is partially embodied within the cultural value of its associated artefacts, a theme crucial to making sense of provincial British hip hop and one that underpins much of the following chapters.

Chapter 2

The Relocation of Hip Hop: The Perfect Beat, Duck Rock and Cultural Acquisition

On Saturday mornings after my newspaper round, I began to catch the 339 Devon General bus from the small village of Newton Poppleford where I lived to the metropolis of Exeter some half an hour away. The sole purpose of this trip (which quickly became a ritual that was to last for five years) was to dig through the racks of records in the high street's WHSmith newsagents (who at the time stocked vinyl), HMV and Our Price, scanning record sleeve graphics and designs for some hint that inside may lay a slice of fresh hip hop. It was on one such occasion during the autumn of 1983 when in WHSmith I discovered *Street Sounds Electro 1*, a compilation album released by Morgan Khan's industrious London-based label Street Sounds. As I flicked through the "Various" section my eyes were suddenly struck by a huge, pastel pink number "1" on a De Stijl style background. It was unlike any record I had encountered before, the graphics beguiled me and revealed nothing about the content or context; however I recognized the word "ELECTRO" in large black text—stretching vertically up the right-hand side of the sleeve. I took the gamble and although I had never heard of any of the featured artists, made a purchase. I was staying at my grandmother's house for the school break, and she allowed me to play the record when I returned to her bungalow. I tentatively approached the musty 1950s flat-top hi-fi and slid back the veneered panelling which groaned a low clang, revealing the record player within (which had not so much as glanced at a record since Wilhelm Kempff's rendition of *Für Elise* around a decade before). I slid the wax out of its sleeve, and placed my *Electro 1* on the platter. Anticipation turned to excitement as the crescendo of the first haunting chords of 'I'm The Packman (Eat Everything I Can)' by The Packman reached their peak, sustained through the hypnotic soundscape of Newcleus' 'Jam On Revenge (The Wikki-Wikki Song)', to the conclusion of Captain Rock's Afrofuturist adventure on 'The Return Of Captain Rock'. I was mesmerized, transfixed, captivated. Although this was not my first encounter with hip hop, it remains one of my strongest memories. As the sounds filled my ears I felt as though this music had always been a part of me, yet it was so new, fresh and unprecedented. Every song sounded so different, but equally so exciting as the sonics projected my imagination through the living-room window and into the rugged landscape of Exmoor beyond. I played the record again, and again, and then again. What did the high-pitched, mischievous "wikki wikki wikki" chant mean? Why was this the return of Captain Rock, had he made previous records? Who was this Packman? I yearned for more.

On Relocation

In *Youth Culture in Modern Britain, c. 1920—c. 1970* (Fowler 2008), David Fowler paraphrases Richard Hoggart's essay in *The Guardian* from 1967:

> Hoggart provides in this short essay a model of how Youth Culture, in his view, developed in British society. He argued that it was a London-centric idea and only after a time lag (unspecified) did it reach provincial towns and cities. The vehicles for the spread of this Youth Culture, he suggested, were pop programmes such as *Ready Steady Go!*, radio, magazines, fashion and records (Fowler 2008: 125).

The ways in which hip hop travelled through the British provinces is of course similar, but, as I intend this book to argue, hip hop in provincial Britain did much more than simply arrive there from the metropolis. Furthermore, hip hop is often described as a "youth culture", which I consider to be blatant misrepresentation; rather, hip hop can be cultivated in youth, but it charges its participants with continual reflective and contextual learning which increases with maturity.

The cultural context of hip hop in Britain requires locating with respect to two critical relationships: firstly, the relationship between Britain (as an entirety) and New York, and secondly, the relationship of urban Britain vis-à-vis provincial Britain. In turn, the interrelationship between these reveals a dynamism of some complexity, a cultural triad from the locus of the provincial dweller which I will unpack later in this section. This triad supports the remainder of this chapter via the primary transatlantic exchanges of hip hop's practices and reifications. As outlined in the introduction, hip hop culture had gathered a critical mass and momentum by 1982 and from New York's point of view was already experiencing moments of stylistic change and global reach. In Britain by now Kurtis Blow had appeared on BBC's *Top Of The Pops*,[1] 'Rapper's Delight' had opened the gates to the era of the disco-rap record, Grandmaster Flash & The Furious Five's 'The Message' had peaked at number eight in the UK official charts on 28 August 1982 and broke into the top ten in Austria, New Zealand and Holland,[2] while Charlie Ahearn's hugely significant film *Wild Style* was released in theatres that autumn. However, in Britain hip hop was still unidentifiable as a cultural movement, and rap was perceived incidentally as a gimmicky alternative to singing (illustrated in the pop records of Adam Ant and The Ants' 'Ant Rap' [1981], and Wham!'s 'Wham! Rap' [1982]). Hip hop's invisibility may well be attributable to the visual presentation of Kurtis Blow and Sugarhill Gang—they were bright, jolly and shiny, conveyed as disco acts with no suggestion of the underlying culture they represented. 'The Message' was not performed live on British television, but the video was broadcast, albeit late at night. The song remains an exemplar of political rap, and the video (a game-changer as the first true hip hop music video) illustrated the destitution of New York City, rapping on the street, the stoop and generally hanging out until the police harassment scene at the close, "the track is a jeremiad about inner-city unemployment, underdevelopment, poverty, and blight—its central 'message' that if structural racism continues an uncertain threat will materialize" (Rollefson 2017: 97). Despite the great political weight of the song, the video was devoid of anything obvious that suggested a new culture was on its way to audiences in Britain.

During 1982, rap records were beginning to diversify from purely disco rhythms to the sounds of electro, championed by the interplanetary Arthur Baker production 'Planet Rock' (1982). The year 1983 was one of seismic expansion for hip hop culture generally; as well as pirate copies of *Wild Style* leaking through Europe, Tony Silver's equally important documentary *Style Wars* was pivotal to the spread of the culture, for the first time presenting all four physical elements with some clarity and categorization to a British audience. Closer to home, the fascination with Malcolm McLaren's 'Buffalo Gals' video and Morgan Khan's *Street Sounds Electro* series launch offered consumers tangible touchstones of the culture that was to become known as hip hop.

Reflecting on the popular music scene in 1982 Britain, the popular phase of new romanticism was fading. Amongst The Jam's revivalist mod sound epitomized in 'A Town Called Malice', Human League's representations of narcissism, and the disposable pop of Bucks Fizz, 1982 was a year of transition. The anxiety embedded within the overtly complex 'My Camera Never Lies', the subtle revealing of delusion in 'Mirror Man', and Paul Weller's observational lyrics on life in Woking, "A whole street's belief in Sunday's roast beef / Gets dashed against the Co-op / To either cut down on beer or the kids' new gear / It's a big decision in a town called Malice", were metaphorical for the state of the nation. In broader society, the Falklands conflict had resurrected, for some citizens, the fallacy of the British Empire and reignited the delusion of colonialism; Canada repatriated its constitution, and Gibraltar reinstated the pedestrian gateway to mainland Spain. A year after widespread riots, the effects of Thatcher's monetarism tactics led to the dissolution of British National Oil Corporation in favour of privately owned Britoil,[3] and the closure of Round Oak Steelworks resulting in an enormous loss of jobs. Immigrants became scapegoats for deprivation, fuelling the hallucinations of John Tyndell which led to the formation of the British National Party (BNP). Football hooliganism was rife with the first related death occurring during a riot between Arsenal and West Ham United (Davies 1983). There was anger rising in the nation yet, despite all this, the conservatives were still ahead in the opinion polls. The Tories' claims that the economy was the strongest and unemployment the lowest since 1979's winter of discontent was certainly a contributing factor here; however the support was far from universal. Britain was blatantly split geographically, culturally and economically. Thatcher's main priority was very much focused on revitalizing London and the South-East, which concurrently ostracized major regions in the North, Scotland, Wales and parts of the West Country. This divide was also much more complex and abstruse than it may first appear, particularly from the experience of British youth. On the question of British identity, Mark Cowan (DJ Science) felt a strong disconnection from Britishness living in Stenhousemuir, Scotland:

> That was the time of the Thatcher and Tory domination in politics. It was great for London and the south as many people prospered but it was very different at the other end of the UK. Pretty much everyone I knew felt they were treated as second class citizens and looked upon as a class below (email to author, 30 April 2017).

However, it was not as binary as a north-south divide, as Deliverance's Remark suggests: "I lived in Tooting Broadway, as a child growing up in multicultural South London it was intense at times, vibrant and energetic with an air of political uncertainty around us, it was the cold Thatcher years, when shops were closing due to the recession" (email to author, 24 April 2017). Exeter-based Eraze explains: "It was quite a revolutionary time anyway, with Scargill...the political unrest of the Thatcher years...there was a lot of stuff going on. It was hard not to be affected by it, but it's also hard to pinpoint exactly why" (i/v, Exeter, 13 March 2017). The adolescent demographic was exposed to an increasing and intensifying media presence, and with the arrival of Channel 4, MTV and the popularization of the VHS player, the early 1980s provided an unprecedented accessibility to a diverse set of cultural references delivered largely through the media. Through the music video and other televisual representations, those youths that chose to explore hip hop found themselves questioning their own cultural heritage and very essence of Britishness.

Popular music was largely represented and delivered through the sound of new wave, post-punk and the plasticized spawn of glam rock, which in the mainstream had all but smothered the worthiness of Jerry Dammers' ska and Paul Weller's mod revivals.[4] In television, cultural reference points were presented to the youth via shows such as *Blue Peter*, *Grange Hill* and *Rentaghost*; and while *Blue Peter* effectively charged viewers with how to be a model citizen in British society through its various portrayals of exemplary behaviours,[5] Phil Redmond offered as earthy a rendering as he could through the tribulations of everyday London school life in *Grange Hill*.[6] *Rentaghost* filled the void between these worlds in true British slapstick style, parodying the stress of capitalist work-life through the escapism of a comedic spirit world. Of course, these were not the only television programmes broadcast, and neither did the youth necessarily consider them in this way, but they were regarded as great British staples of children's television production (Davies and Kelley 1999). If *Blue Peter* and *Rentaghost* safely represented the fallacious aims of the BBC and the government, *Grange Hill* was dangerous, and perceived as a threat to social stability, with the press branding Redmond as "the devil incarnate, a Marxist trying to break down the structure of society" (Dickson 2015). These three television shows uncannily emulated the real-world environment, and in the provinces, *Grange Hill* was as close as one could get to experiencing everyday life in the metropolis, however artificially staged it may have been. In 1980 I was banned from watching *Grange Hill* amidst fear that I would emerge from the brown MFI settee as a disobedient, cigarette-smoking, loose-lipped truanting child upon its closing credits. However, rather than transpire as an incarnation of Tucker, I reluctantly accepted this ban from my mother; although I was bewildered at the time as to why this ban was placed, I can now reflect that media propaganda was largely to blame. I am also certain that there was some notion that (aspiring middle-class) parents in provincial areas did not want their children mimicking the perceived stereotypical actions of inner-city youth they believed they were witnessing on television. The ideologies embedded in traditional provincial regions deceived even its own dwellers.

There exists an estranged dialectic between "city" and "non-city" which is far from facile. This estrangement derives from a form of cultural distancing, speed and transmission. The provincial environment is a complex beast, in many ways more complex than that of the metropolis. The provincial portrays calmness, reservation, maturity and control, fuelled gently by docility and a lack of ambition yet its reality can be intense, intimidating, cruel and hostile. Its attitudes are rooted in tradition and amplify some of the most extreme ideologies in both socialism and conservatism, within the traditional social structures of mining and farming communities, diluted and fragmented with the temporal relocation of the daily commuter. However, broadcasts (television or otherwise) slice through space at great speed directly into the hub of the home, delivering various forms of cultural propaganda and representations, creating tension as much as saturation. Lefebvre describes the role of the television as a component of linear rhythm in life: "you can leave the TV or radio on and go about your business, distractedly following the ocular and verbal chatter" (Lefebvre 2004: 47). Simply by depressing a button or dial, one can connect to a different rhythm, which by simulation and broadcast seems to, in part, operate in the same space-time, yet without the opportunity for dialogue.

In this way, representations of the urban are immediately presented inside the domesticity of the provincial, slicing across the environment. Returning to *Grange Hill*, there was no discourse, no discussion as to what constitutes the experience of a London secondary modern school, no debate as to its merits, its shortfalls or even its existence. Its portrayal was delivered into the provincial sitting room to be consumed; children absorbed themselves in this world, captivated in the edited and packaged story, while parents passed judgement from afar on the use of slang, undone school ties and playground fighting, under the delusion that these behaviours do not display themselves in the provinces. The early evening news programmes that followed children's television accentuate these phenomena, although here real people's lives are chopped and edited, and through some paradox of play the media becomes part of the everyday, but the media portrayal of the everyday is spun to be illusory—through over-communication. The hyperreal takes over: "The hyperreality of communication and meaning. More real than the real, that is how the real is abolished" (Baudrillard 1994: 81), something I will return to later. As part of the complex rhythm of life, these forms of propaganda can act as agents for the shaping of an imagined habitus. This imagined habitus is constructed of a cultural bricolage which, when discussed in the evolution of provincial hip hop, envelops the direct experience of the provincial everyday, the indirect urban representations, and the alien forms of hip hop.

The Cultural Triad

The first phenomenon of the cultural triad is experiential and relates to the direct lived experiences of dwelling in the provincial realm (Figure 2.1). Previously I defined the provincial in terms of a rooted spatio-cultural value system that linked to both rural and urban thinking and living, and I also suggested that provincial life operated with both extreme conservatism and socialism. I should qualify these statements here, insomuch that I grew up in Devon during the 1980s, a tourism, dairy and crop farming county that is traditionally anchored in conservatism. People did not tend to relocate, there was minimal postwar immigration, and the area was sparsely populated compared to other provinces, with less than half the national population density. Any change was slow in comparison to that of the cities, and the unhurried passing of time through a spacious landscape provided a living experience of some passivity. Through the decade's increased consumption, much of the working class aspired to middle-class values; the middle class sought one-upmanship on their peers yet were complacent enough to exemplify the epitome of bourgeois life. In material culture, what mattered were status symbols and tradition; those of thatched cottages, land drains and pheasant shooting. Compare this experience with the challenge of living in a mining village suffering from the actions of the National Coal Board's colliery review procedure: intent on closing inefficient pits following Thatcher's plans to close 23 pits across the country in February 1981, the National Union of Mineworkers led by Arthur Scargill embarked on moves to put in place a large-scale strike which at its peak saw 142,000 miners on strike during 1984–85 (van der Velden 2007: 352–54). These very contrastive experiences of provincial life share one common denominator: a cultural distancing from the metropolis, a distance that made for a very different hip hop education from that of its city counterpart. However, despite this distancing to urban places, the language of urbanism embodied within construction elements in provincial space (for example, electricity pylons, steel bridges, concrete drainage dykes and concrete bus shelters) offered an urban taster that many rural hip hop headz migrated towards, often becoming backdrops for photographs, places to write graffiti, rap, or just hang out.

The second and third moments of this triad relate to representations of the urban, which are both directly lived and perceived but are also imagined through secondary forms of representation and symbolism. These urban representations can be described in two ways: firstly, in a Lefebvrian sense, as the temporal lived and perceived experiences of provincial dwellers during encounters with the city, and secondly, through the imagined experiences

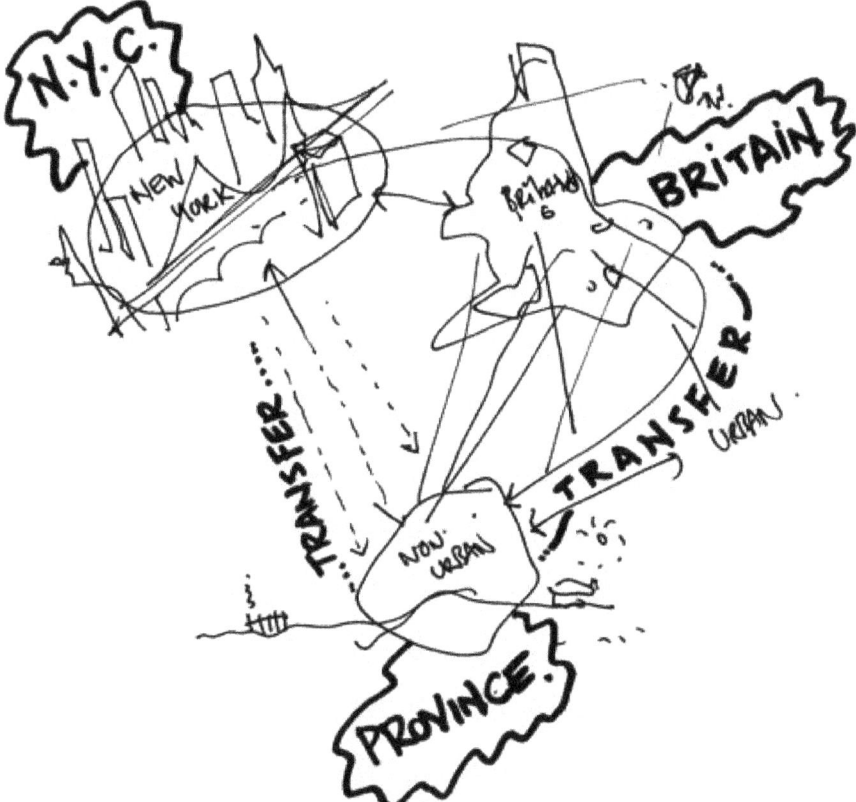

Figure 2.1: The imagined hip hop habitus in respect of the British provincial, as an acquired cultural and conceptual triad. Diagram by author.

embedded within the artefacts of music, film and non-moving imagery. Provincial dwellers drew upon temporary engagement and observations with the city and American hip hop through these imagined secondary experiences, expedited by engagement with its reifications and artefacts to frame their own less urban position. Both forms of exposure reveal a further complexity as they are by no means disconnected. Of course, British city dwellers would also have experienced secondary forms of hip hop representation; however, there is a distinction here that is twofold. Firstly, urbanites, particularly those living in London and other major cities, were in closer proximity to imported records, and exposed to local pirate and licensed radio shows.[7] By 1983 London's Groove Records, Soho, was stocking the hottest American 12″ singles on import, and an advertisement in an August 1983 edition of *Blues & Soul Magazine* listed Project Future's 'Ray-Gun-Omics', Time Zone's 'Wildstyle' and 'Jam On Revenge' by Newcleus in their top 20 electro/funk chart (all of which featured on the *Street Sounds Electro* series discussed in the next section).[8] While provincial dwellers occasionally caught a glimpse of the Groove chart, they might have only heard a small number of these records. By 1984, Mike Allen (The Boss) was hosting his renowned thrice-weekly hip hop shows, which grew out of his jazz, funk and soul shows on Capital Radio that started in the early 1980s, and a number of other urban stations aired similar programmes (for example Stu Allan on Manchester's Piccadilly Radio and Key 103).

Secondly, family was an important linkage between urban Britain and urban America, and largely due to postwar immigration and the Windrush generation major cities now had almost 40 years of Caribbean, black diaspora and black cultural heritage, which was almost nonexistent in the remoter provinces.[9] Even in some of the provincial larger towns there was minimal non-white culture, as Tom Darnell[10] recalls: "there was definitely a void of black influence in Brighton… According to the 1991 census, Brighton had a population just shy of a quarter of a million people. The non-white population at that time made up only 3.1%, with the Black Caribbean, Black African and Black Other population constituting only 0.5% of Brighton's population"[11] (email to author, 2 April 2017). According to Simon Denny, Norwich was more extreme: "Norwich was regarded as the last white city—I had heard about there being NF [National Front] head office in Norfolk and the education was geared to a white Catholic/Christian value base. The chance of bumping into black and minority ethnic groups were very remote" (email to author, 30 March 2017). Boston, Lincolnshire was in a similar position, as Scott Coombes remembers: "the population was roughly 45,000 at this time, of which very few indeed were of multicultural origin" (email to author, 12 December 2017).

British Hip Hop and Britishness

The first true British hip hop record was 'Christmas Rapping' recorded by Dizzy Heights and released on corporate label Polydor in 1982. Despite a handful of records between 1982 and 1986, 'Christmas Rapping' was his only rap song, with his later releases aiming for the commercial disco market. During the mid-1980s, a trickle of British artists achieved recording contracts and released some notable records, although these were mainly geared towards commercial success by record label management (established British record labels did not know how to handle British rap music, and still struggle with it), and were received with mixed responses on street level. Artists included Newtrament, Three Wize Men, Fission, Private Party, and City Limits Crew, but the weight of British hip hop arrived with Simon Harris and his London-based label Music of Life, home to Derek B, MC Duke, She Rockers, and later Demon Boyz, Hijack, and Hardnoise. In other major cities, Manchester was home to the seminal Bboy crew Broken Glass, whose 'Style Of The Street' (1984) was hugely influential across the country, while in Bristol The Wild Bunch's presence in the city helped solidify the future of Massive Attack and the Bristol scene.[12] It was not until 1990 that artists from outside the major cities began to gain recording contracts, two of the most noteworthy being Caveman (from High Wycombe, Berkshire), and Krispy 3 (from Chorley, Lancashire), although to headz further afield, these artists were perceived as hailing from London and Manchester respectively.[13] The turn of the new decade saw the arrival of the formidable Shepherd's Bush-based label Kold Sweat, which released over seventy records in its short-lived existence until 1994 and was the only strong contender to rival Music of Life.[14]

Were there any representations of Britishness presented in the careers of these pioneering British artists? Newtrament's only release, the vocoder-laden 'London Bridge Is Falling Down' (1983) and London Posse's self-titled record (1987) both incorporate the culturally contextual nursery rhyme: "London Bridge Is Falling Down / My Fair Lady" in the lyrics.[15] While Newtrament recite the lyrics as in the original nursery rhyme, London Posse adapt most of the wordage but retain the tune: "London Posse we don't choke / We don't smoke, speed or coke / Or the charlie or go broke / My fair lady…". MC Duke's fourth single 'I'm Riffin' (English Rasta)' (1989) brought the English reference into the chorus hook, and a myriad of other references appeared such as "My posse and I had to do it again / Make sure you all know who's number one in England" in Derek B's 'Good Groove' (1988). Regional and local references were also common, one of the standout moments being the crisp delivery of Kamanchi Sly's shout outs at the end of 'Hold No Hostage' (1988), where he acknowledges his local and urban geographic status: "Extra special thanks goes out to the people of Brixton, Stockwell, Clapham, Vauxhall, Peckham and Streatham. South London serves again". Forman discusses the obvious emphasis on locality and places in hip hop lyrics:

> Rap's lyrical constructions commonly display a pronounced emphasis on place and locality... Rap artists draw inspiration from their regional affiliations as well as from a keen sense of what I call the extreme local, upon which they base their constructions of spatial imagery (2002: xvii).

The sense of pride in one's turf is clearly evident in K. Sly's shout-out, much akin to the call and response dialogue in the original New York block parties, but before attempting to further the distinction between territories in British hip hop, it is important to discuss the question of Britishness as a cultural value system.[16]

How does the question of Britishness position itself within British hip hop culture? Irene Morra asserts Vron Ware's comment that the English are the only cultured nation without their own music (Morra 2014: 2). However, Morra continues to declare that: "the musical heritage of Britain is established and diverse" (Morra 2014: 2). Furthermore, Morra discusses the themes central to Britishness and popular music culture that emerged from the 1960s linked to classlessness and national pride. This position is illustrated clearly with reference to mod culture, the followers of which accepted the ambitions of working-class British band The Who's classically informed concept albums within a "self-consciously classless society" (Morra 2014: 52). Talking of the 1960s mod era and its social and cultural identity, Pete Townshend, quoted in Levy, states: "It was the closest to patriotism that I've ever felt" (Levy 2003: 132). Mod, however, carried with it a paradox; it displayed the clean-cut characteristics of Modernism, the authoritarianism of the elite, and the conviction of the establishment that they were reacting against (Weight 2013: 9). With respect to punk rock, Morra suggests that punk extended the idea of the unlearned and unskilled natural expression (found in skiffle), and was further liberated through the crudeness of punk's do-it-yourself approach (Morra 2014: 71). What is interesting here is that the value, identity and representation of Britishness in popular music appears to become British through some virtuous act or practice, having been acquired and appropriated from some other place, and packaged as British product for mainstream consumption. But what of hip hop? In many ways, British hip hop carried a similar value system to punk. Young (2008: 239) drives a compelling argument that the value system of Englishness is developed outside the geography of the nation and is in fact ideological in its construct of national identity.[17] There is clearly a form of multiculturalism embedded here, and this construct made up of many cultures does not simply operate in a linear fashion, but operates simultaneously, cyclically and dialectically, and I would point again to London Posse and Hijack's early releases as clear examples of this. In Ben Pitcher's discussion about multiculturalism as forms of social practice, he states that:

> While it is sometimes useful to think about multiculturalism as a local phenomenon, and particularly of contemporary urban life, states ultimately concern themselves with the nation as a fundamental horizon of identity and belonging. As such, the politics of multiculturalism are ultimately a national politics, and are concerned with what it means to identify with and belong to a society as a whole, even if this belonging takes a particular form (Pitcher 2009: 23).

By proposing that the various forms of local multiculturalism eventually become of national interest (in terms of the nation-state), he continues: "The state's claim to represent or speak for the nation is, I want to suggest, absolutely essential for an understanding of the contemporary politics of multiculturalism" (Pitcher 2009: 23). It may be the case that forms of multiculturalism can be designed into policies for social cohesion, for example; however I would respond by advocating the value of multiculturalism in the locale, and that it is the local and regional phenomena of multiculturalism that drives the identity of British hip hop. This local identity is crucial to the (de)regionalization and post-globalization of hip hop culture, as the state cannot signify the spatio-politics of hip hop; when Butler and Spivak talk about the state as something that: "can signify the source of non-belonging, even produce that non-belonging as a quasi-permanent state" (Butler and Spivak 2007: 4), they talk about exactly the politics of region that woke hip hop headz encounter. These ideas are discussed further in Chapters 5 and 6, but here I would state that the multiculturalism of provincial hip hop is primarily spatial and material, and becomes variably non-material through acquisition, practice and reflection. This spatio-multiculturalism is connected to displacement, migration and juxtaposition with other cultural reference points, and the representations embedded with this spatio-multiculturalism are experienced and valued differently according to the cultural conditions and positioning of those that produce and consume these constructs, making them essentially local and regional.

There are three relative ways in which to explore the acquisition of hip hop in Britain. The first is to examine what I will term "the Buffalo Gals Effect", where Malcolm McLaren witnessed the vibrant cultural emergence of hip hop in New York and reframed it for broader consumption. Coupled with his reputation as the establishment's antagonist, he was enthused by the idea of "making music out of other people's music".[18] However, when McLaren's approach and product are unpacked, there arises questions connected to imperialism, colonialism and exploitation, and ultimately the production techniques of capitalist-consumerism. The second is what I dub "the London Posse Effect", where the diasporic histories of multiculturalism and the plurality of social identity are explored through Jamaican heritage, reggae influences and life in London during the formative years of hip hop which led to a formation of a particularly British hip hop identity. The third, I call "the Street Sounds Effect", which frames the idea of the distancing and remoteness experienced by provincial headz, the slow traditions of regional life with the secondary representations carried within the compilation albums released by labels such as Street Sounds, Tommy Boy, Charisma and Jive. The relationships between these three effects are what drives the very essence of Britishness and the provincial within hip hop, and discussions throughout the remainder of the book relate in some manner to these effects.

The Perfect Beat

The 1982 release 'Planet Rock', by Afrika Bambaataa & the Soul Sonic Force (music by Planet Patrol) and produced by Arthur Baker was a monumental record indeed.[19] It epitomized the seismic shift of hip hop's sound from disco-rap to the newly embraced sound of electro and had an enormous impact worldwide. So high was its regard, that between its initial release and 2016, it has been released via 70 different official issues, and at least eight unofficial, in the US, Europe, Japan, Brazil and Canada.[20] It has been remixed and reinvented to suit hip hop, rave, house, electronic and trance audiences; appeared on over a hundred official compilation albums, and has been a Bboy anthem for nearly 40 years, although is played less frequently at the time of writing due to allegations against Afrika Bambaataa.[21] One of the compilation albums that had the greatest impact in Britain, although almost two years after the initial release of 'Planet Rock', was *Street Sounds Crucial Electro 2* (1984). Renowned graffiti writer, Kilo, living in Devon at the time, specifically recalls:

> We were sat around listening to 'Planet Rock', I'd never heard anything like it, it blew me away, and I had to find out about this electro. I didn't even really know the kid who had the tape, but I went back to his house the following day to ask him about it, that sound was so exciting (i/v, Cambridge, 23 May 2017).

Two other important compilations featuring 'Planet Rock' was *The Perfect Beat* (1983) and *Tommy Boy—Greatest Beats* (1985), the latter containing 14 songs released on the Tommy Boy Records label which closed with a megamix by 3-D (Ralph D'Agostino, Tommy Musto and Tommy Sozzi).[22] Swindon's Stepchild recounts his first encounter with the Arthur Baker produced Tommy Boy sound, through an American boy called Snowy whose father had been stationed at the nearby US Air Force base: "He used to get radio shows on cassette sent over and showed me tunes like 'Cheap Thrills'[23] and 'Planet Rock', there was a depth to those tunes that riddled me with worms, imagination blown, by the time I heard 'Looking For The Perfect Beat'[24] I thought I'd found God" (i/v, Swindon, 3 December 2017).

One of the qualities that makes 'Planet Rock' so fascinating is that producer Arthur Baker had resynthesized Kraftwerk's 'Trans Europe Express' from 1977. The exquisite synth patterns accompanied by innovative Roland TR-808 percussion and the confidence in the sparse, frugal rhyme patterns challenged the disco-rap convention, resulting in a fusion of electro, rap and electronic funk. Baker illustrates the depth of rhythm he achieved by using this instrument: "The rhythm of an 808 has its own internal groove".[25] The 12″ version stands at over six minutes in length, and epically builds as Bambaataa, M.C. G.L.O.B.E., Pow Wow and Mr. Biggs encourage one to socialize, to get down and "let your soul lead the way", with key references to Mother Earth, nature's children and "livin' dreams" on a "land of a master jam". These lyrical territories lace the atmospheric music perfectly, and as one listens, one is transported to this place and time where chasing dreams is possible. 'Planet Rock' undoubtedly reached people in club-land, but its impact (along with the other three Afrika Bambaataa & Soulsonic Force singles)[26] touched young British hip hop headz too young to go clubbing. The context of 'Planet Rock' is (outer) space rather than (inner) place; and the provincial youth caught up in its space-age soundscape experienced a different form of reality, one which exists in "such a place that creates such a melody".[27] Deliverance's Remark[28] attests: "For me it was hearing 'Planet Rock' being played on a boombox[29] by an older boy in the school canteen at Ernest Bevin. I could hear and feel its vibrations stirring in me…deeply" (email to author, 5 May 2017).

For me, it was another Soulsonic Force record, 'Looking for the Perfect Beat', that drew me closer into hip hop. I first encountered this song on the compilation album *The Perfect Beat*, curiously released in 1983 within the UK, Greece and Brazil only (due to Tommy Boy's relationship with 21 Records and Polygram Records) and consisted of only five songs.[30] Another epic adventure, much like 'Planet Rock', but more urgent, intelligent and exhilarating, drenched in heavy electronic synths, tough beats, vicious cuts and complex arrangements, 'Looking for the Perfect Beat' confirmed my love for hip hop. Each time I spun the wax, the shift in drum programming on the shout "BEAT THIS!" twelve-pattern breakdown released a rush inside me that compelled me to pop and lock,[31] before the rhythm switched back to that of the opening bars. Hollers of "it's working, it's working!" by Soulsonic Force suggested that something long in the making had eventually clicked, that the planets, moons and stars had aligned exactly as they should for this bright new phase of electro-rap charged hip hop. One of the reasons this song may have had such an impact on me is that three of the other songs on *The Perfect Beat* were slight variations of 'Planet Rock', including 'Play at Your Own Risk' and the instrumental version, 'Rock at Your Own Risk', and with the moody vibes of 'Pack Jam' closing out the album, it became clear to me that the energetic, fast, cut-laden dynamic was what I desired. I hunted out the futuristic—those sounds were so thrilling as I sat within what at the time felt like the cultural vacuum of hip hop; alien and other-worldly, I fully embraced the soul of the sonics without any form of context apart from a fondness for science fiction, and I was not alone. Evil Ed, a DJ and producer growing up in Leighton Buzzard remembers: "I was a sci-fi fan as a kid and so I instantly took to tunes like 'Planet Rock' and anything with a vocoder or laser sounds in it" (email to author, 14 June 2017).

Arthur Baker also delivered a further three songs which were to anchor the idea of hip hop culture in Britain, these being Afrika Bambaataa & Soulsonic Force's 'Frantic Situation' (1984), 'Battle Cry' (1984) by Rocker's Revenge, and 'Breaker's Revenge' (1984) with full artist's credit to Baker himself. Not only do these three songs amplify the elation and intensity of 'Looking for the Perfect Beat', but for aspiring British headz they also promoted the landscape of Bboying under the holistic sky of hip hop. 'Breaker's Revenge' and 'Battle Cry', similar in essence (albeit 'Battle Cry' is a darker piece of music), echo urgency and the mindset of forthcoming breakdance combat. 'Battle Cry' launches with calls to war; distant explosions trigger a density of percussion, furious scratches and Zulu Nation style chanting which increase the temperature as the song progresses. Imminent engagement in combat becomes certain as the lyric "I know what's in store, because I'm headed for a dancin' war", is sung over sounds reminiscent of repetitive laser guns. References to the moonwalk, and then the exclamations: "freeze!", "dance sucker!", "fresh, fresh, fresh, fresh, fresh!", and as the song begins to conclude, "slide...glide...dive" and "headspin!" are delivered disturbingly, breathy and sinister, reinforcing various battle moves and tactics of subversion. Soundbites of "keep on pushing", "do it" and "hey!" are cut and scratched throughout adding to the song's menacing vibe.

'Breaker's Revenge' is slicker and jazzier (largely due to the inclusion of a dynamic jazz piano solo) although its polished sparkle does not distract from an equally demanding percussion and rhythm freestyle arrangement. From the opening, high-pitched a cappella shrills of "Break!...break!" precede heavy percussion laden with snares, claps, rim shots and hi-hats; an insistent bassline backs the cuts and scratches of "beat this!", "party people", and other Soulsonic Force chants. Relentless sound drops of "break", "huhs", and "breakdance is where it's at!" splatter the song, seemingly at every opportunity. These vocal stabs act almost like percussion themselves, which follow an incredibly complex drum roll and conga pattern, a shrieking "Say what? Eeeeeeeee....hit me!" and precede the only pure lyrics that namecheck New York City, Atlanta GA, San Francisco, and Zimbabwe, illustrating hip hop's growing geographic reach and cultural-historic acknowledgements to Africa. Locations of black diaspora puncture through the electronic pulses of the 808 and into the ears of the provincial British youth.

'Frantic Situation' plays to a similar agenda, yet with deeper context in the lyrics. Soulsonic Force educate that hip hop was a "state of mind", "in a musical sense", timely in its arrival, inventive and electric, and that this "musical drive" is a worldwide phenomenon. The hip hop state of mind is discussed later in Chapter 6, but I would state here that the work of Soulsonic Force planted the seed that was to foster an awakening within the minds of British provincial headz. What these songs were communicating was a model whereby the landscape was one of "peace, unity, love and having fun",[32] yet one that challenged the expected conventions of life conveyed assertively and with determination, supported by empowering call and response motifs. "Everybody say… Say! Say what?" and chants of "zing zang a-zihzang zang…zing zang a-zangah" drew one into the song, and much like how the audience become part of the performance during Sun Ra Arkestra shows, Soulsonic Force records embraced and welcomed the listener to be part of this movement. At this point I began to make the connections between Bboying, battling and the style of the music, but like many in provincial Britain, was still naïve to the cultural context of why the invention of hip hop and the metaphorical messages in these records were paramount to the progression of an oppressed way of life.

Alien Forms

I describe hip hop at this point as alien, in two senses of the word. Hip hop was foreign to the British, not only invented overseas in New York but during its formative seven or eight years wholly belonging to it. Moreover, hip hop existed conceptually in another space; it was an incredibly unprecedented art form which was so exciting and beguiling that to the provincial British youth who fell in love with this culture, it felt like it was created by beings from another world as its sonics had no earthly precedent. Britain did not experience the thrill of the original park jams, the disco-rap era, or witness the decade-long evolution of hip hop culture between 1973 and 1983, but instead was given snapshots of cultural moments presented in parallel—edited highlights of hip hop's key developments—and these were the true points of arrival for hip hop in Britain. Wood (2009) observes that during his experience growing up in Scotland, the electro-fuelled hip hop records of the early 1980s "sounded both alien and familiar to a generation of youths growing up with computer games and music. This was not the sound of an essentialized black America, but a curious, compelling hybrid style" (Wood 2009: 187). This spattering of a new, beguiling culture was enough of an olive branch for much of the British youth, who felt so distant from the social, political and cultural structure of Britain, that hip hop was a dynamic agent for change.

It is no coincidence that much of the narrative within hip hop music produced in the early 1980s embodied alien concepts. Sinker (1992) explored the links between black science fiction and Afrodiasporic soniculture, and van Veen (2016) observes Sinker's mappings of "the tropes of armageddon and alien abduction as they shaped the shared imaginaries of the dispersed, yet connected cultures of what Paul Gilroy would memorably theorize—in nearly the same year—as the black Atlantic (1993)" (van Veen 2016: 68). These alien and science fiction tropes strongly align to the reimagining of the Atlantic slave trade (van Veen 2016: 68); armageddon has already happened according to Sinker (1992). The Atlantic conduit returns these accounts through the reorientations of hip hop, building message upon message into the culture. On discussing Sun-Ra and the space he created for the synergy of activism and innovation, Youngquist points to Afrika Bambaataa as the one who "stepped into that space with the commanding twelve-inch single 'Planet Rock'" (Youngquist 2016: 248). Sun-Ra, as the "original brother from another planet" (Youngquist 2016: 8), is crucial to Afrofuturist thought in hip hop—particularly soon after its inception, when it began to bleed past the bounds of New York City.

As well as Afrika Bambaataa & Soulsonic Force, artists such as Captain Rock and Newcleus presented themselves as either from outer space, or in dialogue with beings from other worlds. These science fiction driven concepts are far more than purely literal. Framed within the ideas of Afrofuturism, songs like Captain Rock's 'The Return of Captain Rock' (NIA Records, 1983) and 'Jam On Revenge' (Mayhew Records, 1983) by Newcleus exemplify the notions of nomadic spiritualism, and present contextual counter-positions to mainstream western culture. Songs like these were valuable commentary on the evolution of hip hop within a broader, oppressive societal framework, and reinforced hip hop's own existence in an alien world—but from this viewpoint the alien world constitutes that of urban dilapidation, the nomad (the marginalized being), and hip hop the culture that was born from the experiences of cultural diaspora and displacement (de Paor-Evans 2018b and 2018d). The term Afrofuturism was not coined until a decade later than these revolutionary records,[33] but these songs draw inspiration from earlier artists linked deeply to Afrofuturism such as Sun Ra and his Sun Ra Arkestra, and George Clinton and his ParliaFunkadelicMent movement, who each respectively challenged socio-political contours through their reimagined artistry. One of the most enlightening moments of the informal British hip hop education is the opening sequence of *Beat This!: A Hip Hop History* (1984), where Afrika Bambaataa speaks of Afrofuturist ideas surrounding autokinesis, Jupiter, and interplanetary happenings: "who controls the present controls the past, who controls the past controls the future; funk". What was originally alien became less alien and more understood, and in turn the immediate context in Britain became more alien—hip hop revealed to the provincial adopter how far removed from the youth the nation-state of Britain was. Headz began to wake.

Seeing Hip Hop

It was not purely the sound that captivated young provincial headz, though; the visual spectacle of hip hop ensured it was perceived as a continuous, joyous creation. Record sleeve design captured certain facets and moments of hip hop, offering a glimpse into this world which still remained beguiling but incredibly exciting. Eraze points out that for him, the representations that are most vivid "aren't moving ones in my memory, they're record covers" (i/v, Exeter, 13 March 2017). Peter Barrett's sleeve design for *The Perfect Beat* compilation is a montage of stills seemingly photographed on a television screen as blue hues and fuzziness distort the images, exemplifying the agency of technology. The main image on the front is of DJ Jazzy Jay's hand mid-scratch on a turntable, outlined in electric white lightning. This notion of electric charge echoes through the border of two other images bound by jagged electric blue and yellow lines; other imagery suggests the scientific, the artistic, and the metaphysic. Text definitions of hip hop language subtly blend across the whole sleeve, with five examples highlighted that define "chilly the most", "gear", "kicks", "word up or word", and "Rap attack", intent on educating potential hip hop headz from afar through representation. This last definition: "Rap attack…a quick-paced onslaught of 'def' expressions delivered with stylish verbal dexterity. Example: 'Magic's rap attacks are the last word in wild style'", is clearly intended to emulate dictionary conventions, and through these I not only learnt to broaden my hip hop vocabulary, but discover more hip hop figures, and in this case I was forced to question this individual named Magic, whom I later discovered hosted his Rap Attack show on New York City's WBLS-FM…or was it Mr. Magic the disco-rapper from Connecticut? I frequently inspected and absorbed every word of the text, and would begin to relate names and words with those appearing on other records, for example one definition from *The Perfect Beat* reads: "the new record by Man Parrish is positively treach!" to define "treacherous or treach". Reading this definition and its reference to Man Parrish was the catalyst for my purchasing of Man Parrish's self-titled album at Caterpillar Records, North Street, Exeter, on one of my weekly visits to the city. My world broadened as I joined the dots. The televisual stills of Jazzy Jay, Rock

Steady Crew, Pow Wow, and Afrika Bambaataa were formidable; the musicians adorned Native American head dresses, African jewellery and clothing mixed with westernized leather jackets, while the Bboys wore sweatshirts and kicks.[34] These teachings on record sleeves offered an essential primary hip hop education not found elsewhere in the provinces.

I was not alone in poring over record sleeves to educate myself about hip hop. A peer of mine from the small village of Sidford, Devon, replicated the graphics from the sleeve of *The Perfect Beat* with Berol Coloursticks on the white inner bag, a practice many youths living in quiet, rural areas would carry out (Figure 2.2), which suggests a true hermeneutical experience on the part of the consumer, and early evidence of consumer-as-producer. The act of replicating the sleeve artwork (which visually represents the music encased

Figure 2.2: Bespoke replicated inner-sleeve drawn by consumer. Photograph by author.

within) while simultaneously listening to the music representations themselves presents cultural meaning and experience concurrently, potentially an embryonic trigger for the hip hop state of mind. Hans-Georg Gadamer discusses the aesthetics of art tangential to the analytic conventions within modern philosophy, favouring a phenomenological approach (Gadamer et al. 2004: 66–87). When drawn into the discussion here, Gadamer's tactic underpins this idea of the acquisition of cultural knowledge through passive and active experiences gained through exposure to secondary forms of representation, which also relates to the proximity of composition and interpretation (Gadamer et al. 2004: 70–87). The aesthetics of audio and visual in hip hop are a means to reveal cultural reality, and these realities are, in turn, distinct within the creative practice and output-artefact. Here I turn to Gadamer's argument that within translations between languages, a gap forms which even with the most studious intention, cannot be fully closed (Gadamer et al. 2004: 386). He states that, "where there is understanding, there is not translation but speech. To understand a foreign language means that we do not need to translate it into our own" (Gadamer et al. 2004: 386). This is an important idea when framed within the emergence of hip hop culture, and I propose that the mastering of hip hop language takes place through secondary representations, as Gadamer continues:

> When we really master a language, then no translation is necessary—in fact, any translation seems impossible. Understanding how to speak is not yet of itself real understanding and does not involve an interpretive process; it is an accomplishment of life. For you understand a language by living in it... (Gadamer 2006: 386).

This is the essence of the hip hop state of mind which I will revisit in Chapter 6, but I draw attention here to present not only the idea of the linguistic language of hip hop through lyrics and speech, but of the visual language of apparel, dance, and graffiti; and the invisible and intangible aesthetics and language of attitude. Provincial British headz were not merely acquiring music from America in a passive manner, but acquiring a complete culture, which even from the outset of its arrival spawned practice, albeit tentative and in miniature. It would be foolish to doubt that urban youth did not experience the arrival of these artefacts discussed above; however what is important is how they were received, and the value that provincial youth needed to attach to these reifications due to different and limited exposure to material and experience; these artefacts became precious.

Portrayals of Hip Hop in Film

By 1984, representations of the culture through film had a drastic impact on how the youth of Britain was to practise hip hop. *Wild Style* (1982) and *Style Wars* (1983) were undoubtedly the films that embodied and anchored all aspects of hip hop culture and were rooted in a sense of realism. *Beat Street* (1984) and *Breakdance: The Movie* (1984),[35] although more staged and less convincing, reached larger audiences as they were both screened widely in cinemas across Britain. *Wild Style* and *Style Wars* were shown on television in 1984, and those fortunate enough to capture them on VHS shared copies of them and these pirated tapes were essential lessons for provincial hip hop growth. Michael "Spider" Hooper, a disco DJ from Devon remembers, "The beginning for me was summer 1984. I was meant to meet a friend and watch *Breakdance: The Movie*. He didn't show but I still went on my own and was hypnotized by what I saw" (email to author, 1 November 2017). Si Spex, one half of Cornwall's The Creators, recollects:

> Yeah, you know what, wow; I've must've been really young because I've suddenly had another memory of trying to get a (VHS) tape of *Breakdance: The Movie*. I can remember watching *Beat Street* in my old house with my mum. She thought it was very good but was a bit worried because there were a couple of rude words in it. Basically, I was exposed to it at that age, eight or nine, and a friend of mine had *Breakdance: The Movie* so we'd tape it; and I suppose at that point maybe the earliest junior discos, so from that point, about age nine…I was definitely one of the first people into it (i/v, Truro, 6 December 2017).

Breakdance: The Movie was screened in Britain from 22 June 1984, and I too remember watching it in the cinema that summer. It was during the seemingly endless six-week school holidays following my first year at secondary school (*Grange Hill* seemed like a lifetime ago), and *Breakdance: The Movie*, as the first hip hop film I watched, began to partially consolidate the ideas I was experiencing through *The Perfect Beat* and other hip hop compilations the year before. Upon returning to the second year that September, there was a buzz about *Breakdance: The Movie* as those that had watched it over the summer tried to impress their peers with Bboy moves at school. Rola[36] discusses his first memory of hip hop with some perspicuity:

> My Mum was on low income, so I never had the luxury of the latest toys or a BMX bike like all the other kids at school seemed to have. Something was missing in my life. Then in 1984 I started back at school after the summer holidays, and in the break time all the kids were gathered together in this area under the stairway, I had to go check it out, and they were breakdancing to electro music and it was just like "Oh my goodness, this is it" sounds crazy but it was probably one of the most life changing moments I've ever had. This is what I was missing, I was hooked! (email to author, 25 March 2017).

Richard "Rumage" Cowling[37] furthers this observation, when discussing how he was enticed into hip hop:

> It was seeing the older boys at school popping, locking, and breakdancing…it was more robotics at first, the popping came slightly later…they must have been doing robotics to New Order's 'Blue Monday', and that just blew my head away (i/v, 17 December 2017).

Bboying was already well underway in Britain at least 18 months before *Breakdance: The Movie* arrived, but the impact of this film strengthened hip hop's presence to deep in the provinces and affirmed the cultural snapshots we had previously received. The choreography in *Breakdance: The Movie* is generally much commercialized, although there are moments of excellence, such as Turbo's (Michael "Boogaloo Shrimp" Chambers) pop and lock solo serenade with his everyday broom to Kraftwerk's 'Tour De France', and Ozone, Turbo and Kelley's battle with rival crew Electro Rock. The film's light and conventional pace ensured it was popular across a broader spectrum of society than the slightly later *Beat Street*, but in terms of hip hop culture, Ice T and Chris "The Glove" Taylor's cameo appearances in the club scenes were critical access points to scratching and emceeing, particularly their performance of the 'Reckless' vibe.[38] Ross Adams of Dorchester, Dorset, while describing his growing up in a "quiet market town…with very little access to anything 'urban'" (email to author, 30 March 2017), recalls the impact the film had for him:

I was 11 in 1984 and a couple of mates and I decided to go to the local Plaza cinema to watch the film *Breakdance: The Movie*. We were immediately blown away by the trainers, amazing dancing, and most of all the scene with Ice-T and Chris "The Glove" Taylor where they perform 'Reckless' during an uprock.[39] The scratching up of the vinyl on a turntable was something we had never seen before, it sounded like nothing else, brand new, fresh, exciting (email to author, 30 March 2017).

Nathan Loynes (Nat Drastic) from Pontefract, West Yorkshire, simply states: "The standout jam from *Breakdance: The Movie* was Chris 'The Glove' Taylor and Ice-T's 'Reckless'" (email to author, 4 December 2017). One can clearly picture Ice-T clad in a burgundy-grey Nike tracksuit top, accessorized with a ski-mask around his neck, blue baseball cap, studded belts, and The Glove wearing black with white rimmed shades, a white studded belt and a black studded glove on his hand that shimmered as he cut the record. Ice-T's "yes, yes y'all, you know emcee Ice is fresh, y'all" and The Glove's cuts jamming over The Art Of Noise's 'Beatbox', wilfully draws one in to this world as the camera glides from the club entrance to the dancefloor where clubbers, hip hoppers and party-goers are beginning to jam and dance. On the background walls one catches a glimpse of stage set graffiti, which works as it is not central to the shot. This 30-second fragment of film before the structured dialogue recommences was a pivotal gateway to further exposure to hip hop's visual and sonic context.

Beat Street followed a similar conventional structure to *Breakdance: The Movie*, although the representations of hip hop delivered a more realistic impression. Set during a snowy winter in The Bronx (as opposed to the perfect, sunny LA location of *Breakdance: The Movie*), *Beat Street* includes appearances by hip hop pioneers Afrika Bambaataa & Soulsonic Force, DJ Jazzy Jay, Rock Steady Crew, Doug E. Fresh, Treacherous Three, Melle Mel, DJ Kool Herc, New York City Breakers, Furious Five,[40] Lisa Lee, Sha Rock and Debbie Dee, as well as soul-funk artists The System. The storyline largely follows the character Ramo's life struggles as the greatest graffiti writer (although one can render the plot somewhat insignificant here: what is of much greater value is the footage of hip hop practice). The Bboy battle scenes in the subway and at The Roxy, between fictitious crew Beat Street (played by New York City Breakers) and their rivals Bronx Rockers (played by the Rock Steady Crew) epitomized the delight of Bboying. Both battles take place to 'Battle Cry' and 'Breaker's Revenge' respectively, adding to the exhilaration. Having not heard 'Battle Cry' before watching the film, the excitement was unsurpassable as the song commenced in tune with the subway battle. As the Beat Street crew spot Bronx Rockers across the length of the subway concourse, the whispering vocal of 'Battle Cry' slides into the audio as Lee (Robert Taylor) commands the screen: "Let's do the right thing, let's serve these dudes, man!" The scene is relatively short compared to the battle in The Roxy—both crews square each other up, set up camp by throwing tracksuit tops down and placing the boombox on the floor, before an ensuing battle where several moves are exchanged before they are raided by the police. What follows is a confused scramble resulting in Lee and several other members of both crews arrested. 23DeepDish comments: "I'm laughing my ass off remembering this scene. Deep down inside, this scene was so fucking dope; where they see the other crew on the opposite side of the subway and walk up to them. That shit was too dope. BATTLE CRYYY" (YouTube comment, 15 November 2016). The idea of the NYC subway was far removed from the provincial environment, yet as I sat in Sidmouth's Radway Cinema,[41] fully immersed in this hip hop world, this scene resonated with me deeply. I would attribute this to the spatio-temporal intensity of the film scene: although I was taken by the graffiti, trains, cityscapes and club representations, there was something about the quality of space and its being in the everyday, yet concurrently it was a space of supermodernity,[42] "the non-symbolized space of non-place" (Augé 1995: 82). Marc Augé suggests: "Clearly the word 'non-place' designates two complementary but distinct realities: spaces formed in relation to certain ends (transport, transit, commerce, leisure), and the relations that individuals have with these spaces" (Augé 1995: 94), as the characters temporarily transformed the subway into a surge of hip hop culture and past the realm of "non-places, or rather, imaginary places: banal utopias, clichés" (Augé 1995: 95). This scene encouraged many headz to consider other alternatives to places where they might breakdance, building on the leftover space under the stairs that Rola describes above. A quest to be "more urban" had commenced, and the search for new territories of hip hop had begun.

It was not until after *Breakdance: The Movie* and *Beat Street* that the provincial British were to receive *Wild Style*, despite its production almost two years prior, due to it not receiving a UK release. In fact, it was only aired within Europe in West Germany (ZDF TV, 7 April 1983) and in Denmark almost a year later, and it took some time for VHS copies to circulate in Britain. Part scripted and part documentary, the resulting docufiction of *Wild Style* was a further influence, and much more valuable to viewers than previous films in terms of how it documented the mechanics of hip hop practice. Performances were not faked and were choreographed by the Bboys themselves, the graffiti was produced by actual graffiti writers unlike the designer-led simulations found in *Breakdance: The Movie* and *Beat Street*, and the emcees and DJs executed their own routines and rhymes. *Wild Style* contains an impressive cast of hip hop pioneers who served as inspirations to many British headz (more so than *Beat Street*, certainly in terms of graffiti writers), and features "Lee" Quinones, Lady Pink, Fab 5 Freddy,[43] Busy Bee, Daze, A.J., Grandmaster Flash, Grand Wizard Theodore,[44] The Fantastic Romantic Five, Cold Crush Brothers, Double Trouble, and Rammellzee. The earthy, everyday realism with which director Charlie Ahearn captures hip hop life is paramount to understanding hip hop. Watching *Wild Style* was a revelation; suddenly British audiences were given a docufiction that presented hip hop before the arrival of the electro sound and delivered as a holistic culture which integrated the four elements of graffiti, Bboying, DJing, and rap.

Similarly, Tony Silver and Henry Chalfant's TV film *Style Wars* includes a host of prominent graffiti writers and Bboys, and presents the same four elements as the pillar of hip hop culture (yet with slightly more bias to graffiti and Bboying) even more palpably, and for us in Britain we were immediately convinced by Sam Schacht's opening, authoritative narration:

> They call themselves graffiti writers, because that's what they do. They write their names, among other things, everywhere. Names they've been given or have chosen for themselves. Most of all they write in and on subway trains which carry their names from one end of the city to the other. It's called "bombing", and it has equal assertive counterparts in rap music and breakdancing (*Style Wars*, 1983, Public Art Films).

This construct is later reinforced when explaining the relationship between the terms "style" and "rocking": "The idea of style, and competing for the best style, is the key to all forms of 'rocking'. For the rap emcee, it's rocking the mic. For the Bboys, it's rocking your body and breakdancing; or for writers, rocking the city with your name on a train" (*Style Wars*, 1983). I would argue that amidst the images of awe-inspiring graffiti, conflict between writers, the authorities, and the personal stories weaved throughout the narrative, the two pieces of narration quoted above firmly positioned hip hop culture to outsiders as four core elements. Furthermore, the products of these elements were audible and visual, and *Style Wars* fundamentally confirmed that graffiti was the essence of hip hop culture.[45]

For provincial Britain, these films became a compressed simulation of the previous decade's evolution of hip hop, and contemporaneously paraphrased material into edited sources which unintentionally supported the embryonic, exploratory and tentative actions of hip hop practice remote from its original site. This second point is especially crucial for the provincial, where hip hop had begun to exist only in small pockets. Furthermore, the roots of the culture itself were simplified and watered down during 1983–84 and labelled as a craze. In its infancy, classifying British hip hop as a craze was, in many respects, apt; it quickly achieved widespread popularity by the middle of 1983 and as rapidly had become unpopular by 1985, peaking just after *Breakdance: The Movie* and *Beat Street* arrived in British cinemas. I would argue that this was a definitive and positive turning point for hip hop, for after the followers of mainstream popular culture had moved on to the next fashionable phenomenon, those of us who remained interested in hip hop culture and keen to master its practices began to deepen our understanding, and here I will introduce hip hop's fifth element, knowledge.

The BBC's pivotal documentary *Beat This!: A Hip Hop History* (1984) slipped past much of the youth upon broadcast, but thankfully the technology of the VCR again ensured the message was spread far and wide, as those that captured the film shared it among their peers. Screened as part of the *Arena* series on 12 July 1984 (only 20 days after the British release of *Breakdance: The Movie*), director Dick Fontaine's framing of hip hop culture through the lens of Afrika Bambaataa (animatedly narrated by Gary Byrd),[46] explores the intangible cultural heritage of hip hop. For the first time, British headz were discovering the roots of hip hop in respect of black history and its cultural and political origins—Cab Calloway, Muhammad Ali, Martin Luther King, Malcolm X and Nelson Mandela were drawn into the great discussion; Malcolm McLaren, graffiti writer Brim and even (bizarrely) Mel Brooks[47] were included to demonstrate hip hop's broader societal reach, and again, key pioneers from groups Soulsonic Force and Cold Crush Brothers anchored the contemporary position of hip hop. Parker, a DJ from Plymouth, Devon, attests the film's importance: "1984, and I randomly catch the BBC documentary *A Hip Hop History*, this was a life changing moment, everything clicked into place and I loved hip hop from that night on." He revisits this point later when asked why he was attracted to the culture: "The simplest and most honest answer is that when I saw the BBC documentary I fell in love with hip hop, it was the best thing in the world" (email to author, 6 May 2017). For many headz, *Beat This!: A Hip Hop History* also resulted in everything clicking into place; they gained clarity about the elements of hip hop—especially knowledge—and could continue their hip hop education with more purpose. One pivotal scene is the footage of DJ Kool Herc driving through destitute streets accompanied by Gary Byrd's semi-rap story:

> But the story of hip hop doesn't belong, in New York, LA or London, that's wrong; the true story begins in devastation—bad housing, gang wars and desperation. In The Bronx ghetto, or Planet Rock, let's take a minute and turn back the clock, to the first hero of the hip hop groove, the man that made the people move. From Jamaica he came with a sense of rhythm, and what he brought to The Bronx was a sound system. Music he played made life work, and made him a legend, Kool DJ Herc (*Beat This!: A Hip Hop History*, 1984, BBC).

This was the first time Britain had been introduced to DJ Kool Herc, and as importantly, one could observe the deprivation of The Bronx which contrasted with the romance and thrill of the graffiti narrative. When hip hop arrived in Britain, it was assumed by provincial headz to be a new culture—how could it have already accrued history? The ensuing stories of Kool Herc being stabbed, street gang warfare and the destitution faced daily by black and other minority groups would gradually become visible to British, white majority provincial hip hop consumers. For headz desperate for knowledge, hip hop now had greater meaning, intention and purpose, and there was much more to embrace than pure spectacle and exhibition. For the more engaged followers, it was a signal to dig back into history, and fill the gaps by reaching out to others, as Kilo illustrates:

> If you look at the time scale of things, my knowledge of the late '70s only came later, when the knowledge of the late '70s really came about, because obviously in '83…it was basically from connecting with people like Skam and people like that had knowledge that went further back than mine.[48]

Followers of this culture were now gaining insight to the black diaspora, and the continual oppression, adversities and racism that black and minority groups were experiencing in America. None of this was taught at provincial British schools, therefore *Beat This!: A Hip Hop History* offered a preliminary education and was a key agent for viewers to make sense of hip hop's emerging position within the broader socio-political world.

Duck Rock

In the previous section I discussed a range of recorded and filmed artefacts that brought hip hop to Britain through cultural tamping (the concept of which is explored in the next section), but one of the clearest moments of arrival embodying all four physical elements was the music video of 'Buffalo Gals' by Malcolm McLaren and the World's Famous Supreme Team, released just before Christmas in 1982.[49] This is a commonly acknowledged point of arrival and is corroborated by many pioneers of British hip hop, notably London Posse's Rodney P, who when discussing the birth of hip hop culture on BBC Four's documentary *The Hip Hop World News* (2016) with DJ Premier, states, "In the UK, we credit that record ('Buffalo Gals'), as the record that introduced us to hip hop culture."[50] In reference to the video, Rodney P then narrates:

> Now we knew exactly what the culture looked like, in terms of the dancing, how they dressed, and how the art looked, two turntables and a microphone. The imagery for that comes from the 'Buffalo Gals' video…that was a real eye-opener for me. This English guy, who introduced the world to punk rock music, is also the same guy who introduced the world to hip hop (*The Hip Hop World News*, 2016).

Rodney P's rhyme partner from London Posse, Bionic, furthers the significance of 'Buffalo Gals', and comments:

> I was introduced to the whole hip hop culture by…'Buffalo Gals', mate. Yeah we see 'Buffalo Gals' video; fucking, Malcolm McLaren, yeah and that's it, innit, see the whole flex, New York and all that, and that's it, that's when we first see the flex and then, bang—we was on it one time mate, we was down Covent Garden in seconds…Rock Steady and Mr. Freeze doing their 'ting. That's my first memory of that whole 'ting (*The Hip Hop World News*, 2016).

Covent Garden, London, was the most significant place for the pioneers of London-centric hip hop, and although Bionic references the importance of 'Buffalo Gals', he also talks about other people in his life that acquired an understanding of Bboying through direct experience, and continues "when man see that ['Buffalo Gals'], then my bredrin[51] William come back from New York at the same kinda time, yeah, with fresh moves…he came back with this difference style, that's when man really got interested into the 'ting" (*The Hip Hop World News*, 2016).

This crucial time in Covent Garden illustrates clearly the importance of Bboying that helped set down hip hop roots in London. As 'Buffalo Gals' hysteria took place, the jams[52] grew and started to become predominant in the large cities. In these cities, it was not uncommon for inhabitants to have family in America whom they would visit, and who would visit them, which also propelled the evolution of hip hop. This is important to note, as a different contextual beginning emerges here between urban and provincial hip hop in Britain, and my experience is very different to that of Bionic. The closest I came to encounter someone who had first-hand experience of hip hop was meeting a new pupil at school whose parents had emigrated to Devon from Canada. I was seduced by his accent (wrongly assuming he was from America), and asked him if he was "into hip hop", to which he replied that he had heard of Grandmaster Flash but did not care for the music, which disappointed me greatly. I missed Jeffrey Daniel's famous backslide dance move on *Top Of The Pops* during 1982, but the absolute spectacle of 'Buffalo Gals' was unlike anything I had witnessed before. So refreshing was this spectacle amidst the escapist glamour of pop, that it captured the minds of a generation bored with songs about the usual pop tropes.[53] 'Buffalo Gals' was alien, abstract and obscure in its content yet enthralled those who consumed it, and for many it was the perfect introduction to a lifelong engagement with hip hop culture. McLaren followed up with 'Jive My Baby/World Famous' which was only issued on a 7" single in the US, and concurrently his mini album *D'ya Like Scratchin'* also saw a US only release, until 1984 when it was issued in the UK with the different title *Would Ya Like More Scratchin'*. This six-track EP is a total scratch fest, with crazy cuts by the World's Famous Supreme Team tearing apart 'Buffalo Gals' throughout, although the standout track remains the sublime 'World's Famous' ridden over elegant piano sections. However, in between the initial success of 'Buffalo Gals' and *Would Ya Like More Scratchin'*, the *Duck Rock* album (released January 1983) delivered a cultural bricolage that many headz were not prepared for.

Duck Rock features 11 songs inspired by a wider range of musical styles than those immediately enveloped in the sounds of hip hop. Inspired by bluegrass, folk-country, Latin, ambient, isicathamiya, and mbaqanga among other world rhythms, McLaren takes the listener: "Around the world in 40 minutes", according to the Billboard advertisement (Figure 2.3). McLaren

Figure 2.3: Billboard advertisement for *Duck Rock*. Photograph by author.

had been convinced by Steve Weltman to work with the Charisma label, and agreed on the proviso that he made a hip hop record: "all he could say was that he still wanted (somehow) to work with the hip hop scene, which he sensed was the closest thing America had to London's subcultures of resistance" (Bromberg 1991: 257). McLaren's comment about "London" specifically and not "Britain" in terms of subcultures of resistance is revealing and illustrates the cultural chasm between the capital and the provinces. 'Soweto' (the first single after *Duck Rock*'s release) entered the top 40 official singles charts, but slipped by largely unnoticed, yet six months later 'Double Dutch' peaked at number 3 and enjoyed 13 weeks in the chart. 'Double Dutch' is not a conventional hip hop record by any definition, yet this release resurrected an interest in McLaren amid the British provinces, due to the song's relationship with New York Double Dutch troupes. Double Dutch skipping resembles Bboying in terms of spatial combat and, coupled with McLaren's sonnet as he shouts out the name of several troupes, "The Ford Green Angels", and most prominently "The Ebonettes", a strikingly similar structure to the emcee namechecking Bboys becomes apparent. Coupled with the obvious link to the first city of hip hop—"they might break and they might fall / But the gals from New York City don't"—spoken over the Zulu rhythms of mbaqanga, 'Double Dutch' appealed to and broadened hip hop's rhythmic palette.

One year on from 'Buffalo Gals' and the fifth and final single from *Duck Rock* failed to enter the top 40. That release was 'Duck for the Oyster', a barmy rearrangement of the traditional square dance figure, 'Duck for the Oyster, Dig for the Clams'. McLaren's version builds into a frenzy, complete with manic sample stabs of "Duck!", "Rock!" and concluding penultimately with a bow of "thank you, partners!" and finally an earth-shattering reverbed scream of "DUCK!!!", which seems a fitting end to such a culturally eclectic album. Interestingly though, despite hip hop fans showing an antipathy to 'Duck for the Oyster', McLaren once more takes the position of the emcee, commanding the dance troupe, yet this time over fiddle, banjo, accordion and concertina. The broad diversity of *Duck Rock* contributed to both its success and its failure, yet McLaren's concept was to deliver a true contemporary folk album, and he did exactly that. This idea was held by McLaren before he had even signed to Charisma:

> There was no time to waste if this new black punk scene was to be exploited, so when Steve Weltman asked McLaren what he wanted to do, he blurted out that the more he thought about it, the more he had realized that the key to it all wasn't the music—in

six months every kid would be rapping, he said—but the dancing. And not the contorted twisting of the breakdance crews, not the vernacular get-down-and-boogie dancing of everyday parties, but *folk dancing*. All the world knows how to dance, said McLaren, but only in folk dancing is everyone united in the *same purpose*. Folk dance was the perfect bet for the eighties (Bromberg 1991: 258; original emphasis).

McLaren may have gained a reputation for his exploitation, and exploit he did; however the results of his exploitation techniques enabled explorations of hip hop practice—through the richness of folk that *Duck Rock* delivered, the message became: *new folk was hip hop*. McLaren reframed hip hop within more sociologically understood forms of culture, which increased its standing, while concurrently introducing the European audience to a plethora of music and dance rituals. I have grown to love this album over the past 37 years; however, this took time, and I did not fully understand McLaren's intentions at first. My experience exemplifies that of many in the provinces, and as we were bombarded by the electrifying sound of early hip hop, the passivity of 'Obatala' and 'Legba' and the power of the Lucumi cult on 'Song For Chango', the sonic collage clouded full comprehension of the gravity of McLaren's concept.

The music, however, was only half the story of *Duck Rock*. Recruiting style-master general Dondi White and Keith Haring—two prominent artists working in New York City—*Duck Rock* as a visual artefact also became a cultural bricolage. The backdrop to the sleeve consists of a single complete panel (in shades of burgundy, front, and shades of blue, rear), created by Haring in his trademark symbolism, patterning and dancing figures, and here he also includes two dancing snakes. The rear also features a Haring television set, screening an image of a tribe (collaged in by Egan) tuning in to McLaren's infamous *Duck Rock* boombox—named the "Duck Rocker"— as well as a woman clad in African wax fabric carrying the boombox on top of her head, and McLaren himself donning headphones and enthusiastically tuning a dial. Splatterings of various fonts in a plethora of colours shout "Webo", "Double Dutch", "Z-Zulu", "break" and "electric boogaloo" (clearly inspired by McLaren's New York experience), and the unmistakable hand-style of Dondi's lettering that reads "Duck Rock". This imagery attracted headz to the record in the first instance, but the boombox itself was an artefact to behold. Under the coordination of Nick Egan,[54] the boombox took shape. Emulating the motifs of Bboy's boomboxes and Latin American car customization as well as the (re)appropriation and recycling practice of Zulu tribes, the creative team developed the "Duck Rocker" which became the epitome of hip hop artefact. The boombox itself was a JBL model, and its customization featured spray painting the dials in primary and secondary colours, wrapping the handle in leopard print fur, cut outs of Dondi's "Duck Rock" letters mounted to the speakers, and a pair of car indicators and additional lamps mounted to the top. Other accessories were a wing mirror upon which hung headphones, a traditional bike horn, microphone and no less than 13 radio aerials and a TV aerial, topped off with a long, grey and white feather. The "Duck Rocker" becomes its own performance, akin to the idea of the peacock that McLaren noted in his observations of teddy boys' exhibitionism. This fetishized the idea of the customized boombox and became an inspiration across the UK, as headz began to customize their own. Figure 2.4 shows the Ill Beat Productions boombox customized by Rola, sprayed completely red and displays the "Donnay"[55] logo on each speaker, a "Roland" sticker and "GL" mounted letters, topped with the crew name over the tape decks. While this was much more understated than McLaren's, it affirmed the idea of the bespoke and spoke of a rising provincial identity.

The "Duck Rocker" is as important as the album itself. Not only is its spectacle representational of several modes of cultural (re)appropriation, but

Figure 2.4: The author with the IBP boombox, Exeter, 1987. Photograph by Eraze.

the boombox also travelled, reframing the sounds it played in different contexts, an assemblage in itself. Egan states: "The Zulus in South Africa were the most affected by the 'Duck Rocker' as they saw it as some kind of deity to ward off evil spirits. What could be more powerful than that?"[56] Egan recalls McLaren's advice in how to approach the visuals for the sleeve:

> "Don't think of it as a square. Instead, think of it as a large wall of which you take the shape of a square and cut one section out and whatever is on that square is the cover, even if my name is hanging off the edge, it doesn't matter. That gives you a much bigger concept; one where people have to try and imagine what the rest of the wall looked like."[57]

In many ways, Malcolm McLaren's formula was perfect. He had set a precedent in bringing subculture to the attention of the mainstream with his provocative approach as impresario of the Sex Pistols in 1976. McLaren had reconstructed the Sex Pistols from being a band with a punk ethos, to a band that was punk as consumption. McLaren capitalized on Johnny Rotten's bluntness, Steve Jones's "what a fucking rotter" moment, and the tragic addictions of Sid Vicious. Post-Rotten and Glen Matlock, McLaren's Sex Pistols circus drew on a plethora of pop-punk post-modernism and furthered his idea of the strutting peacock, so keenly explored during his time with Vivienne Westwood at Sex, 430 King's Road. This reconstruction of punk appeared to parody itself, become a counter-point to the non-materiality of punk, and yet through the illusion of parody generated a series of clear tropes that could be produced and commodified for popular consumption. McLaren's finest hour was the feature-length *The Great Rock 'n' Roll Swindle*, which "interweaves a conventional fictional narrative with documentary and mock documentary footage" (Huxley 2002: 88), to create the illusion of a shocking and radical film.[58] Hebdige determines that: "The punk subculture, then, signified chaos at every level, but this was only possible because the style itself was so thoroughly ordered" (Hebdige 2003: 113). The difference between punk and hip hop, I would argue, is that the Sex Pistols were the beginning of the end for punk, while 'Buffalo Gals' was the beginning of the start of British hip hop. A mere two years after the release of *The Great Rock 'n' Roll Swindle*, McLaren was introduced to the World's Famous Supreme Team who were hosting their radio show on WHBI-FM, New Jersey, and an ensuing collaboration resulted in 'Buffalo Gals'. Hip hop culture found McLaren in 1981 during a tour with post-punk band Bow Wow Wow, where he first met

Afrika Bambaataa and experienced a South Bronx hip hop jam. His account of witnessing hip hop mixing for the first time surely resonated with the postmodern conflict of punk's context:

> The sound I realized was coming from the way they were messing around with their hands on the decks, moving records backwards and forwards. But they weren't just doing it with one record; they were doing it with two, and they were mixing across one to the other. In fact, it was making music out of other people's music (*Beat This!: A Hip Hop History*, 1984).

McLaren saw hip hop as an art and act of serious play. Gadamer considers art as a disclosive practice, disclosing realities, but doing so according to its own parameters, and art is capable of seriousness in the very essence of its playfulness (Gadamer et al. 2004: 110–16). The hermeneutic spirit of 'Buffalo Gals' is one of mischief, yet behind the playful façades lay the subversion that McLaren desired. "Making music out of other people's music" (*Beat This!: A Hip Hop History*, 1984) particularly excited McLaren, whose appreciation and commodification of counter-culture had underpinned so many of his previous projects. During his experience in the South Bronx, McLaren witnessed graffiti, rap, mixing and breakdancing as respective parts of hip hop culture, and constructed a series of emulative representations through the 'Buffalo Gals' video. Recruiting the production skills of Trevor Horn, the scratching ability and vocal presence of the World's Famous Supreme Team, and the breakdance experience of Rock Steady Crew, he orchestrated cultural representation. It is important to consider 'Buffalo Gals' as one component of the much larger project, in that *Duck Rock* extends McLaren's impresario role into one of the anthropologist, who by visiting the origins of the album's musical styles, somehow feeds back his discoveries to the World's Famous Supreme Team, who, in turn, broadcast a musicological bricolage to the listener as the album is cut-in with radio skits. This audible anthropological study, executed through the album's entirety, resonated with its young audience, and although some of us youth may not have fully comprehended the album's agenda, it ensured hip hop culture was positioned alongside world music cultures, as 'World's Famous', 'Buffalo Gals' and 'Double Dutch' sit within an album juxtaposed with the recognized regional world music cultures of mbaqanga and Cuban merengue, and to that end helped to increase the value of hip hop from subculture to culture. The roving, giddy boombox-hugging anthropologist generated not only a point of arrival for hip hop in Britain, but a British conduit for hip hop to reach Australasia, as Blaze attests:

> Hip hop culture also migrated here, but not purely by boat or plane. It also came via television, cinema and radio, circa 1983/4. Like most other countries it came in a loosely held package. Strangely enough it manifested itself here via an Englishman's version of New York. Yes it was Malcolm McLaren's doing, more so it was the film clip to his 'Buffalo Gals' track. Although the song isn't all that, the visuals were. We heard the sounds of the World's Famous Supreme Team scratching, the Rock Steady Crew breakdancing and…Dondi piecing up a Buffalo burner (Blaze, quoted in D'Souza and Iveson 1999: 58).

McLaren delivered hip hop as consumable culture, and within a little under four minutes had presented the four physical elements in equal measure, succinctly and evocatively. It is perhaps not so surprising that McLaren's imported cultural representations were also exported to ex-British colonies Australia and New Zealand (among other European countries) as part of the imperialist hangover continued. McLaren's acquisition and framing of hip hop was at odds with the death of post-modernism.[59] Discussions on the 'Buffalo Gals' video consistently fixate on McLaren's presentation of New York hip hop but overlook the representation of McLaren himself. As compere, he dons an outsized Vivienne Westwood mountain hat and a brown sheepskin jacket from McLaren and Westwood's Buffalo Girls Collection and chants: "Two buffalo gals go around the outside, round the outside, round the outside", reworking the North Carolina folklore song 'Lubly Fan', which had over time evolved into 'Buffalo Gals' as a traditional American folk song. 'Lubly Fan' was originated in 1844 by the blackface minstrel John Hodges, who performed as Cool White, which of course, is hugely problematic. McLaren's 'Buffalo Gals' subverts both the song's narrative and the traditional square dance to create a hip hop record, and by doing so captures the very essence of hip hop's reclaiming and (re)appropriation tactics. To this end, a song that initially appears to promote the archaic notions and absurd ideas of imperialism in fact practises an art of post-coloniality, paradoxical as that may appear considering the commercialist facet of McLaren's agenda. 'Buffalo Gals' was the first hip hop music video that convinced its non-American audience, and as George Lipsitz states: "Hip hop expresses a form of politics perfectly suited to the post-colonial era" (1994: 36). 'Buffalo

Gals' is a political act that served as the perfect conduit for hip hop to reach the provinces.

Further to Rodney P and Bionic's acknowledgements above, the phenomenon of 'Buffalo Gals' was even more important to the arrival of hip hop outside London. DJ Smiz aka Krash Slaughta, growing up in small post-war new town Livingstone, West Lothian,[60] and recalling the 'Buffalo Gals' video, remembers: "It just made me start spinning round the room immediately. Seeing the World's Famous Supreme Team scratching and also the graf[61] in these videos was eye opening." Dwelling in a place where the population of the whole district was less than 140,000[62] (a little more than 2% of the population of Greater London)[63] the idea of urban culture was remote. Nice One, a writer from Heanor, Derbyshire,[64] remembers a similar experience:

> My first encounter with hip hop came in 1983. My mate Dave said, "I've got a video I want you to check out." He put the video in and I didn't move for the three odd minutes that it was on, it was Malcolm McLaren's 'Buffalo Gals', I just said "what the hell are they doing?" "It's called breakdancing; they're The Rock Steady Crew." That was it, I needed to see more. I think I watched it ten more times trying to get my head around what I was watching. Dave and some others had been popping and breaking for a few weeks outside our local Boots on a Saturday, so I went; I was hooked (email to author, 29 March 2017).

Finally, on 'Buffalo Gals', a comment on the buffalo itself. The many species of buffalo, members of *bubalus*, a genus of bovines, inhabiting Asia, Africa and North America, appear in rural imagery; there is always a herd of buffalo being rounded up in the first act of spaghetti westerns, for example. The most common bovine in Britain is the cow, and in 1980 the UK had 3.2 million cows producing milk on dairy farms.[65] In 2012, the national herd was almost half that number at 1.8 million. When I first heard 'Buffalo Gals', cows were everywhere. Wherever there was no built environment, there were cattle. The accessibility and difference of McLaren's lyrics repeatedly present rural connotations embodied throughout the song, and the cuts and vocal stabs of "Dub-dub-dub (ba) / Dub-dub-dub (ba) / Dub-dub-dub dub-dub-dub ba-ba-ba-ba (ba) / Dub-dub-dub / ba-ba-ba-ba-be (ba) / Dub-dub-dub / ba-ba-ba-ba, ba-ba-ba-ba / Dub-dub-dub, ba-ba-ba-ba, ba-ba-ba-ba", were that of a ruralistic hypnosis.

Rose states that: "Hip hop emerges from complex cultural exchanges and larger social and political conditions of disillusionment and alienation" (Rose 1994: 59), and these cultural exchanges are both immediate and obvious. The complexities of cultural exchange are synonymous with the political conditions that charge them, which, outside the context within which they are created and in terms of the relocation of hip hop to provincial Britain, were gradual and obscured to its audience. Through the birth of the hip hop artefact and the construct of hip hop narrative it is possible that the intangibility of disillusionment and alienation can become tangible, even on the cusp of the tangibility of hip hop itself. The triad of provincial British hip hop began here: the interwoven experiences of sustained regional and local cultural heritage, the temporal, occasional and momentary urban experiences, and the imagined experiences within representations and artefacts provided the platform for the cultural acquisition of hip hop.

Cultural Acquisition

Previously in this chapter, I explored a multiplicity of representations responsible for hip hop's initial impact in provincial Britain. Shifts in the everyday, observational and direct lived experience, exposure to factual and fictional film narratives, and various recorded and sonic artefacts and products all contributed to hip hop's arrival and manifest themselves through the coded cultural triad. This steers me to two issues I will now focus on in this concluding section of the chapter. Firstly, the difference between hip hop's cultural relocation and its contextual juxtaposition within provincial Britain compared to the city, and secondly the brief time span within which this cultural relocation took place.

To expand the first point, I would like to solidify the ideas of location, relocation and acquisition of culture. In *The Location of Culture* (2004), Homi Bhabha presents his concept of mimicry, its causes and effects within colonial discourse. In cardinal terms, mimicry occurs when groups or individuals of a colonized society emulate the cultural motifs, tropes, codes and representations of the colonizer. These actions of replication are intended to draw the colonized closer to the colonizer, with the aim of achieving peer status. Bhabha frames mimicry within Edward Said's *Orientalism* (Said 1978: 240), and states:

In this comic turn from the high ideals of the colonial imagination to its low mimetic literary effects mimicry emerges as one of the most elusive and effective strategies of colonial power and knowledge (Bhabha 2004: 122).

He expands on the strategy of mimicry by describing it as an "ironic compromise", which for me suggests that there are moments of fluctuation and difference between mimicry which is intended and that which is accidental or involuntary. These differences and fluctuations of mimicry operate around shifting uncertainties, and require constant reframing:

> Within that conflictual economy of colonial discourse which Edward Said describes as the tension between the synchronic panoptical vision of domination—the demand for identity, stasis—and the counter-pressure of the diachrony of history—change, difference—mimicry represents an *ironic* compromise…which is to say, that the discourse of mimicry is constructed around *ambivalence*; in order to be effective, mimicry must continually produce its slippage, its excess, its difference (Bhabha 2004: 122; original emphasis).

The actions and practices of mimicry are not purely to do with submission or pacification. Bhabha suggests that through the actions of mimicry, one's position, or how they might present themselves, can be seditious (often without intention), and has the potential to expose the representations of structured fallacies of power and oppression:

> The *menace* of mimicry is its *double* vision which in disclosing the ambivalence of colonial discourse also disrupts its authority. And it is a double vision that is a result of what I've described as the partial representation/recognition of the colonial object (Bhabha 2004: 126; original emphasis).

Mimicry often is loaded with negativity, yet the bilateral nature of mimicry can be positively engaged to unearth socio-political and cultural flaws in the colonized-colonizer dialectic. I would like to extend the bilateralism of mimicry into a trialectic approach, and here follows an explanation of what I will refer to as the three positions of hip hop mimicry, these being where the acts of mimicry are practised, to:

(1) seek an understanding of and a closeness to the origins and pioneers of American hip hop culture
(2) reveal the slippages and fallacies within the realities of everyday life and the challenges of localized and regionalist contexts
(3) question the validity, quality and accuracy of received representations of hip hop.

The first position is where the coagulated elements of hip hop are mimicked by provincial British youth following their exposure to certain fragments of culture through the various reifications, experiences and artefacts such as the ones described earlier in this chapter. The practice of mimicry here is extremely rudimentary, and during this infantile period, hip hop's elements (breakdancing is the clearest example) are practised with intention but without cultural criticality; rather, any level of critique is connected solely to the level of skill or closeness of imitation. The excitement experienced upon hearing and seeing hip hop leads to a desire to imitate, as Chrome[66] explains:

> I remember watching *Top of the Pops* on Thursday evening as me and my older brother always did, and a video came on for the song 'Buffalo Gals' by Malcolm McLaren and the World Famous Supreme Team. I remember blanking everything else out and just focusing on the whole video and thinking, "what the hell is going on in this video?" It didn't seem to make much sense as a 7-year-old, but it was incredibly interesting and addictive to watch. After it finished, I remember me and my brother looking at each other in amazement and I think he even tried to do some robotics or popping (email to author, 8 December 2017).

On the question of initial engagement with hip hop, he continues: "After seeing 'Buffalo Gals' it seemed like everyone at school had seen it too, so we were all trying to break at lunchtime. I suppose that was probably my first engagement" (email to author, 8 December 2017). Ross Adams' experience is similar and extends the notion of the desire to imitate:

> Trying to learn to breakdance and scratch on a standard record player after watching *Breakdance: The Movie*, to the soundtrack of *Street Sounds Electro 5*. We just wanted to be like the DJs and Breakers we saw in *Beat Street* and *Style Wars*. I was no good at Breakin', I tried but the other lads were better. So, I stuck to Graffiti (I was quite good at art) and a bit of DJing but that was

difficult on the substandard equipment we had at home (email to author, 30 March 2017).

National music magazines like *Record Mirror* covered some aspects of breakdancing, such as an article published on 24 September 1983 entitled 'The Men with the Four Way Hips' which perceptibly depicted a step-by-step guide to the dance moves of the electroboogie, the smurf and general breakdancing. These kinds of articles sporadically appeared throughout 1983 and 1984, as imitated static fragments of culture which, in turn, let those that consumed it to mimic themselves, although these were not as successful as the representations of Bboying in the moving image. Si Spex also talks about the presence of other elements within film: "*Beat Street* was a great introduction 'cause you get all the elements in there so I was probably digging the whole thing, it was obviously completely new, but it was definitely the breakdancing to start off with, that was the main thing" (i/v, Truro, 6 December 2017). While breakdancing was a moment of arrival for many, others rapidly moved onto other elements, as Ross Adams suggests. Following periods of self and peer criticism and reflection, practitioners made informed decisions upon which practices they would pursue. Much of these informed decisions were paramount to the accuracy and skill with which one could mimic. With the concurrent advent of VCRs appearing in a large proportion of UK homes, it was possible to freeze images, to pause a moving train to examine that Dondi or Blade piece, or analyse Crazy Legs' moves—forward and back, rewind and pause. Headz examined these films and by such acts would, in time, generate the roots of hybrid cultural heritage.

The second point of mimicry addresses the challenges of one's immediate context vis-à-vis hip hop praxis and uses the act of practice to form a sense of criticality or a critical regionalism about one's locale. Those that attempted the practice of one of the elements[67] were regularly ridiculed, as Gloucester's Darren Norris aka Big Tunes D[68] describes:

> My first engagement into the scene would have been breakdancing, I remember starting off in the bedroom practising body popping and trying robotics in front of the mirror just imitating moves I'd seen on TV. I got involved with others that same year—I'd say 1983—we would meet up and try our knee-spins on cardboard, I remember the local skinheads laughing at us but this was the future. Yes! (email to author, 7 June 2017).

Parker reiterates and extends a similar experience of derision:

> A bunch of the hard, cool lads in school saw me doing some popping outside a local pub (this would be during 1984) and came over to take the piss out of me but instead they got into it (after a bit of piss-taking). Over the weeks we got serious and formed a breaking crew with these guys, it was real odd as apart from breaking we had nothing in common with them (the hard guys) (email to author, 6 May 2017).

Parker's engagement here is illuminating as it illustrates not only the dynamic between the developing practitioner and the ridiculing observer, but a notable shift as the observer turns involuntary practitioner during their act of ridicule. The ridiculer mocks as a response to a cultural practice that is perceived as inappropriate or silly within the conventional everyday rituals of the province, but when the ridiculer accepts the practice, and commences practice themselves, they begin to challenge the very traditions and socio-cultural structures that they had previously sat comfortably within. The second moment of mimicry is not limited to engagement with people, however. Returning to Ross Adams' comment that DJing "was difficult on the substandard equipment we had at home", many emerging practitioners learnt about the techniques of scratching the hard way. Evil Ed states: "I tried to scratch records, but I didn't know about slipmats, so I scuffed up the vinyl" (email to author, 14 June 2017). With no mentors to teach headz about needing slipmats between the record and the platter, many aspiring DJs ruined their vinyl as the platter abraded the underside of the record as one pulled the record back and forth to scratch. By mimicking a sound or an edited film visual, how could one know about slipmats? In these cases, the act of mimicry exposes the lacuna between the realities of practice and the perfection of presentation.

The third moment of mimicry relates to Bhabha's "ironic compromise", and somewhat to the gaps mentioned above in terms of representations of hip hop. Here, through acts of mimicry, practitioners make demands on the quality, validity and accuracy of the cultural product. Discussed in detail in Chapter 4, a strong example is that of the ill-conceived rap record or poorly researched hip hop film. By analysing these representations as forms of mimicry through acts of mimicry, the provincial British practitioner could explore the quality of the representation, and where necessary unmask its low mimesis, thus progressing the nature of practice locally, while concurrently revising one's source material. Each of these moments of mimicry operates variably and in flux but exists in a memetic state within which the praxis of hip hop can mature.[69]

Cultural Tamping

Rather than a developed, homogenous and indigenous culture, the cultural acquisition of hip hop not only stems from its origins being rooted elsewhere, but also its cultural development evolving over time, some ten years before it landed in Britain. Yet the culture became embedded across Britain within less than two years, masquerading as a fashionable trend, craze and fad. The breadth and depth that hip hop culture developed during its first decade owes much to experimentation, happy accidents and social and political triggers as well as the African, Caribbean and African-American cultural heritage, experience and influences, which became tamped to form a wedge of culture presented and consumed in Britain. The cultural tamping process consolidated hip hop culture's birth, existence and ten-year development of practice and coagulated its elements and released it to new audiences and cultural conditions through the various reifications and representations discussed in this chapter. These films, videos and made artefacts both compressed the period of evolution and reduced the developments of practice to the final product and by doing so the less obvious phenomena that create cultural shifts and social change become invisible. Furthermore, this cultural tamping seeped into the provinces at a slower rate and with a slight time lag, taking longer to leak fully into its new sites. One of the most interesting facets of cultural tamping is time-based, and while there are differences in time for the leakage of culture into its new sites, something of greater interest is the order in which certain moments were released and reached the provinces.

The result of this leads to two clearly defined trends in hip hop's provincial arrival: firstly, certain moments in hip hop's history were released and discovered not only in a tamped time frame, but unchronological. Hip hop had existed in the provinces for almost two years before Gary Byrd had made DJ Kool Herc known to hip hop consumers; thanks to the *Street Sounds* series the arrival of electro and electro-rap was synonymous with hip hop culture. Of paramount importance is that the term hip hop did not become common usage in provincial areas until 1984, despite the consumption (and preliminary practice of hip hop), as Big Tunes D recounts: "Funny, we were calling it electro funk at that time. The term hip hop came later for us—we were always a little behind because of our location" (email to author, 7 June 2017). Secondly, the editing out of key and non-obvious development stages required consumer-producers to reinvent the processes of practice. This is evident in the accounts of primary Bboying and scratching presented earlier, which unearth the embryonic nuances between the consumption and production of hip hop discussed in depth in Chapters 4 and 5. A further ramification of cultural tamping was the speed with which the physical presence of hip hop manifested itself in the provincial environment. The mimicked practices of Bboying and graffiti writing challenged the existing form of regionalism and normalization acutely. This sharp shift in spatial practice was accentuated by the physical presence of hip hop's commercial and readily available products—by 1984 alone there were in excess of 30 compilation albums on the UK market with a hip hop inspired focus. Although most of these records included songs that were not hip hop or made by hip hop artists at all (but acted as fillers), the visual compression of hip hop and breakdance moves, motifs and myths emphasized the culture, which in turn reinforced the excitement the British youth felt as they spun on their heads, popped and locked.

Chapter 3

The Territories of Hip Hop: Domesticity, Occupation and Appropriation

It was a sunny Saturday afternoon in Exmouth, Devon during the late summer in 1984. Along with about ten other aspiring Bboys, I caught the 334 bus from Sidmouth as we had heard that there was a crew from Exmouth who wanted to battle us. When I say "us", I refer to the group of lads I had met at Sidmouth Youth Centre about a year earlier, who on a Wednesday evening would practise Bboy moves on the shiny timber floor to various electro sounds.[1] They were all around two or three years older and much taller than I, and for the first few weeks I attended the youth centre I watched from the sidelines, the shy 13-year-old who was unsure about approaching the group as they slid, span, laughed and joked clad in their Nike bi-colour windcheaters,[2] Puma Lendl and Puma G Vilas trainers,[3] until one evening they decided to bust out the "top hat".[4] A move best executed with a shorter person as the top hat, I was called over and asked if I could break, and "did I want to do the top hat?" Nervously I agreed but tried to act blasé as a tall lad hoisted me up over his head, flipped me horizontally and started to spin on the spot. I stretched my arms and legs out like da Vinci's "Vitruvian Man", the world spinning, sounds morphing and kids wailing as we span. We succeeded, much to the delight of the others. This became "our thing", and when we battled or practised, out came the top hat. I had claimed my place in the crew (as much as it was a crew), and here I was, sat with the others by the bus terminal in Exmouth, showered in watery sunshine. A buzz rolled around the street that the Sidmouth breakers were in town and looking for a battle. After what felt like a week (but was more like half an hour), a couple of local Bboys approached us and confirmed they were indeed ready to battle at the old warehouse out-of-town. This warehouse was a redundant, dilapidated mid-1900s brick building located halfway up a semi-rural hill sat in an overgrown and abandoned site. It was a fair stretch out of town, and one of the locals showed us which bus we needed to catch. As the bus rolled up the winding hill, a lad on roller skates passed by us; "There's Locky!" someone on the bus exclaimed. Locky, by all accounts, was the star popper of the rival crew. We alighted the bus and walked the rugged, broken footway to the building. As we approached, I could hear the morphing pulse of 'Clear' by Cybotron oozing through the apertures; I was anxious and excited. This was the first time I had experienced firsthand the thrill of battle. As we entered the building our rivals were well prepared, lined in a semi-circle facing the entrance and behind a large oblong of brown and taupe kitchen linoleum garishly splattered with huge mirrored sunflowers, bobbing to the music in unison. Almost immediately my excitement turned to fear; I was in awe of their presence. This was not our turf, and I felt intimidated. The battle commenced to the tune of 'Breaker's Revenge', and mid-way through we performed the top hat, executed perfectly, but then Locky took to the floor. He transformed the battle, popping and locking sublimely like some kind of alien cyborg. The home crew worked up into a frenzy, cheering, busting moves themselves from the sidelines, dust and smoke filled the space; it felt like some dystopian *Mad Max* war scene. Our crew were outshone by our rivals who thrived in their space with such control, aggression and elegance; they owned the entire afternoon. Territory was everything.

On Territory

In the last chapter I discussed certain occurrences associated with the relocation of culture, and particularly the formative hip hop phenomena responsible for its introduction to Britain. This chapter deals with hip hop's spatial and territorial manifestation in British provinces, its contours of appropriation, occupation and demarcation as it transformed within its new contextual terrains. The spatiality of all cultures, which one might initially consider to be less tangible than the material-artefacts of culture, is produced in numerous ways through the execution of rituals and practices, formal and informal, structured and unstructured. The spatial productions of hip hop are immediate, vibrant and bold, yet concurrently appear slow, languid and subtle. However, the production of space in hip hop is always territorial. In this chapter I have structured the tactics of territoriality in two parts: domesticity, and occupation and appropriation, as the overlaps between "occupation" and "appropriation" work in such close synergy that it is necessary to discuss them together. The section furthers the discussion of re-use and alternate-use of existing material culture and offers examples of each that are particularly regional such as Barclays Bank, simply known to local headz as "Barclays" in Exeter, Devon, where a small, external entrance foyer to a high street bank was appropriated in the mid-1980s on Saturday afternoons for breakdance battles and jams. The Barclays experience was a socio-spatial construct of appropriated architecture, where for a brief period of time each week the polished stone entrance communicated hip hop rather than capital and finance. This follows an exploration of territories and terrains of British hip hop through graffiti and their shifting landscapes between urban and rural as headz began to make sense of and control hip hop's emerging regional and national spatial languages.

Forman states that: "A highly detailed and consciously defined spatial awareness is one of the key factors distinguishing rap music and hip hop from the many other cultural and subcultural youth formations currently vying for popular attention" (Forman 2002: 3). He continues to stress: "In hip hop, space is a dominant concern, occupying a central role in the definition of value, meaning and practice" (Forman 2002: 3). Forman's in-depth analysis of space and place concerns in the American context is rich and provides excellent examples of this from actual space to textual space. Hip hop's complex spatial experiences engage in conflict, negotiation and synergy with the complexities of the city, the rural, and the liminal spaces of the in-between. It is the latter relationships that are of key interest to this chapter. Forman maintains that:

> In hip hop's physical and localized expressions and in rap's narratives, the authority of the individual experience is generally built upon what is conceived as the self-evident truth of natural or material spaces, where events occur and experience is registered (Forman 2002: 23).

Forman's work within hip hop's territories from the 'hood to the global industry provides certain points of reference for this chapter, which reimagines similar concepts within the unexpected locations of Britain's provinces. Drawing upon the formative synergies of hip hop's emergence, these provinces behave as a kind of liminal zone, a realm between that of the vernacular and the regional, and the nation-state of the United Kingdom.

Territorial Practice

These territories are physical, textual and metaphorical, and I previously affirmed that in spatial terms, the territoriality of hip hop initially appears most obvious through the representations of graffiti and Bboying. While the former holds more permanence than the more transient nature of Bboying, both practices occupy and alter the territories of spaces. Drawing upon Bhabha's "Third Space" theory (Bhabha 2004: 53–56), Soja's furthering of third space principles in *Thirdspace* (1996) and Lefebvre's spatial production (1991), aids my grounding of the territorial practices of graffiti and Bboying in primary, secondary and tertiary terms. Embodied within the concept of hybridity, Bhabha's third space is a mode of navigation and enunciation—employed by the colonized—which operates in the liminal space between the representations of the colonizer and the colonized. This third space offers opportunities for high-level cultural criticality and production, but not bound by preexisting cultural motifs or tropes, and resists practices of normalization. Similar to mimicry, the third space occupies sites of uncertainty and incongruity "which makes the structure of meaning and reference an ambivalent process, destroys this mirror of representation in which cultural knowledge is customarily revealed as an integrated, open, expanding code" (Bhabha 2004: 54).

While Bhabha's third space is defined within literary and cultural production, Lefebvre presents "three moments of space": representations of space, spatial practice, and representational space (Lefebvre 1991: 38–40). These describe the conceptions of planners, architects and designers; the perception of those conceived spaces and how the citizens of a society as a whole respond to them through routine, the habitual and the event; and the space of inhabitants, users and individuals within the lived moment and their appropriation techniques of everyday spatial engagement. To a degree, Soja triangulates Bhabha and Lefebvre's conceptions of space, which he calls "an efficient invitation to enter a space of extraordinary openness, a place of critical exchange where the geographical imagination can be expanded to encompass a multiplicity of perspectives" and declares that "Thirdspace" (adjoining Bhabha's "Third" and "Space") is "rooted in just such a recombinatorial and radically open perspective" (Soja 1996: 5). All three of these concepts place weight on that of the individual, the subjective, and the lived and negotiated experience, which during the 1990s emerged as counter to the western convention and certain linearities within human geography, cultural and spatial studies.

These theoretical triads have since been applied in a myriad of works, but within hip hop theory, and in particular this book, what is required is the development of an inquiry that is fourfold. Firstly, it must frame and present the territories of hip hop culture as a set of contextually and spatially engaged practices. Secondly, the existing contexts require defining; and thirdly, the negotiations that take place between existing context and hip hop practice present a panorama for critique necessary to project hip hop's position. By this point, the inquiry has gathered a complexity that might align to Soja's Thirdspace; however, the fourth tier to this inquiry involved deeper negotiation and navigation as practitioners in provincial Britain grappled with hip hop's urban representations and their own cultural heritages. This territorial hip hop praxis began with the initial engagements of provincial headz and is synergetic with the three positions of mimicry discussed in the previous chapter, but also leads to the question of how did hip hop configure in white majority spaces?

Spatial Practice

In *Consuming Architecture*, I argue that the origins of hip hop lay in the roots of graffiti practice and were the first visible signs of territorial gain and ownership for broader hip hop culture. I positioned the formative period of graffiti bombing not as pure acts of vandalism, but that graffiti bombing "was the earliest point of producing space with an intentional spatial and material identity and consuming of the city, a counter-narrative to the conceived city" (Evans 2014: 193). To further frame this idea:

> Initially the actions of the graffiti writer can be read as the production of social space; the actions of graffiti production create a new space and spatial identity within that lived moment (Lefebvre 1991: 39). As the writer actively writes on the surface, the surface is in turn re-defined, re-identified and re-coded with a value system and subsequently re-experienced by the writer, other writers and other users of the space, and is therefore the spatial context within which the surface is also physically altered by this act (Evans 2014: 193).

Furthermore, the spatiality of graffiti gathers complexity through time:

> The exploration of spatial production through the actions of graffiti writers becomes more complex when the actions of graffiti

writing are interrogated over time. This is also the moment to dispel the myth that graffiti is merely an act of spontaneity. Graffiti writers conceive, perceive and socially produce space… (Evans 2014: 193).

The practice of graffiti writing matured rapidly through the 1970s, and I further argue that strategies akin to those of the spatial practice of architecture were developed as a way to make critical sense of the city:

> The conception of a work of graffiti requires planning, thought and experimentation. It is a process of development, often discussed with other writers, and involves the evaluation of site, surface, location, time, climate, environment, population, practicality, impact, experience, colour, form and meaning: interestingly the qualities of the city which the city planners and architects addressed poorly (Evans 2014: 193).

I would extend this argument to suggest the spatial practice of writers, and the displaced cultural values and practices of non-white diasporas, were a far more successful spatio-cultural response to the city than the low-quality municipal modernism of Robert Moses' plan. Further displacement was triggered due to Moses' refusal to revise his Cross Bronx Expressway plan, and "over fifteen hundred families would be forced to relocate" (Flint 2011: 142). While parts of Moses' new build program in the 1940s offered black families an opportunity for new housing, fresh air and better schools, and as DuBose-Simons argues, "the South Bronx represented a better way of life during the 1940s and 1950s" (DuBose-Simons 2014: 543), the poorly considered urban solution had splintered and cracked by the time of hip hop's birth. From the perspective of the people, a focus on the youth made for a primary topic for airing the anxieties of the post-war public, and: "Young people themselves gradually became objectified and reified as the source of the problems, and new public policies directed at young people were put into effect" (Austin 2001: 29). Additionally, the social structures of the very nature of practice have parallels between avant-garde architectural practice of the 1980s and 1990s (deconstructivism and new-pragmatism largely inspired by Derrida and Foucault), and graffiti practice of the 1970s (already predicting a Spivak-esque response to place):

> Writers consume the margins of the city as a laboratory, studio, workshop and gallery. These actions, over time, are not purely linear; there is a continual reassessment of identity and meaning as the spatial and material activities of writing are critically practised (Evans 2014: 193).

In terms of its new life as part of hip hop and broader urban culture, graffiti (and its spuriously related cousin, street art),[5] has existed as a global phenomenon for more than three decades. However, there are critically regionalist nuances that exist within graffiti. In the introduction to *Graffiti and Street Art: Reading, Writing and Representing the City*, Avramidis and Tsilimpounidi confirm:

> Despite the continuous and often aggressive "wars on graffiti", and while the surprisingly persistent "broken windows" theory still enjoys popularity…this subculture survives and migrates from the streets of Philadelphia and subway cars of New York to almost every city around the world. There it is transformed and mixed with the historical, aesthetic and cultural particularities of each place (Avramidis and Tsilimpounidi 2017: 8).

Avramidis and Tsilimpounidi continue to suggest the textual and physical widespread network of graffiti: "Authors from other regions start examining their local scenes in relation to the particularities of their specific cultural and urban contexts" (Avramidis and Tsilimpounidi 2017: 8). There is also interesting work being done on the digital network and presence of graffiti, particularly by Evan Roth and Graffiti Research Lab,[6] and Lachlan MacDowall (2017) who discusses the production of graffiti as a digital object within the ever-increasing digital realm.[7] In *The Cambridge Companion to Hip Hop* (2015), Ivor Miller offers a useful framing of the key historical moments in graffiti's development aligned to the work of Rock Steady Crew member Doze's practice (Miller 2015: 32–41), and there are many other historical and critical monographs that address graffiti in the urban realm from various positions (see Ferrell 1993; Powers 1999; Macdonald 2001; Snyder 2009; Gastman and Neelon 2010). But what of the work in the British provinces? The existing published work to date focuses solely on urban environment (which has been much needed), yet since the arrival of hip hop in Britain adopters of graffiti have practised in the metropolises and provinces alike, and before the internet era stories, outlines and photographs were discussed formally at graffiti jams and informally at writers' benches. Networks and crews were established across the country which led to writers meeting up to paint and trade photographs through Royal Mail. But prior to these reticulations of writers, the pioneering practitioners of graffiti in the provincial realm were self-educated and took, as their starting points, existing works presented in the books *Subway Art* (Chalfant and Cooper 1984) and the later *Spraycan Art* (Chalfant and Prigoff 1987), both commonly referred to as "the bibles of graffiti" by old school British writers. Unfortunately, Norman Mailer and Jon Naar's pioneering graffiti book *The Faith of Graffiti* (1974) rarely received acknowledgement from provincial British writers. I would suggest the apparent lack of value in the latter relates somewhat to the cultural tamping of graffiti and the location in time that graffiti writing arrived in Britain (as Kilo attested in Chapter 2). Graffiti had evolved vastly during the decade between *The Faith of Graffiti* and *Subway Art*, that if writers had confronted Naar's graffiti photographs they may have passed them over as outdated, while Chalfant and Cooper's images presented the most advanced and contemporary styles of the time.

Following the arrival of the VCR and the freezing and pausing of images, careful and forensic examinations took place. The paused trains—frozen on screen—painted by legendary New York writers became the absolute precedents and mentors that new writers in provincial Britain were seeking. Would-be writers examined every inch of tape in *Wild Style*, *Style Wars* and even *Beat Street*, for the pieces they wanted to analyse and copy. Writers redrew pieces such as Seen's 'Hand of Doom', Dondi's 'Children of the Grave Again, Part 3' (with the Vaughn Bode characters either end), and pieces by Blade, Revolt and Case 2. Furthermore, the textual messages within some of these New York works expressed the view that graffiti was not actual crime—"stop real crime" on Lee's self-titled piece, "All you see is… crime in the city" by Skeme, Dez and Mean3, and even the staged Ramo's "If art is a crime, may god forgive me!" Other messages about the broader sociopolitical context were a revelation, too: "We are the sons of the ghetto and we will survive" (Skeme, in 1982), "The children of tomorrow can't love this world if we the people of today destroy its beauty before they even see it…" (Lee, in 1979) and just simply, "Knowledge!" (Izzy Caz, in 1982). With the tape frozen in time, graffiti was copied from the territory of the city on the screen to the page of the sketchpad. These territories, re-represented on paper, were then used as points of departure for developing an updated version, and emulated the original to greater or lesser degrees depending on the experience and confidence of the adopter. Occasionally, these pieces would succeed to be painted in the public realm and occupy a new territory. The sources for these precedents were not always confined to film and books; record sleeves also contained a rich pool of graffiti imagery and were used as a visual mine for many graffiti experiments. Growing up in Hythe, a village on the edge of the New Forest, Hampshire, writer Ricky Also recounts his first engagement with graffiti:

> It was when I first saw a copy of *Spraycan Art* that I really connected. Someone brought it into school and a bunch of us were crowded around in complete owe at the pieces in there. I was into drawing cartoons at that point and had tried some very basic graff letters but had no idea what it really was all about, until seeing that book. Lee was the one who stood out for me at that point, his pieces were so rich and detailed, they just looked totally complete, filling every inch of the wall. From then on, I was obsessed and would try to emulate the full colour pieces and crazy backgrounds (email to author, 21 January 2018).

Young aspiring provincial headz, desperate for new exposure to hip hop, would also spot references in much less obvious places. With fewer physical examples to examine than that of their urban counterparts, precedents and inspiration also came through television programmes like *The Equalizer*, based in the graffiti-drenched streets of New York City. Brent Aquasky, a writer and recording artist, who grew up in the New Forest in Hampshire "in a really, really small village, probably 30 houses in this village, it's three miles to the nearest train station, buses stopped at 5.40pm, there was one bus an hour, and two street lights; forest everywhere" (i/v, Bournemouth, 12 December 2017), recalls the opening sequence of *The Equalizer*:

> *The Equalizer*, Edward Woodward, I was obsessed, I used to love the music and I used to get that little cassette player and I think we had the VHS then, and what I used to do, I used to love the music, I would record the music; doo-doo-doo-doo-doo-doo-doo…and I used to loop it and wait 'til the following week and get it perfectly timed and then record it again, and make these loops of *The Equalizer*, but because I sort of loved the music, as we all know, that train comes in with Tragic Magic, and the [subway] car as the door shuts and that woman…and there's all the graf there as well. That was a big influence on me (i/v, Bournemouth, 12 December 2017).

Brent's obsession with *The Equalizer* spawned a relationship with two kinds of territory: the territory of New York City and its painted trains, and the sonic territory of the theme music, both of which increase in tension throughout its 92-second sequence. One of the most revealing examples of learning through product still exists in Devon (Figure 3.1, albeit faded; this photograph was taken in 2015). The anonymous piece is believed to date from 1984, and one can make out three distinct representations here, all painted in a single burnt orange colour, most likely to be from the Dupli-Color range (which was the only freely available range of spray paint in provincial Devon). The ground for the work is a side wall of a humble pebble-dashed, single-storey mass-produced garage which sits in a suburban street. Despite its faintness, one can read "FRESH", a single word of hip hop language; and a dancing figure executing the King Tut dance move (a staple for poppers and lockers). Compare this to the sleeve artwork for Malcolm McLaren and the World's Famous Supreme Team's *Would Ya Like More Scratchin'*, and a direct relationship is apparent between the dancing King Tut figure and Keith Haring's famous dancing figures which adorn McLaren's record cover (Figure 3.2).

Figure 3.1: "FRESH" with Keith Haring-inspired character, Exeter, c. 1984. Photograph courtesy of Benny Bronx.

The Territories of Hip Hop 89

Figure 3.2: Malcolm McLaren and the World's Famous Supreme Team, *Would Ya Like More Scratchin'*, 1984. Front and rear sleeve. Photograph by author.

Figure 3.3: Zulu Nation inspired "Hip Hop" graffiti, Exeter, c. 1983. Photograph courtesy of Kilo's collection.

90   *Provincial Headz*

The King Tut figure attempts to replicate Haring's style, painted in a single, thick monotone line; featureless, but in motion. The second reference affirms this piece took inspiration from *Would Ya Like More Scratchin'*, as the letters "FRESH", painted in a slightly curved formation, again echo the single word "BREAK" from the back of the sleeve, also presented on a curve. The next stage of writing development in Devon would be to take further departures from the images of hip hop's transatlantic reifications and begin to add one's own ideas, such as the Zulu Nation inspired "Hip Hop" (Figure 3.3) which takes the sleeve design of Shango's *Shango Funk Theology* (1984) as its point of departure.

Another fine example of the shifting territory between representation through artefact and spatial representation is a piece entitled "Is Art Really A...Crime?" by Wiz, on Exeter Central "A" Signal Box (Figure 3.4), which drew heavy inspiration from Ramo's "If art is a crime, may god forgive me!" piece from *Beat Street*. Significant similarities here include the rhetoric surrounding the notion of graffiti as crime, but the clearest influence is demonstrated in the spray can, spraying paint in action. The *Beat Street* piece has additional text wrapped like a banner on a tattoo which reads "dreams of

Figure 3.4: "Is Art Really A...Crime?", by Wiz, Exeter Central Station signal box, c. 1983. Photograph courtesy of Kilo.

glory", while secondary words in Wiz's piece dedicate "for the Bboys", and a cheeky challenge to the authorities with "guess who?". The spray can in Wiz's piece is also held by a character of a writer, although the spray can in Ramo's piece is free floating, yet they both appear to hover in an almost saintly, ephemeral world.

These Devonian pieces illustrate the complexity of the shifting landscape between location and relocation, and the territories within. In terms of rural sites the targets were barns, garden walls and garages and the technological infrastructural interventions of flood drains, railway sidings and signal boxes. In responding to Daniels' comments on the duplicity of landscape (art) (Daniels 1989) and Wylie's connected observations (Wylie 2007: 67), Woods suggests that "the challenge to 'landscape' as a way of seeing makes clear that they also extend to ways of viewing the rural that reduce complex rural environments to the rather two-dimensional and simplifying notion of 'landscape'" (Woods 2011: 109). Rural graffiti, however, rises to that challenge, if we consider graffiti in the rural environment as landscape art as well as a political act. The later interventions illustrated in Sce's piece "Sce" (Figure 3.5) and "MysonSuch" by Myson and Such (Figure 3.6) exploit the spatio-material situation of the rural, emphasizing the infiltration of urbanist architectonics. These works also comment on opportunity; both the trailer and the notion of the flood drain are metaphorical sites for the temporal, suspended life of urban graffiti. This temporality also pushes back on what Foucault would call "power as a diversity of force relations that organize a territory" (Raunig 2007: 49) and makes blatant these force relations exist as potently in the rural realm. Rural graffiti expands the experience of the rural as it embraces "the possibility of directly, 'situatively' resisting the objectively positioned 'situations' of capitalist societization" (Raunig 2007: 174). Halfacree (2006) comments that: "We must note how the material space of the rural locality only exists through the practices of structural processes, and how the ideational space of rural social representations only exists through the practices of discursive interaction" (Halfacree 2006: 48). In which case, the interventions of graffiti become rural acts, and not urban acts placed in rurality; concurrently the acts of graffiti are a meshing of urban and rural, reframing the "ideational space of rural social representations" (Halfacree 2006: 48).

Woods attests that: "The rural gaze is hence a political act, and conflicts can break to the surface if the expectations of the gaze clash with economic or other imperatives driving change in rural areas" (Woods 2011: 109). These pieces of graffiti challenge the rural and work with the urban material,

Figure 3.5: "Sce", by Sce, an agricultural trailer next to the M5 motorway, Devon, c. 2005. Photograph by Scarse, courtesy of Such.

abruptly invading the rural gaze. Yet the work of these writers is positioned somewhere between the local politics of service and infrastructural space and the politics of countryside idylls. Writers were producing and recoding rural space while concurrently consuming it, and by doing so making apparent the differences of consumption of rurality by other groups. The quest to find urban materialism in the rural was not so much the task; the challenge became how to become invisible as a writer in the provinces. Any new production would be much more obvious to the authorities than if it had been painted in a typical dense urban fabric graffiti site, and anonymity was arguably more crucial for provincial writers to maintain. Other pockets of regional style were evolving across the country, Brighton being an example of some substance. During correspondence about the ways in which the locale influenced headz, Tom Dartnell explains:

> if you mean in terms of Brighton's hip hop scene influencing me, then absolutely. The Brighton graffiti scene has always been distinct and that can be attributed to just a handful of writers. While London had a thriving scene from the get-go, Brighton's developed in its own special way. Writers like Req, She, Slab and Fire

The Territories of Hip Hop 93

Figure 3.6: "MysonSuch", by Myson and Such, at the juncture of Marsh Barton weather drains and the River Exe, Devon, c. 2006–2008. Photograph by Such.

forged the town's distinctive letter style, which writers in other parts of the country started emulating in the mid-1990s. And Nema's ascent to become train king of England was obviously a major influence (email to author, 2 April 2017).

Figure 3.7 illustrates the first known piece of graffiti in Northern Ireland by Sherry, "UR", painted in his father's garage. The sparsity of graffiti in the provinces during these early years brought the pieces that did exist much greater significance and impact, both literally in terms of their visual presence and culturally as they became worthy markers of cultural emergence. Over time, these pieces have also acquired greater presence in the local and regional history of hip hop for similar reasons, but also act as important exhibits of evidence attesting hip hop's existence in these terrains. The reduced density and saturation of graffiti and hip hop culture as a whole had a huge impact on its territory and presence, each piece, each tag, each throw-up was paramount. The provincial graffiti network also provided a platform for discourse, often carried through the existence of the pieces themselves, enhancing and reinforcing its own narrative and the narrative of the urban network of countrywide infrastructure. The provincial graffiti writer's most important space, however, was the domestic space of the bedroom.

94 *Provincial Headz*

Figure 3.7: Sherry, "UR", the first graffiti piece in Northern Ireland, c. 1983. Photograph courtesy of Craig Leckie.

Domesticity

As the variances between the graffiti of the metropolis and the province gain a certain clarity, I would like to zoom in and focus on the small scale: the domestic. The reframing of place and the emergence of non-material and territorial spatial practice discussed previously may reveal a divergent evolution of graffiti, but one space that was common to all writers was the space of the bedroom. Upon the rising question of territoriality and ownership of space when talking about graffiti, conversations are always fixed in the public realm, but the dialogue between domestic, small-scale private space and public space is crucial to understanding the spatial practices of provincial writers. The space to plan, to hide, to conspire and to design—and all the other rituals associated with the practice of graffiti writing—unremittingly occurred within the privacy of the home. Even those writers whose home life demanded the need to share a bedroom with a sibling managed to craft some safe, private to stash the tools of their trade; in addition to paint and pens, shoeboxes, pencil cases, biscuit tins and sketchbooks contained a portfolio of process, production and evidence of territorial gain. In discussing graffiti in public bathrooms, Haslam states that: "All graffiti writing requires a certain amount of secrecy" (Haslam 2012: 114–15); however here I am not only talking about writing, but the practices and processes that support the actions of writing itself.

In *Style Wars*, Skeme's mother comments: "Meanwhile, he has destroyed his room", to which he responds: "I'm testing out my paint". The opening sequence in *Wild Style* follows Lee Quiñones as writer "Zoro" as he abseils down the wall displaying his famous "Graffiti 1990" piece; moves through the train yard at night, cuts through hidden apertures in wire fences, and tags with Lady Pink before stealthily moving through another part of the yard, sliding under trains illuminated partially by the teal and grey metallic light. Alarmed by persecutors, he makes a break, over a live line, drops along a wall, and makes good his exit through another hidden hole in the fence. Sniggering at his fortune, he nonchalantly hops over to the street, where he casually ambles back home in the wet, dark night. He scales the iron fire escape stairs at the side of his typical five-storey brick tenement block, and crouched by the sliding sash window, sidles it open and slips into a bedroom. Zoro's brother is waiting on the bed, clad in army gear with Latino music playing in the background, and upon hearing the window creak, aims a pistol to the window. Startled by this sight, Zoro exclaims rather than questions: "Hector! I thought you was supposed to be in boot camp?" Hector lowers the gun, alights the bed and replies: "You know I was gonna shoot your ass? I oughta rearrange your face, that's what I should do." The confrontation continues and turns to the subject of graffiti. Hector is sending money home for Zoro and their mother but becomes greatly displeased that Zoro has spray painted his room: "What the fuck is with that durag on your head anyway? I don't know what the hell you were doing in my crib, but I want this shit..."—he gestures around the room, pointing to the graf—"...out of my room." Heated exchanges are made, and Hector refers again to the graffiti, "there ain't nothing out here for you", to which Zoro replies: "Oh yes there is. This." As well as echoing a parental situation, this domestic scene is metaphorical for the actions of graffiti writers, and "reinforces the theme of entering prohibited spaces by recalling the opening shots of the film" (Monteyne 2013: 103). The staged confrontation is reminiscent of the arguments teenagers experience with their elders, where the space of the bedroom is the agent for conflict. The next scene cuts back to the public realm, and pans across train lines, painted subway cars, demolished sites and destitute streets.

The bedroom itself is a space common to all dwellings, a space where intimate domestic rituals are performed. Forman states: "The 'hood exists as a 'home' environment" (Forman 2002: xix) and continues to argue brilliantly that: "The 'hood does not replace the ghetto but is, rather, a displacement of a more discursive nature" (Forman 2002: 64). There remains, of course, a distinct series of identifiable thresholds between public, semi-public, semi-private and private spatial realms. The bedroom space of the hip hop head, and perhaps more accurately the graffiti writer, becomes a "radical reworking of domestic space", and in *Wild Style* presents "an intervention that seeks to resist the conformity and limitations of inner-city tenement housing" (Monteyne 2013: 103), yet its bounds are not so clear-cut.

If one can imagine a tomography that scans the private spaces of the dwelling through the semi-private spaces of the entrance lobby, the semi-public space of paths, stepways and yards to the public spaces of the street and the square, one might imagine how that most private and protected territory of the bedroom relates to the most open space of the square.[8] Not only are the visual vernaculars of the built environment revealed, but also haptics and non-materiality of space and their interconnectivity. Consequently, it is these relationships that require investigation, and by starting with the archaeology of the bedroom, it is possible to construct the bedroom of the writer as a commentary on the processes of territorial gain.

In the second observation, Skeme and Zoro have turned their bedrooms into multi-purpose spaces. Skeme's becomes a studio/laboratory for testing paints, and Zoro's a studio/gallery displaying complete work. This reveals some of the hidden processes of graffiti, those that are not apparent when graffiti is present in the public realm. In Zoro's case he has capitalized on Hector moving away to boot camp, and it can be determined that either Zoro upgraded to Hector's room in order to occupy a room of higher quality than his own (or maybe that they shared in the first place, and Hector being the eldest sibling assumes ownership of it), or he is occupying the room purely as studio and a secret entrance/exit to the street. It could also be both, but my main point here is that the bedroom becomes a stake in the subterfuge of graffiti, and its identity transformation of the city.

The bedroom confrontation in both Skeme and Zoro's cases is of course nothing new to family life, and common triggers for altercations between parents, siblings and their offspring often revolve around the state of one's bedroom. Here though, a defence is structured more obviously by the writer;

Skeme attempts to justify the damage to his room by a process of practice, in testing his paint. Here he may have been examining the thicknesses of marker pens, their speed of flow, as well as intensity of paint, colours, nozzles and can pressure. As well as the practical testing of equipment, Skeme might also have been testing his techniques through letters, tags, arrows, in fact any visual element in a writer's personal catalogue of styles and motifs. The *Wild Style* scene is clearer to the viewer, when Hector instructs Zoro to: "Stop fucking around and be a man!"; he is not only insinuating that Zoro should find a job and start contributing to the household economy (in the next scene we see Zoro halfheartedly attempt to obtain work at Connie's Superette), but that he should cease graffiti practice. Zoro attempts to justify his position by gesturing at the graffiti-drenched bedroom; for him the ghetto is working—it is giving him graffiti culture. If those whose position was against graffiti, did their concern grow when graffiti invaded the spaces of domesticity? If graffiti belonged anywhere, it surely belonged in the public urban environment, in a space or on a surface that was the responsibility of the authorities, a space that could be pointed at or signalled to, a place where it is the responsibility of others. Could it also be that the presence of graffiti within the private domestic space is more invasive than when it exists in the public realm, suggesting the family space is as broken as the public space? A further question: could it be that the parents or guardians made links between graffiti inside their house and the graffiti they witness in public space, and that their offspring became part of the pandemic? After all, when one is behind closed doors it is possible to ignore the public realm.

If the bedroom of the metropolis connected writers to the urban fabric upon which they were to paint, how did the bedroom of the provincial writer operate? Brent Aquasky's earliest form of graffiti practice was to reimagine cityscapes from his bedroom through the practice of drawing:

> I used to get sheets of A4, my dad used to come back with A4 paper from work, printed on one side, so we had the back side of it to draw and I used to stick all these A4 sheets together and I'd start… I'd literally draw a street scene, like a block, with a B-Boy and a stereo, some litter and a rat. And then I'd add another sheet of A4 and another building with more, and then I'd add another, and then I'd put the sheets above and I'd create the tops of the buildings and I'd end up with this huge picture on my floor, 'cause I'd just be drawing and drawing; there was nothing else to do in the Forest (i/v, Bournemouth, 12 December 2017).

98   *Provincial Headz*

Brent's representational construction of the cityscape acted as a basis upon which to imagine not only the territories of graffiti, but the tangibility of urban life. Through the act of drawing, a spatial discourse is formed which holds double value: it is an inquiry into the nature of urban space as much as it is a formative practising of graffiti, an envisioning of hip hop growing up "in a tiny little village, in a little forest cottage on a goat farm" (i/v, Bournemouth, 12 December 2017). Kilo recounts the value of the bedroom as studio as more about honing skill and technique: "You know back then you kind of tried everything… I liked breaking and graffiti, so I kept doing them; with graffiti practicing in my bedroom, outlines and letters, and I became the sort of writer for Master Blast at that point" (i/v, Cambridge, 23 May 2017).

Figure 3.8 shows Eraze (donning his Master Blast customized tracksuit top and posing with a can of matt black paint) and skater, Rob, in Kilo's bedroom, and in a similar way to how teens display pin-ups and cut-outs of celebrities they admire (in fact, a poster of Samantha Fox, a central figure in 1980s British pop culture is fixed over part of the graffiti-soaked soffit), Bboys and writers adorned their bedroom walls with imagery associated with

Figure 3.8: Kilo's bedroom, 1983. Photograph by Kilo.

hip hop culture. This of course is typical of most teenagers; however, the customization of the room's surfaces draws the notion of practice into the space. Here, the bedroom operates as a kind of paraphrased space; dominated by a full colour piece running at high level over the bed complete with character, lettering, stars, 3-D, and highlights, it shows a set of tropes and details and suggests the maker's comprehension of graf. The piece appears to have been tagged over in black spray paint and marker pen, which indicates it is not new. To the right over Eraze's shoulder, evidence of line-hugging methods and spray-can control is present: line weight, form, outline, highlight, 3-D techniques and colour can all be spotted in a lilac, burnt orange and matt black squiggle which is the result of a conversation with paint. Older and more basic graf is shown in the "NWP" at the top of the wall, and in the same red paint, "ELECTRO" can be deciphered running behind the magazine poster pull-outs. Seven marker pen tags are visible, executed using two different pens, and from the hand style these were made by at least four different writers evidencing further the wider graffiti discussion. Flyers for five events can be seen above the bed at low level, one directly above Eraze, assumed to be flyers for early hip hop events in Devon, and finally two stickers for clothing brands Fila and Puma are mounted on the left-over wall space, valued sports labels for mid-1980s Bboys. The bedroom surfaces become a palimpsest, a shrine of sorts, accruing not only visual information, but developments in practice. The writer's room was a truly curated place which would morph from studio to exhibition space to hidden archive according to the dynamics of a certain moment. Collections of marker pens, nozzles (not so much spray cans themselves as they were not easy to hide due to their bulkiness and odour), sketchpads and blackbooks,[9] as well as shoe boxes and photograph albums containing finished pieces of graffiti, would be carefully maintained and archived for much of the time. The photographs would be inspected, analysed and discussed with other headz, but would rarely be on display, particularly if the writer in question was carrying out illegal practice, which most writers were.

In the aftermath of Operation Anderson on 20 March 1989 (at the time, the largest anti-graffiti bust in the history of British policing), writers took extreme measures to remain anonymous and practise in secret. During the bust, the privacy and domesticity of the bedroom space vanished instantly as police trawled through personal belongings hunting for incriminating evidence. Writers from the most rural areas were drawn into the same pool as those not only from provincial cities Bath and Exeter, but also the Welsh capital Cardiff and neighbouring Bristol. Instantaneously, a shared experience blurred the lines even further between the urban and the rural. Although illegal activities continued to build and rebuild post-Anderson with many writers assuming new nom de plumes, one less predictable outcome of the raid was a focus on legal sites and commissioned work for some. Following court appearances, four members of South Side Alliance who admitted "300 graffiti-related offences in the city" (local newspaper, *Express & Echo*, 1989), received a grant from the Prince's Trust and much media attention, representing graffiti and hip hop on BBC's *Daytime Live* and *Newsround Extra*. Furthermore, they painted regionally, taking part in workshops and supporting local businesses and community projects, such as the Surf and Skate Centre, Exeter (Figure 3.9). As well as national television coverage, these writers were also the subject of a piece in *The Independent* (Figure 3.10).[10] This national exposure affirmed the writers' position as serious practitioners in British graffiti culture, building a new and different fame spot from the street-level reputations previously strived for. However, Remer attests that being busted did not alter things: "It didn't make any difference to how I felt, or felt how I was perceived. I had two regrets, firstly association with others and getting caught, secondly wishing I'd done more" (p/c, Exeter, 1 June 2018).

Operation Anderson still affects those who were convicted, as Remer continues: "I try to forget it but yes, I was unfortunately a 'crown courter'; a criminal record forever. No solicitor can remove it, I've tried!... It's made a mess of my life when I've applies for jobs. As I have to disclose it as it's never spent, I may as well have gone to prison!" (p/c, Exeter, 1 June 2018). The bust meant that writers' birth names were revealed to the public, opening up writers' anonymous fame to the infamousness triggered by local, regional and national press. The idea of "maintaining a form of 'anonymous fame'", which is "central to graffiti and street art practice" (Iveson 2017: 97) took a curious twist, as did the commonly assumed schisms of legal versus illegal, or art versus vandalism. While "name and fame-based graffiti" (Snyder 2017: 268) returned underground, represented through writers' reimagined pseudonyms, it concurrently related to the popular forms of graffiti celebrated in the media. Regionally, this had an interesting impact on the local spatial occupation of graffiti. Post-Anderson, there were new names on the graffiti scene, which to those outside the graffiti underground suggested that there were more or newer writers, leading the local authorities and the public to believe there was a much wider graffiti pandemic than the reality. Although the visual evidence was dense, only a relatively small network of regional writers was in production.

Figure 3.9: Scarse, Marka, Kilo and Case outside Surf and Skate Centre, Exeter, 1989. Scan courtesy of Kilo.

Figure 3.10: Cue, Scarse, Marka, Eraze and Kilo at The Wall of Fame, Exeter, 1989. Scan courtesy of Kilo.

The Territories of Hip Hop 103

Figure 3.11: DJ Krash Slaughta's bedroom, Livingston, Scotland, c. 1988. Photograph by Mark Cowan.

Figure 3.11 tells a similar story, although here a full piece is completed, the length and breadth of the wall. The idea to graffiti one's bedroom with a complete piece became commonplace by the end of the 1980s, yet interestingly not so much in the bedrooms of writers, but produced by writers for their Bboy peers who specialized in other elements. I am not suggesting that these bedrooms were exclusive to the provinces by any means, but rather championed their importance and value to the growth of more rural British hip hop culture. In terms of regional territory, these bedrooms fulfilled a significant function as nodes for a multiplying network of headz which tentatively connected headz across large expanses of landscape. In East Devon during 1985, for example, a network of three nodes existed in Sidford, and a further network of approximately eight nodes in the surrounding Exeter area. By 1988, the East Devon network had increased, enveloping Sidford, the surrounding Exeter area and new nodes in villages Feniton, Whimple, Newton Poppleford, Cowley Bridge and Crediton. The bedroom was also a very private and safe space, Rola remembers: "After watching the kids breakdancing at school I didn't have the confidence to have a go in front of anyone so at first I just used to practice in my bedroom at home" (email to author, 25 March 2017), and Big Tunes D: "I remember starting off in the bedroom practicing bodypopping and trying robotics in front of the mirror just imitating moves I'd seen on TV" (email to author, 6 April 2017).

As these bedrooms became layered with new meaning—curated spaces of cultural production—their inhabitants too were exploring an unfamiliar territory of relationships as they met other headz. The second time I met Kilo, I had come into town in the morning and the plan was to meet some of the other members of Black Jack Posse outside Barclays, our now familiar street territory. In my keenness, I arrived too early, and he still had some family chores to take care of, so he suggested I stay in his room for an hour or so. Equipped with a boombox and a stack of tapes, I was only too glad to be able to scour through his cassette collection and check out some new beats. I was sat on the edge of his bed, my head tilted sideways scanning along the spines of his tapes, as Freeze Force's 'Boogie Down (Bronx)' pumped through the boombox, when in walked someone I had not met before. He introduced himself as Mark from BJP, and he was also waiting for Kilo. He took the chair opposite, and we both head-nodded along to the track. When the tune ended, an awkward silence filled the space, neither of us being quite sure what to say or select next, and as neither of us owned this room, we were playing polite. The ice-breaker was talking through the graffiti imagery on the walls, pulling out cassettes and discussing the track lists, and the flyers mounted around the boombox. These hip hop artefacts and representations offered us points of discussion and an alternative territory for engagement, and concurrently the territory of the room provided a space to facilitate these conversations between two headz from different places.

The bedroom-as-node also became meeting points for the discussions of broader hip hop practice and were pivotal to the evolution of the first provincial hip hop music and demo tapes, as well as offering the territory for new practitioners to refine their craft. DJ Smiz recollects: "We were coming out with a lot of the same styles at about the same time. I was always in my bedroom developing my own unique scratches and was first to make it to vinyl with some of my cuts, that's something I'm very proud of" (email to author, 6 April 2017). As these territories became flexible from bedroom to studio, ad-hoc methods were introduced to make the best use of the space. Figure 3.12 shows Chris Richardson, cutting on a Technics 1210, sat on the bed hunched over the turntable positioned on the bedroom carpet. Due to lack of horizontal surface area, the floor was the next best thing to a table, and provided the stability required for cutting and scratching, despite the method requiring the DJ to sit in such a position. Figure 3.13 also shows another

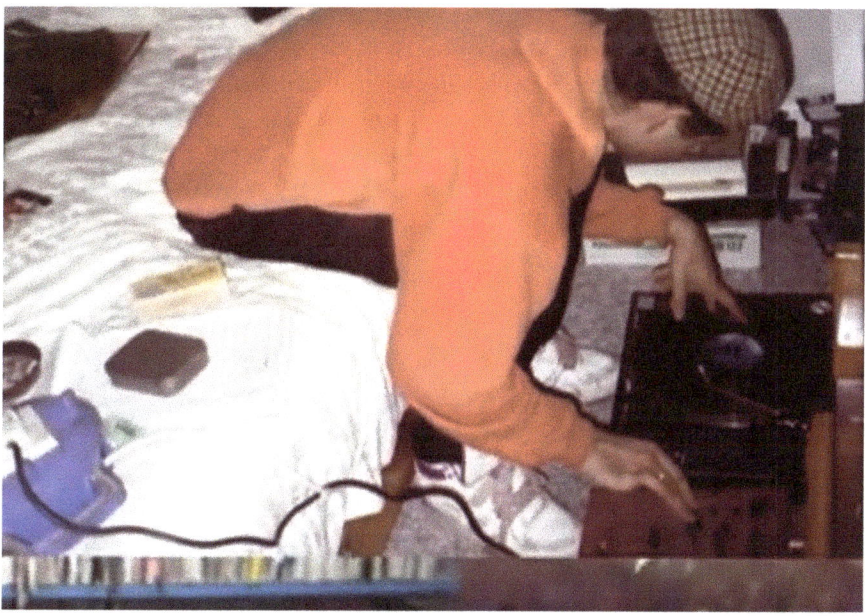

Figure 3.12: Chris Richardson from Bolingey, Perranporth, Cornwall, cutting with the turntable on the floor, at Dave Brinkworth's[11] house, c. 1988. Photograph by Dren Throwdown.

crude spatial organization with the mixer balanced on the side of the synth, the turntable on a lower coffee table and more sound equipment hugging the space behind the synth over the bed. This produces a new kind of vernacular interior architecture, one that restructures the spatiality of the bedroom and its traditional furniture and fittings into one that accommodates music technology and hardware, cables, leads and microphone stands. Crude these domestic spatial appropriations may have been, but they were paramount to the developing language of provincial hip hop as they not only provided the physical space to produce work, but also a fixed base, as the emotional notions of dwelling and place meet the tectonics of a new culture.

Heidegger discusses the experiences of the horizon within his ideas of identity and place, which for him is greater than merely the physical boundaries and edges of space. His example utilizes the bridge to explain the concept of place contained within space, where neither space nor place are measured quantitatively:

> The bridge is a [place]. As a thing, it allows a space into which the earth and heaven, divinities and mortals, are admitted. The

space allowed by the bridge contains many places variously near or far from the bridge. These places, however, may be treated as mere positions between which there lies a measurable distance... an intervening space or interval. Thus nearness and remoteness between men and things can become mere distance, mere intervals of intervening space... What is more, the mere dimensions of height, breadth, and depth can be abstracted from space as intervals (Heidegger 1993: 155).

This phenomenological view that the thing offers a richer experience than the object, when translated into the territory of provincial British hip hop, uncovers much of the sensibilities of the domestic space and its relationship to the public realm. The space illustrated in Dren's photographs is a setting for industrious production, and while the bedroom is enclosed to the outside unlike Heidegger's bridge, the experience of it as both a territory of and for the rituals of dwelling and working require interrogation. The idea of dwelling and working in the same space presents itself with multilayered spatial experiences, which may be more intense for the one who dwells in the space with greater permanence.[12] For the one who lives there, there will rarely be a clear schism between dwelling and working. Before crew members arrive at the room, there might be a need to set up the space, to pack away the things of dwelling and unpack the things of work; equally there may be a need to do the opposite when colleagues have departed. Also, this physical need to create shifts between the place of bedroom and the place of studio has emotional attachments. These emotions are based on the experience the dweller has of the two places, but also these two places might conjure differences in meaning. As a bedroom, the dweller identifies with all the domestic rituals surrounding sleeping, waking and everyday formalities of preparation, which crew members will not associate with this place.

The schism between dwelling and working is also not so abrupt for the visiting crew members. The visitor, then, also has a closeness with the room, fuelled by emotions and experience. To return to Heidegger's bridge:

We do not represent distant things merely in our mind...it belongs to the nature of our thinking of that bridge that in itself thinking gets through, persists through, the distance to that location. From this spot right here, we are there at the bridge... I am there, that is, I already pervade the room, and thus I can only go through it (Heidegger 1993: 156–57).

Figure 3.13: Dren Throwdown cutting on the limited edition Vestax mixer with his Korg DSS-1 sampling synth, at Dave Brinkworth's house, Bodinnick-by-Fowey, Cornwall, c. 1988.

This emotionally charged attachment to how we identify things, for Heidegger, transcends scale and place. The boundaries are not so exact between inside and outside, and in this way, we become near to the place regardless of its spatial distancing. Considering approach and retreat: the bedroom studio is located within the house, which in turn sits in the landscape. In the case of Dren's crew in Cornwall, the house is upside-down with an inverted plan (with the living accommodation above and the bedrooms at the lower level) and is located on a corner site on the side of a hill. The house is enclosed by stone garden walls, mature evergreens, grassy banks and palm trees.[13] Green banks invade the road, and treetops among treetops cover the landscape, their canopies almost enclosing the road creating a thick, green tunnel. As one approaches, one is directly experiencing the territory of the cultivated landscape, one can feel the coolness of the River Fowey and catch a hint of the Celtic Sea. As one arrives or departs the dwelling house, one is physically and emotionally connected to this landscape. At the same time, one is connected to the bedroom studio, for all its anticipation and reflection on the hip hop practice it contains; the territory of the room radiates out into the Cornish topography. Once hip hop is pulled into this Cornish experience, for Dren and his crew, the idea of remoteness becomes "mere distance", and the spaces between Bodinnick-by-Fowey and The Bronx "mere intervals of intervening space" (Heidegger 1971: 155) as the crew exist within a hybrid space of acquired culture and concrete culture. This mindset, in turn, hugely affects the reading of territory, and I discuss the Cornish example as exemplary due to the obvious opposing spatial and material qualities between the Cornish terrain and the urbanization of New York. Returning to Forman's observations, in terms of the local and the physical, the stories of hip hop are "the authority of the individual experience" and structured around those spaces within which "events occur and experience is registered" (Forman 2002: 23). The narratives in hip hop are fundamentally linked with that of territory, and the territories of the British provincial are constructed through the actions, emotions and experiences of a hip hop thirdspace; nowhere is this more obvious that in regions of sparse population, low density and greater natural landscape.

The contours of the provincial domestic space are shifting and transient insomuch that they pull graffiti and hip hop music into the privacy of the bedroom from the imagined and real urban and public realms. Bedrooms were curated, becoming galleries, studios, archives; organic spaces with particular tactics and methods of practice attached to them. With fewer graffiti locations and fewer writers, bedrooms became more important as nodes of a network across a larger, less-urban area. The inhabitants of these spaces became artists-in-residence, responding to their contextual framing in terms of hip hop and locale. The practices of hip hop have reimagined and transformed the city, and "the particularities of urban space are subjected to the deconstructive and reconstructive practices of hip hop's cultural workers" (Forman 2002: 71), but in the British province the practices of hip hop reveal the idiosyncrasies of the rural. The visuals and sonics of hip hop fill the provincial bedroom creating a microcosm of hip hop, a true urban set of representations which, upon recreation within the space of domesticity, become myth and exemplify the major tenet of "Thirdspace" (Soja 1996). If the "firstspace" is the real and the material, it is domesticity and the ordinariness of the province; if the "secondspace" is the space of interpretation and the imagined, then it is the space of hip hop. The Thirdspace then navigates and negotiates between them, recoding the spaces of hip hop which Soja might refer to as "thirding-as-Othering" (Soja 1996: 5). This "Othering" (Soja's capitalization) is an opening up of "our spatial imaginaries to ways of thinking and acting politically that respond to all binarisms, to any attempt to confine thought and political action to only two alternatives, by interjecting an-Other set of choices" (Soja 1996: 5). Here Soja talks about restructuring rather than dismissing the first and second spaces, an act that I have referred to as recoding. To use Lefebvre's terminologies (Lefebvre 1991: 38–39), this recoding makes sense of a new world of provincial hip hop through the spatial practices of its practitioners as they interrogate and critique the (imagined) representations of space and the representational spaces of both hip hop's reifications and the provincial British landscape.

These practices ignited the fuse of provincial hip hop Britain's critical regionalism, particularly at a time when Thatcher was denouncing the notion of society. In an interview for *Woman's Own* she stated: "Who is society? There is no such thing!",[14] and with the revised Public Order Act 1986, which introduced new offences under the titles of "riot", "violent disorder", "affray" and "fear or provocation of violence", Thatcherism's gradual instilling of fear into mainstream society was working.[15] However, as much as scaremongering and demonizing the inhabitation of public space, and the emphasis on the tightly-structured family unit and the drug of television seemed to be reducing national socialization, headz were taking ownership of public provincial territories, planned in the private spaces of domesticity (Figures 3.14 and 3.15).

Two Turntables and a Microphone

When discussing the elements of emceeing and DJing in spatial terms of the physical, a shift to the micro scale is necessary.[16] The success of practising these elements depends largely on technique and attention to detail by emcees and DJs. The emcee's tool is the microphone, and each emcee will

110 *Provincial Headz*

have a preference for use at live shows and jams, although the Shure SM-58 has become the main choice. Emcees will also have their own style of stage presence, and microphone technique plays a subtle yet important role here. The microphone is an extension of one's voice, and if the ergonomics are understood, a prosthetic to enhance performance of the vocal abilities of the emcee. Pioneers like The Fantastic Five would hold their microphones delicately as they oozed charisma; the Funky 4 + 1 often left the microphones on the stands while they performed, freeing them up for movement across the breadth of the stage; and perhaps most interestingly, Rammellzee would cup the microphone in his two hands covering up its ball to change its polar pattern which added resonance and reverberation to his voice, altering its sonic spatiality. When the spatial is considered in respect of the practice of DJing, the DJ needs to know the physical structure of the records used to enable deft handling of the music. As well as knowing the audible structure of the songs played, the DJ must be able to distinguish the start and end of breaks, the breakdowns themselves and other patterns of sound visually. Upon close inspection, it is possible to pinpoint by eye the change in sound structure

Figure 3.14: Eraze and Rola organizing audio equipment and records in Eraze's bedroom, c. 1988. Photograph by Kilo.

Figure 3.15: Dren Throwdown, Si Spex and MC Tony gathering ideas for a track at Si Spex's home, Camborne, April 1990. Photograph courtesy of Dren Throwdown.

of a record; as the pattern of sound changes, the groove in the vinyl will become darker or lighter, slightly wider or narrower depending on the pressing. DJs would inspect their records, and when the break was located, check the visual location with how it sounded. Once confident the useful parts had been accurately located, DJs would often mark them visually with small strips of tape or stickers (usually from cassette inlays) for more secure identification, which is especially useful when playing in dark spaces. Knowing one's records intimately and coding the critical moments in this way aided much slicker, quicker and confident mixing.

Occupation and Appropriation

The acts of occupying and appropriating are central to the practice of hip hop and are as much a mental manifestation of these acts as the physical occupation and appropriation themselves. These acts strengthen ideas of identity, ownership and territorial gain. In 1984, I first experienced the Saturday Bboy meets at Barclays Bank, Exeter, Devon (renamed by the Bboys simply as

"Barclays", which already indicates ownership through the semantic). The architectural language of this high street bank communicated its capital: it was located on a corner plot with the High Street and Princesshay (much of which was rebuilt in a municipal modernist style after World War II) which was constructed three storeys high from the building line, although the street-level entrance to the bank was set back with considerable depth. This afforded a spacious faceted entrance loggia with a shiny marblesque floor that welcomed customers into the branch and oozed confidence and security, reassuring patrons that their business was safe with them. There were tall, double mock-Georgian hardwood varnished doors at the threshold to the internal space of the bank, adorned with large brass doorknobs fitted centrally on each door leaf. This pastiche design again instilled a sureness for the consumer, at a time when the bank's UK and international operations were brought together to form Barclays PLC.[17] Traversing the shiny floor, one could catch a glimpse of the inside workings (as the doors were only shut when the bank was closed) if one peered around the security guard who often stood by the doorway, and glows of orange light radiated from the green-hooded Emeralite lamps sprinkled around the timber fitted interior. To a ruralite, this bank was the centre of the big corporate city, yet in reality it was a modest, provincial branch despite existing as the largest in the region. It was here, one wet Saturday afternoon, that I first caught sight of the local Bboys who had targeted the space for its material and spatial merits. Herbie states: "Back in the '80's a hip hop scene grew in Exeter UK—the raised marble tiled entrance to Barclay's Bank in the High Street provided a perfect stage for nightly hip hop gatherings, with Saturday shoppers and tourists filing past to the beats of New York and LA".[18] Revaluing and rethinking the corporate space of the bank transfigured it to a new spatial meaning. Recoded messages are contained within the representations of spatial acts; bank becomes jam.

Exeter's formidable breakdance crew was called Master Blast, a crew invented by Herbie (a pioneer of hip hop in Exeter) who brought Centre Force, Street Law and several other formative Devonian crews together. Clad in matching BHS tracksuits,[19] blue terrycloth with a yellow trim, and red iron-on letters across the back that read "MASTER BLAST", they looked incredible as they breakdanced, popped and locked to the sounds of *Street Sounds Electro 5* blasting from a slightly battered boombox: "Put on your dancing shoes, get, get, get ready to get a-loose, to a beat that the DJ found, it will make you get on dooooown…it's time to rock, rock rock! Rock-R-R-Rock!"[20] The crisp sound of 'It's Time to Rock' drew me straight into Barclays by some sonic osmosis—I had never heard this song outside of my small Sidmouthian[21] circle before—and filling the octagonal loggia were a circle of Bboys and a few bystanders watching. I shuffled my way through and watched for what felt like twenty minutes. Master Blast radiated a level of confidence I had not seen in my breakdancing colleagues before, and I realized they were way ahead of us from the sticks, but what elation I felt upon discovering hip hop was thriving in Exeter. Rola attests the value of similar experiences:

> From hanging out under the stairway at school I got chatting with others and we got to know each other well. On Saturdays some of us would hook up to go into Exeter city shopping for music and checking out the Exeter breakdance crews that would meet up for battles outside Barclays Bank after it closed at 1pm (email to author, 25 March 2017).

As a member of Master Blast, Kilo remembers: "Barclays was obviously the pinnacle point, and I remember going to Barclays and that's when we first saw Centre Force, you know the crew that Herbie mentioned" (i/v, Cambridge, 23 May 2017). Barclays was pivotal not only for its physical construct in hosting the direct spatiality of Bboying, but also acted as a temporal cultural hub for the development of regional hip hop. The gatherings, which included Centre Force, Street Law and other satellite crews and Bboys, provided a social construct for the solidifying of the Master Blast super-crew. Herbie corroborates this point, tracking back to the very first occupations of Barclays:

> Due to us hanging around outside the former Barclay's Bank in the high street daily, virtually anyone going anywhere would pass that point. As we were making early attempts at breaking and popping, we met others that had stolen their mother's kitchen floor lino and the first crews were born, "Center Force" and "Ex-Static" (p/c, Tunbridge Wells, 23 October 2014).

Herbie was the linchpin for the Barclay's jams, on occasion setting up a complete rig powered by caravan batteries, appropriating everything possible to make the event work from car speakers, domestic hi-fi equipment and furniture to the physical space of Barclay's loggia (Figure 3.16). Herbie would also use the microphone, hyping up Master Blast and the crowd to generate a strong vibe, and often dropping the *Coronation Street* theme in between electro anthems. This was more than pure gimmick—mixing in an earworm from

Figure 3.16: Herbie setting up the sound system at Barclays, Exeter, c. 1984. Photograph courtesy of Kilo.

the most highly watched British soap opera caught the attention of everyday folk and helped muster a crowd. This was one of the first moments of provincial practitioners fusing American hip hop with British popular culture sonically, a theme that I will return to in later chapters.

However, the Barclays experience was not without conflict. The daily loitering that Herbie touches upon actually took place in the high street, outside the ownership boundary of Barclays, and it was only on Saturday afternoons and night-time that the Bboys slid into the loggia. This afternoon slot was the only opportunity to break on the perfect floor, and the anticipation of this spatial empowerment gathered intensity during Saturday mornings. Hearing word about crews arriving from neighbouring towns to battle, what new cassettes would be played to break to, and the steadily increasing buzz as time ticked closer to the moment the bank's doors closed until Monday morning, grew close to hysteria. As the great doors swung shut, we would bum-rush the space, throwing bags and jackets into the corners of the walls, as the boombox started to play. Then occasionally, and within a matter of minutes, the security guard appeared, challenging our presence. At other times the police were called, and I distinctly remember an instance when some of the crew refused to leave following security's demands. "Fuck you, you twat!" one Bboy yelled (the most simple but powerful insult of the time), during a few awkward minutes prior to the arrival of the police. Mostly, these gauche moments dissipated the hangers-on, but the hardcore Bboys remained obdurate, with some staring back at security and others continuing to breakdance in attempts to rile them further. When the police swung around Princesshay at the west side of Barclays, every Bboy would gather their bag or coat and the group would dissipate.[22] The alternative location need not be discussed; we were all headed to the sheltered, shiny first floor of the Guildhall Shopping Centre. We believed we were looking for something urban, and Barclays and the Guildhall was it.

Street Beats

Wherever there were Bboys, there existed their own version of Barclays. For DJ Bex, hailing from Camborne, a small Cornish town, it was Tesco:

> Around leaving school in Summer of 1984 I noticed a few kids that were in the year above me and had already left school, were wearing Patrick wind cheaters, then at an under 18s disco was a guy in a denim jacket and white gloves body popping—I wanted in. During that winter Camborne Breakers were born. Outside Tescos until one in the morning with our ghettoblaster and lino; we also started graffing[23] in and around Camborne in the dark winter nights (email to author, 27 March 2017).

Although only 11 years of age, Scott Coombes remembers a similar moment in Boston, Lincolnshire:

> Though it was only about 20 minutes' walk, trips into town on my own at that age were frowned upon, but due to my mate being 13 he managed to persuade the old dear to let us go up one Sunday afternoon. Obviously back then nothing was open, but that wasn't the point. As we approached the centre there was music emanating from a sheltered shop doorway, and as we got closer we could see a group of lads, maybe four or five of them about 16 or 17, dancing, but not like normal. It was a bit surreal looking back but I was absolutely taken in by what they were doing. There was a kind of uniform too, red and blue raincoats. I didn't quite get the

whole thing, but I knew I wanted to do the cool stuff that they were doing and that music! Eventually I plucked up the courage to ask what they were doing, and they told me "Breakdancing… we're the Crazy Crew". We just watched. For ages (email to author, 16 December 2017).

What headz were searching for was the urban adventure, having seen the daytime Bboying locations in *Beat Street*, *Breakdance: The Movie* and *Style Wars*—those highly urban places that exist on the threshold between semi-public and semi-private—and positioned in time and space between the institutional (school, youth club) and domesticity. There was something edgy about breakdancing in this realm, from the mixed receptions by the public to the flirting with trespassing, but as well as the element of risk, what was desired was that feeling of "being street", a sensation hard to achieve in the countryside. Although the territory of the street was represented in film, the more beguiling representations were embedded within hip hop music. By the end of 1985 a barrage of records containing the word "street" had entered the provincial—blatantly and obviously in the song titles. Purely on the *Street Sounds Electro* compilations alone (and that in itself was a clear signpost) there was: 'Beethoven's Fifth (Street) Symphony' by The VHB and revered Mancunian Bboy crew Broken Glass with 'Style of the Street'. Further afield, Sugar Hill Records released compilations entitled *Street Beat* and the highly commercial group Break Machine with 'Street Dance'. Slightly harder-to-find records in the provinces included 'Street Wars' by Palmerforce Two, 'Street Justice' by The Rake, 'Street Love' by Twilight 22, 'Street Girl' by Spoonie Gee, and Choice M.C.'s 'Beat of the Street', some of which found their way into collections in villages and hamlets as a result of carefully planned record shopping excursions into the cities: "Looking at it just from the time I lived in Sidford, we went to visit Bristol a couple of times because they had better record shops" (Rola, email to author, 25 March 2017).

The themes of "street" and the urban also appeared recurrently within the graphics of certain record labels, perhaps the most prominent and widely known being Sugar Hill Records, whose label design features the profile of a dense city, with a street-like spiral tapering into the flamboyantly colourful and flowing words "Sugar Hill" which hover effortlessly above the bitonal urban outline. Duke Bootee's Beauty and the Beat Records label design portrays a subway train sliding through the megalopolis on a raised bridge, with "BEAUTY" and, "and The BEAT" painted on two subway cars, the whole scene reminiscent of a detailed tableau, drawn immaculately in pencil, yet thick with texture echoing the grime of the urban fabric (Figure 3.17). Almost like a miniaturist painting (the record label is only 100mm in diameter), one is drawn into the urbanist space of the image as one pulls 'Triple Threat' by Z-3 MCs from the sleeve.[24] Other labels with urban names that emerged during the 1980s included City Beat Records, Tuff City, Strong City, Street Beat Records, Urban Rock Records, Easy Street Records, Street Scene Records, and of course, Morgan Khan's Streetwave.

The semantics and semiotics of these record labels connected the notion of the metropolis with the creation of hip hop. Lefebvre claims that: "Semantics and semiotics hold a respectable but limited place in our general understanding, and in our understanding of space in particular" (Lefebvre 2014a: 123), and defends this statement by suggesting that the proper name given

Figure 3.17: Centre label of 'Triple Threat' by Z-3 MCs, 1985. Photograph by author.

to a place may position it within a coded network (of other places), but the emphasis on semantics and semiotics to embed a certain message which champions communication, places understanding of information in jeopardy (Lefebvre 2014a: 124). This is certainly the case when considering the housebuilding culture in the UK, where scores of new twenty-first-century developments construct house typologies such as "The Stratford", or "The Cambridge" as part of "The Heritage Collection".[25] These buildings are usually scattered around cul-de-sacs named "Royal Way", "Queen Anne Close", or "St. George Drive", with the expressed purpose of adding an over-coded semantic-driven regal value to the properties, which does not seek to impart any understanding or knowledge to the consumer. However, within the evolution of hip hop, I would argue that the semantic and semiotic argument Lefebvre proposes is, in fact, synonymous with the ideas of communicating and informing. He continues:

> Those who unthinkingly apply such concepts to space...assume that that space contains a message. The message can be decoded. Because it is addressed to people it can be read. It can be compared to writing. It is based on several more or less common codes, the code of knowledge, the code of historicity, the code of symbolic interpretation (religious, political) (Lefebvre 2014a: 125).

Lefebvre then relates this statement to the idea of transmission, illustrating that humans are the transmitters of messages, not the spaces that humans occupy. Space responds to and realigns the complexity of human transmission. If it is assumed a coding is contained within a space for humans to decipher, for Lefebvre: "This theorization reverses practice" (Lefebvre 2014a: 125), and by returning to his theory of spatial practice, he contends that: "Space decodes people's impulses, in we choose to employ that term; it is not people who decode space" (Lefebvre 2014a: 125). However, Lefebvre's position here is only a part of the structure of understanding space in relation to my argument. What complexly extends the notion of transmission in hip hop are the modes of representation in different sites of occupation: the sonic site of sound and lyrics, the semantic and semiotic site of the record label and sleeve design, and the spatial sites (both perceived through hip hop films and directly experienced). These sites were valued and reevaluated by Bboys, and by triangulating these representations led to a decoding and recoding of (urban) space, that made sense in the world of provincial hip hop.

Active and Reflective Occupation

The bus shelter was also a space/place of occupation and appropriation, and of territorial gain. Particularly in the depths of rurality, the bus shelter offered a double-symbolism: firstly, as a public, municipal urban structure, and secondly, as a spatio-material device that suggested the location of a bus stop, a node among a line of nodes that led to the transport hub or terminal in the town or city. The shelter became an attractive hangout space; when occupying the shelter, one felt closer to the destinations at the ends of routes and could catch a hint of urbanism as passengers alighted on their return journey carrying high street shopping bags, fast food or flowers.[26] These meanings of shelter also resulted in it becoming a strategic target for rural writers, as Brent Aquasky recalls:

> We had nowhere to tag, I lived in the middle of a forest, so I just went and tagged all the tree stumps that had fallen down across the road. They cut them up and cleared them off the road and there were all these exposed stumps there and I was tagging those up. And obviously the bus shelter and everything where I was, the bus shelter was hit up over and over (i/v, Bournemouth, 17 December 2017).

Locally, the tagged-up shelter gave writers a sense of ownership of the shelter, and furthermore a claim in the hip hop stakes by communicating the existence of writers in rural areas. Writers from elsewhere may pass-by, taking note of these tags, a documentation of the process of writing and evidence of its existence in the province (this idea is explored further in Chapter 5). The shelter also took on the role of "writer's bench",[27] and for music practitioners as much as writers.

Previously in this chapter when discussing the domestic, I proposed that when linked across the province, "bedrooms as nodes" supported a growing network of hip hop activity. The shelter becomes part of this network, a mediating space between the open rural realm/dense urban realm and the privacy of the bedroom, a creative space which supports opportunities for reflection. The shelter in Sidford operated as one such space (Figure 3.18). It was not the tiny timber shack associated with most village bus shelters, but a handsome brick and render building, which also housed the village public lavatories. In true Victorian style, these are celebrated buildings, although the example here is too far off the Devon tourist track to have been extravagant; however it does boast a garden and hanging baskets that split the paths to the toilets into the traditional "Gentlemen" and "Ladies" routes. The shelter lies on a corner junction where bus routes pass through to the larger destinations of Honiton, Seaton, Exmouth and Exeter. The design of the shelter was a success, although aesthetically mundane: in plan it was rectangular, and the space left over between the dog-leg entrances to the male and female toilet spaces was given over for a long timber slatted bench for seating. The seated area offered superb shelter from the elements and a decent amount of privacy suggested by the threshold structure of three arched openings. Much to our delight, the hard-rectilinear surfaces of this semi-enclosed space ensured substantial echo and reverb when the boombox was played from within. Although it was situated near two rows of small terrace houses, the car park to the rear offered enough distance that when the boombox was present complaints were rare. It was also opposite the village pub, The Rising Sun, which served take-away from the jug and bottle entrance to the side, and on Saturday evenings we would buy a bottle of Devenish Bitter and a bottle of dry cider each, and blast rap music until around ten-thirty.

My crew had been occupying the shelter in this way for almost two years before we began producing our own music; it had become a familiar territory

Figure 3.18: "Sidford Shelter". Photograph by author.

we associated closely with hip hop, our recoded piece of urbanism. We were not the only youths to use the shelter; the village was small, and everybody knew everyone else—all the youths attended the same school. Others from our peer group would also hang out here at times which led to an interesting set of spatial negotiations. They had their own coding for the space; it was a space to smoke, to flirt, a piece of privacy outside the home with no fear of being overheard by parents. Musically, this peer group were fanatics of U2, Simple Minds, AC/DC, Bob Marley and Prince, and would scorn and mock the sounds oozing from the boombox and equally we would retort with jibes aimed at Bono. However, on occasions where all the youths that used the shelter (approximately 15 in total) got together, the shelter's occupation was negotiated on an ad-hoc basis. Ten-minute breaks from boombox-blaring hip hop, twenty minutes (one cassette side) of a Prince album, back to a John Peel homemade compilation, relocation of the boombox to one end of the shelter, music off again, and so on. These impromptu negotiations helped us learn how to use the space, such as tilting the boombox towards the soffit under the arches for the best reverb effect, and they also facilitated discourse across genres of music. The location of the shelter was also quiet, and with few distractions was a perfect location to analyse music. The schism between boombox and the passivity of rural life is shared by Evil Ed:

> It probably made it more exciting for me that hip hop was something alien to Leighton Buzzard. It was mostly coming from the USA to begin with and then to the cities and bigger towns then to me walking around fields blasting it on a Walkman or boombox. Tunes like 'Shout' by M.C. Craig "G" being blasted in the Bedfordshire countryside I didn't really think of as being odd back then, I just needed my fix of music, but it is quite funny looking back (email to author, 14 June 2017).

The shelter was a two-minute walk from our recording base, so was ideal to appropriate as a critically reflective space. The shelter had become a territory we had associated with hip hop, so when we began to produce our own sound, it was a natural progression to test out our music in the shelter: our appropriated fragment of urbanism as a context for self-evaluation and reevaluation of rural hip hop. When discussing the spaces of academia and critical regionalism, Powell observes that when academics "disconnect scholarship from the place it occurs" (Powell 2007: 193), an alienation of ideas, practices and eventually of academics themselves takes place. He continues: "An awareness of place in political and cultural critique, on the other hand, claims local ground, the immediate surroundings, as the starting point for change, moving from reflection to action by making the local a site of vigorous cultural struggle" (Powell 2007: 193). The educational spaces for provincial hip hop were the appropriated territories of the bedroom, shelter, the bank foyer, the market forecourt, and the assemblages and networks of the village and man-made interventions in the fields beyond. Brent Aquasky remembers attempting to urbanize the fabric of village life:

> I used to take old bike tyres and try and throw them up over the lamps, over the street lights, and there was only two street lights in the village —I was determined to get things hanging off them because I saw that in some hip hop music video I watched, or maybe it was *Hip Hop History* or something, so I thought, "ah yeah, that's something I could do". I was trying to turn my village into New York, but the one-man crusade didn't really work (i/v, Bournemouth, 12 December 2017).

Brent's memory might appear extreme but removed from the assumed aesthetics and spatiality of hip hop, awareness of one's immediate place and space of hip hop enables the interactions and dialogues that lead to an alternate placing of oneself *within* hip hop. Richie B from the small mining village of Langley Park, County Durham, states: "Where I live had an effect on me as it's miles away from urban surroundings and any type of hip hop scene, so it made loving all of this more special and personal" (email to author, 29 March 2017). Distancing from the city added a further dynamic to action, production and reflection on one's own practices. Ross Adams alternatively describes the softness of provincial life as a space for developing practice in Dorchester:

> It was a small market town, quiet. But for some reason we had a really passionate, talented bunch of young lads who were eager to learn about all the elements and also had a wide range of talents between them. Brilliant breakers, emcees, DJs, and artists who all came together as one. The scene allowed you to do this and had no nastiness. It was an exciting time and learning process for everyone (email to author, 28 March 2017).

These kinds of reevaluations were arguably a more polyvalent process for provincial headz, as they were required to detach themselves from the urban spaces of hip hop to a greater degree than that of city dwelling Bboys, yet this may have afforded them a greater vantage point for reflective decoding and recoding. In "Soft Tension: Reimagining Urbanism and Rurality through the Spatio-cultural Practices of Hip Hop"[28] I introduced the idea of distancing for decoding and recoding (an idea also discussed in Chapter 4). By retreating from the city, one can reconsider one's urban experience within the context of the non-city. This removal of oneself from the urban environment enables one to consider the transmission of the codes of hip hop with greater equivalence (de Paor-Evans 2018c: 186–93). This act of detachment generates a thick threshold of some weight between the rural/village and urban/city. By traversing the threshold back to the urban, one occupies space and time to synonymously critique the provincial. These oscillating sites of physical occupation are decoded and recoded in tandem as one's own hip hop practice develops, leading the practitioner to arrive at a critical position of his or her own. In the mid-1980s, this reimagining of urbanism and rurality through the spatio-cultural practices of hip hop served as a platform for future provincial practice. Although experienced on a much-reduced scale, the art of Bboy and graffiti combat brought a realness to the conflict with the spaces of capitalism that Harvey discusses in *Spaces of Global Capitalism* (Harvey 2006). He states:

> The corporatization, commodification and privatization of hitherto public assets has been a signal feature of the neo-liberal project. Its primary aim has been to open up new fields for capital accumulation in domains hitherto regarded off-limits to the calculus of profitability (Harvey 2006: 44).

Harvey continues to signal the commodities, infrastructures and services that have suffered the neoliberal effect, which of course includes space. Yet the takeover of public spaces, at least in the mid-1980s British provincial towns, was much less obvious than the phenomena in the polis, and far too subtle to trigger any form of direct resistance. Barclays and the Guildhall reproduced capitalist space and represented it in the everyday under the disguise of public space, inviting potential consumers to spatially occupy this architectural spectacle, provided one operates according to the neoliberal agenda. The resistance to the structured neoliberalization of space that Bboying and hip hop brings is significant: not only did the practices of provincial hip hop forge a heterotopia by challenging spatial ownership and power, they also revealed and made apparent the systematic consumption and confiscating of public space from society, through the new style of the street.

Chapter 4

The Consumption of Hip Hop: Commercialization, Distinction and the Subaltern

During a conversation in the school playground one Monday lunch break in 1985, I had heard that a BBC Radio 1 DJ by the name of John Peel played hip hop records on his night-time show. That very same evening and enthused by the prospect of hearing some new tunes, I went to bed just before ten o'clock (a usual time for a school night), but excitedly lay in bed wearing a pair of cheap Sony earphones plugged into my modest Sharp GF-7400 E boombox and tuned the FM dial to Radio 1. Armed with a blank TDK D60 tape, I was ready to record in case the rumours were true, and I waited patiently. Just after ten, Peel arrived on the air. The first couple of songs I did not recognize, and after several more songs of some obscurity, I began to realize that I would know none of the music Peel was playing. In some way, the unusualness of his selection increased my faith in him playing me some new hip hop as I lay in bed in our quiet, dark bungalow in the dimly lit village. Half an hour slipped by, then longer; my eyelids became heavy with tiredness and I was becoming increasingly disappointed. Despite fighting my fatigue, I drifted off slowly to sleep (stirred only by the harsh rasps of occasional FM interference), when suddenly I bolted upright in my bed as Peel announced "…and this is The Organization" before dropping 'The Big Beat'. The huge chords and beatbox intro triggered me to consciousness. My finger had slipped off the pause-button previously as I had fallen asleep, which resulted in the whole of one side of tape being recorded, so frantically fumbling I ejected and flipped the cassette over to record as much as I could of this incredibly popping electro-rap jam that I had never heard before. My head was rushing. Did he just rap the Unknown DJ's name in the first line? I definitely heard: "Chillin' not illin' in the place to be / DJ Unknown with the big big beat and…" I was freaked. Was that the same Unknown DJ from '808 Beats' on *Electro 7*? Who was the emcee? I only missed the first few seconds and indulged in every beat, scratch, rhyme, beatbox and stab throughout the song, wide awake, animated and buzzing from this discovery. The next morning could not come soon enough when I could meet my crew and ask them if they too had caught it. I barely missed a John Peel show for the next five years.

On Consumption

British hip hop was consumed initially through products and artefacts which adorned the recurring themes, tropes and signs that had become established and accepted forms of hip hop culture from New York. Although some of the key records and books—the paramount artefacts perceived as bringing hip hop to Britain were discussed in Chapters 2 and 3—this chapter draws on some arguably less informed and exemplary examples of early hip hop commercialization through the compilation album. It first explores the cultural values of three albums *Hip Hop—the Original and Best* (Charisma, 1984), *Breakdance Fever* (Jive, 1984), and *Rap Graffiti* (Charly Records, 1985), which are then discussed in comparison with Morgan Khan's *Street Sounds Electro* series. One important reason for selecting these albums is that none of them were issued in America, and purely targeted a British and European market. These are analysed in detail in the section "Commercialization", below, which also picks up on the notion of the urban myth. In reference to the analysis of cultural products by Huet et al. (1977), de Certeau observes: "it seems possible to consider these products no longer merely as data…but also as parts of the repertory with which users carry out operations of their own" (de Certeau 2002: 31). Users absorb products; and the ways in which this process of absorption is undertaken subsequently becomes a driver for production. In this chapter I will argue that provincial headz worked with their limited range of consumption through a creative practice of accumulation, absorption and critique to aid the formative productions of provincial hip hop. In the chapter's section "Distinction", I argue that an interpretive process of consumption played its part in triggering a sense of taste and distinction in provincial headz. This sense of taste and distinction was key in shaping the habitus of provincial hip hop, which in turn helped inform the first lo-fi recordings by practitioners in less-urban areas. The chapter continues to explore notions of habitus and taste through local, national and regional radio transmission, and concludes with an interrogation of the everyday, underground and DIY cultural drivers that shaped a critical regionalism/de-regionalism in the final section, "The Subaltern".

Commercialization

During the early to mid-1980s, certain record labels in the corporate music industry reacted to and capitalized on the boom of breakdance and graffiti culture via the vehicle of the hip hop compilation album. There was a wealth of breakdance and rap-oriented compilation albums that appeared in record shops across Britain during the breakdance explosion, many of them taking inspiration from the *Beat Street* and *Breakdance: The Movie* soundtrack albums. The compilation was a swift way for labels to release an album and broaden and diversify their genre and product portfolio. Wikström and Burnett discuss the benefits of portfolio theory: "Music firms use many different strategies to reduce their exposure to risk and to limit uncertainty. One such strategy is to follow the principles of portfolio theory" (Wikström and Burnett 2009: 508). When this theory is applied to the compilation album, it potentially reduces risk and cost as labels are not signing artists or paying for studio time, but rather buying a licence for the content, which was highly attractive during the emergent and uncertain days of hip hop in Britain. Also, at this point Britain's contribution to hip hop music was negligible, so releasing a compilation of whatever American songs could be licensed was a fast-track method for exploiting breakdance to generate capital consumption. Of course, any music rights costs decrease considerably if the label already owns the content: "Releasing a compilation album involves significantly less risk than releasing a traditional album and, in times of financial difficulties, compilation albums may be a tempting way to meet the sales budget" (Wikström and Burnett 2009: 512). A further factor that figured in the making of these compilations was a misperception of hip hop's temporality: the visually dynamic yet ephemeral qualities of breakdance and graffiti could be exploited, but needed to be acted on before it disappeared, and the next craze arrived. Wikström and Burnett also discuss the importance of packaging and repackaging to sell songs that have been issued repeatedly, the most cost-effective way in which to deliver product (Wikström and Burnett 2009: 507–22). This is certainly true in the case of hip hop songs such as 'White Lines (Don't Don't Do It)', which has featured on over 90 compilation albums in the UK alone.[1] Although this type of album was widespread among global

The Consumption of Hip Hop 127

record corporations,[2] this section focuses on three albums designed in Britain and aimed specifically at British and European youth, with mixed success.

The Famous Charisma Label's offering to the field of hip hop compilation albums is the 1984 release *Hip Hop—the Original and Best*, which was released in the UK on Charisma and by sister or partner labels in Germany, Italy, Yugoslavia and Portugal (Figures 4.1 and 4.2).[3] Only three artists appear on this compilation, these being Malcolm McLaren, the World's Famous Supreme Team and the Rock Steady Crew, artists already signed to The Famous Charisma Label. McLaren's contributions here are the songs 'Buffalo Gals' and 'Double Dutch', the latter again produced by Horn, but not featuring the World's Famous. 'Double Dutch' is not a hip hop track but rather more mbaqanga in genre, but was perceived to be hip hop at the

Figure 4.1: Front cover, *Hip Hop—the Original and Best*, 1984. Photograph by author.

Figure 4.2: Rear cover, *Hip Hop—the Original and Best*, 1984. Photograph by author.

time by its association with 'Buffalo Gals' and its inclusion on this album and *Duck Rock* (see the analysis in Chapter 2). The previous relationship between the World's Famous Supreme Team and Malcolm McLaren ensured that the World's Famous were also signed to Charisma, to whom they provided their debut single release, 'Hey DJ',[4] to much less commercial success than 'Buffalo Gals'.

The Rock Steady Crew was arguably the act that was the most active in terms of hip hop culture. I use the term "act" specifically, as the Rock Steady Crew contained no musicians, but dancers and writers. Formed in 1977 in The Bronx, New York City by Jojo and Jimmy Dee, they became the most active and formidable breakdance crew worldwide, and still continue to perform, teach and progress practice. However, in terms of their musical output, similarly to the World's Famous Supreme Team, both tracks '(Hey You) The Rock Steady Crew)' and 'Uprock'[5] that feature here were produced by others: Ruda Blue (Kool Lady Blue of The Roxy fame) and Stephen Hague produced these two Rock Steady Crew's songs, and although there are rich roots of hip hop culture within the crew, the music itself is a fabricated commercial construct of hip hop music. However, the less fluffy of the two, 'Uprock', is packed with breaking related lyrics, as Baby Love's introduction rides the one-note synth before the beat drops: "Uprocking, stabbing the air, if you wanna battle 'cause the beat's all there", signalling the punchy stabs "Uprock! Sureshot! Never stop! The body rock!" then, "uprock, uprock, uprock!" Similarly, their debut single repeats this four-bar chorus no less than eight times:

> Hey, you, the Rock Steady Crew
> Show what you do, make a break, make a move
> Hey, you, the Rock Steady Crew
> B-boys, breakers, electric boogaloo

The lyrics far outshone the cheese of the pop-synth music in respect of the message, but the real interest of these singles for British and European hip hop fans were the sleeve designs, both of which featured graffiti-style caricatures of the Rock Steady Crew drawn by Doze. Additionally, the sleeve for 'Uprock' featured the characters stood in front of a painted wall that read "Uprock" surrounded by tags, above which the profile of the city panned behind a graffed-up train. In small, silver letters emulating a throw-up on the side of a building in the background, reads: "Uprock—warlike dance. Object—to take out your opponent without physical contact". ShelltoeMel, from Milton of Campsie, East Dunbartonshire, Scotland, draws upon the memory of these characters as one of the first things that enticed her into hip hop: "I had a *Number One* magazine breakdance special.[6] It featured members of the Rock Steady Crew who were also around at the time with their record '(Hey You) The Rock Steady Crew'. I copied the graff figures off the record onto my bedroom door" (email to author, 22 June 2017). DJ Smiz, Specifik, and Tom Dartnell also cite the Rock Steady Crew directly as an influence, and with their appearances in *Wild Style*, *Beat Street* and *Style Wars* arriving in Britain at a similar time to their records, it was the culture they represented rather than their music that inspired the youth of Britain.

Charisma did not look past the extent of their own licensed music to enhance the curation of this album, but rather made the decision to produce an album with only three tracks on each side, and furthermore one of the six tracks (on side two) is simply an instrumental version of 'Hey DJ'. This was somewhat justifiable by the current vogue of 12″ singles at the time, and in terms of duration of play, the inclusion of the extended versions ensured that the release did not fall much short of a standard album. There was a short-lived trend of launching compilation albums with so few tracks (arguably due to the length of the 12″ single), and in the same year Island Records released the UK-only compilations *Crew Cuts* and *Crew Cuts 2* also with only six tracks on each release. These featured Run-D.M.C., Beatmaster, and Grandmixer D.St., although a majority of the songs included were from the broader field of dance music (Nuance, Jocelyn Brown, Screamin' Tony Baxter), expertly blended by Mancunian DJ Chad Jackson, taking a lead from the *Street Sounds Electro* series. Additionally, these were marketed as part of Island Records' specially priced mini-album series, which were denoted by a postage stamp logo on the top right of the sleeve which read "MINI-LP 33.3" (this series also included *(The Woodwork) Squeaks* by Was (Not Was), U2's *Under A Blood Red Sky (Live)*, and The Waterboys' *The Waterboys*).[7] However, *Hip Hop—the Original and Best* is neither blended nor remixed; the content consists purely of the tracks from the previously released 12″ singles. All five of the singles achieved commercial chart success in Britain (with 'Hey DJ'[8] the least successful but still reaching number 52 and 'Double Dutch'[9] peaking at number 3), prompting Charisma to create this album; however, following its release, it appeared nowhere in the Official Albums Chart Top 100. One of the reasons for its low sales could be attributed to its lackadaisical curation which was no match for its hip hop compilation rivals. Rather, Charisma relied on previous chart success to sell the album, whereas consumers wanted new, different or remixed sounds.

In terms of the product's packaging, the album is far more successful. If one had not heard the music therein, the cool confidence in the title: *Hip Hop—the Original and Best* seems to suggest exactly that. However, this is a much spurious claim, as 'Buffalo Gals' is as close to genuine hip hop as any of the music reaches. One could ironically argue that the music is "original" in a bizarre way—insomuch that it did not actually represent hip hop of the time accurately at all—and there are equal problems with the assertion that this album contained the "best" hip hop music. This point is useful, however, as it does raise the difficult subject of legitimacy in hip hop, and the value in the position of what hip hop "should" sound like (which is discussed in the next section). There was a value in the title though; for many, it was the first time (apart from *Beat This! A Hip Hop History*) that the words "hip hop" had been clearly spelled out through written representation on a recorded product, which was greatly important to the provinces. Curiously, the music may not have been a true reflection of hip hop's sonics, but those two words communicated the culture's name to its audience. Alongside the words *Hip Hop—the Original and Best*, the sleeve design incorporated several images that acted as key indicators to hip hop. The front cover depicts a filtered photograph of a single breakdancer in a freeze position underneath the large font title and above a list of the artists' names. This single, strong image clearly communicates that this is an album one can breakdance to and promotes the message that the Bboy in the photograph is breaking to the music therein. On the back cover, a photograph of each of the artists contextualizes the notion of breakdancing further and introduces the element of graffiti. The first photograph of Malcolm McLaren documents him again rocking his mountain hat (from his and Vivienne Westwood's "buffalo girls" or "nostalgia of mud" collection) and posing with the famous "Duck Rocker". Additionally, there are photographs of the Rock Steady Crew in an urban park holding Bboy postures and accessorized with two boomboxes, and the World's Famous Supreme Team modelling turntables and mixing equipment with a graffiti backdrop. Even the catalogue number FRESH 1 amplified the message that this *is* hip hop, it is original, and it is the best: misleading signification but carrying a very important sign.

Jive's *Breakdance Fever* follows a similar pattern in terms of its visual presentations (Figures 4.3 and 4.4). It features two Bboys on the front cover, Dolby Dee from The Crew: Sidewalk and Killian (Elliot Popper) from The Capricorns donning Kappa tops and pastel-pink cardigans (a look belonging somewhere between Bboy and casual),[10] frozen in full windmill and headspin mode respectively.[11] The dynamism of the motion-blurred photograph captures the dynamic of the dancers, breaking on the street in front of a corrugated iron fence which occupies the entirety of the space. The fence is fully painted in graffiti with the words "BREAKDANCE FEVER" decorated with typical graffiti tropes: several coloured arrows, white popping gloves, stars, and other vague symbols rippling over the corrugation painted by an artist called Aero-Soul, whose name did not appear on any other hip hop reification. The track list was located on the rear, hovering over the barbed wire that hung atop the corrugated fence, the purple hues of the perfect sky exaggerating a much-staged feel.[12] The credits were drawn rather than written, in fat lettering (although far more illustrative than any graffiti style), arrows instead of dashes between song titles and artists' names, more stars and a white glove, with solid colour fills of bright yellow, peach, salmon pink and white—typically fashionable colours of the time. The ersatz of these tokens lead to a representation whereby: "The casual observer could be forgiven for thinking that breakdancing was devised in an advertising agency pressure session" (*Rap Graffiti:* liner notes). However, to the provincial youth, this sleeve spoke "street", and "capitalised on hip hop's urban symbolism which was represented through product" (de Paor-Evans 2018c: 192).

These visual tokens may have swayed some consumers to buy into this album, but if any punters were wavering, surely the first track on side one would have convinced them. The opener 'White Lines (Don't Don't Do It)' by Grandmaster & Melle Mel is the only song on the compilation to have required licensing from outside the Jive/Zomba group, and it peaked at number 6 and stayed in the official singles chart for an interminable 60 weeks. The next artist to appear is Whodini, staple Jive artists and a crew of high quality output, who had experienced marginal British chart success in December 1982 (the same month of 'Buffalo Gals' fever) when 'Magic's Wand' reached number 47 (although curiously none of my 45 interviewees mentioned 'Magic's Wand', despite its status as one of hip hop's greatest old school songs). The Willesden Dodgers' two offerings are superb examples of electro and Gifted 4's funky 'Temper (Gotta Keep Cool)' reinforces the strength of Melle Mel, Jalil and Ecstasy's raps with some tight punchlines, although the remainder of the curation is problematic. The other three songs arrive courtesy of Richard Jon Smith (one third of The Willesden Dodgers and a 1970s soul artist), Funk Machine (an Italian electronica duo), and Trinidadian singer Kate Kissoon, all of whom had previous success outside the genre of hip hop music. Kissoon's offering 'I Need a Man in My Life' is effectively a commercial pop song which sits uncomfortably at the close of side one, and Funk Machine's song is a cover of the mercantile Break Machine's second single 'Break Dance Party', and never released as a single—this cover version was created purely for this compilation and acts merely as a benign filler of some six plus minutes. Smith's contribution fares slightly better and employs lyrics such as "breakdancing in the clubs and on the street", advising the listener that "once they get started they'll blow your mind / They spin like tops and their bodies unwind" as toms, synths, and mechanical, robot-like crashes litter the rhythm track; yet the music of these last three tracks finds itself in the same position as *Hip Hop—the Original and Best*, a commercialized unadventurous sound, and attempts to mimic basic cultural tropes rather than explore a genuine sound of hip hop.

Charly Records' compilation *Rap Graffiti* presents artists Grandmixer D.St. and The Infinity Rappers, B-Side, The Smurfs, and (also graffiti artists)

The Consumption of Hip Hop 133

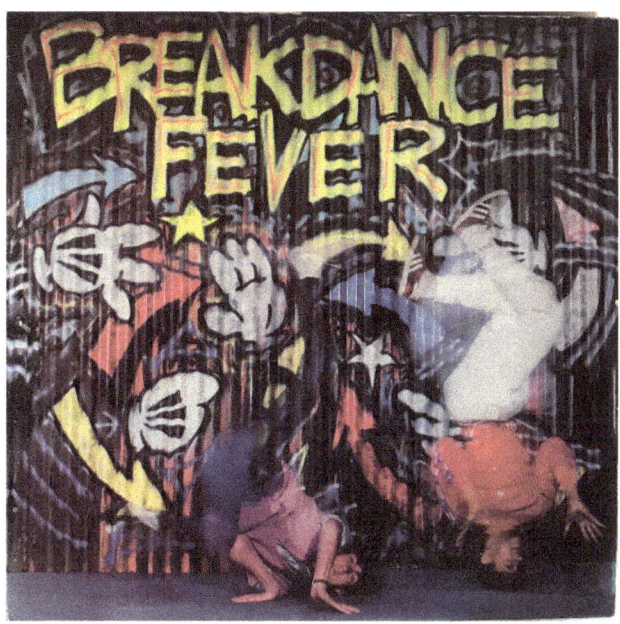

Figure 4.3: Front cover, *Breakdance Fever*, 1984. Photograph by author.

Figure 4.4: Rear cover, *Breakdance Fever*, 1984. Photograph by author.

Fab 5 Freddy, Phase 2 and Futura 2000 (Figure 4.5). This album clearly relates hip hop to graffiti practice through not only the obvious title, but through the work of the artists (overseen by Bill Laswell)[13] which visually, sonically and texturally brought a glimpse into the world of The Roxy and the multiplicity of style and origin found in hip hop and graffiti culture. While it was puzzling at first to discover that these hip hop artists were linked with The Clash, Material and other post-punk musicians, the sleeve notes by David Toop were a shrewd move and of great benefit to the young British provincial consumer in contextualizing not only the compilation itself, but also hip hop's position in respect to the Manhattan disco scene and the post-punk era:

> At that crucial moment in the middle '70s when the party music of mid-town Manhattan and Fire Island was inflaming discos from Dubrovnik to Doncaster and punk was in training to kick progressive rock into a temporary wilderness there was another music—in style, attitude and from somewhere between disco and punk—rocking the "unfashionable" boroughs of New York City (*Rap Graffiti*: liner notes).

The importance of James Brown and Dyke and the Blazers, but also rock artists AC/DC, Billy Squier and Aerosmith, began to inform consumers that the makers of hip hop indulged in a much broader palate of sounds and dug deep for its sources. Charly Records, a label that generally specialized in funk and soul reissues, were comfortable with *Rap Graffiti*, as the songs included there were all released three years previously in the US on Celluloid Records, but largely missed the provincial audience (despite several receiving a UK issue in 1983 through Charly) due to distribution. Effectively, what Charly Records presented was very much in theme with the idea of the reissued compilation and offered further historical insights, which helped extend the panorama of British hip hop culture past the electro and rap delivered by the early Street Sounds albums.

The album presents seven songs, and textually "side one" and "side two" are recoded as "Upside" and "Sidewalk", immediately linking the audience with moments of urban America. The album's opener is 'Une Sale Histoire' by B-Side, where the introductory lyrics command, in a French accent, "change the beat, change the beat", leading into a vocoder-laden rap delivered in French. Closely followed by Fab 5 Freddy 'Change The Beat'—effectively the same percussion with slightly different sounds and production with Freddy rapping in American-English—the synthesis between these two

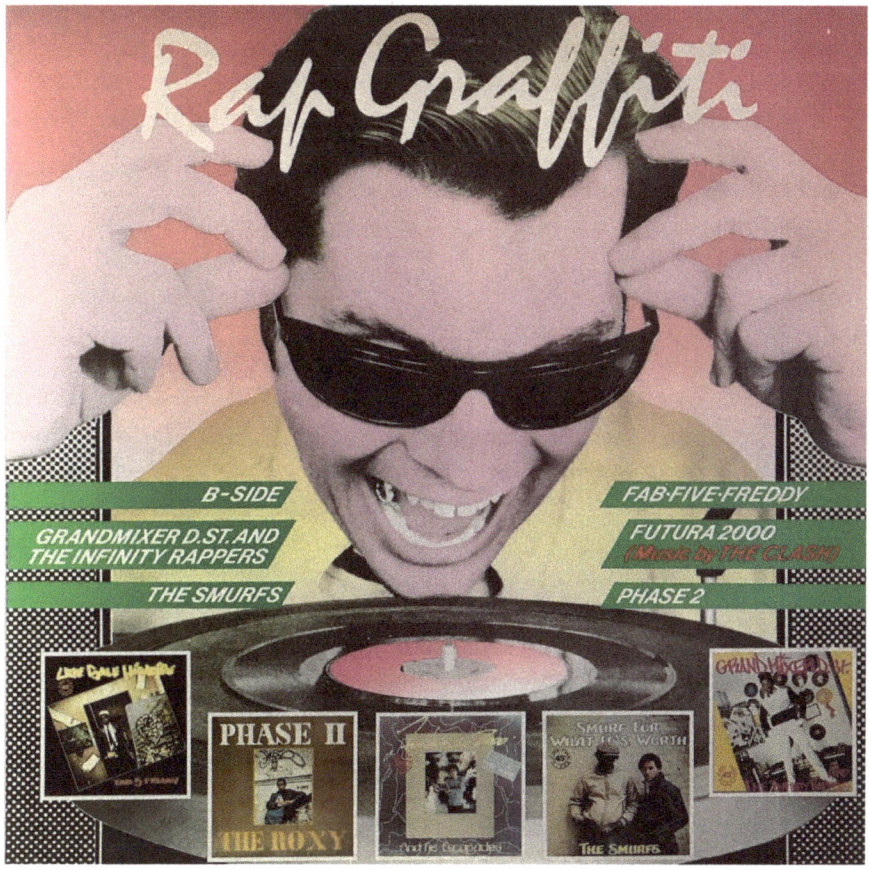

Figure 4.5: Front cover, *Rap Graffiti*, 1985. Photograph by author.

tracks conveyed the inspiration from the melting pot of the downtown scene. Freddy had linked with Patti Astor (who, with Bill Stelling, started The Fun Gallery, the first art gallery in the East Village) and Charlie Ahearn some years earlier, and his broad palate of creativity is evident here. "Upside" continues with graffiti writer Phase 2's 'The Roxy': an ode to the venue, this jam is a collection of sound and lyric bites, snippets of "The Roxy", vocoder-heavy cuts of "fresh" and "Ahhhhh", sparse rhymes ("Roxy the hottest spot in town"). Amid the experimental industrialism of Laswell's production, one can make out "The Fun Gallery", "cash money", and the eerie "Wheels of steel the DJs spinning all night long / Everybody's in the party rockin' strong / Rapping breaking cutting taking all the night / Roxy is the place to be it's out of sight...yeahhhh". "Upside" closes with Grandmixer D.St. and The Infinity Rappers' 'Grandmixer (Cuts It Up)', which continues the montage of tune patterns in unexpected keys, mechanized sounds and fragmented raps. "Sidewalk" opens with 'Krush Groove', exclusive to *Rap Graffiti*, which sits somewhere between a posse cut, a segue and a megamix. This track is an orientation through each of the independent songs on the album. The Smurf's 'Smurf For What It's Worth' follows, a sonnet to the dance by the same name, and closing out the album is 'The Escapades Of Futura 2000' by graffiti writer Futura 2000. By this point Futura 2000 had visited London and inspired a number of pioneering British writers such as Skam. The opening verse again reiterates the relationship of graffiti to hip hop: "Futura is my name and I said / Graffiti is where I got my fame / But it's not my fame that I'm here to claim / I wanna tell the real story about my game". Delivered over a rolling bassline and deep, robust percussion and with the music credited by Mick Jones from The Clash, the song affirms the album's agenda, communicating hip hop's stake in the in-between space of downtown and uptown, post-punk and post-disco.

However, by far the most important aspect to this compilation was contained in the first six seconds of the record. This was the first time the famous vocoder sample "Ahhhhh this stuff is really fresh" was pressed onto UK vinyl, and more interesting is that some consumers did not necessarily know this until they got the record home. This was a monumental moment for hip hop in the provinces as none of the celluloid pressings had reached the far lands of rural Britain. The value of this sample to hip hop was strengthened further when, only a few months after *Rap Graffiti* was released, Doug E. Fresh and The Get Fresh Crew's 'The Show', laden with Barry B and Chill Will's cuts and scratches of "Ahhhhh" and "fresh" reached number seven in the UK singles chart. Almost without exception, every electro and hip hop record from 1982 to the early 1990s that incorporated a DJ, scratched, cut-up or sampled that soundbite, and furthermore, with this pressed onto a UK album, aspiring DJs could use it to practise.[14] It *was* hip hop, and remains positioned as one of the strongest sonic hip hop tropes in history.

For consumers of *Rap Graffiti*, the pre-industrial soundscape was quite unexpected, but began to make sense alongside Toop's descriptive liner notes and the accompanying eight highly contextual photographs which included the insides of subway trains and outside The Roxy. Most importantly, these photographs were populated by Bboys, Bgirls and hip hop artists in action: to provincial headz, *Rap Graffiti* was a complete reification of hip hop. Toop's words filled a gap between the compilation album as convenient consumption of music and hip hop education:

> In the Bronx, Harlem, Brooklyn, Queens and Staten Island, even out to New Jersey, upstate or the Carolinas, the black youth alongside a sprinkling of Hispanics were cutting beats and writing rhymes—making a new kind of music to fill the vacuum that they sharply felt (*Rap Graffiti*: liner notes).

The Raven Design Group's graphics epitomized the mainstream styles of the time, and the front cover's pink-skinned, quiffed, shades-donning trendy, frozen in ecstasy as he leans into a turntable platter, seemed bizarre. However, this pink-skinned figure added an important facet to the face of the British hip hop compilation album as he stares at the original record sleeves montaged below, and acts as a visual metaphor: "The records compiled for *Graffiti Rap* [sic] were made during a previous period of *volte face* for rap" (*Rap Graffiti*: liner notes). Toop's words also served as affirmation that graffiti was firmly part of hip hop culture, confirming and extending what was learnt from *Wild Style*:

> What we now know (only too well) as hip hop culture was one of New York's best kept secrets. Its only downtown manifestation was the graffiti of folk heroes like Taki 183—scrawled tags which blossomed over the ensuing years into panoramic spray paint murals with a degree of high art credibility. Otherwise it was a quiet revolution, dispersed on cassette tapes and contained within legendary dancehalls such as Harlem's Audubon Ballroom (*Rap Graffiti*: liner notes).

Scott Coombes educes the value of *Rap Graffiti* as a catalyst for his personal development within hip hop culture, prompted by purchasing *Rap Graffiti* on one of his frequent family visits to north-east London from the small market town of Boston, Lincolnshire:

> It was also during one of these trips that I bought my first ever hip hop LP from a record shop in Chadwell Heath. It was a new Charly compilation called *Rap Graffiti*, which featured the Escapades of Futura 2000. 1985 would see the birth of several personal lifelong obsessions, a pair of turquoise Gazelles scored

from a discount shop above the Co-op in town for the bargainous price of three whole pounds would sow the seeds for what would become a footwear passion which would become almost as important as food (email to author, 16 December 2017).

Rap Graffiti solidified graffiti's position and made a strong contribution to the perception of hip hop in Britain, as Scott attests:

That record just jumped out the rack at me, base instinct really, rap plus graffiti, stuff I'd recently taken on board as a kid, I had heard of Futura 2000 by then and was already intrigued by his style. It was less street and, I don't know, just something more progressive, in adult terms I guess (p/c, Lincoln, 12 June 2018).

Scott's suggestion that *Rap Graffiti* "was less street" presents an interesting question about the nature of "street". Previously I discussed the plethora of early products which solicited the literal semiotics and semantics of "street" as a proponent for the perceived urban identity of hip hop. However, Scott's reflective description of the album as progressive indicates the social reform of music and culture inherent with this production, emphasized by the exposure of the broad roots of hip hop through Toop's words and reified through Laswell's production and the Raven Design Group's graphics. *Rap Graffiti* offered an alternative slice of hip hop knowledge to provincial consumers. But despite the connatural avant-gardism encapsulated in this album, the urban myth of hip hop lives purely through the subtle use of the term "Sidewalk".

Consuming the Myth

Barthes describes myth as "a type of speech", opening his "Myth Today" essay with: "What is a myth, today? I shall give at the outset a first, very simple answer, which is perfectly consistent with etymology: myth is a type of speech" (Barthes 2009: 131). He continues to synthesize a theory of semiotics wherein the myth is dependent on a series of conditions which are connected to the signified, signifiers, and ultimately signs. The type of speech of the myth is not so literal as to be purely verbal but can also be visual: the myth evolves from what Barthes names "meaning", "form" and "concept". The "meaning" is that meaning attached to a sign which is the result of the relationship between the signifier and the signified (the language). Barthes uses an example of a rose and how it signifies passion:

> on the plane of analysis, we do have three terms; for these roses weighted with passion perfectly and correctly allow themselves to be decomposed into roses and passion: the former and the latter existed before uniting and forming this third object, which is the sign (Barthes 2009: 135–36).

The rose is the signifier, the passion is signified by the rose; the resulting relationship between the rose and the passion becomes the sign. He continues to explore this idea in terms of experience and analysis:

> It is true to say that on the plane of experience I cannot dissociate the roses from the message they carry, as to say that on the plane of analysis I cannot confuse the roses as signifier and the roses as sign: the signifier is empty, the sign is full, it is a meaning (Barthes 2009: 136).

To follow Barthes' analysis and apply this to the product of *Breakdance Fever*, this album embodies a language, as the sign of the productivity of hip hop. This productivity, in its complex processes and productions, becomes tangible through the painted semiotics of graffiti and of movement through breakdancing. The pictorial speech of *Breakdance Fever*, those representations of Bboying by Dolby Dee and Killian, and the representations of graffiti by Aero-Soul are the signifiers, carrying the signified (productivity) to create the sign. There is further meaning here though: the corrugated iron fence and the barbed wire are also signifiers of urbanism, the signified, and the sign of the relationship between the notion of urbanism and the tangibility of the material; but it is the corrugated fence that carries the result of the productivity of graffiti practice, and the motion-blurred photograph that evidences the urban engagement of the Bboys as they break in front of the fence. The combination of these signs produces a language about the site of the productivity of hip hop and urbanism.

How does this reification of the urban productivity of hip hop become a myth? Within the myth there are two semiological systems that overlap. The discussion above explains the "*language-object*", that is, "the language which myth gets hold of in order to build its own system" (Barthes 2009: 138), and the myth in its own right, which Barthes calls "*metalanguage*, because it is a second language, in which one speaks about the first" (Barthes 2009: 138). Within this metalanguage, the sign becomes another signifier, which he names "meaning" (that which holds the meaning to the myth), so when considering the language-object of *Breakdance Fever* it already presupposes a meaning. However, when it becomes altered into form—that is the basis of the myth—the myth here being the productivity of hip hop practice exists in the urban realm. Once this sign is considered myth, by common use, it loses its historical content and combines with the signified to create the "signification": the myth itself. The myth then becomes a neologism, a new language which over time acquires a new history. The meaning, however, is not lost: "the form does not suppress the meaning, it only impoverishes it, puts it at a distance, it holds it at one's disposal" (Barthes 2009: 141). The myth does not take away the language of the urban fabric, the graffiti or the breakdancers' moves, but it does communicate the creativity of hip hop as urban, as "*myth hides nothing*: its function is to distort, not to make disappear" (Barthes 2009: 145; original emphasis). The myth embodied in *Breakdance Fever* is one example of the large and diverse network of metalanguage that continually reinforced (and still does) the myth of urban hip hop.

Electro is Aural Sex

The *Street Sounds Electro* series was the brainchild of Morgan Khan, founder of Streetwave and the Street Sounds brand and record label in 1982.[15] While Streetwave mainly released licensed singles, Street Sounds became established as the market leader of compilation albums specializing in music of black origin and all styles of dance music, and in 1983 the label introduced the pioneering hip hop styles of electro and rap to a British audience (and much of Western Europe) via *Street Sounds Electro 1* (Figure 4.6). The *Street Sounds Electro* compilations became the label's most successful series and were paramount to the arrival of provincial hip hop culture in Britain. The *Street Sounds Electro* series embedded more than just the sonics of hip hop and reframed and redefined an era of hip hop. The currency of *Street Sounds Electro* in British hip hop culture is vastly greater than that of other compilations, and their value is still retained 37 years later. Morgan Khan's editions selected the most current American import 12"s and due to Khan's connections with the various dance scenes in London, the *Electro* series was largely curated based on the hottest records in clubland. There were particular American labels that Khan had licensing deals with, and until 1985 most of the songs that appeared on the series were licensed from NIA Records, Sugar Hill Records, Profile Records, Sunnyview Records and Vintertainment, although not solely. Every *Street Sounds Electro* album broke the top 100 album charts, with volume seven peaking at chart position number twelve (Figure 4.7).[16] Considering this chart success vis-à-vis the individual records themselves that made up *Street Sounds Electro 7*, from the hard New York sounds of Roxanne Shanté and The Fearless Four to the 808-laden electro sounds of California's Egyptian Lover, Unknown DJ and The Knights Of The Turntables whose records were not available outside the major cities, Khan had made a significant advance for hip hop in Britain. The pathbreaking *Electro* series took electro and hip hop records only known in the underground of the polis as well as some even lesser-known or unheard songs,[17] and remixed, repackaged and represented them to the British consumer. This advancement was especially valuable for dwellers outside the urban scenes and major cities, as these compilations were readily available in mainstream shops such as HMV and Our Price, but equally so within local towns at WHSmith and Woolworths, ensuring that the pick of current hip hop reached the smaller pockets of Britain. The impact of Khan's series carried enormous weight, as Whirlwind D clearly remembers:

> In around '83 my mate MSD (Manjit) who was my old beat box, who designed the original Liberty Grooves logo,[18] said to me "mate you should check these *Electro* albums out, they're wicked". And that was it! I literally dumped all my Adam and The Ants records (i/v, Salisbury, 15 October 2017).

Specifik corroborates and suggests this series generated a wider impact and acted as precedent for others:

> The Electro series was hugely important in the development of hip hop within the UK. I also believe that the diversity of these records also laid the foundations for other genres of electronic music. With the sudden wave of popularity, you also had a number of compilations that were clearly targeting a wider audience (p/c, Bournemouth, 1 May 2018).

One such compilation series which took a strikingly similar form of representation to the *Electro* editions was Serious Records' *Upfront* series which ran between 1986 and 1988, and contained a broader palate of hip hop, house, soul and funk. Many other interviewees cited the *Electro* series as pivotal in

Figure 4.6: Front and rear cover, *Street Sounds Electro 1*, 1983. Photograph by author.

their foundation of hip hop knowledge; DJ Smiz considers them an obvious point of reference: "All the *Electro* albums from the Street Sounds series helped a lot as well of course" (email to author, 6 April 2017), and Evil Ed places their use in context:

I was lent some cassettes of the *Street Sounds Electro* albums. Also, my friend had a cousin who came to visit from London now and then and brought tapes of the latest rap and electro tunes. We used to hang out in a park and one of the older kids had a huge boombox, with big detachable speakers and I used to just hang out around that listening to the tapes, hungry to hear every track on them. I had a Walkman too and was listening to the tapes nonstop, walking to and from school, on my paper round, at any opportunity (email to author, 14 June 2017).

Dren Throwdown further frames this context through the *Electro* series, which also acted as a trigger for proactivity: "When I eventually stumbled into the *Street Sounds Electro* compilations I was hooked, all my mates were into The Cure, The Smiths and Prince; most people laughed at me over my musical taste, so I bought a cheap ghetto blaster and started taking it to school". But most importantly the *Electro* series acted as agent for linking with other like-minded folk: "The main spark to kick it all going properly was bumping into a young DJ Assassin, aka Simon Gilbert later to be Si Spex from The Creators, in Camborne. I was playing *Street Sounds Crucial Electro 1* and he just came over and said hello" (email to author, 20 June 2017). Uncle Colin The Funky Diabetic, living in the market town of Highworth, Wiltshire recalls: "One Sunday afternoon some friends came and called for me, we went out to my mate Michael's house and they played me *Electro 6*, the two Doug E. Fresh tracks changed my life"[19] (email to author, 3 April 2017). The vividness of the interviewee's memories in pinpointing exactly when the *Electro* series made an impact evidences their importance, so why is it that the *Electro* series were so successful compared to the previous compilation albums discussed in this chapter?

The execution of *Street Sounds Electro 1* was not produced by a simple practice of product bundling. Apart from the conventional 12″ of pressed vinyl and card jacket, this record was unlike any compilation that preceded it, and the appeal of *Street Sounds Electro* to a young British audience can be attributed to three fundamentally innovative factors: affordability and availability, innovative design, and pathbreaking production. Firstly, this album was delivered complete with eight full-length tracks for the same price as one 12″ single imported from the USA. This made it very attractive as to purchase eight import 12″s at this time would have been in the region of £40 and too costly for most consumers. Khan's previous distribution deals ensured that the Street Sounds product was available countrywide in independent record

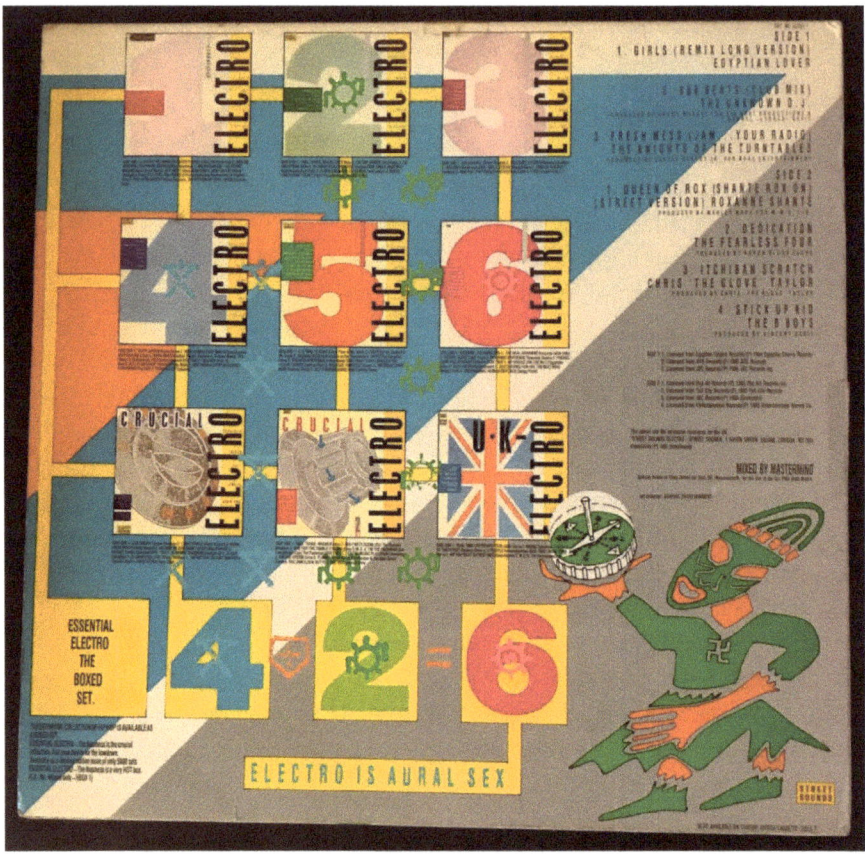

Figure 4.7: Rear cover, *Street Sounds Electro 7*, 1985. The series strongly suggested the idea of the collection as each edition presented the previous releases in chronological order on the rear cover. Photograph by author.

shops and certain mainstream stores such as Our Price and HMV. Consumers no longer had to pay in excess of £5 for a single imported record, as they could buy the Streetwave issue for half the cost, which was favoured by many consumers despite the Streetwave issues following some weeks after the imports were released. Those few British record shops that did deal in stateside 12″s tended to order very few copies of imports, due to availability from the US supplier, the high outlay cost, import duty and risky chinks in the supply and demand chain as there was no sale or return arrangement on imported records. Related to this, the Streetwave label also alleviated disappointment to consumers if a desirable import was unavailable due to the label's insightful decisions to mainly issue the records that were creating a buzz on street level.

While a key objective of Streetwave was to emulate the stateside 12″ record typology which championed extended dance mixes and remixes of songs, *Electro 1* was a masterstroke in compilation development, altering not only the landscape of dance music, but of how consumers in the UK perceived and experienced this transatlantic culture of electro and rap music. Furthermore, the single album was convenient, and also available on cassette which opened up these songs to consumers who did not own a record player. Following on from this, the tracks selected for *Electro 1* were not only costly, but in short demand in the UK. In some cases, several of the tracks included had not even been heard before. The quality and breadth of the songs included, ensured that these compilations were trustworthy as the Street Sounds stamp guaranteed excellence. The majority of records used on the *Electro* series were scarce even in the cities unless they received a UK issue; Khan ensured key American labels and artists were represented across all the editions, and while there were labels whose artists were recurrent (Marley Marl and Vincent Davis productions, for example), they also included random greats such as 'We Come to Rock' (1984) by Imperial Brothers, 'Star Raid' (1985) by 19th Fleet and 'The Party Scene' (1983) by The Russell Brothers. Without *Street Sounds Electro*, these exemplary hip hop records would not have been heard in the more remote rural environment. Due to national distribution deals with P.R.T. Records Ltd, Street Sounds managed to reach more consumers and drastically increase the demographic of new electro fans. The 12″ singles featured on *Electro 1* were only available in very limited quantities and in very few independent and specialist record shops at locations in London, Manchester and Birmingham, and Street Sounds brought electro to the provinces and remote corners of the UK.

Secondly, the product itself was an extremely seductive and beguiling package visually. The sleeve design was a spatial assemblage of colour, text and symbol, organized with architectural precision and slickness. A pale-yellow background supported a vertical strip of bright yellow to the right-hand side, a large pastel pink "number 1" sat slightly off centre to the left, with a bold block of red, centre-left, adorning the artists' names. A thinner, flying vertical strip of grey adorned the words "AS SEEN ON TV", while the Street Sounds emblem sat firmly in the top left corner. Over each vertical letter of the word *Electro* read the words: "SPECIALLY MIXED FULL LENGTH VERSIONS". This minimal, almost De Stijl approach suggested something fresh, new and bold was inside, just waiting to be played. The rear of the cover intentionally gave only the necessary additional information in terms of track titles, artists and licensed record label acknowledgements, yet also for the first time included the time lengths of each track. All of this factual information was aligned to the right-hand margin in black text. To the far left, hovering about the tail of the reverse image of the number 1, reads in bold, red lower-case lettering, "Electro is aural sex". What did this even mean, electro is aural sex? This album was alien, and its pathbreaking design beguiled. These compilations, with their blocks of colours, and no pictures of people, contained a complete air of mystery, as Whirlwind D vocalizes: "The first *Street Sounds Electro* album I had was probably *Electro 2*, I didn't get the first one, but those sleeves were incredible, they just made you ask, 'what was in those records?'" (i/v, Salisbury, 15 October 2017). John Carver states:

> Carver's art directed all the early Street Sounds sleeves... I used to work with two very talented designers who called themselves Red Ranch. Morgan heard some tunes being played in the studio I used to share with a film production company called Standard Pictures. One of the producers used to share a flat in W11 with DJ Noel Watson. They were some of the first people to learn about Electro, buying import 12″ singles from the USA at £5 each. Morgan put out an album with 12 tracks on it for £5! *Electro 1* entered the UK Pop chart (not dance chart) at 18 going on to sell 60,000 units. The album featured tracks no-one had heard of. Neville Brody was inspired by our design to create a cover for The Face...not the other way 'round. I invented the line ELECTRO IS AURAL SEX that you see on all the sleeves. We created a boxed set which is hugely collectable. I lent mine to Banksy's mate Paul Insect when he worked for me many years later and haven't seen it since. For the record Morgan had the idea for a series called Street Music and I suggested it was called Street Sounds. The rest is history (John Carver, in a Facebook post by Jon Tansley, 23 April 2012).

Greenberg argues that modernist art champions flatness, the uniqueness of which is exclusive to the art itself (Greenberg 1961: 100–10), and, as Berman says, "strives to withdraw from modern life" (Berman 1983: 29). Writing in 1953, Barthes discusses this notion in the context of literature, where a writer of modernism "turns his back on society and confronts the world of objects without going through any of the forms of History or of social life" (Barthes

1970: 52). In discussing Barthes' essay "The New Citroën" (Barthes 2009: 101–104), Hebdige argues that "For Barthes, the real can only be inserted into language as a 'silence'—'a silence which belongs to fairy tales'. But instead of the 'silence' of the object, we might like to stress its solidity, its materiality, the simple fact of its 'being there'" (Hebdige 1988: 79). The persuasion of these observations of modernist aesthetics suggests the disparity between the context of life and its modern image. In the case of the *Electro* series, this disparity is indeed present and celebrated—the sonic content and its Afrofuturist and African-American context removed from the visual. If this visual does turn its back on social life, it is for stressing its solidity, and its own presence. The problem of representation in the *Electro* cover art is in fact not a problem at all, and as Hebdige points out, Barthes was a litterateur, and as such, "the problem of representing the material world remains paramount...the relationship of speech to silence—because the problem is itself immaterial" (Hebdige 1988: 79). To this end, the relationship between consumer, visual and sonic product is immaterial; the existence of the object itself is responsible for its success. Yet my argument is to place Carver's design as an alien form, a visual that strikes absolute empathy with the sounds contained within. For the everyday consumer not knowing Carver's history, the beguilement continued; but "aural sex" indeed, as one experienced the increasing fade of the introduction to 'I'm The Packman' by The Packman which opened side one.

Thirdly and arguably most importantly, the selected recordings were mixed and blended into each other with no silent pause between the tracks. As The Packman draws to a close, the third and arguably most important phenomenon of *Electro 1* becomes evident. The listener did not experience the end of the first track, then several seconds of dead vinyl before the start of the second track, as every other compilation album before it. Rather, The Packman is blended perfectly into the second track, 'Jam On Revenge (The Wikki-Wikki Song)' by Newcleus, which in turn is mixed into West Street Mob's 'Break Dancin'-Electric Boogie', which drops perfectly into 'Get Wet' by C-Bank to conclude side one. The idea was to simulate the club/block party experience by mixing the song selection (a practice perfected throughout the 1980s but pioneered in the 1970s). Herbie Laidley (aka Mastermind) was the DJ responsible for mixing *Electro 1* and a majority of the *Electro* albums, transforming the listening experience from that of a sequence of compiled imported tracks to, effectively, a single sonic encounter. The ingenious idea to deliver the albums as a mixed production was a paradigm shift not only for record production, but also for the consequential impact on the audience—these mixed albums gave the provincial audience an experience of witnessing a DJ mixing. This curatorial invention also bore a significant impact on some of the earliest forms of provincial practice as aspiring DJs attempted to emulate Mastermind's mix, a practice that also relates to pause-button mixes, discussed in the next chapter.[20]

Other editions employed the skills of D.J. Maurice, DJ Noel, Bunny Roc Inc., Froggy, Simon Harris, Mixmaster Tee, and R.J. Scratch whereby these DJs became artists in their own right—the *Electro* series became more than the licensed music, and masterclasses in blending and mixing. Without knowing many of the original released mixes, independent studies were required to ascertain where the juxtapositions of songs were. Some were obvious, such as the colossal vocoder drop of 'Break Dancin'-Electric Boogie' from the mesmerizing 'Jam On Revenge',[21] but others were finely intermingled with careful play on melodies, beats and even vocal phrases, as in the meld between 'The Buck Stops Here!' and 'B-Boys Breakdance'.[22] Unpacking these mixes was practice-based research in itself, as Dren Throwdown explains: "I became intrigued with the way the tracks were blended on the *Street Sounds* LPs after hearing the original records on John Peel, I had a tape-to-tape recording hi-fi and began making pause-tape mixes" (email to author, 20 June 2017). These moments pinpoint the nascent DJ's shift from consumer to producer. A similar process was undertaken by Evil Ed: "I was really into making pause-button mixes. My grandad had a hi-fi with a record deck and tape deck built in, so I could make these mixes at his house. I would take some of the Electro LPs and other records I had and make the mixes" (email to author, 14 June 2017). Concurrently, it was as much of a learning process when the original arrangements were known, as in the segue of 'Ultimate III Live!' through 'M.C. Story' to 'Girls (Rulin' The World)', all of which had been played on John Peel's shows.[23]

The *Electro* series not only offered the seduction of an affordable and visually fresh and beautiful product, but the innovative way it took the idea of the remix/extended mix, and blending and mixing practices from the block party to the home stereo. It introduced provincial headz to mixing and to analyse for themselves what was mixed and how. *Street Sounds* continued to release 27 compilation albums from the *Electro* series between 1983 and 1988,[24] reinventing the titles and brand slightly throughout this five-year period. One of the most noticeable shifts echoed that of the culture. On *Electro 11* (1986), the phrase "hip hop" was introduced subtly alongside the word "electro" and increased in visual presence up to edition 16. Simultaneously the graphic presence of "electro" decreased, and by edition 17 (1987) had disappeared;[25]

the series was given a complete visual overhaul, the slick graphics were replaced by graffiti-soaked visuals, and it was named *Street Sounds Hip Hop 17*.[26] It is curious that this shift in name took so long, particularly in light of *Beat This! A Hip Hop History*, and *Hip Hop—the Original and Best*. I would speculate that this was due to Khan's building of *Electro* as a brand. The very naming of this series reinforced hip hop being referred to as electro music in provincial Britain, and headz only fully made the switch to "hip hop" as a genre term during the demise of electronic sounds and increase in the presence of emceeing and sampling during the mid-1980s.

Drawing from this analysis, what was happening here appears to produce a strong synthesis between culture by design and culture by evolution. The cultural experience of hip hop consumed via the compilation, including the *Electro* series, differed from consuming the original 12″ singles and provided a much alternative set of representations to the primary source of culture. Through a set of cultural assemblages that relate cultural production and consumption through commercialism and an authenticity of mimicry, the *Electro* series constructed a combinatorial productivity which in turn established and re-established, affirmed and reaffirmed cultural significance through its graphic and audio coding. Hebdige talks about how youth cults begin to aspire to "the flatness and stillness of a photograph…completed only through the admiring glances of a stranger" (Hebdige 1988: 31); however the *Electro* series did not rely on photographs of hip hop tropes, Bboy stances, graffiti, and urban imagery, but rather signposted hip hop practice and content through the mixed curation of the music. The visual representations of "the Buffalo Gals Effect" (cherry-picking the tropes of hip hop in New York and reframing them for broader consumption) may have triggered the first breakdance and graffiti practices, but Carver's graphics and Khan's distribution ethos fostered and furthered hip hop culture across provincial Britain. The consumption of the *Electro* series is responsible, in part, for the evolution of the hip hop habitus and the production of provincial hip hop music practice.

Distinction

In Bourdieurian thought, the cultural capital of individuals within a society has three facets—the institutional (Bourdieu 2010: 74–75), the objectified (Bourdieu 2010: 69, 172) and the embodied (Bourdieu 2010: 70; 1993: 270 n. 24). The institutional is the capital of conventional marked achievement, of qualifications and certificates. These act as benchmarks for progression through life for the individual, but also for measurement against others within society. Furthermore, the cultural capital of the institution forges representations of the individual. The objectified is that capital of the material object, artefact or thing, which also provides representations about the individual and depends on ownership, acquisition and collection. The embodied, then, is the cultural capital of one's thoughts, disposition of mind and actions, and how these accrue as one develops. It might seem natural that these three facets of cultural capital synergize at certain moments throughout one's life, and there are, of course, a multitude of combinations of these. However, there exist divisions of success within these facets of cultural capital and these divisions are measure-dependent on taste, class and societal expectations. Furthermore, it is not necessarily so that someone from a privileged background (for example) will succeed in life purely based on upbringing, yet the notion of privilege based on cultural capital triggers a prediction which assumes that that member of society will be successful. The evolution of the habitus is directly informed by these three facets of cultural capital, as the habitus is constructed from one's tastes, selections, achievements, beliefs, loves and values. Bourdieu's notion of the habitus is also constructed from the space between family, social structures and the choices and wills of the individual. The habitus, then, is revealed through practice: "The habitus is both the generative principle of objectively classifiable judgements and the system of classification (*principium divisionis*) of these practices" (Bourdieu 2010: 165–66). So, what does the habitus of the provincial British hip hop devotee look like, and how does it relate to the representations of hip hop presented in this book?

The cultural capital in question at this point may appear less connected to that of the institutional, but rather is created from the relationship between the objectified and the embodied. Of immediate main concern is the capital of the object—the material culture of the recorded artefact and the practice of radio broadcast. However, in terms of taste, Bourdieu suggests that music representations derive from two modes of acquisition—domestic and scholastic. Bourdieu describes the music of record collectors as "an expressive, dramatic, sentimentally clear art of communication" (Bourdieu 2010: 69) and points to Barthes' discussion of music. On the coding of records, Barthes states:

> Provided they be clear, that they "translate" an emotion and represent a signified (the "meaning" of a poem): an art that inoculates

pleasure (by reducing it to a known coded emotion) and reconciles the subject to what in music can be said: what is said about it by Institution, Criticism, Opinion (Barthes 1977: 185).

Following both Bourdieu's and Barthes' views, the recorded artefact is a communication device but also a piece of art, and a tangible piece of culture: "Every material inheritance is, strictly speaking, also a cultural inheritance" (Bourdieu 2010: 69). The records that provincial headz were collecting were a form of inheritance: in a strikingly analogous manner to how Bourdieu describes the acquisition of taste through the material objects collected from antiques dealers or galleries (Bourdieu 2010: 69), headz were collecting music and photographs of graffiti. These collections were continually built upon acquisition of culture through regular analyses and transmission of the core values of hip hop, subsequently drawing upon them to generate their own productions which, in turn, became material objects themselves transmitting further messages to the pool of hip hop artefacts. Records and photographs became more valuable than objects of collection or archive, but objects that aided the formation of provincial hip hop culture and practice. It is imperative to point out that the domestic and scholastic in hip hop are closely linked: the taste of authority (scholarship), as delivered through the recorded and curated artefact enters a conversation with the taste of the consumer group (domestic), and the results of those conversations either accept and value those given artefacts or dismiss them as having low cultural value (as in the case of casually curated compilation albums).

Miller indicates that: "A particular society elaborates its cultural practices through an underlying pattern which is manifested in a multitude of diverse forms. By learning to interact with a whole slew of different material cultures, an individual grows up assuming the norms that we call culture" (Miller 2014: 53). Miller's study positions the habitus within a much broader frame, one of the conventions of everyday life; however, it is exactly these conventions, this assumed habitus to which Miller refers, that is the habitus that provincial headz were beginning to challenge through their acquisition of hip hop. In the provinces, this acquisition was based on a habitus of hip hop crafted from cultural editing. This editing was not the result of a practice or process carried out by headz, but rather the result of processes and practices by two key active (or not) related parts of economically-driven capital in the wider sphere of hip hop. In her study of house and rave culture, Thornton (1996) determines: "Just as books and paintings display cultural capital in the family home, so subcultural capital is objectified in the form of fashionable haircuts and well-assembled record collections" (Thornton 1996: 137), and continues to describe limited edition and 12″ records that are "well-chosen" (Thornton 1996: 137). However, in provincial hip hop it is crucial to recognize that such collections were built from a smaller pool of quality records than those collectors in the major cities. She continues: "Just as cultural capital is personified in 'good' manners and urbane conversation, so subcultural capital is embodied in the form of being 'in the know', using (but not over-using) current slang and looking as if you were born to perform the latest dance styles" (Thornton 1996: 11–12). These objectified and embodied cultural capitals that Thornton describes certainly contribute to the habitus of provincial hip hop. Williams (2011) paraphrases Thornton within his study of "identity and authenticity"; focusing on subcultural hierarchy, he surmises that: "Each form has its own value, though those afforded the highest status in subcultural scenes often possess significant quantities of both" (Williams 2011: 137).

While both Thornton and Williams' observations serve a particular framing of subculture, I would posit that the cultural capital of scholarship (the institutional) figures strongly in the similar hip hop scenario. It was not enough solely to be "in the know" and appear to *be* hip hop—this is potentially dangerous territory when the sense of the real in hip hop is considered. Furthermore, the habitus of hip hop is first and foremost about practice—and although collecting records is a practice in itself, it is how one uses those records as a source for their creative practice. In hip hop one cannot afford to be a tourist or a bystander, as Junior Disprol attests: "Early on it felt like you couldn't just 'enjoy' hip hop without being involved" (email to author, 2 June 2017). This notion is furthered by Stepchild:

> Not being around it [hip hop] physically it was easy to believe that what was out there was on such a high level that we could never achieve so we immersed ourselves deep, thinking of it then as we did in package terms we felt obliged to be versed in all the elements, being downwind from the Chinese whispers in our wilderness naivety we became 360 degree Bboys and anything less was wack; you'd hear comments like "yeah he's a good popper, breaker, rapper, graf writer, DJ…but he doesn't beatbox", "DOESN'T BEATBOX?" oh the shame…ha-ha (i/v, Swindon, 3 December 2017).

Stepchild's remarks suggest that outside of London the need to be an all-round practitioner was paramount, which could be attributed to fewer headz practising. In the introduction to *Hip Hop Authenticity and the London Scene* (2017) Laura Speers acknowledges: "Although I had considerable knowledge of hip hop and key artists, as well as friends in the scene, it became apparent just being a 'fan' and not being able to rap or DJ limited my insider status in the scene because I did not practice or 'do' hip hop" (Speers 2017: 7). For me, this territory is the marked difference between what one views as "subculture" and "culture"; the seriousness of practice and all it embodies positions British hip hop firmly as a culture.

The cultural capital discussed previously was the agent for two modes of distinction for London vis-à-vis the provincial, that of radio coverage and record distribution. By starting to explore the habitus from this position, I will establish that the provincial British hip hop habitus was not born solely from the spatial and material practices discussed in Chapters 2 and 3, but also and rather critically from consumption; and as end consumers of the editing phenomena. First, I will explain what I mean by cultural editing via these two modes of distinction. During the early British hip hop years, it was difficult to access a broad and rich range of hip hop music in most provincial areas. I previously discussed the limitations of imported records from America as being a central trigger for Khan's various *Street Sounds* series, and this was especially true of the latest electro and hip hop records. Specialist shops such as London's Groove Records in Soho's Greek Street were meccas for the hottest imports, but these shops did not exist in every city, let alone in the further provinces and smaller towns. These imported records were not without demand, but the critical mass of consumers compared to that of the major cities was not financially viable for any retail outlet. The imports that did arrive in Britain were distributed directly to shops like Groove Records in very small numbers, sometimes only receiving one or two copies of a record from the distributor. This was inevitable, as in many cases the American label may have only sent to press a small run of units in the first instance, so in this context it was remarkable that copies even ended up on the shelves of British shops. On rare occasions imports did find their way to regional high street outlets, one fine example being 'Triple Threat' by Z-3 M.C.s (1985), which seemed to be supplied to every HMV across the country, but these cases were extremely atypical. The hip hop records that were stocked in the provinces were those licensed through a UK-based label, and labels Cooltempo,[27] Champion[28] and Streetwave[29] were a blessing for provincial dwellers. A further way in which hip hop records reached the less-dense regions were if a label was big stateside and could afford a UK base, as in the cases of Tommy Boy (licensed to Island) and Sugar Hill Records (which held a UK distribution deal with PRT); however, this meant that consumers were limited to the artists signed to Tommy Boy and Sugar Hill Records.

In terms of the reach of records, a fourfold cultural editing process took place. The first point of edit appears stateside in the numbers of copies earmarked for export to Britain, and the second point of edit exists at the exchange between stateside supplier and British importer. Through the mechanisms of economic and material cultural capital, the editing process is carried out by direct and indirect dialogues between exporter and importer, label and retail outlet, and/or distributor. The economic drivers and risks to be considered are obvious—demand for the product, ability to supply, cost of shipping, export and import duty, success or failure of sale, and potential for follow-on orders. The cultural drivers, however, are of more interest here—why would an imported record succeed or fail? Is there a difference in the British attitude to hip hop music compared to American audiences, and is there an assumed attitude on the part of the manufacturer, supplier, distributor and retailer? Is the imported product of a high quality, and at what moment can one distinguish between a record that is high quality and one that is inferior quality? I will return to these questions later, but for now I will continue to explain the third and fourth points which are connected to UK-based labels.

The third point of edit is the British label that licensed records from American labels—where the various stages of acquiring an American record to issue under licence in the UK contained various forms of editing. Whatever the dynamic of licence, the agreement, exchange and resulting release, British issues of certain American records acted as a diversion from those American records not licensed in the UK. There is a dual ramification of this diversion: first, these British issues would have appeared in shops after the initial import was present and, in some cases, this may also have been after the initial buzz of the record had settled, particularly in the cutting-edge hip hop world of London. Conversely, in the harder to reach areas where the import rarely landed, the major UK-based licensed issues could be found. What I am suggesting here is that the presence of the major UK-based licensed issue in the provinces diverted attention away from seeking out import records, as headz settled for these UK issues, at least during the early years of consuming hip hop.

The fourth point of edit is connected to distribution of US labels that held a stake in the British market. Both Sugar Hill Records and Tommy Boy retained a partial monopoly on circulation in the provinces, which, again, diverted consumers from seeking alternative records. A further editing occurred within the artist roster of these labels: the popularity of lesser-known artists such as Keith le Blanc and Special Request (Tommy Boy), and Kevie Kev and Farrari (Sugar Hill Records) was largely due to their presence in the provinces, and not necessarily due to the quality of their music. The combination of these four points of editing resulted in a very different consumer landscape in the provinces, and the further one was located away from the metropolis, the slimmer the offerings. This had a significant impact on not only how hip hop in the provinces was consumed, but in how the provincial hip hop habitus developed.

Much of hip hop culture in Britain was also consumed through radio, which also experienced a similar cultural editing phenomenon. Pioneering radio DJs such as Tim Westwood (KISS-FM), Greg Wilson (Piccadilly Radio Manchester) and Mike Allen (Capital Radio) brought electro and hip hop to the airwaves of London and Manchester, spawning a multitude of pirate and localized hip hop radio shows in urban areas across the nation, but due to the signal range of pirate and local radio, these shows seldom reached further than the immediate suburbs of the polis. Headz living in more rural areas were effectively occupying dead spots, where the freshest tunes just did not reach. Mike Allen's Capital Rap Show developed from September 1984 "into a more urbanized music policy"[30] and was well established by 1986, when TDK initiated a sponsorship deal that would fund a wider-reaching show—National Fresh—hosted by Allen and recorded weekly at Radio Luxemburg studios in Hertford Street, London. At last, further regions outside the capital could be kept informed of weekly developments in stateside hip hop. As DJ Food attests in a post following news of Mike Allen's untimely death in 2015:

> Without him many of us who lived outside London and couldn't pick up the pirate stations would have had no weekly access to new releases, never known about Groove Records, the famous import shop in Soho, and never gone to events like UK Fresh '86 or Freestyle '85.[31]

However, National Fresh was not broadcast by a national station, but rather via a selection of local and regional stations, which resulted in much of the more remote areas of Britain being omitted from the Allen experience. Many rural areas were less engaged with the idea of contemporary urban sound and had no interest in broadcasting Allen's National Fresh. Stations like DevonAir broadcasting largely to East Devon were actively distancing themselves from the larger cities, with managing director Maurice Vass voicing: "We want DevonAir to be less remote than the national radio stations, very much a local station which people could communicate with."[32] One wonders to which people and what kind of communication Vass was alluding? My suspicion is that when Vass made this statement, communication with the youth, and particularly the youth attracted to hip hop, was very much devoid from the agenda. While presenter Tim Arnold came close with a Saturday evening show "Dance to the Music" as did Chris Dinnis with "The Rhythm of the City", more than a hint of superciliousness radiated from DevonAir if it ever got too close to hip hop. During the early 1990s, DevonAir's later incarnation as Gemini FM (now replaced by Heart Exeter), further ostracized any hopeful relationship with Devon hip hop headz by including an hourly jingle that concluded with an assertive tone: "…AND WE DON'T PLAY RAP!" This jingle carries a firm judgement of taste—there was (and still is) a solid conviction in rural areas that hip hop is "not proper music". Gemini FM appropriated and acted as proponents of this belief through the jingle as almost a conversational technique (Bourdieu 2010: 279), and for listeners, to consume Gemini FM justifies and affirms their personal taste.

Allen's Capital Rap Show and Groove Records strengthened their position in promoting hip hop in London by collaborating to deliver the Groove Hip Hop Sales Chart.[33] To analyse, the first hip hop chart dated 15 February 1986 (after the name change in February 1986) epitomizes the cultural editing in the remote provinces. Out of the top 20 records, only one was released primarily on a UK-based label (Masquerade's 'One Nation Def Mix' on Streetwave),[34] seven were American issues that subsequently received issue on UK-based labels (for example Cutmaster D.C.'s 'Brooklyn's In The House'), and eleven featured on *Street Sounds Electro* compilations. This meant that, eventually, provincial headz did gain exposure to eleven of these tracks while nine remained unheard, amongst the latter records by MC Ade, Byron Davis and The Fresh Crew, and Lightning Rich, Big John & The Maniacs. This was not untypical: upon inspection of all available Groove charts during Mike Allen's hip hop broadcasts,[35] many records were aired that have become exemplars for this period of hip hop. Standout records that missed the rural voids included Arcade Gang featuring Rich Cason's 'Radio Activity Rapp', Awesome Foursome's 'Funky Breakdown', and 'Breakdown New York Style' by Rusty P (The Toe Jammer) and The Sure Shot 3.

However, there was a saviour of radio for hip hop consumers in the far provinces in the form of BBC Radio 1's John Peel. During the 1980s, Peel was regularly playing a small selection of hip hop records on his shows.

His DJ style, eclectic and sporadic, led to a deep anticipation as a listener, and so beguiling and genuine was his approach to music and audience, that hearing a tough hip hop jam alongside The Fall or The Bhundu Boys felt so natural. When I first started listening out for hip hop on Peel's show, I would fast-forward through the indie, dub and world music until I heard the familiar sound of hip hop, but after a while I became so seduced by his manner and incredible breadth of music that I listened to as much of the show as I could. In some ways, the John Peel show shared a conceptual journey akin to *Duck Rock*, and through my thirst for hip hop I discovered a richer palate of sounds. Furthermore, this broad sonic palate echoed the sensibility of hip hop music itself: a music culture formed on the strength of a diversity of other music genres that eventually became its own was tantamount to this experience. The preciousness of Peel's shows was edifying, and I was not alone in my bedtime quest for hip hop, as Ross Adams recalls:

> A friend's Dad who was into his music told us that John Peel would regularly play this type of music on his evening show, so we would listen and record it. I can remember it started at 10pm, so being quite young at the time; I used to listen to it on my headphones in bed, hovering over the record button and pressing it when John introduced Schoolly D or Marley Marl. We would then record the rest of the show and make our own compilations (I still have mine to this day!) (email to author, 30 March 2017).

Growing up on a farm in Buckland Monachorum, Devon, Mike Mac pinpoints the Electro series as important to cultural knowledge, "the obvious ones are *Electro* and soundtracks like *Wild Style*", but states "John Peel was my compilation album. RIP" (p/c, Westbury, Wiltshire, 1 May 2018). One can imagine a constellation of teenagers in their bedrooms, scattered across the country, awaiting a fresh hip hop track to record. This was particularly important for those in rural regions, as Dren Throwdown attests: "I was an avid listener to John Peel, pretty much the only outlet anywhere in Cornwall at that time to hear hip hop, usually a couple of tracks in a two-hour show, tape deck on record/pause ready to go" (email to author, 20 June 2017). The impact of Peel's shows also reached past the edges of Britain to Northern Ireland, as Craig Ellis Leckie says:

> Radio was a huge deal, it was arguably our first connection with the raw excitement of what was happening in the US, and on the

British mainland, and yep, like yourself, John Peel was arguably the key figure for a bunch of us, allowing us to keep up and stay current with all things hip hop (email to author, 22 March 2017).

Si Spex further confirms the void of hip hop radio and attests the monumental impact of Peel's eclectic shows on provincial hip hop followers:

Obviously, there was nothing, we were starved of music, so we had to listen to John Peel and he played two tracks a night. I'd be half asleep trying to stay awake with my finger on the tape—that's how it used to go with music, trying to record and having to sit through hours of Cocteau Twins and Half Man Half Biscuit and crazy thrashy nonsense (i/v, Truro, 6 December 2017).

John Peel was playing hip hop from the outset of its availability, and knowingly so, that unless he played them these records would not gain exposure nationally. In his semi-autobiography, he explains his advocacy for new music: "Over the years my programmes have often been the first to play music which subsequently found a wider audience and, very occasionally a niche on Radio 1" (Peel and Ravenscroft 2005: 351), and offers a solid example through his defence of airplay for hip hop:

For example, I started playing hip hop when the first records, imported from New York, arrived in this country. I did all this despite the fact—perhaps, on reflection, partly because of it—that a producer and presenter both came to me independently and told me I should not be playing what was, in their view, the music of black criminals (Peel and Ravenscroft 2005: 351).

The Peel experience was a major contributing factor in the construction of the provincial hip hop habitus, and despite his sparse selection of tracks, they were excellently judged in delivering a gamut of styles. West Coast electro to Miami bass and the hardcore New York sound were well represented via The Organization's 'The Big Beat', Egyptian Lover's 'Scratch Force One', Rap-O-Matic Ltd.'s 'Lies, Lies' and High Potent's 'H.P. Gets Busy'.[36] I offer these examples specifically, as four records that remain important moments in 1980s hip hop styles yet may never have been heard in rural areas without John Peel's show.

The producer and presenter that offered ill-informed advice to John suffered the common error and vast misjudgement of hip hop through their literal perceptions, failing to grasp the real roots of hip hop; moralistic positions have always been central themes in hip hop, and a simple reflection on the records named above reveals stories of some didacticism. In 'The Big Beat', Cli-N-Tel's disappointment is blatant as he tells the story of reuniting with a girl he met "back in '82", yet now in 1985 she was: "Rocked up all clocked out / She had a big sore in the corner of her mouth / I said 'hey baby what the **** happened?'" to which she replied, "understand it wasn't my plan / I got caught slippin' by the rock man". Rap-O-Matic Ltd. also exhort a moralist stance in 'Lies, Lies', offering a myriad of examples of how lies damage individuals, community and society, with a chorus hook "Lies are the root of all evil / Stop bullshitting tell the truth to the people". Even the traditional brag-raps of Egyptian Lover, "I'm telling you straight out that your scratching is sleazy / You're missing you're not on beat at all", and High Potent's "I'm Jay-Z and I will do work"[37] contain moral standings surrounding the practices of hip hop. Through his playlist Peel helped crystallize the sound of hip hop for those outside the catchment of pure inner-city hip hop radio. Furthermore, he championed the emerging sounds of British rap through early crews such as Three Wize Men and Fission, but here I want to establish the provincial hip hop habitus further. Returning to Bourdieu's cultural capital of habitus—the institutional, the objectified and the embodied—I will reinforce the idea that the habitus in question here strongly relates to all three facets, although it may at first seem that the objectified cultural capital is most prominent. The prominence of the material object, and here I include the consumption of John Peel's show as material object, is evidenced above, and links directly to the embodied as embodiment of hip hop grows within the individual. I propose that this embodiment is synonymous with both taste and knowledge. Bourdieu states that:

> Taste is the practical operator of the transmutation of things into distinct and distinctive signs, of continuous distributions into discontinuous oppositions; it raises the differences inscribed in the physical order of bodies to the symbolic order of significant distinctions (Bourdieu 2010: 170).

If the artefacts of records—imported, home-released/distributed, and compiled—are offered up as signifiers of hip hop culture through the spatial mechanisms of radio and retail outlet, then is it the consumer who distinguishes and chooses what is deemed to be of good taste? The answer is only partially affirmative. The habitus of the marketplace, commerce and industry presupposes what is tasteful in the construction of objects in the first place. This "universe of objective properties" (Bourdieu 2010: 170) where such artefacts are conceived, constructed and distributed across the space of the everyday experience, that is the "universe of life-styles" (Bourdieu 2010: 170), has already decided what hip hop looks and sounds like before it is presented to consumers. One of Bourdieu's conclusions here is that: "Taste, a class culture turned into nature, that is, *embodied*, helps to shape the class body" (Bourdieu 2010: 188), and while his discussion on the habitus through the homologies of class spaces is clear, I want to continue an interrogation that develops the above idea of habitus-by-taste with the idea of differential social positions and distancing, challenging the idea of provincial hip hop as a class-based practice. In turn, what is produced is "taste as cultural driver" which draws upon urban forms of hip hop through processes of discovery, evaluation and distancing.

Taste as Cultural Driver

The processes of discovery, evaluation and distancing, while tentatively started upon hip hop's arrival in Britain, became solidified through the mid-1980s. The process of direct discovery in terms of radio and retail has already been discussed but turning attention to what I would call indirect discovery, there were other, more organic ways in which hip hop seeped into the remoter areas. Through family links and occasional jams and trips to the larger urban centres, one could add to one's growing hip hop habitus—often signified through swapping of tapes, particularly tapes from pirate or local radio that were not available in the provinces. These tapes would then be dubbed-off (duplicated via a tape-to-tape device), second, third, fourth and fifth generation and beyond, until every member of the crew had a copy.

In late 1986 my father took me to London for a weekend, as I was so desperate to dig in Groove Records and hoped that there might be a chance of recording Mike Allen's Capital Rap Show. Being the estranged father that he was, this trip was an attempt for us to reconnect as father and son, but the truth is the trip was all about hip hop for me. I took my modest boombox (the Sharp GF-7400 E) and a pack of three TDK D90 cassettes in preparation, and two of my crew mates had given me some money and a list to buy them import records from Groove.[38] This weekend trip was to be my only experience of both Allen's Capital Rap Show and Groove Records, yet still over 30 years later I can vividly remember every detail, the records I flicked through (I still regret not purchasing M.C. Chill's album), the taxi ride from Groove to the Holiday Inn (it was hammering with rain, and neither my father nor I were confident navigating the London Underground), and the faux-timber laminated work station-come-table in the Holiday Inn bedroom as I sat, mesmerized, as Allen punchily announced: "Hit it, Cheese!" as he introduced the first artist of the special show, DJ Cheese and Word of Mouth. I also recall being slightly disappointed that both the Friday and Saturday night of that weekend I did not get to hear Allen count down the Groove Hip Hop Sales Chart, but in retrospect it was the perfect weekend's radio to capture. There was something very subversive about sitting in a Holiday Inn bedroom, plugged into Mike Allen presenting UK Fresh '86 while my father slept, five months after and three miles away from the Street Sounds actual event. Upon returning to rurality, my crew mates were much more interested in the UK Fresh '86 recordings than the records I had bought. Although two of my crew mates had persuaded a parent to drive them to the actual UK Fresh '86 event, I was not so fortunate, yet I had experienced this through the recordings and act of recording Allen's shows. This indirect discovery of the UK Fresh '86 performances demonstrates a moment of cultural distancing; while I was removed from the real performances, in some ways it seemed as though I had travelled to the source to hear Allen and visit Groove, yet in the case of this particular weekend the radio source was already distanced from the event.

The perceived distancing from hip hop's city phenomena generated a desire for provincial headz to get closer, so strategies and tactics were developed as a kind of practical practice—whereby methods designed to procure music ultimately accrued taste. Stepchild explains: "We'd drive to the top of the surrounding hills to tape Westwood when he was on Capital, a couple of years later Acme saved us the petrol by wrapping a length of copper wire over his roof, he could get KISS-FM too, good lad" (i/v, Swindon, 3 December 2017). Ricky Also, who grew up in Hythe village, Hampshire, experienced similar strategies:

> My main buddy at school was Nick aka DJ DSK, he was one of the main influences for me in terms of music and was always a step ahead of the game. He lived on a hill and was able to just about catch the Westwood show on Capital FM, by hanging long aerial wires from his radio out of the window. Capital tapes became like currency at school and the best way to keep up with what's happening (email to author, 21 January 2018).

These diversions and interventions were edifying and enhanced the notion of taste. The thrill in successfully capturing a track that exists outside the provincial realm becomes symbolic: the sign of the actual song captured on tape, with its hiss and interference, topped and tailed by dialogue from Mike Allen or Westwood, embodies not only the richness of the new song itself, but of the act of its capture, as a motif of taste. No matter how poor the recording, for Evil Ed connecting into the show was where the value lay:

> I started listening to Mike Allen (RIP) on Capital Radio, although as he was on late, I would stay up to hear the start of the show and would record it and play it back the next day. I could only just get a signal where I lived and although it was really hissy, I loved hearing the latest tracks. I became an overnight hip hop fiend (email to author, 14 June 2017).

Similarly, Tom Dartnell attests the significance in capturing radio shows, and the creativity entailed in receiving a signal:

> Even though Brighton is 50 miles from London, I lived on the northern edge of the town on a hill, so with a wire wrapped around the light on the ceiling and connected to my hi-fi I was just about able to pick up London stations—specifically Westwood on Capital and Max and Dave and Richie Rich on KISS. Without this, I don't think my knowledge of records—particularly British hip hop ones—would have been so broad (email to author, 2 April 2017).

For those whom these radio shows did not reach, targeted taping strategies were in place, as Scott Coombes illustrates:

> Trips down to Nan's now took on a whole new dimension. Not only did I now understand that the amazing artwork I was seeing was linked to the dance we were working so hard at, it was heartening to learn that some of the kids I had befriended down there over the years had also got into it, but they had access to seriously good music too, presumably through older brothers. I was getting tapes nobody back home had heard of, to be fair we only had dubbed copies of a few early *Electro* albums (email to author, 16 December 2017).

In his memoir *Wiggaz with Attitude* (2017), Andrew Emery recollects: "Shops dedicated to selling only hip hop vinyl were popping up in the UK, storied retailers like Groove Records in London, a focus for the scene, a place of far-away dreams for us Northerners" (Emery 2017: 82). Craig Ellis Leckie adamantly attests to the tactics of capturing radio shows:

> Each trip we'd make, I ALWAYS ensured that blank tapes were purchased beforehand, and whatever radio show was blasting hip hop, it was recorded in high fidelity. If there was a new rap track I hadn't heard, play and record were impatiently but carefully pressed (email to author, 29 April 2017).

Recorded radio shows were essential agents for provincial headz to learn about the hip hop that was escaping them and what to keep watch for, as occasionally releases leaked out into the provinces. Uncle Colin illustrates the relationship between the trading of tapes and high street music stockists: "As we were so far from London or Bristol keeping up with music was usually done with tapes copied from friends and then maybe being able to buy stuff in the local Our Price in Swindon" (email to author, 3 April 2017). The tapes that were circulating in the provinces were curated in three ways: by taping John Peel's national show which required patience; relocating to a place temporarily (for the duration of the show) where one might obtain a signal from a regional hip hop show; and by taping regional shows during longer trips to friends and family that lived in a suitable catchment area. These cassettes were then often personalized, most commonly with graffiti-style font, tags and motifs, with some curators building a series which were traded and swapped across crew networks. This exchange of cassettes extended hip hop's seeping into the remoter areas which could be added to one's growing hip hop habitus.

The consumption of hip hop music in the provinces was paramount to the development of the hip hop habitus. Bourdieu describes the habitus as:

> both the generative principle of objectively classifiable judgements and the system of classification (*principium divisionis*) of these practices. It is in the relationship between the two capacities which define the habitus, the capacity to produce classifiable practices and works, and the capacity to differentiate and appreciate these practices and products (taste), that the represented social world, i.e., the space of life-styles, is constituted (Bourdieu 2010: 165–66).

He expands on his explanation of the habitus as both "structuring structure" and "structured structure" (Bourdieu 2010: 166), whereby the former organizes the perceptions of practice and practices themselves, and the latter the logical class divisions which organize social classes and the perceptions of the social world. The habitus reconciles and negotiates between these two forms of structure, and "apprehends differences between conditions" (Bourdieu 2010: 167), which in turn produces the lifestyle, or in hip hop terms, the "state of mind" (discussed in Chapter 6). This lifestyle is tangibly manifest through the artefacts of taste, these being the products and practices of hip hop which occupy the sites and spaces of the province. The curated reifications of the compilation album and the self-recorded cassette discussed above offer affirmations of taste from the positions of the record industry, radio DJs and provincial headz. The making of the self-curated cassette becomes the ultimate reification of the hip hop habitus, as curators assessed what they deemed as tasteful to construct their tapes, through the improvised and designed editing of radio recordings as necessary. I would further Bourdieu's discussion here that while the practices and product of the curated cassette represented a distinctive life-style choice (state of mind), it also represented a shift in the development of the provincial hip hop habitus. The structured structure of conventional working-class and aspiring middle-class provincial life did not account for hip hop culture's presence—the provinces were limiting in exposure and access to hip hop; however, the structuring structures of hip hop practice and its perception by those within the culture and of those outside resulted in a hip hop habitus that reframed hip hop within a provincial context using tactics triggered by limitation. Brent Aquasky testifies: "If anything maybe we had to work harder, we were remote, in the country and had to make the effort to connect into the cities and build a scene" (i/v, Bournemouth, 12 December 2017). The process of habitus-building was, on one hand, carried out at a distance from the apparent heart of the culture, yet on the other hand—and of paramount importance to provincial hip hop culture—the evolution of an emotional centre, constructed through connections between polis and the provincial. Neil Taylor discusses this emotional sense of centre:

> Putting the pieces together, and comprehending that there was a unifying culture, being interpreted differentially by geographic location, was another way in which I felt connected even though I was separated by distance and circumstances from the core of hip hop (email to author, 3 October 2017).

This assemblage of hip hop acknowledged its limitations in terms of urban exposure, but also recognized its own context. The issues surrounding identity, production and the spatio-geographic are discussed in Chapters 5 and 6, and here it suffices to state that by interrogating the limits and liberations of both commercial artefact and spatio-geographic position, provincial hip hop consumption morphed into production. Its very processes initiated a dialectic with both the commercialization and contextualization of American and British-bred hip hop.

The Subaltern

Through acquisition and critical evaluation of commercial artefacts and radio broadcasts, provincial headz were cultivating a form of hip hop distinction, which considerably shaped their taste in hip hop and, in turn, impelled a desire for the subaltern, the underground—for some kind of truth in hip hop. The presence of hip hop in the provinces had expanded from the formative mechanisms of relocation to a broader consumption of artefact, sound and space, yet this broader offering was still in deficit when compared to the major cities. A critical facet of one's continual developing hip hop practice is represented through the act of digging. To dig, to search for, to find and to acquire with the aim of extending one's music and cultural knowledge is inseparable from the art of hip hop. I introduced knowledge as hip hop's fifth element in Chapter 2, and knowledge of self and one's own history has been paramount to the evolution of hip hop since before it began. Most clearly, the Universal Zulu Nation have championed the element of knowledge across almost five decades, amplified in the late 1980s through various critical-historical approaches by artists and collectives such as KRS-One, The Native Tongues, X-Clan and Lakim Shabazz.

Public Enemy revolutionized concept and content and awoke many headz with their rigorous approach to consciousness, although there is clear evidence of knowledge and consciousness of the African-American experience through earlier rap records. In the pre-Public Enemy era, there are fine examples (Brother D with Collective Effort's 'How We Gonna Make The Black Nation Rise?' (1980), Afrika Bambaataa & Soulsonic Force's 'Renegades of Funk' (1983), and 'Stick Up Kid' (1985) by The B Boys) that talk about African and African-American histories, experiences and the socio-political both from collective and individual positions. Furthermore, there are the subtle, yet palpable messages embedded within songs like Rammellzee and

K-Rob's 'Beat Bop' (1983), Duke Bootee's 'Broadway' (1986) and 'Crack It Up' (1986) by Funkmaster Wizard Wiz, all of which presented observational social commentary on urban life and the issues faced by inhabitants of New York's deprived areas. K-Rob's verses throughout 'Beat Bop' construct the story of struggle, with poignant lines relating to the urban experience: "Make you feel real bad every time I see / Another bum or brother sleeping on the street / New York City is a place of mysteries / Drug addicts dope dealers taking over the streets". The despair in K-Rob's lyrical content and his mundane yet eloquent delivery build over the course of the track and in the third verse, deflated from lack of opportunity, he rhymes:

> Now things are hard and you're really depressed
> And your mind can't function 'cause you can't pass the test
> You're saying to yourself "what can I do?
> I can't go home; I might as well quit school"
> Jobs are hard to find everybody knows
> And you can't do crime 'cause you're on parole
> No education is a big disgrace and
> So you might as well work at the sanitation
> Can you get my drift?

K-Rob defines the low income and no income lives of many here, and to answer K-Rob's rhetorical question, one could get his drift. Duke Bootee extends this commentary and offers observations on the realities of life on 'Broadway', opening with the chorus:

> Broadway the talk of the town
> From the top to the bottom everybody gets down
> From Washington Heights to Battery Park
> Broadway like a snake wiggles after dark

This contextualizes not only the architecture of the street, but suggests its personality; Bootee spatters his verses with activity: "Running three card monte over by the station / Selling Gucci shirts of some cheap imitation", "Nothing's real because everything's fake / Even the chicken ain't fried it's just shake 'n bake", "A tourist with a camera 'bout to get capped / Got a Rolex on his wrist he must have lost his map". After Bootee storyboards life on the street with wit, he turns to the transatlantic and offers similarities with Europe's urban promiscuity: "In London it's the circus Soho or Piccadilly / In

Paris it's Pigalle or a girl named Lily". Funkmaster Wizard Wiz's cut 'Crack It Up' has a darkly sarcastic manner:

> From nine to six girls turning tricks
> Putting their lips on brothers' tips
> They don't care who you are
> They'll do yo head right in your car
> In the back seat they'll beat yo meat
> Until you cum like 'Cream of Wheat'
> Then up the cash and watch and see
> How fast they run right down the street
> In the morning when they get up out the sack
> They pull the same old clothes off the rack
> They won't even eat a bowl of Sugar Smack
> They're always running out the door to get a crack

The celebratory chorus chants the ritual, "Crack it up (crack crack it up) / You gotta put it in the pipe (put put it in the pipe) / I wanna crack it up (crack crack it up) / Then smoke it (let's get smokin'!)". As the crack-cocaine epidemic grew within inner cities, a spate of anti-crack rap records were produced,[39] although the listening public and media mis-interpreted 'Crack It Up', and neglecting the sarcasm and reality Wiz was trying to portray, KISS-FM pulled the song from DJs' playlists. In an attempt to rescue the record, it was edited by adding a vocal drop "Ya better not" as a prefix to "Crack it up" in the chorus, but by that point the record had been shunned. At the time of its release, I knew nothing about the record. It wasn't on any British compilation, was not played by John Peel, or available in the shops in my locale, but I managed to purchase a copy during one of my rare trips to Bristol, the nearest metropolis from my home, some 87 miles away. Not knowing any of the independent record shops in Bristol, I headed for HMV, which stocked a better selection of import 12"s than the HMV in Exeter. As I flipped through the record racks, the clues were there as I came across a single copy of 'Crack It Up'; the explosive "TUF" of the yellow and turquoise letters leapt off the brilliant red Tuff City company jacket. My eyes zoomed into the label which saw a comic book fist ripping through the centre of the label, splitting the words "Tuff" and "City", underneath which read "Modern Urban Music". How could I resist. My heart pumped faster as I read the artist and title: FUNKMASTER WIZARD WIZ, and below "CRACK IT UP" and "CAN'T YOU TAKE A HINT (Bellevue Patient) (R)".[40]

It was usual for provincial headz to target their local and regional shops regularly, with occasional and prearranged trips to larger cities further afield, but all digging required strategic planning. Specifik outlines its magnitude to the culture: "Digging for records in the 1980s was essentially the only reference point to the source of the culture. Whether that be a James Brown break or an import rap 12″, these important discoveries helped us rural folk understand hip hop's DNA" (p/c, Bournemouth, 16 May 2018). He describes the buzz between his peers and the tactics involved: "In fact, it was almost a scrap to get there first. We would get off the bus and literally run to the shop to get to the rack first. Sometimes I would pull a sneaky 'let's go into this shop' and then do a back-door bunk to HMV. Often there was only one copy" (p/c, Bournemouth, 16 May 2018). Specifik's singular use of the word "rack" suggests the limitation on general hip hop stock and corroborates my recollection that outside the polis there was rarely more than one copy available of any import release per town. Interesting too that Specifik's location for digging is also HMV, highlighting the lack of independent record shops. Cleethorpes' DJ Jamez Gant took a different approach: "I was always at the only record shop we had before it opened. I helped the guy take his stuff in, and I could check for imports" (p/c, Cleethorpes, 16 May 2018). Similar patterns of digging in the provinces were occurring simultaneously, and as the hunt for records grew more intense into the 1990s, diggers were thinking laterally and targeting jumble sales and car boot sales. Particularly in the provinces, this increased the possibilities greatly, as Si Spex recalls: "As far as digging, there was loads of digging going on down here. I kind of get the impression from people I speak to all over the country that each little area's got their own, almost identical, scene". The West Country was one of the first regions to experience the car boot sale trend in fields and meadows, as Si Spex continues: "We had some of the earliest car boot sales, I remember the golden era of car boot sales and I would just be getting amazing records that wouldn't last ten seconds now, everyone would be swiping all the good stuff" (i/v, Truro, 6 December 2017).

As some diggers like Si Spex turned professional producers, the dig was crucial to collecting material for sampling, and these marginal spaces of consumption provided a source for cultural production. Crewe and Gregson (1997) explore the boot sale as a social act, for both vendors and buyers, suggesting the boot sale context provides: "The informality of such marginal consumption where the character and texture of the gathering are paramount" (Crewe and Gregson 1997: 42–43). They further discuss the idea of commodity sourcing and geographical knowledge, stating that "selling at a car boot sale is frequently a follow-on from participation as a buyer", and "many vendors draw almost exclusively on the knowledge gained from car boot sale participation" (Crewe and Gregson 1997: 44). Digging for sample sources or hip hop records at a provincial car boot sale is advantageous due to fewer headz digging; however this equally means that there may be less material on offer. To this end, provincial diggers began to think more laterally about their sources, taking gambles on records that showed some visual clue to its content (before serious diggers equipped themselves with portable turntables to attend car boot sales). Diggers are not seeking Elvis or The Beatles but discovering the breaks on James Last and Herb Alpert & the Tijuana Brass records. Crewe and Gregson further state: "consumption practices reflect individual perceptions of taste and discernment and how the boundaries between good and bad taste are both subjective and constantly open to reinterpretation" (Crewe and Gregson 1997: 46), particularly in the field of hip hop culture's digging practices. These reinterpretations of value are driven by the attributes any record discovered at a car boot sale has on the production or practice of hip hop—a record may be considered in everyday culture to be in bad taste, garish or kitsch if considered as a whole, but if it contains a fabulous fragment which upon successful sampling contributes to a hip hop project it acquires new meaning and value.

The practice of "blind-digging" remains commonplace among diggers, but my point here is not purely that the deeper one digs, the more one reaps rewards in the form of rare or undiscovered music, but moreover, one deepens their knowledge. Schloss (2014) discusses the inspirational values of "digging in the crates",[41] in robust, broader terms, but the digging practice that provincial British headz carried out pulled them closer to the culture that had originated across the Atlantic: firstly, digging refined their taste in hip hop through the accruing material and cultural inheritance, and "transmitted the values, virtues and competences" (Bourdieu 2010: 69) embedded in well-received records in terms of sonic quality; secondly, it increased knowledge of spatio-political, social and geographic contexts which remained out of reach. The material and cultural inheritance was not solely about the music knowledge and the powerful messages entrenched within; detail about artists, titles, labels, catalogue numbers, etchings in the run-out groove, even knowing the pressing plants where the issue was pressed, were all valuable to the provincial digger to further historical understanding. For example, Davy DMX's 'The DMX Will Rock' and 'Wrong Girls To Play With' by Papa Austin with the Great Peso were both released by Tuff City in 1985, and both feature on *Street Sounds Electro 8*. However, when one inspects the catalogue labels, Davy DMX's record carries the catalogue number TUF 120003, while Papa Austin with the Great Peso's carries catalogue number TUF 120004, confirming the Davy DMX record was released first. Minutiae of this nature was a tremendous aid to the deepening knowledge pool of unreachable American hip hop culture. Equally, the cultural inheritance of the socio-political content expanded provincial headz' knowledge base to challenge their own context. The true value of digging deepened one's historical, cultural, political and social knowledge and equipped headz to manufacture their own representations in the hip hop habitus, which I argue in the following chapter.

Chapter 5
The Production of Hip Hop: Process, Empowerment and Cultural Repositioning

It was an early summer Sunday evening in 1988, the breeze which had cooled my skin for the past hour or so seized abruptly as I pulled the bedroom window shut with a clunk, which even seemed to startle the blackbirds in the small, semi-rural terrace street in Sidford. "Come on then, let's get these raps down", Rola said with a smile. Although I had rapped for about two years, I had never recorded anything, at least nothing that I wanted anyone else to hear. We were making our first demo tape, but although we thought of it more as a test for ourselves, we also talked about maybe making some inlay cards and selling them at school and the youth centre. Rola and I stood in the bedroom, while our DJ fiddled with wires and jacks, eventually handing Rola the light, cheap Tandy Realistic microphone. Taking turns to rap, a process dictated by the clunk of the hand-me-down two-track recorder, we dropped our verses over the beats created on the Yamaha RX-21 and a simple melody à la Skinny Boys played on a Yamaha VSS-200. After two takes, we sat on the lumpy sofa in the corner of the room and listened back in silence. When the track finished, Rola bounced up and flicked the switch; the reels stopped. More silence. We looked at each other, and reservedly exchanged approving murmurs, and that was it. Our first demo song as Ill Beat Productions.

Over the following two days, we clubbed together and bought a pack of ten C-15 computer tapes. We considered them perfect for the manufacture of a cassette single—at seven and a half minutes per side it made sense—although, as we were so inexperienced, we failed to realize that the quality would be less than brilliant for audio. Nevertheless, we proceeded to manufacture the product. The inlay card was designed using black pens and some cut-out images from a magazine, and I photocopied them at my mother's place of work after it closed. By Wednesday, a neat stack of ten units were ready for public consumption. We each took three, and one was saved for the archive we were yet to create. I took two to the youth centre that night and showed them to a couple of my friends. By this time, the older lads I was Bboying with in 1984 had long moved on, most were not even attending the club anymore, and there was no hint of hip hop left in this sleepy town's youth centre following the demise of breakdancing. However I felt a spark of interest as our 'Return Of The Funky Fresh Bell' cassette single was passed around and gawped at. A few people egged me on to play it, so I approached the club's boombox in the TV room and popped in the tape. As the beat started, I felt a nervous, sickly feeling and averted all eye contact—especially during my verses. A few people sniggered, a few heads bobbed a little, then it finished, and that was that. Reflecting on my walk home through the dark, tree-hugged lanes, I felt good that people had heard me rap. I wasn't bothered that nobody had bought a copy: what mattered to me was I had taken the first step in presenting my music to an audience. My mind was racing as I dreamed of a record deal.

On Production

The aim of this chapter is to explore the evolution of the cultural agents in provincial British hip hop responsible for driving its national, regional and de-regional growth. Through previously undocumented processes of experimentation, first attempts at engaging with performance and recording, to self-releasing records on private press and negotiating with record labels, this chapter seeks to affirm the juxtaposition between the emerging language of Britishness and locality in hip hop productions. The next section "Process" explores in depth the processes of music production from the lo-fi to the arrival of MIDI and the digital vis-à-vis the power shifts between spatial and sonic editing in pause-button mixes and the dromosphere. The following section "Empowerment" discusses the dialectical operations and tactics of counter-cultural production vis-à-vis the super-crew and conventions of social power structures. In "Cultural Repositioning", the discussion is furthered, and presents evidence of regional and de-regional cultural ecologies which evolved through the practices and productions of British hip hop. The work in this chapter draws particularly upon Foucault's theory of heterotopia, Virilio's theory of dromology, and moments of thirdspace.[1]

Without its own production system, provincial hip hop would surely have died. Indeed, many of the early hip hop followers in the mid-1980s drifted away from hip hop and into rave culture by the end of the 1980s. Rave is by no means at fault, although it was used as a scapegoat and blamed for the reduction in hip hop's presence, certainly in the provinces. I clearly remember during my formative years of clubbing what felt like an overnight paradigm shift from DJs playing house, hip hop, disco and rare groove at the same night to club events playing pure acid house. I am convinced that this seismic shift was more apparent regionally for three reasons: firstly, there was much more of a Pavlovian response to the cultural developments of major cities, and this reactionary way that many provincial club nights were handled led to a misrepresentation of rave culture; secondly, rave culture was perceived by many non-urban hip hop headz as a threat to hip hop culture, and this perception was inflated as more headz "defected" to rave; and lastly, larger cities continued to run hip hop oriented nights, radio shows and record shops. Additionally, raves in the larger cities (and of course in the rural areas during the illegal rave scene of the late 1980s and early 1990s) actually did still play certain hip hop records, provided they were fast and danceable (in rave terms).[2]

The operations of hip hop production started to gather notable momentum in the provinces during late 1983 through to early 1984. These operations followed exploratory and tentative Bboying and graffiti writing practices, and while they were productions of sorts and provided many points of departure, I take the forming of crews as a starting point here as a range of evidence locates the initial moves towards creative collective identity. Craig Ellis Leckie states: "the first events I can recall taking part in were around 1984. I was the kid in the crew that had all the tapes" (email to author, 29 April 2017). DJ Bex remembers his first engagement in Cornwall: "in the late summer of 1984 we as Cambourne Breakers performed every Sunday at the Penventon disco in Redruth and did a couple of demo displays at local social clubs" (email to author, 27 March 2017). DJ Krash Slaughta refers to:

> The Mint Family, who was a crew of Indian brothers around 1983, you had four brothers all dressed in green Adidas tracksuits and seeing these guys battle in the street was just mind-blowing. They would battle against Paul White and his crew; I think they were called The Livi City Breakers (email to author, 6 April 2017).

Although these formative practices were discussed in detail in Chapter 2, it is beneficial to consider these as a point of departure for a more robust cultural structure which developed during the mid- to late 1980s. Where these embryonic practices were an exploration of new culture, the development process led to a point of arrival whereby practices were becoming mastered and the resulting outputs became a ballast for provincial hip hop.

Process

Developing from the first engagements of production by compiling and curating cassettes, the pause-button mix was the first intentional editing and mixing technique practised by hip hop adopters, and the only equipment required was either a twin-cassette boombox or a cassette and record player system. One deck would suffice, as snippets of music would be chopped into one another, the creator aiming for a perfectly timed drop from one beat to the next. Further progression saw the inclusion of stabs, which were painstakingly crafted requiring the tiniest amount of tape for each repeated sound in order to build up a triggered stab exemplified in records such as Paul Hardcastle's '19' or the "D-D-Don't Don't Do It! Do-Do It-Do It!" stabs in the final phase of Grandmaster & Melle Mel's 'White Lines'. Pause-button mixes were ammunition for production battles too, with budding producers and DJs swapping them within crews and at school. However, what is fascinating is that the evolution of the pause-button mix seemingly had no precedent or guidebook but was invented through empirical inquiry in two ways: firstly, via the self-compilation of radio cassettes, and secondly through analytical research of an existing mix or edit.[3] In both cases, and often as a synergy between both methods, what was required on the part of the practitioner was working directly with the results of either the self-made radio recording or an existing edit or megamix.[4] Soon after these pioneering discoveries, methods of manufacture and production were exchanged within the community. In terms of the first inquiry, Evil Ed recalls his own progression from selective radio recording to pause-button mixes:

> I was really into making pause-button mixes. My grandad had a hi-fi with a record deck and tape deck built in so I could make these mixes at his house… I knew a kid at school who showed me how to make pause-button mixes, I have no idea how he knew, I think it was just knowledge that was passed around between kids, one person showed another. It was borrowing cassette tapes from other kids that started it for me in late '84 and shortly after I was recording records onto tape to play on my Walkman and

recording Mike Allen's show and pause-button mixes went hand in hand with that (email to author, 14 June 2017).

Following these primary pause-button experiments, Ed developed an appropriated mixing construct: "I would take some of the Electro LPs and other records I had and make the mixes. I also devised a system for making tracks at home which involved an old reel to reel recorder, a Walkman a turntable and a mic" (Evil Ed, email to author, 14 June 2017). Specifik suggests that a lead was taken from the blending on the *Street Sounds Electro* and *Crew Cuts* series (the latter of which Chad Jackson mixed):

> We also ended up doing pause-button mix tapes because at the time, people like Chad Jackson and other such DJs were doing… on records you'd have the tracks but you'd also have the megamix on a lot of those compilations, so we were trying to emulate the music and those megamixes by doing pause-button mix tapes (i/v, Bournemouth, 27 November 2017).

Mancunian Chad Jackson held the title of DMC World Mixing Champion 1987, and thanks to a short appearance on *Blue Peter* and guest megamix release 'Master Mix Medley' on *Ultimate Trax* (going head-to-head with DMC World Mixing Champion 1986, America's DJ Cheese), had become a valuable source for promising producers and DJs to analyse. Furthermore, his appearance on other TV shows provided a clear visual for learning, although analysing these was certainly a later method as pause-button mixes had existed in the provinces for at least three years prior to Jackson's TV appearances, proving that analysis was carried out audibly. With no visual clues, teachers or precedents, analysis had to be well focused, as DJ Krash Slaughta testifies:

> I was hearing stuff with more and more cuts on there, making me search within for the answer as to how these DJs were making these sounds. Without a visual representation or guide you had to work it all out yourself. Pause-button mixing came before getting my first set of decks (belt drive realistic and mixer) so you or anyone else doing this pause-button stuff at the time were already building a sense of timing. Using a double tape deck and pause-button to make mixes or repeating the phrase in a favourite track (email to author, 6 April 2017).

The first megamix that captured my imagination (following the discovery of D.St.'s Herbie Hancock 'Megamix') was the 'Tommy Boy Megamix' by 3-D from 1985. The lessons here were clear, thanks to my existing knowledge of many of the songs contained in the megamix, but also other songs I was less familiar with were included in their entirety on the Tommy Boy compilation album. This presaged my analysis and enabled me to clearly decode the mix, deciphering where, when and how patterns of music were spliced together. Following repeated analysis of this megamix, I ensued with my own. Using *Street Sounds Crucial Electro 1* and *Breakdance Fever*, I chopped and spliced Warp 9's 'Light Years Away' and 'Nunk', 'The Smurf' by Tyrone Brunson, 'Gunsmoke Breakout' by The Willesden Dodgers and Grandmaster & Melle Mel 'White Lines'. The finale soundbite was "That's my man throwing down", ripped from the end of the Tommy Boy Megamix, and its full length was a little over seven minutes. One of my tactics to increase the dynamism of the mix was to incorporate the existing blend of 'Light Years Away' and 'Nunk' from the album as mixed by Mastermind and multiplying the 'White Lines' "D-D-Don't Don't Do It! Do-Do It-Do It!" stabs tenfold. I made many more pause-button mixes thereafter, and while some were more successful than others, this practice taught me much about the coding-decoding-recoding of hip hop music.

DeLanda offers three continuums for the role a component plays within an assemblage, and these are connected to the expressive, the territory and the code (DeLanda 2013: 8–25). Drawing upon DeLanda's realist approach, a hip hop record acts as a component within the broader assemblage or strata of hip hop culture which may decode, recode and code a certain sonic language which in turn point and reference other elements and components within its assemblage. Taking 'White Lines' as a case in point, the record decodes the bassline, riff and haunting vocals of Liquid Liquid's 'Cavern' by replaying its patterns via the Sugar Hill house band. The original song loses structure and meaning and becomes abstracted as it is reframed as a backing track for a completely different song. Constructed under both a new arrangement and new sound, this backing track is then recoded with the addition of Melle Mel's anti-cocaine narratives, and following production, coded as a hip hop song sonically and visually with the manufacture of the vinyl and its Sugar Hill Records company label and sleeve design. The result is a product born through these coding processes which reifies its own position as hip hop artefact and also a part of hip hop's cultural assemblage. The record's level of cultural and commercial success gives weight to its position, in terms of stratifying hip hop—'White Lines' becomes a very stratum of the culture, a core benchmark for what truly represents hip hop.

Makers of pause-button mixes were reorganizing and representing cultural messages. What happens, then, when fragments and patterns of 'White Lines' are spliced into a pause-button mix? On one hand, 'White Lines' is decoded—the fragment that is extracted and brought into the mix loses meaning without context. The stabbing exclaims of "D-D-Don't Don't Do It! Do-Do It-Do It!" lose their significance with respect to cocaine abuse and become abstracted. Simultaneously, the same fragment enters a new structure and acquires a new meaning as the stabs are not only relocated between slices of other music but also are repeated, emphasizing the new message of the edited and recoded snippet. Juxtaposed with the organic atmospherics of 'Gunsmoke Breakout' the snip enters a dialogue with notions of battle, as the mix flips between "D-D-Don't Don't Do It! Do-Do It-Do It!" and the vocal drop "Gunsmoke Breakout!" The neoteric message is one of defence in the form of threat, a common trope in hip hop warfare, and here aimed at other makers of pause-button mixes. This manoeuvre creates a further stratum of the pause-button mix and the assemblage of hip hop, building on the formative understanding of hip hop's codes (discussed in previous chapters), but by experimenting with the creation of one's own decisive practice. In Piper's discussion on political art and its place within the paradigm of innovation, his point on how: "A work of art can innovate in many ways that thus conflict with the foundations of unrestrained free-market capitalism" (Piper 2008: 123), suggests that: "it can subvert the act or process of consumption itself" (Piper 2008: 123). These pause-button mixes became artworks in their own right, and became strata upon which many practitioners built their work. For Craig Ellis Leckie this method of production built a reputation:

> The pause-button tape fascination came straight from 'Adventures' by Grandmaster Flash.[5] I was an impatient kid, I couldn't wait for anything... I became well known for my tapes too. The concept of pause-mixing was fairly unknown, but I didn't care, I just made as many non-stop pause-tape mixes as possible. By the mid-80s, I'd practised my art to a point where they were good enough to be played in Dublin. That was another part of the country, but it was a big deal to know that kids in "the South" were jamming to my mixes (email to author, 29 April 2017).

Leckie's comments here offer insight into possibly the first version of homemade hip hop independent of London and consumed by audiences outside his immediate network. This is crucially important, as historically the demo tape of one's own music is the starting point for the wider circulation of regional hip hop. Of course, this does reveal the issue surrounding authorship and the threshold between where artistry begins and ends, and while it is not the intention here to delve into the creative bounds of editors, engineers and remixers, the point of where creative practice commences is important to locate. I would argue that the involvement of all practitioners in a creative process contribute to the quality of the production, and although this may be assumed to variable degrees and dependent on the respective output, it is unquestionable that the sole practitioner making pause-button mixes is not embarking on a creative act. Perhaps it is even more clear as the terms of engagement are so obvious—as to the listener the raw materials are well known, and the equipment used is so lo-tech that there can be no smoke and mirrors or effects trickery to conceal any editing flaws. Leckie also employed this technique on his mixtapes:

> 'Spoonin' Rap' by Spoonie Gee was another doozy I exhausted, the opener of "Ya say a one for the trouble, two for the time / a come on y'all lets rock the…" got heavy rotation. It was clean [no music underneath it] so it was perfect for dropping just before a tune, if the following tune had a tough beat as an opener. I'd lay the Spoonie intro onto cassette, then go back and pause it so that it sounded like the Spoonie intro was part of the next track on the tape. I'd simply park them in between cuts every few tracks. I hadn't even heard a pause-button tape, but that is what they were (email to author, 29 April 2017).[6]

Pause-button mixes also offered a structure for one's own jams, in the formation of lo-tech backing tracks for raps, as Nat Drastic recounts: "We would create backing tracks using my friend's dad's stereo, using the 'pause tape' method of looping instrumental sections of the hip hop LPs we had" (email to author, 4 December 2017), continuing practice into what was a natural progression from pause-button mixes of other artists' material to taking greater ownership and authorship of the output by including the emcee. Adjunctly, pause-button methods were also used to test out new beats and loops. Being the emcee and with limited production skills and equipment, I would often make a two-minute loop of a beat or potential sample on my domestic hi-fi that I had discovered at home and take it to play the rest of the crew in the studio, a practice I continued until well into the late 1990s. These primary engagements were very empowering. Before the conventional technology to make music was available, that of the drum machine, sampler and 4-track recorder, and before that, even on the double decks and mixer, the humble record player and tape deck enabled this first tier of sonic creativity. In the *New York Rocker*, Malcolm McLaren declared: "You're using technology in a way that the industry doesn't want you to use it…you are therefore claiming part of that culture for free. There's a possibility to control a lot of the cultural forces around you right now" (McLaren 1981: 13). Here, McLaren is referring to turntable-as-instrument, but pause-button technology was even more primitive, with an even lesser relationship to the commodities of the music industry.

Pause-button mixes also carried ramifications with regard to how one understood broader music culture and cultural conditions, particularly with reference to provincial life. Such was the banal and formulaic structure of the everyday, that all things from the length of a pop song to the length of the school day was perceived as standardized and predictable. Pause-button mixes changed that, and while we had been introduced to the 12″ single as a medium that challenged the convention of the three-minute song, these still averaged around seven minutes—and still bore a formulaic pattern of "intro-verse-chorus-verse-extended break-instrumental outro". The pause-button mix was endless—seven minutes, nine minutes, ninety minutes—time and creativity stretched over 130 metres of tape, the maker was in full control.[7] Creators of pause-button mixes were challenging the conventions of time in music culture directly, which I would argue had an impact on hip hop culture and broader society. As well as these mixes travelling across country as in Leckie's example, they promoted an alternative experience of music in both the abrupt shortening and extending of edits and splicing. Furthermore, they provided prompts for budding producers to contest the conventions of constructing music and became a self-led journey of discovery. Through the practice of pause-button mixing, a closer understanding of the work of editing champions The Latin Rascals, D.St., Double Dee & Steinski, and the UK's Coldcut could be made. This offered a confidence to young producers in their experiments—the reality that one did not have to be trained in reading music or playing an instrument to create music became apparent—all that was needed was a passion for hip hop, a sagacity of rhythm and a sense of timing.

The alternative practice-based and often self-taught music education of the pause-button mix became metaphorical for other approaches to an emerging hip hop way of life in the provinces. So how did it impact on the provincial experience? To explain some of these approaches, I would like to draw upon Virilio's theories surrounding the dromosphere. Dromology as presented by Virilio is an important anchorage for the production of non-urban hip hop, and although his notions of picnolepsy and dromosphere are rooted in the technological world, the related experiential conditions that he explores support my arguments here with some clarity.[8] Virilio proposes that the city is fundamentally constructed of a technology of obstruction, and this complex obstruction is one that decelerates the effects of the dromosphere. The dromosphere is essentially formed around Virilio's concept of dromology, based on the phenomenon of speed. The dromosphere comes into existence when human beings alight the surface of the ground, either on or in a vehicle or other device, and the technologies of that device (engines, axles, gauges, and even, I would suggest, windscreen wipers, air conditioning and satnavs) gain speed, the surrounding world becomes more chaotic as the human mind attempts to adapt to this dromospheric experience. As these technologies advance and multiply, into the realm of nano and digital technologies, speed and ensuing chaos increases, and one's mind needs to continually fathom new strategies of operation and adaption to deal with this increase in technologically-driven speed. The consequence of this is that the more speed increases, the further removed from reality one becomes within the dromosphere. Reality then becomes phenomonologically twisted and imprecise as one is enswathed in the dromosphere. The city then counters the dromosphere by obstructing its speed, a tactic to decode, recode and slow down to a point where it can control the dromospheric entity.[9]

The provincial head needed to acquire the latest music by regularly visiting retail outlets or recording them from the radio. I have previously spoken of travelling to Exeter on the bus to hunt for records, a weekly ritual that many headz living in less urban areas carried out (see Chapter 2).[10] This ritual is important to understanding the part that the dromosphere must play here, and links to notions of increased anticipation and contentment, both of which I would argue were far more accentuated than that of the urban digger. In a similar way to the adrenalin rush from hearing a new jam on John Peel, the journey from village to city contained spikes of excitement along an ever-increasing anticipatory feeling as the bus drew closer to the terminal. This growing anticipation is fuelled solely by speed and distance. Along the journey of 16 miles between village bus shelter[11] to city terminal one traversed along a single road through several small, low-rise villages, soft rolling hills which open out to present meadows stitched together by Devon banks and timber fences, up onto the plateau of the common, littered with a floor of bracken as open sky gapes above, the moorland in the distance, before one can spy the white and grey pixels of the city ahead. The bus journey would take around an hour in total, and each of these shifts in surroundings triggered expectations and hope. Excitement grew as the revolutions of the engine became louder, its rattles and clanks accumulating as it sped through the countryside. From the moment one climbed onto the double-decker, ritualistically turning into the tight spiral stepway up to the top deck, one felt a planing across the landscape to the city. Through the intense dromosphere of the bus one could develop a double-edged strategy, one that firstly coped with the dromospheric experience of the journey, and secondly, targeted searches of record shops (see de Paor-Evans 2018c: 186–93). The strategy I devised was to give myself several markers in the landscape which would help me determine the distance the bus had covered, and how much remained. The other technique I used was to consider the products that hopefully sat waiting for me in the record racks. I would build a mental picture of the records I might purchase which were based on two key things—the new jams I had heard that week on John Peel's show (this was uncommon as most of the records he played were imports, but I lived in hope) and the educated guesses which would be made based on visual clues through an artist's name, song title or sleeve design.

Anticipation often moved dangerously close to anxiety. It was a big deal to make the trek to Exeter once a week, and the worry that more local urban headz had already snapped up the cream of releases that week was consistently concerning. It was sometime later that I discovered that most of the new records would be delivered on a Monday and would be present on the racks either later that day or on a Tuesday once they had been logged, so catching the earliest bus I could seemed a somewhat futile attempt to beat the crowd to the freshest tunes; I was already five days late. Despite this, I often came away from the city with fruitful purchases, and the return journey would be a very different experience, one of contentment, yet again fuelled by speed and distance, but this time the markers in the landscape appearing in reverse order. On the return leg the dromospheric experience is similar: the speed of the bus as it traverses across its 16 miles of suburbia, village and countryside distort one's haptic awareness of the life one is cutting through, yet simultaneously the blurring of visual-geographic thresholds as they shift from grey to brown to green generates a greater feeling of detachment from the city. This suspension of spatial tactility feeds the focus on one's purchases, and time is spent examining one's records while sat on the bus. The hour journey would be spent reading sleeve notes and centre labels and observing the graphics and images, with only a sporadic regard to the world outside the window. If ever I glanced up from my reading and noticed the bus had travelled further than expected (past an estimated marker), a feeling of spatial separateness and disjunction would materialize in the moment, heightening the continually increasing distance between the bus and the city. This dromospheric experience could only be gained by those dwelling outside the city centre, and the further away one lived, the more intense the events of the dromosphere would become. These two hours (in my case) provided a time frame suspended from reality, which both accelerated and decelerated a desire, closeness and intensity with hip hop records and concurrently increased and decreased the physical distance between village and city. Upon completion of this cycle and located back in the village, one felt more distant from the city than before the journey commenced, yet more connected to hip hop.

Returning to the pause-button mix, these experiences of dromology are pertinent to the processes of hip hop production in the provinces. The dromosphere provided an experience of time, space and distance set within everyday life, but skewed the phenomenology of life's spatio-materiality, thus stretching and compressing the reality of life. Furthermore, the dromosphere acted as an agent for spikes of emotion within the space-moment and a focus on particular targets through time-distance. I would argue that these experiences fed into the creation of pause-button mixes made in the non-urban realm, and these mixes are representational of many a journey, as much as journeys are metaphorical for the mix.

Casual Shadows and Open Skies

I discussed above the shift between village and city via the dromospheric experience, but to further the discourse on the non-urban production of hip hop, I will turn to perhaps something of more stasis. DeLanda discusses the idea of the "casual shadow" as a benign byproduct of the city; that the city, as a large assemblage, may be "inhibiting the formation of new towns within their sphere of influence by depriving them of people, resources or trade opportunities" (DeLanda 2013: 37). He emphasizes that the shadow is not literal: "But, of course, it is not the cities as physical entities that can interact this way, but cities as locales for the activities of their inhabitants, including merchants, investors and migrants, as well as market-places and government organizations" (DeLanda 2013: 37). He continues to suggest that the assemblages from city to city achieve similar shadowing, but it is the determination of the locale that is important to the production of provincial hip hop. When the locale is far enough removed from the pull of the polis, rather than existing under a casual shadow, I would advocate it lives under open skies; however, these open skies do not escape occasional clouds. These open skies are apparent when the actions and processes of hip hop's production take points of departure from their non-urban locale as much as (if not more than) the products of the city. The concept of the casual shadow and open skies forms something of an armature for provincial hip hop production. Sonically, the primary structure of this armature is beats, while contextually it is one's environment, both of which have a range of starting points. As discussed earlier in this chapter, in the formative production phase beats were often bitten from existing hip hop instrumentals or longer instrumental passages and spliced using the pause-button technique.

By 1986, some headz had been able to either afford a pair of turntables or fashion double decks from separates, although, due to a lack of guidance or money, many headz began their DJing careers on belt-drive turntables, which were extremely difficult upon which to blend beats. They did provide a steep learning curve for scratching and cutting, however, as Mark Cowan illustrates:

> My dad did however manage to get me a small cheap 4-channel mixer which had no cross fader but did have some on/off tilt switches which I became rather deft at doing transformer scratching with. The decks he got me were just old belt drive ones that were pretty useless for scratching but I somehow managed to learn on them (email to author, 30 April 2017).

DJ Krash Slaughta remembers the first time he witnessed scratching on a low budget belt-drive record player:

> I got into Scratching and decided this was what I wanted to learn after seeing a friend called Sprocket (Stuart) scratching on one of those box type record players, the type that could select a stack of records (Fidelity or something). It had volume control faders and he had the volume faders taped halfway up (as they were like 10" or something) cuttin' a 7" of Whistle's 'Just Buggin'' and the phrases on this record. This freaked me out as I had never actually seen anyone scratch before. I was hooked immediately (email to author, 6 April 2017).

These appropriated and primitive agents for practice are a critical part of the processes of hip hop production, and while there is little surviving evidence of these practices in terms of audio recordings, comparable stories describe in some detail the similar techniques that were invented across the provinces. Before I owned Technics 1210s, my own setup comprised a belt-drive BSR deck and a belt-drive Garrard deck, both prized from their original casing and set into an upturned bottom drawer from an old chest of drawers, becoming a homemade DJ console of sorts. I attached a further smaller drawer to the right-hand side which housed a Realistic 4-channel mixer (from the High Street's Tandy shop—the saviour of many DJs), with a 3.5mm mono jack output that fed into my boombox's microphone input for amplification. I painted the console with blue spray paint to match my customized boombox, and it was upon this rig that I taught myself rudimentary scratch patterns.

However, those practising scratch techniques on these homemade contraptions soon hit a glass ceiling, so headz turned to cheap drum machines to advance their beat making skills and provide a backing track over which they practised their DJ artistry. Entry-level drum machines became the staple equipment for fledgling producers in the mid-1980s. For most headz, expensive and exemplary machines such as the Roland TR-808, the SP-12 and the DMX remained a dream, but lower specification machines such as Yamaha's RX range were more affordable. The first machine my crew used was the BOSS Dr. Rhythm DR-55, a basic step-time machine with only four sounds, three variations and three hi-hat patterns, but this machine provided a sonic backdrop for the exploration of our rap and DJ practice. I would describe this process of making music as having two phases: the first is the creation of rhythms and beats with the drum machine, and the second the writing, rehearsing and recording of raps and the digging, testing and recording of record snippets as scratches and cuts. The beats were almost always crafted first, and after these were made came the concept for the song. My explanation here returns to the point that as a step-write-style machine it was impossible to freestyle beats, so the beat-making effectively became a planning or design phase which resulted in the armature to enable the other elements to be freely explored. It was a natural progression from the pause-button mix to try to emulate certain beat patterns in existing hip hop music. Very soon after the purchase of the Dr. Rhythm, a Yamaha RX-21 was acquired which was more empowering as it could be played and programmed in real time. This was a revelation as for the first time we could test ideas freely, and the process of music production began to feel much more organic. In late 1988, we acquired a Yamaha RX-5 which transformed our music production techniques massively. We also recognized that the RX-5 was used by Tim Simenon of Bomb The Bass on 'Beat Dis' (among other hip hop records) which affirmed for us the status of the equipment we were working with; somehow this offered a further confidence in our sound. With a much larger data bank of original sounds and with attack and delay envelopes, additional sound assigning capabilities and enormous flexibility in customizing of pre-installed kits, we developed what remains as some of our most experimental beats.

This free exploration of beats, rhymes and scratches, executed under the casual shadows and open skies, leads me to a discussion of environment. Our base for producing music was in a bedroom in Sidford village, in the centre of a Victorian terrace row, nearby to the village shop, butcher, public house, bus shelter and playing field. The view through the window was of the small old people's home and modest row of council houses opposite (typical of the post-war expansion seen in most villages in Britain), green verges and treetops, and felt incredibly domestic. The only sounds one would hear were those of occasional seagulls as they retreated the two miles inland from the coast if harsh weather was approaching. Rarely did a vehicle pass down the street, and when one did, net curtains would twitch. This was the epitome of provincial experience, yet within the confines of a bedroom, we were striving to make the hardcore, urban sounds of the hip hop we loved. My journey from home to our recording base was a 20-minute walk through a bungalow estate (built to accommodate the expanding aging population) and a winding country lane enclosed with Devon banks (since named Dark Lane by the local authority; Figure 5.1), hardly the context to produce hip hop, one might think. As I walked to meet the rest of the crew, I would listen on my Walkman to our beats, my John Peel edits or other compilations passed to me by my peers, and as I returned, if our recording session had been successful, I would be analysing what we had just made. This was all part of the production process, as following individual analysis we would often reconvene and revise our work.

The physical and ontological qualities of both urban and rural variably intertwine to produce the hybrid hip hop experience, which become more acute depending on their juxtaposition (see Evil Ed's reflection on p. 121). Situations like these did much to frame hip hop in a new light. It was becoming clear that although there were major differences between the rural British experience and the American context of hip hop's roots, this abrupt schism was becoming increasingly blurred as the everyday practices that Ed describes became more regular and commonplace. The practice of carrying a

Figure 5.1: Dark Lane, Sidford, Devon. Photograph by author.

boombox or even a Walkman in the external provincial environment brought hip hop into that realm and becomes a part of the ontological process of hip hop development.

Microcosmic Production

The early provincial productions of hip hop music extended past purely the manufacture of sound. Although commonly referred to as demo tapes, the DIY recordings were not only made for posting to the city-based record labels in the hope of achieving a record deal but were also made as products to sell locally and regionally. These products were designed, manufactured, promoted, sold and consumed within a small geographic area by each crew, but also crew members outside the immediate music-makers would act as designers, promoters and retailers. In effect, a microcosm of the music industry evolved in the locale. In late 1989, we changed our crew name to Def Defiance, and in 1990 we produced *Music Fusion!*, the first four-track cassette EP under that name. This was the first product proper that I was confident in pushing; the songs covered a range of sonic styles typical of the hardcore British sound of hip hop. By this point we had obtained an AKAI SL-900 digital sampler which saw a paradigm shift in our production practice. Despite still using somewhat limited equipment we cunningly hooked up the sampler to the RX-5, thus utilizing the drum machine to trigger and sequence samples. This meant we could make complete song arrangements using this technique, which we would then transfer onto the two-track reel-to-reel. Sampling and looping full patterns of beats had become an absolute game changer in the world of hip hop during 1988, and our mastering of sample techniques (although two years behind the pioneers) made us feel as though those producers we idolized were somehow within reach.[12]

A critical source for samples came by way of the *Ultimate Breaks & Beats* compilation series,[13] which we would order from Spin Off's mail order record shop (the only way to regularly keep up with purchasing American releases). In a comparable way to the consumption of import records discussed in Chapter 4, these stateside compilations reached us, and the value of the *UBB* series to music production is as important as the *Street Sounds Electro* series is to consumption. Each volume of the *UBB* albums comprised six to eight original songs (usually funk and soul but occasionally psych or rock) which each contained either a breakbeat sampled in a well-known hip hop record, or a breakbeat which was yet to be used in a hip hop record.[14] Often, the break was extended on the compilation as in the case of 'Ashley's Roachclip' by The Soul Searchers, or in a more extreme example, the break of 'Amen Brother' by The Winstons is slowed down to a pitch similar to 'King Of The Beats' by Mantronix.[15] These edits offered precious lessons to producers and DJs operating remotely as now there was access to the "original" sample source which they would have rarely (if at all) discovered in the provinces. This fostered a comparative analysis of the original source (albeit a representation in the form of an edit) with the hip hop record that used the sample in question, resulting in a series of conclusions about how the sample was used.[16] These conclusions would then be taken back into our own beat-making practice which formed the armature for *Music Fusion!*

The opening title song 'Music Fusion' is drum-heavy and created around a Sly and the Family Stone sample, and remains raw throughout with no bassline or melody, and laden with four verses of rap and laced with 'I'm a kilo'[17] cuts and a slight haunting chorus. Rola's opening line: "Welcome to the dominant South-West" is an immediate attempt to locate the EP in a hip hop geography, followed by my own opener: "Next up, the Project with the know how / Better and faster than a mad cow know how" (a diss[18] which was aimed at a rapper from Plymouth who had taken the name MC Mad

Cow, discussed in Chapter 6). 'Cruising at 30,000 ft.' increases the pace, constructed on an armature of Kool and the Gang 'Jungle Boogie' samples with furious battle cuts intended to position ourselves within the broader scope of British hip hop. 'Terrified Faces' builds upon the synth breakdown sampled from Herbie Hancock's 'Hang Up Your Hang Ups' and drum break from Isaac Hayes' 'Joy (Part 1)', and, following a melancholic intro comprising an air-raid siren underlaid with the piano patterns of Lil' Louis & The World's 'Brittany', delivers a narrative about the challenges of landing a recording contract based remotely from London. With this song particularly, I recall experimenting with my voice. I wanted it to sound eerie yet assertive, and so I rapped in a slightly deeper voice. Furthermore, I desired a reverb effect on my vocals, although at this point we only had the effect available on the two-track recorder which was too invasive, so I rapped all my verses wearing record boxes over my head to create a miniature echo chamber. We could not afford echo chambers, and when we were making our earliest recordings in about 1986 to '87, we were in awe of Schoolly D's 'P.S.K.' and that dope murky reverb, and when I heard 'That's Deep' by Dr. J.R. Kool taking it one stage further, I really wanted to make something like that. I used two empty LP record boxes; one was positioned half over my head, and the other I pressed the microphone and then my face into, to try to create an echo. It worked marginally, but those were the kinds of things we did when we lacked the knowledge or the equipment to make what was in our heads. Due to a lack of a proper sound booth, we would rap pressing ourselves into the corners of the bedroom, wrapped in curtains, holding up pillows and cushions, or hanging the microphone from the pendant lamp to shape the sound of our voices. These spatio-technological appropriations contributed greatly to the process of making rap music and shaped the sound of this DIY aesthetic. 'One Way To Reach' closes the EP with fast-paced traditional freestyle rap, emphasizing skills and high quality practice over samples from KC and the Sunshine Band's 'Let It Go'.

Timing was particularly important in terms of when we could record vocals. Being based in such a quiet place, strategy was everything. What accentuated the importance of getting the vocals right on as few takes as possible was that each take led to a deterioration of sound quality, so it was paramount not to be interrupted while rapping. Constructing beats and even laying down cuts and making the final mix could be done at a low volume so this was less of a concern, so these operations were ordered around our voice recording sessions. We identified 4–5pm weekdays as the optimum time, a tiny window of opportunity after college and before parents and neighbours returned from work. However, we had just launched into a session when there was either knocking from next door or parents shouting up the stairs "Put that racket quiet!" and "You can hear that noise right down the street!" which did everything to lower the mood in the recording session and put increased pressure on us to execute our raps well and as swiftly as possible. Sunday afternoon recording sessions were the most intense; as I walked to our base I could feel the curtains twitching as I passed windows, imagining those lurking behind them becoming angry at the prospect of us disturbing their quiet day. This made for increased anxiety before any raps were even laid down, and the combination of limited takes on tape and being interrupted mid-flow by agitated neighbours placed further pressure on the rapper concerned. Despite this, these obstacles helped shape our recording practice in two ways. Firstly, the increased pressure upon us accelerated our accuracy in rap; we simply had to get it right as quickly as possible. Secondly, if we had passed the optimum point of a take (usually when neighbours and/or parents had invaded our mental space) we would walk to the fields, the bench or the shelter. These breaks offered a distancing from the job in hand, but also a reframing opportunity under the clear skies. Being empowered to experience a cultural distancing sometimes helped massively with our creative process.

Thirty copies of *Music Fusion!* were made. Once we had agreed the running order, the design was considered, and a black and white strong graphic was decided upon, which was appropriate for two reasons: first it made for easy and cheap copying, and second it was very much in keeping with the graphic styles of hardcore British hip hop of the time (discussed in detail later on). Rola and I recorded each tape in real time over a 15-hour period using the best quality twin-cassette machine that we knew of, owned by Ritchski, a fellow head in Exeter. The following day we took the complete EPs into Exeter and sold them in the street, mainly to people we knew, but also some strangers. One potential customer was flicking through the hip hop records in HMV, when Marka (one of our hip hop associates) approached him and (slightly forcefully) inquired if he wanted to buy the new Def Defiance tape rather than the record he was eyeing up in the shop. Feeling slightly peer pressured, he bought a tape. Our paths crossed again, some fifteen years later at a jam in Exeter, when he told me he was glad he bought the tape and that he had digitized it and still played it. A less aggressive promotional tactic was carried out by Eraze, who the previous year (along with Rola) had hand-delivered a demo tape to Nicky Ezer, who in 1989 hosted a Monday evening radio show called 'Street Level' on DevonAir, playing a range of soul, rare groove, funk and rap.[19] She played our song twice that evening, and although

I did not hear it, it seemed we had become overnight local celebrities as strangers excitedly approached me at college the next day offering positive comments and asking when the record would be released.

The *Hazardous* album then arrogated *Music Fusion!* as a point of departure, learning much from the experience of curating and producing a hip hop artefact. Again, 30 copies only were made, but we were aiming for a more professional appearance. It was early 1992, and the previous black and white trend had been superseded by full colour imagery and slicker graphics, excelled by the visuals of British albums such as London Posse's *Gangster Chronicle* and Hijack's *Horns of Jericho*. Logos had been designed by Rola, Kilo, and Sce for Def Defiance, South Side Alliance, the D.D. Shack (the name of our recording base, which by this point had moved to Broadclyst, a village on the outskirts of Exeter) and Music & Arts, all of which appeared on the back of the cassette's J-card. The aim of this was to illustrate the various stakeholders, and with no formal record contract or production house behind the release, we constructed our own stakeholders and logos. The J-card was again handmade, but this time reproduced on a colour laser copier with a laminated finish. The body of the cassette was also considered; plain black cassettes were used upon which we adhered handmade labels, cut to shape to fit within the border of the cassette face to emulate the appearance of a factory manufactured product. All 30 copies had been sold or given away within a few days of completion, and while two copies were sent to Tim Westwood and Music of Life respectively (who both replied with similar stories of rejection—a theme discussed in the next chapter), our aim was more to produce an album for ourselves and our extended hip hop family rather than as a mechanism to achieve a recording contract.

This DIY process to production was not new—almost two decades earlier punk bands had followed a similar approach—however, what did make for a new kind of practice in terms of music manufacture was the hip hop ethos that all headz practised the elements of hip hop, and carried a greater awareness of such elements. True to this form, graffiti writers and those that practised the more ephemeral element of knowledge gain were part of the process of production. Rather than the chaos and reactivity of punk, a reinforcing of intentionality is present at moments throughout the album's lyrics. On 'Perpetrating Frauds', aimed at deceptive promotions and duplicitous A&R men, Rola proclaims: "I get physical vocally and nothing choking me / And when you're playing the tape I guess you're smoking me / So that's the reason that we're doing it so why the hell you ruin it / By being a fraud you're making mistakes", suggesting that the A&Rs are enjoying the music but unwilling to take the risk on signing provincial artists. My own line "welcome to the planet of the music makers / Making a melody fit for authority" intended to receive such people by producing outputs that were appropriate for industry, but also recognized the authoritarianism within. By the process of DIY production and manufacture, we were aiming to dismantle the strictures that had informally been imposed on non-urban hip hop music, illustrated by my opening line on the title track: "Open all the power while the project pushes deeper / Deeper deeper into your system". The system again being the semi-formal structures and strictures of the hip hop record industry. The system is a recurring theme here; recorded in October 1991, 'Poetically Lyricin" predicted an ambitious new year: "1991 another year gone another one come so here's a new song / Future complex ejects the future system, future system". We had gained buoyancy in our own work which embraced the visual and sonic with equal value, and set our vocals higher in the mix as confidence grew in rapping in our own dialect. The sonics were improving as we practised, and so too were the visual representations. Our counterparts in graffiti were also refining their practice, and the three years between 1989 and 1992 saw a much-enhanced synergy and trajectory between the audio and the visual productions of hip hop. However, this phase of production of hip hop was not limited to sound and vision; the physical and ontological were also critical components in empowering the processes of music production.

Empowerment

It was the experience of many that a sense of empowerment was exaggerated by holding membership of a multi-faceted crew. While crews that were rappers, graffiti writers or breakers were plentiful, there were fewer crews that fully developed all the elements, particularly in semi-rural environments. The most important culturally contextual agent for these early hip hop productions was the evolution of the super-crew.[20] Devon's South Side Alliance (SSA) was one such crew, initiated during a park bench conversation after several bottles of cider. Kilo had recognized that there were three crews operating in the Exeter area of Devon and, reaching out into the villages as far as Taunton and Okehampton, and eventually Southampton, further loose collectives of like-minded individuals existed. A recruitment process got underway and within a few weeks there were in excess of 30 members of SSA donning a full hip hop skillset. Under the social structure of SSA, empowerment and a sense of strength in numbers became apparent, and so began for many the most major cultural repositioning of their lives. While SSA was without a manifesto, there was a common approach to hip hop, and the production following this cultural repositioning was the result of a core set of non-material cultural values, translated into ideas and manifested into artefacts. This chapter continues with a theoretical critique of the South Side Alliance social structure, and its political freedom exerted through music and graffiti during the ultimate months leading up to Operation Anderson, the UK's largest graffiti bust which saw 72 arrests made on 20 March 1989 across the West Country, several of which were members of SSA (see Chapter 3). In the aftermath of Operation Anderson, the political climate altered drastically, and a more considered yet politically charged approach to the counter-culture of hip hop began, discussed as part of the next chapter.

Here I will present the idea of the super-crew as agent by dissecting South Side Alliance (SSA), the super-crew formed during early 1989 in Devon (Figure 5.2). SSA was a collective of emcees, DJs, dancers, graffiti writers, and promoters. There were existing crews within SSA: Ill Beat Productions/ Ill Brother Posse/Def Defiance, and Black Jack Posse/Wild West Posse. These crews contained most of the core members of SSA, who produced music and graffiti respectively, and individuals were located in Exeter (largely the village-like areas of Mount Pleasant and St. Thomas), and Sidford, Whimple and Feniton, villages in East Devon within 16 miles of Exeter's centre. At the time of SSA's initiation there were approximately 14 core members covering all practices within hip hop, and by the time of its demise in 1992 SSA had peaked at almost 50 members, with many more satellite associates based along the UK's southern east-west axis from Truro in Cornwall to Tunbridge Wells, Kent.

The super-crew was paramount for headz living in less urban and rural areas. Since the arrival of hip hop in Britain seven years earlier, it had moved through periods of being a trend, fad or craze, to unfashionable and passé, and in the provinces hip hop was still perceived as something kids used to breakdance to. The golden year of 1988 did much to solidify a new direction for hip hop music in both America and Britain, with the impact of a vast number of exemplary debut albums from artists such as Big Daddy Kane, EPMD and Jungle Brothers (among many others) as well as sterling 12" offerings by British artists Hijack, Demon Boyz and London Rhyme Syndicate. However, the British records that made the most impression were all by London-based artists, and it would still be another year before the likes of Bristol's 3PM and Manchester's Ruthless Rap Assassins would make noise outside their metropolitan areas. The SSA connected as many active members of hip hop

Figure 5.2: Still from SSA filming, 1989. Film courtesy of Kilo.

culture together as possible, which not only had a drastic impact on the presence of hip hop in Devon, but also on its cultural production. The foundations for SSA were laid during and in the lead-up to a pivotal jam at Exeter's Arts Centre during April 1988, when Kilo asked Rola if IBP would be interested in performing. The Saturday before the event, I was in Pitts (a record and stationery shop in Exeter), where I noticed the poster for the jam which Kilo had designed (Figure 5.3). This was the first time our names had been on a poster for an event, but furthermore it reified that before we had even performed, we were a part of something larger. The poster is designed in an extremely British style, the left-leaning letters with small counters and short stems being typical of mid- to late 1980s graffiti development (typified by writers such as Bristol's 3-D and The Chrome Angelz). Incorporating references to contemporary hip hop phrases of the time with the terminologies "in effect" and "bring da noise" (relating to Public Enemy's 1987 record 'Bring The Noise'), the poster successfully hyped the event. What is of further interest is the inclusion of a magazine image of an advertisement for Groove Records, montaged into the right-hand side of the page. The intention here is to offer some kind of endorsement, or validity to the jam. If read literally, the message in this poster speaks of a link to Groove Records; however, the purpose of the image is to legitimize the jam's very existence, and to place it on equal standing as jams in London.

Rola and I arrived at the afternoon session. The recreation room jams were as I had imagined must have been like in New York's old school era: there were long trestle tables set up at one end with decks and a mic, a PA system running underneath the tables and a few Bboys had started to gather and show each other moves, all dotted around the edges and gathered in corners. One of the writers from Black Jack Posse was mixing two copies of 'It Takes Two' by Rob Base and DJ E-Z Rock, and we aimed straight for behind the decks. The value of this jam was not in its existence as an event, but as a catalyst for what the group of headz in attendance was to become. It was sparsely attended, but a keen sense of taking part in something bigger than Ill Beat Posse was felt by both Rola and I, and it was exciting to feel included in something with potential outside our tiny village clique. Something had been produced that afternoon which was deeper and further-reaching than the raps delivered, the mixes executed, the dance moves performed, and the graffiti displayed: the production of a community network was in process.

This community was to be built of a sense of empowerment, yet different from the ownerships discussed in Chapter 3. Although the production of space and territorial gain was still very much present through the work of writers and dancers, I would like to turn attention to social structure. SSA evolved organically, and although unwritten did carry a powerful sense of support, peer-review and a core set of values. SSA was initiated by Kilo; however, he is keen to point out that its evolution was spontaneous rather than designed:

> With the South Side (SSA) we weren't really thinking like that (it wasn't designed really), but from the outside looking in, it looked like we were this kind of collective force, which we were; but we weren't really deeply organized, were we? But even so, we had quite an impact, because we linked people together that were out there doing stuff, and we united them, even the Plymouth lot, which was quite different because there was the rivalry associated with football. The whole thing united people together and it was significant in the South-West (i/v, Cambridge, 23 May 2017).

Figure 5.3: Flyer for jam at Arts Centre, Exeter, 1988. Designed by Kilo. Image courtesy of Rola.

Kilo's rhetoric here is highly metaphorical for the super-crew's evolution. While it was initially very loose in terms of structure, its unification over time led to establishing something of significance, and something quite different to the conventional social, domestic and civic structures of everyday life. Hebdige discusses the structures of subcultures and their relationship to established social structures and asserts: "Subcultures are therefore expressive forms but what they express is, in the last instance, a fundamental tension between those in power and those condemned to subordinate positions and second-class lives" (Hebdige 2003: 132). In chapter 9 "O.K., it's Culture, but is it Art?" of Hebdige's book *Subculture*, he takes issue with Nuttall's observations regarding cultural production as high art. Nuttall suggests: "Very little has come out of the whole teenage development that has more beauty than decorated rocker-jackets" (Nuttall 1970: 31), and stresses that: "Without any sentimentality, it is possible to say that they constitute art of a high degree" (Nuttall 1972: 31). Hebdige counters this to reinforce his art-within-culture vis-à-vis subculture argument, stating:

> Subcultures are not "cultural" in this sense, and the styles with which they are identified cannot be adequately or usefully described as "art of a high degree". Rather they manifest culture in the broadest sense, as systems of communication, forms of expression and representation (Hebdige 2003: 129).

I sympathize with both views here. The issue in terms of provincial hip hop is twofold: firstly it must be recognized that the period from 1988 to 1992 is essential in British hip hop for locating a power shift from subculture to culture, and secondly that the notion of artistic merit embedded within a culture or subculture must connect directly with its processes and methods of production. Hebdige continues:

> In the same way, subcultural styles do indeed qualify as art but as art in (and out of) particular contexts; not as timeless objects, judged by the immutable criteria of traditional aesthetics, but as "appropriations", "thefts", subversive transformations, as *movement* (Hebdige 2003: 129; original emphasis).

This argument appears to distinguish high art and its value system from the art of subcultural movement, the latter of which of course does not fall into the established art canon. The complexities of subculture, culture and society are crucial in discussing production and its associated repositioning and have everything to do with hierarchies. Both the production of art and the tensions between hip hop culture and broader society were tantamount to hip hop's provincial evolution. In terms of the SSA, the processes and artefacts of production were affected by its growing network, identity and reputation, its jarring relationship with the cultural heritage of the locale and broader hip hop, and the authorities, police and law enforcement. Bourdieu's model: "The field of cultural production and the field of cultural power" (Bourdieu 1993: 37–40) positions the literary and artistic field within the field of power, "while possessing a relative autonomy with respect to it, especially as regards its economic and political principles of hierarchization" (Bourdieu 1993: 37–38). The artistic field is dominated within the field of power, which in turn occupies a dominant position within the field of class relations. "It is thus the site of a double hierarchy: the heteronomous principle of hierarchization" and "the autonomous principle of hierarchization" (Bourdieu 1993: 38). This double hierarchy is evaluated by either book sales or satisfying its own logic (for example degrees of recognition by only those who recognize). Bourdieu continues to suggest that the more autonomous a field becomes, the more a distinction can be drawn between mass scale production and restricted production (producing for other producers). This, in turn, increases the symbolic power in favour of the autonomous:

> Thus, at least in the most perfectly autonomous sector of the field of cultural production, where the only audience aimed at is other producers (as with Symbolist poetry), the economy of practices is based, as in a generalized game of "loser wins", on a systematic inversion of the fundamental principles of all ordinary economies: that of business (it excludes the pursuit of profit and does not guarantee any sort of correspondence between investments and monetary gains, that of power (it condemns honours and temporal greatness), and even that of institutionalized cultural authority (the absence of any academic training of consecration may be considered a virtue) (Bourdieu 1993: 39).

Bourdieu's framing of these hierarchies is of great benefit in evaluating the position of provincial British hip hop culture. I would argue that, certainly in the SSA community, its initial aim was to become as autonomous as possible in its cultural production, and its main pillars of production were generating work, these being graffiti, dance and music. 1988 was also a pivotal year for how creative processes were viewed by their producers. The notion of art as mimesis or representation was surpassed, and a distinction became clear between how we had created our early productions and a new direction for lifelong productivity. Thus, the disciplines of music, dance and graffiti were as much, or perhaps more, concerned with the practice of making work, the narratives and accounts of experiences, than that of the end representation. SSA member Remer, a writer from Teignmouth, Devon, expands on the representation of hip hop's elements within the larger collective:

> There was some decent talent in our area and I felt that we really had it locked down with all the elements, like the rap and DJ thing, the whole posse thing. There were a lot of us. And I look back fondly on those times; it was good to be part of something that has gone on to shape some of us into whom we are today (email to author, 8 March 2017).

Rola recalls the personal impact SSA carried:

> The SSA days were dope; there was a bunch of peeps [people] all wanting the same thing with their own elements of hip hop. This is when we were organizing our own events, doing shows and meeting up with peeps from other towns and cities and it starting to actually feel like we were good at what we did. I was part of something that meant something at last (email to author, 25 March 2017).

Over a three-year period, SSA morphed from a loose collection of headz to a more established group and shifted from making reactionary statements to working within a much more proactive practice paradigm. This cultural repositioning occurred almost by osmosis within the first year, and by early 1990 Ill Beat Productions was performing at The Lemon Grove, University of Exeter supporting important London-based Music of Life artists MC Duke and Demon Boyz (discussed in the next section). However, it was the fallout from Operation Anderson that provoked a reframing of SSA, its values and its aims. With the British Transport Police (and the police in general, who continually and selectively quoted the Public Order Act of 1986 whenever members of SSA were stopped) watching SSA's every move, tactics split between music production, performance and graffiti. The cultural productions of SSA resulted in the creation of a de-global/post-local microcosm of hip hop. Bourdieu reiterates his model of the field of cultural production: "In other words, the specificity of the literary and artistic field is defined by the fact that the more autonomous it is, i.e. the more completely it fulfils its own logic as a field, the more it tends to suspend or reverse the dominant principle of hierarchization" (Bourdieu 1993: 38–39). The activities of super-crews like SSA began to do exactly that—their logic was to produce all elements of hip hop for their direct peers and their own consumption. Once the productions and their associated processes became more refined and consumer ready, a microcosm of economic and political gain developed within the crew. As small as this gain may have been, the gains of the live jams, graffiti writing, and sonic productions were spatial and territorial above anything else, a distinctive feature of provincial hip hop's advancement.

This cultural microcosm reversed the "institutionalized cultural authority" (Bourdieu 1993: 39) which I would consider in two ways: first, this is the authority of the locale, not only the police and lawmakers (that is too obvious), but also the schools and communities who controlled the regional cultural narrative (those who deem what is "art", what is "music"). Second, it is the authority of the global, the record labels and media who share the worldwide narrative, those who view hip hop as a highly urban movement rooted in America with inklings in London and other capital cities (those who deem what is "hip hop"). To this end, the culture of hip hop initially occupied a dominated position within the field of arts, which in turn was also dominated by the field of power. Through the evolution of the microcosm, provincial crews with focused production suspended these misjudgements and gradually reversed some of these dominations, although did not of course take over. Bourdieu continues "but also that, whatever its degree of independence, it continues to be affected by the laws of the field which encompass it, those of economic and political profit" (Bourdieu 1993: 39). The independent productions of provincial hip hop were naturally stimulated and dampened by the economic and political climate of hip hop globally and localized politics, but through the course of the late 1980s and early 1990s marginal negotiations between independent provincial hip hop production and the dominant forces outlined above afforded those practitioners a growing sense of empowerment.

Cultural Repositioning

The semantics that constructed hip hop's identity through the recording were housed in sleeve designs deserving of semiotic inquiry. The sound of London and the context of the real reached the provinces firstly through vinyl and secondarily through occasional jams which would be held in the larger towns. The image of the hip hop artefact carried a definitive style, through brash minimal graphics which thematically hinted at the DIY, simple collage and montage or bold lined illustrations, largely reproduced in black and white. These sleeves spoke of self-empowerment and of utilizing basic graphic tools to produce images that looked as hardcore as the music sounded. The most minimal of these are Hijack's 'Hold No Hostage/Doomsday Of Rap' (1988), Hardnoise's 'Untitled' (1990) and the first self-titled EP by Son Of Noise (1991).

The front cover of 'Hold No Hostage' (designed by Designers Inc.) shows Hijack's logo—HIJACK in upper case ringfenced within the omnipresent yin-yang symbol—occupying almost the entire face (Figure 5.4). Working with the black and white of yin-yang, the logo sits within a white circle on a solid black background, with no other graphic appearance. Its presence is striking, particularly as one flicks through racks of records either in a shop or a collection. The rear of the sleeve lists the track titles, the names of the members and the most reduced down of credits, in upper-case black text on a white background, and space is given over for a quote by "El Shabazz Malcolm X" from Malcolm X's 1964 speech (section V—Social) at the Founding Rally of the Organization of Afro-American Unity. This powerful quote, in reference to the actions and support of black artists, sits over a ghosted image of the Hijack logo. All text is centred save for the small Music of Life logo to the bottom right, suggesting no complex margin justification. To the provincial listener, this cover signalled the arrival of British hardcore underground hip hop like no sleeve before. Released five months after Public Enemy's *It Takes a Nation of Millions to Hold Us Back*, 'Hold No Hostage' rode on the first palpable wave of black consciousness in British hip hop.

In early 1990, Hardnoise supplied the most hardcore, intense and unique British hip hop track ever pressed onto vinyl. The sleeve design, much in the same vein as 'Hold No Hostage', reaches an even more minimal resolution; the front solid glossy black supports two bright white words: "HARDNOISE" fills almost the top half of the cover in what appears to be Impact font stretched to occupy the space and centred below in smaller font, the word "Untitled" (Figure 5.5). The starkness of the cover echoes the track,

The Production of Hip Hop 201

Figure 5.4: Front cover of 'Hold No Hostage/Doomsday Of Rap' by Hijack, 1988. Photograph by author.

the song with an 'Untitled' title. The rear continues the front in approach: small capital letters list the members of the crew, the song titles consist of three versions of 'Untitled' (including instrumental and a capella versions), and three management/label logos to the bottom. Hardnoise member AJ discusses the rationale behind the design: "We wanted the music to speak for us. We had the opportunity to do a picture sleeve when 'Untitled' came out, but we chose not to do one. We believed we delivered a powerful track, so it was not necessary for people to see what we looked like." He continues:

> We wanted the sleeves to reflect our music. Dark and moody. Years ago in the USA a lot of talented black artists that were on

big labels were denied photographs of themselves, so some of the labels at the time replaced their images with an image of a white person. We wanted to reverse that when we dropped our music because we wanted the music to speak for us (email to author, 22 May 2018).

The cultural bleaching that AJ speaks of on record sleeves was also true of certain Latin American, British and European issues of American records. The British issue of Sir Mix-A-Lot's 'Square Dance Rap' depicts a cartoon of three white cowboys playing country and western instruments, which although spinning on the pun of the song itself, delivers a certain message to an audience who had never seen Sir Mix-A-Lot. The European issue of The Younger Generation's 'We Rap More Mellow' uses cropped black and white images of three dancing women, all of whom appear to be white (their faces are not shown, but their hands are clearly pale), and the Brazilian issue is much more blatant in its bleaching by using a photograph of a single blonde female on the front of the sleeve.[21] These cases continue—for example, the hugely influential 'Jam On Revenge (The Wikki Wikki Song)' by Newcleus was released across Europe—none of which represent an image of the band correctly. The UK issue of 'Jam On Revenge (The Wikki Wikki Song)' (Becket Records) depicts a character by Paul Scotton with thick, blonde hair wearing a tennis visor, while the French issue (Sunnyview/Vogue) portrays a caricature of the artist as a thin, gangly singer in a red and black suit with a duck's head and pink hands holding the microphone and stand. Both illustrations make reference to the popular culture of 1983, with the record being released only several weeks after John McEnroe induced fever pitch winning the men's singles at Wimbledon, and the vogue of the sharp suit and skinny tie was donned by Bowie in his 'Let's Dance' and 'China Girl' videos, but these illustrations deny the black history embedded within the product.

Hardnoise addressed this practice of cultural bleaching while concurrently producing a sleeve so starkly beautiful its audience had no choice but to engage directly with the hardcore sounds encased within. The minimal, brutal theme was resuscitated in 1991 when a new line-up called Son Of Noise released a self-titled EP. An identical graphic concept ensured potential consumers would relate this release directly to Hardnoise.[22] This release looks almost DIY as the text on the rear of the sleeve was misaligned, giving the illusion it was crafted with Letraset rub-on transfer letters. These visual representations beguiled some, yet over time have epitomized the period of hardcore Britishness, as Specifik states: "To be honest I was a bit disappointed at the time as they gave no clues about the artists. Now I see them as iconic and a perfect representation of the music and its era" (p/c, Bournemouth, 26 April 2018).

Both Hijack and Hardnoise also released 12″s that included black and white photomontage effects. 'Style Wars' (1988) depicts Hijack in Bboy stances, in an urban street scene with five-storey brick warehouses in the background. With perspective slightly skewed and a high contrast intensity, the black and white image accentuates the coarseness of the urban grain, edges of brickwork, drainpipes, concrete aggregate, but also the stitching on puffer jackets, peaks of baseball caps, hats, fat laces and rims of glasses amplified by intense shadows. The urban fabric and Hijack become one. The cover of 'Serve Tea, Then Murder/Mice In The Presence Of The Lion Part 1'

Figure 5.5: Front cover of 'Untitled' by Hardnoise, 1990. Photograph by author.

204 *Provincial Headz*

(1991) presents a similar suggestion. A streetlamp, wire fences, a brutal brick fragment of the city and spindly trees provide the context as Hardnoise are photographed in the foreground, but the image is an over-exposed negative which luminates the crew intensely (Figure 5.6), resulting in a happy accident:

> To be fair, the guy that took the picture, who also attended the art college Son, Gemini, TLP1 and myself attended, messed up the picture. He was learning photography but over exposed the picture, so we decided to make good use of his error. We were all students back then, so we turned something negative into something positive. We all had group meetings to discuss the art as we were all art students except Mada and Nyce D (AJ, email to author, 22 May 2018).

Figure 5.6: Front cover of 'Serve Tea, Then Murder/Mice In The Presence Of The Lion Part 1', 1991. Photograph by author.

As in 'Style Wars', individuals are not immediately recognizable as they become part of the night city's construct. The shot was located in Peckham, near Peckham Rye station behind the Safeway supermarket, and AJ says that this place was chosen because "there was good light and shadows behind there, so it captured the moody look we were looking for" (email to author, 22 May 2018).

Gunshot and Blade also released records with similar concepts. Gunshot's debut 12″ single 'Battle Creek Brawl' (1990) shows Alkaline, Mercury, Q-Roc and DJ White Child Rix, with eight other extended crew members standing on a rubble-ridden landscape (Figure 5.7). Stood in the foreground amid hunks of broken reinforced concrete with their bent, steel rods spidering out

Figure 5.7: Front cover of 'Battle Creek Brawl' by Gunshot, 1990. Photograph by author.

between broken blocks and bricks, are the four main members of the group, while the other crew members stand behind on the apex of the site. There is no background, just a thicket of grey cloud which occupies the remainder of the front cover. On top of this post-apocalyptic wasteland reads the words "BATTLE CREEK BRAWL", with a ninja/sniper character and barbed-wire running behind the words, and bottom-centre "GUNSHOT", with nine scattered bullet holes across the bottom right of the sleeve. A fusion of Playbill/ Ashwood font screams "Wild West". This assembly of imagery reeked of hardcore hip hop, and the inclusion of verse 12 from the book of Revelations 15:5 on the rear cover accentuated the urgent and impending nature of battle.

Blade's first release with a picture sleeve, 'Lyrical Maniac' (1989), depicts Blade, DJ Renegade and seven other members of his posse walking through a pedestrian underpass, the concrete conduit stained and worn, lined with cracked and broken fluorescent lights. Again, the cover is black and white, and the top centre reads "BLADE" with a thought centred at the bottom: "MANY CONSTANTLY TRY TO MAKE OUT LIKE WE'RE REJECTS OF SOCIETY OR SOMETHIN' – BUT WE'LL SHOW 'EM". These sociopolitically charged cogitations became distinguishable with Blade's next two releases, which stated: "NOTHIN' GREAT WAS EVER ACHIEVED WITHOUT DETERMINATION" ('Mind Of An Ordinary Citizen/Forward', 1990), and "SUCCESS IS TO BE MEASURED NOT SO MUCH BY THE POSITION ONE HAS REACHED IN LIFE, BUT BY THE OBSTACLE ONE HAS OVERCOME WHILE TRYIN' TO SUCCEED" ('Rough It Up', 1991). These cogitations, inspired by Public Enemy,[23] brought home some thoughts on attitude and process. Additionally, 'Mind Of An Ordinary Citizen/Forward' uses a black and white photograph of Blade and his crew in front of an elevated brick overpass, scattered debris and tired graffiti surrounding a police car parked up on concrete slabs. An old tyre in the foreground lies on the slabs. The 'Rough It Up' photograph depicts Blade and his extended family once again (this time 26-strong plus two Pitbull terriers), standing in a London terrace street, as seven residential tower blocks rise in the distance (Figure 5.8).

For Blade, the idea of the hip hop family is central to supporting progress, and as well as the photographs of his collective associates, sleeves feature images of Flako ("Dutch in the ghetto know the deal"), Kobalt 60 ("Comin' soon!!"), No Sleep Nigel ("Roughest engineer in the UK"), and 12 Gauge ("6ft 7in of support"). The inclusion of these people on Blade's record sleeves not only illustrates his valuing of them as individuals, but

Figure 5.8: Front cover of 'Rough It Up' by Blade, 1991. Photograph by author.

of the growing collective identity and structure of British hip hop culture. Similar to the idea embedded in the super-crew, "'the family' is not an irreducible unit, but a way of representing kinship relations" (Martin 2004: 30). Furthermore, there is a value held in the sense of the urban street, and how this relates to the neighbourhood and habitus of hip hop. All these sleeves spoke to provincial headz in similar ways. On 'Serve Tea, Then Murder' and 'Style Wars', Neil Taylor suggests "the raw, hardcore sound fits perfectly with the aesthetic", and regarding 'Untitled' and 'Hold No Hostage', the sleeves were "sparse, like the sound".[24] Mike Mac recalls the strength of the logos, and the plain conviction ensured rigour and longevity, simply stating: "Hijack are incredible".[25]

Please Listen to My Demo

The buzz of British hip hop that the above releases amplified was hugely significant to its emerging identity. These records reached parts of the provinces that the artists themselves were yet to reach (although the live show was not far behind—discussed in the next section), further eliciting faith in provincial artists to aim for similar achievements. Furthermore, the sleeve designs contained two distinct messages: conviction through brutal minimalism and the power of contextualization. The influence of these sleeves on the provincial demo tapes are evident, despite vinyl releases remaining out of reach for regional crews. Stepchild suggests the remoteness to industry, plus a self-press route was out of range: "We didn't have any music industry where we were so pressing vinyl wasn't a viable option, it was all about the cassette tapes, a lot of homemade music got passed around but we'd neither the money nor the resources to get stuff out there like that" (i/v, Swindon, 3 December 2017).

During the summer of 1990, Evil Ed's crew Hidden Identity produced a demo tape entitled *Greenbelt Chronikills*, the first demo tape that featured MC Mistima alongside Evil Ed and Lone Disciple. Playing on London Posse's LP title *Gangster Chronicles*, Hidden Identity's production makes clear rural representations:

> It was recorded in the basement at my parents' house on a 4-track tape recorder. I can't remember how many copies we made, but I made a batch on a double tape deck and photocopied the inlay. They were sent to labels like Music of Life and magazines like Hip Hop Connection. The cover art was by Lone Disciple (Nigel Quinn) who was an original member of Hidden Identity alongside me until Mistima joined us in 1990. The title was a play on London Posse's album which we all loved, and we wanted the art to depict us, three hip hoppers, in the countryside surrounding Leighton Buzzard where we lived, Mistima and LD with spliffs and me munching an apple, straight off the tree (Evil Ed, email to author, 4 February 2018).

Evil Ed's production work extends into the present. Working with artists "from hood to meadow",[26] and releasing the 'Blunted Bumpkin Buskers' EP in 1994, Ed's position and productions contain strong anchorage in the provincial. The content of Hidden Identity's work is discussed in the next chapter, but here I will turn attention to the design of the inlay card. Figure 5.9 illustrates the black and white front cover of *Greenbelt Chronikills*, which portrays MC Mistima, Lone Disciple and Evil Ed silhouetted in a flat, rural landscape typical of East Anglian geography. The characters stand in knee-length foliage (either grass or cereal crops), adjacent to a tree, also in a shadowed profile. In the distance beyond the meadow lies the silhouette of a single farmhouse with a hipped roof and chimney stack (typical characteristics of the local vernacular). The scene is set in what appears to be a summer evening sunset, as the sun hovers above the horizon to the left of the picture plane. All three characters are togged in baggy clothes and caps with the peaks set either backwards or to the side, two of them smoking spliffs (another typical hip hop trope of the time). In terms of text, the graffiti lettering carries the left-leaning style I mentioned when discussing Kilo's Art Centre flyer, the "Chronikills" word surrounded with a melting or dripping background, suggesting either paint or blood, but certainly some kind of fresh activity. The use of the word "Greenbelt" in the title plays on both the rural context and weed culture.

Figure 5.9: Front cover of *Greenbelt Chronikills* by Hidden Identity, 1990. Photograph by Nigel Quinn (Lone Disciple), courtesy of Evil Ed.

Figure 5.10: Front cover of *Music Fusion!* by Def Defiance, 1990. Photograph by Rola.

Turning to Def Defiance and *Music Fusion!* also produced in the summer of 1990, there are striking similarities shared with the visuals of Hidden Identity's demo. Again, in black and white, the three members of the crew are represented through caricatured silhouettes (Figure 5.10). Scarse, an Exeter-based writer (although from satellite village, Feniton) and SSA member, designed these characters, which occupy the foreground of the picture plane, one sporting a hi-top fade, one with a shaved head, and one with curtains and a peaked cap turned sideways. These outlines continue to illustrate the baggy collars of hoodies, before they blend into a minimalist representation of Devon hills. These depictions were intentionally stylized and very much reduced, allowing for the graffiti outline of the letters "DD" (again by Scarse) to punch out from the base of the image. The double "D"s, separated by a star in the foreground, also refer to the left-leaning, laid-back approach of British graffiti letters, stars and spots. In terms of text, the crew name and title employ the same font, all in solid black upper case, with a thin black underline below both DEF DEFIANCE and MUSIC FUSION! centred on the white space above the caricatures.

The bold black and white graphics, most blatant in the cover artwork of 'Untitled' by Hardnoise, 'Hold No Hostage' by Hijack and Black Radical MKII's 'Monsoon' (1989), felt unique to an emerging British identity which provincial headz were attempting to connect into. The representations of human figures of Def Defiance and Hidden Identity also relate strongly to these London artists. Although each figure is presented in a slightly different graphic manner, the overtone is double edged: that one's true identity is, in some way, irrelevant as the musicians represent a broader people, and also that in order to know these artists, you already have to *know*. But nowhere is this silhouetting relationship clearer than in the case of Blade. His second release on 691 Influential 'Mind Of An Ordinary Citizen/Forward' presented a new Blade logo which he was to use on every subsequent release since, a single silhouette in a hat, coat and trainers, striking a Bboy pose (see Figure 5.8). These records had begun to orientate a significant pathway for the direction of British hip hop, and through the production of the sleeves a visual language was emerging that solidified and reified a new national approach to rap, which provincial productions yearned to be positioned alongside.

Live Jams

The self-released demo tape was a key mechanism for self-empowerment, and could be constructed within safe zones of home, bedroom and among a chosen group of peers. The live show, however, offered a very different dynamic for self-empowerment: the spaces in which performances were executed had a formality and an authority, and the shows themselves required planning and preparation much advanced from the ad-hoc and freestyle street performances discussed previously. Furthermore, the live jams held outside London also presented an opportunity for London-centric crews to expand their sense of empowerment. DJ Format recalls the excitement of watching live British hip hop outside of London during that early period:

> It wasn't until we had a friend who was a little bit older than us and he had a car then he could drive us into town, then we could start going to see, for example, Gunshot, Son of Noise, Blade, Caveman, they were the UK Hip Hop acts that came through and played in the back of this pub called The Joiners, that's still there, still a live venue in Southampton to this day. That was quite life changing for me; seeing Gunshot and Son of Noise was like ... especially, to see White Child Rix cutting up, he was this small quiet unassuming guy and he's like a little demon on the turntables, unbelievable. And seeing Son of Noise with two DJs! Every time there was a chorus it would be like, "Mada!" and Mada would do his solo and then it would be like, "Renegade!" and

like, oh my god, our minds were blown! But these events, they were very few and far between. I don't even know how we would always know the details either (i/v, Brighton, 17 December 2017).

The shows that are being discussed here began to take place in the late 1980s when British (largely London) artists were becoming established. As their reputations and fan base grew following not only their vinyl releases but presence in media such as *Hip Hop Connection* magazine and occasional television appearances on shows such as *Snub TV*, *Dance Energy*, *Rapido* (and other offshoots), regional promoters began to stage jams. It was usual practice for a signed London group to headline, and either an associate crew or local artist (or both) would be billed as a support act. These opportunities were paramount for local crews to reach larger audiences in their region and stepping up to the performance plate was not to be taken lightly. The hierarchy of artists would be clearly illustrated on promotional material, usually with the most well-known artist top of the poster in larger font, with the text size reducing in turn of each artist listed (Figure 5.11). This is of course usual practice across live events in most music genres; however, there is potential for hierarchical nuances and conflict in hip hop shows connected to the nature of live rap. The battle mentality ran deep, and even if there was no planned battle, contention would be tested on stage between rival groups of perceived equal stature. This perception of status in terms of where regional groups located themselves and were located by others often came to light through the production of the promotional poster. It was accepted that the visiting London crew would be top of the bill, but in positioning regional crews local politics carried weight. A promoter that was either a part of or close to a crew, through practice, friendship or neighbourhood, might be tempted to position them above another regional crew with whom they did not share a closeness; regardless of the quality of that crew's practice, they would appear lower on the bill. This could cause friction and dissing on a recording: "Sometime a couple of promos put the name on a poster below / Other people, other ones, other men / That are known as my sons" ('I Don't Burn', Def Defiance, 1992).

Something of a two-tiered promotional campaign took place for the Caveman jam. Primarily, the official flyers and posters produced by Ice Cream Promotions were circulated in the usual way, although locally there was a feeling that the London promoters had become complacent with the success of past events. Additionally, the poster that was produced felt extremely lacklustre, which aggrieved SSA. These jams were so impactful in the South-West, there was a concern that the lateness and lack of attention

The Production of Hip Hop 213

in promoting the events would damage the buoyancy of the scene, so SSA employed guerrilla publicity tactics. Scarse produced an alternative version of the poster (Figure 5.12) which was more visually stimulating and particularly captured the essence of hip hop in Devon at the time. The information was almost identical, but with the added text "Live PA's from…" and "South West Projeks"—the former to heighten interest,[27] and the latter to claim ownership over Ice Cream Promotions. All information is delivered in graffiti lettering, the hierarchy of artists still apparent, but with more synergy between them. The word "R" and "W" of "RAW" is split, with the "A" replaced by a representation of Vaughn Bodē's Cheech Wizard character (the work of Bodē was crucial to the development of characters in graffiti throughout the 1980s), and Bboy figures pose either side of the poster. The venue and price information were purloined from the original flyer, collaged into the space below the last statement "The no. 1 jam to reach!", again to induce excitement. This poster was simultaneously distributed across the region, and through these actions of reimagining the visuals, a reclamation of hip hop in the locale took place.

Figure 5.11: Flyer/ticket design for Dance Raw 4, The Lemon Grove, University of Exeter, 1991. Photograph by Neil Taylor.

214 *Provincial Headz*

Figure 5.12: Reimagined flyer design for Dance Raw 4 by Scarse, The Lemon Grove, University of Exeter, 1991. Scan courtesy of Rola.

The Space of Performance

A further hierarchy of the live show depended on the space within which it was held. Jams could be staged in clubs, bars, or live venues located on university campuses, each of which operates under an economic business structure, and in turn under the authoritarian rules and regulations of the local authority and nation-state. In his beguiling essay "Of Other Spaces: Utopias and Heterotopias" (1986), Michel Foucault presents his post-structuralist ephemeral concept of heterotopia—space that is not homogeneous, uniquely structured yet at the same time is conventional and whose conventions are repeated in other similar spaces. He explains the idea of the heterotopia in dialogue with utopia and offers a simple example of the mirror which is both heterotopia and utopia. Utopian in the sense that it is a "placeless place"

(Foucault 1986: 24), an unreal, "virtual space that opens up behind the surface" (Foucault 1986: 24), and that the mirror "enables me to see myself there where I am absent: such is the utopia of the mirror" (Foucault 1986: 24). He continues to define the mirror also as heterotopia: "The mirror does exist in reality, where it exerts a sort of counteraction on the position that I occupy" (Foucault 1986: 24). The heterotopia contests the reality and challenges the myths of space. Foucault outlines six principles of heterotopia and offers up many examples by name of heterotopic sites: prisons, motels, psychiatric institutions, boarding schools, cemeteries and holiday camps among others, which, to varying degrees, are described through his heterotopic principles. In brief, these principles alter the conventional structure of space through crisis (the place of one's first sexual encounter), history (life to death—the cemetery), juxtaposition (the cinema or theatre), time (museum), compulsory, status thresholds (prisons), and illusion/perfection (the colony). In essence, heterotopias are spaces that become places with shifted, flipped or overlapping hierarchies of meaning, social order and authority. Although accused of vagueness (Harvey 2000), the notion of heterotopia is of high value to this exploration; it is not intended to provide an alternate utopianism, but a commentary on the myth and reality of spaces.

Following Foucault's definition of heterotopia space, what is of interest here is the space of the venue, and how the experience of the provincial hip hop jam provided a platform to contest the hierarchies of social order and authority through the processes associated with performance. The five Dance Raw jams in Exeter that were held between February 1990 and June 1991 were promoted by Ice Cream Promotions, a one-man promotional company run by an accountant named Ben, a Londoner who had studied in Plymouth. Ben could see the potential in Devon, and at that time there were no official jams running performances of regular London artists. The first event was at Plymouth Academy (on a Sunday, as weekends were highly charged rave nights) in the summer of 1989, and was a mammoth operation considering it was the first Ice Cream Promotions jam. There were well over 20 performers almost exclusively from London, with Overlord X as the top billing artist. Through meeting headz from Exeter that had travelled to Plymouth for the Overlord X jam, Ben discovered that the East Devon area had a thriving hip hop scene, and at an hour closer to London, was attractive as a location. Hence, the Dance Raw nights were born, with the first hosting MC Duke as the top billed artist. Ben had been introduced to our crew following a first discussion at the Overlord X jam and had invited us to send him a demo tape (which we duly did) as he was seeking support acts for MC Duke. He agreed that we would play on the night and phoning my mother's house to inform me of the news, he advised that he had played the tape to his brother and a few of his friends who were digging the sound. When they asked Ben where this crew were from, and Ben replied Exeter, they exclaimed: "Exeter? Where's that? Don't you mean Leicester?" This anecdote both amused and disappointed me, as it reinforced the belief that Devon was still way off the radar of British hip hop.

The venue for the Dance Raw nights was The Lemon Grove, a live music venue run by the Students' Union on the University of Exeter campus. The campus prided itself on its pristine appearance, located outside the city centre in leafy suburbia, occupying the rolling hills between the villages of Cowley Bridge and Pennsylvania with views over to Exmoor and handsome brick neo-classic and modernist buildings that sat squarely in finely manicured lawns and gardens. Vehicular traffic rolled through the unmarked roads infrequently, save for learner drivers and the occasional student or lecturer; the campus always felt uncannily perfect. Hip hop had arrived in heterotopia. The campus was heterotopian as a whole, offering the perfected spatial and material experience of semi-public space; its exacting and effortlessly spotless make-up reminded one of the coarseness and disorder of rural living and life in the fringe exurbia. The existence of this campus, its reality, "exerts a sort of counteraction" (Foucault 1984: 24) to life outside. As one passes through the black iron gates at the foot of Streatham Drive, one enters a reality of perfection. According to Foucault:

> The last trait of heterotopias is that they have a function in relation to all the space that remains. This function unfolds between two extreme poles. Either their role is to create a space of illusion that exposes every real space, all the sites inside of which human life is partitioned, as still more illusory (perhaps that is the role that was played by those famous brothels of which we are now deprived). Or else, on the contrary, their role is to create a space that is other, another real space, as perfect, as meticulous, as well arranged as ours is messy, ill constructed, and jumbled (Foucault 1984: 27).

I would suggest the campus plays both heterotopian roles in this case. It is a self-contained campus, with a theatre, teaching spaces, bar, cafeteria, restaurant, laboratories, medical areas, car parking, and domestic accommodation; pillar boxes and post deliveries. It is possible to dwell here without passing back through the iron gates. At the same time, it is a series of spaces that collectively make one space, the space of the campus, which is other in its perfect construct and daily execution, other to the world past the gates of disorganization, where cultural production is often the result of combobulation. Dehaene and De Cauter state:

> Academia, for example, absent from Foucault's list, definitely qualifies as a heterotopia. It is the safe haven of the *bios theoreticos* (the vita contemplativa), as both Arendt and Aristotle emphasize...which qualifies neither as economic nor as political (2008: 91).

The physical construct of academia as campus in the immediate experience is what first drives my argument. Headz, artists, promoters, crews and posses that travelled from exurbia, country, village and over the Devon borders from Cornwall and Somerset entered the spatial and material of the campus, and not being students themselves (at least not at the University of Exeter), primarily based their experience in the lived moment. The power structure of academia followed once headz had begun to absorb the differences between inside and outside the campus. Secondly, my argument sits within the realm of the venue. At the heart of the campus lies The Lemon Grove, and as one climbs the winding lane to its entrance the modular concrete box-like structure perched near the crown of the hill radiates nothing but modesty.

    On the night of the MC Duke jam, we arrived early, eager to carry out a sound-check, and possibly meet Duke himself. After convincing the sound engineers that we had been billed to play (aided by a quick telephone call to the manager), we sat in the brightly lit space as the engineers ambled from one end of the venue to the other, carrying the odd lead, microphone, or roll of gaffa tape. Eventually we were called to mic-check and test our backing tape; we were thrilled when our beats blasted through the rig and filled the space. Several times, several lyrics, until the engineers were satisfied. This was a quick process though, and being novices (we had never rapped through a sound system before that demanded a sound check before the venue opened), we contentedly retired to our cluster of plastic seats. Over the course of the next two hours, bar workers, bouncers and cloakroom attendants arrived, then DJ Bex, and eventually, Ben, MC Duke, DJ Leader One and two crew members we recognized from MC Duke's album cover. Lights were dimmed, curtains were drawn; we could hear a crowd gathering outside. I began to buzz with excitement and nerves. Since we arrived we had experienced moments of temporality within a longer event, itself temporal, before it started proper, a series of mini-heterotopian situations: "Heterotopia is the counterpart of what an event is in time, an eruption, an apparition, an absolute discontinuity, taking on its heterotopian character at those times when the event in question is made permanent and translated into a specific architecture" (Dehaene and De Cauter 2008: 92). To the crowd that were gathered outside, the event that had existed on posters for four weeks was imminent. To us, the main event was preceded by a series of shorter events, heterotopian in their social order, contained within The Lemon Grove. As the glazed doors opened and the crowd poured into the lobby, the chatter and a cold wind incited the heterotopia of the event proper. The Lemon Grove, a venue of 800 capacity, began to fill, the empty timber floor area reducing as a sea of trainers, kicks, sneakers, wallabees and the occasional stiletto consumed the space, headz bobbing to the sounds of Rob Base and DJ E-Z Rock's 'It Takes Two', JVC Force's 'Strong Island' and EPMD's 'The Big Payback', and we were live on stage.

We took a Shure SM-58 microphone each from their stands, and walked across the matt-black rostrum stage. I glanced over a ripple of heads, hats and hi-tops to the back, and signalled to the engineers, but our introduction track was already playing. We had made a two-minute intro of "the Soul II Soul break" (based on Graham Central Station's 'The Jam', 1975) and several Alyson Williams vocal samples which would provide space for hyping up the crowd, but little of this was required; the audience were as eager as us. During our 15-minute performance the sense of empowerment was almost overwhelming, the heterotopian experience suspended the perception of real time: "The heterotopia begins to function fully when people find themselves in a sort of absolute break with their traditional time" (Foucault 1986: 26). During this break in traditional time, the time of the performance took over and at once two spaces operated simultaneously, the space the audience occupy and the virtual space of the performance. As the performance is executed, raps and scratches delivered over pre-recorded beats, the emcees stomping across the stage throwing a string of metaphorical rhymes, hand gestures and facial expressions, all coded within the language of hip hop, that real space occupied by the audience is absorbed into the space of the virtual, and it is the performers who appear to control the whole space.[28] Furthermore, the hierarchy of people within the space extends this power-shift: lecturers, university students and hip hop headz, practitioners and artists make up the audience as a whole. Those who frequent the campus daily stand adjacent to those who are virgins to the campus experience, the event mediating and negotiating between their respective rituals and experiences. Dehaene and De Cauter talk about the mediating character of heterotopia: "as a direct function of its position as a dialectical third in the constitution of the polis, between the public and the private realm, animated by an albeit restless dialectics, which always leaves a remainder, a rest" (Dehaene and De Cauter 2008: 94), to which I would add further layers to this spatial palimpsest. The dialectics of lecturer and university student shift as they both become audience, as do the dialectics of the regarded hip hop artist (here, the urban artist booked to top bill the show) and the newcomer (in this case, the rural artist, booked as a support act). A further significant dialectic lies in the university student and the hip hop head; at this time in Devon, to be both was rare. The mediation between urban and rural artist occurs during the rural artist's performance; as the performer takes control of the space, urban artists occupy this controlled space. The performer produces the space, the mediation *becomes* spatial production. This spatial production envelops the established artist, destabilizing social status. These mediation processes rely on spaces "where appearance is hidden but where the hidden appears. The theatrical event, in our argument the heterotopia par excellence, releases all the force of the oxymoron 'hidden appearance'" (Dehaene and De Cauter 2008: 94).

The hidden appearance of the rural performer is revealed as the performance begins. The shift in power relations occurs when the performer begins to command the space through physical actions, sonic interference and vocal delivery. Here the performer is not only taking control of the space and audience, but also of the hierarchical social structure of operation in such a space. Rural contests urban through the medium of hip hop performance. As regional idioms, accents, tropes and motifs are wound into a performance rooted in urban techniques, the hybridity of new critical regionalist hip hop practice is produced and amplified to the audience. Through this performance, a "heterotopia of deviation" is revealed; Foucault identified "heterotopias of deviation" as those spaces "in which individuals whose behavior is deviant in relation to the average or norm, are placed" (Foucault 1978: 139). The phenomenon of the performance in this space deviates from the routine of everyday life, but more importantly marks firmly a deviation from the expectations of rural living. Following the success of the MC Duke jam, Ice

220 *Provincial Headz*

Cream Promotions continued with four more Dance Raw jams at The Lemon Grove, all with "London-based" headliners. These were Demon Boyz, Soul II Soul DJs (Outlaw and Crime), Caveman and Blade (Figure 5.13), and Q-Tee. During the Demon Boyz jam, the heterotopian experience of the previous jam was repeated, and although this was only the second time the venue had been used for this purpose, it was beginning to feel ritualistic, as though attending the Dance Raw jams was a pilgrimage to hip hop. Indeed, this feeling increased as each Dance Raw materialized, and how each London artist also dominated the space of the institution. For headz in Devon and much of Cornwall and Somerset, The Lemon Grove became almost sacred as the place that reified regional hip hop: "The hieratic nature of the ritual time is permanently represented in the specific 'consecration' of a particular building type: a church, a theatre building, a stadium" (Dehaene and De Cauter 2008: 92). The ritualistic pilgrimage was accentuated by the journey made on foot from the exurbia and far reaches of the rural South-West, across the threshold and up the winding hill to the centre of the heterotopian campus where the jewel of The Lemon Grove was located. For the performers (and indeed the promoters and engineers), the heterotopian experience does not

Figure 5.13: Def Defiance on stage at Dance Raw 4, opening up for Blade and Caveman. Photograph by Jay Tomkins.

simply begin at the outset of the jam (as the events leading up to the doors opening describe) or conclude when the liminality of the jam ends: "A stay in liminal space or a liminoid state is, by consequence, mostly temporary. Some people, however, dwell in heterotopia: priests, gurus and wandering philosophers, actors, artists, bohemians, musicians, athletes" (Dehaene and De Cauter 2008: 96).

Similar productions were occurring across the country. As London artists brought their sound to the provinces, local artists would perform as support acts, generating a sonic compound of British and regional hip hop. DJ Krash Slaughta (as a member of Scottish crew II Tone Committee) remembers some of these events:

> If you're talking British hip hop... II Tone Committee supported both Son Of Noise and Katch 22 at Nice N Sleazy a bar in town, which has a basement (it's still there) where we did a couple of shows... Those shows were full of energy and ram packed. All now legendary events. Also, Killa Instinct and Gunshot came to town where we supported both of those acts at Glasgow Art School (email to author, 6 April 2017).

Regional hives of activity were targeted by promoters. The university was a typology that made sense, as there was already the potential for a diverse audience as well as drawing on the wider catchment area. These nodes also evolved more autonomously though, as Cobra P.I. (Agent/Rapid Fire) attests:

> Although we were hit by most crazes, fashions and fads like anywhere else it always felt like we were off the radar. Places like the legendary Barton Hill, St. Paul's, Easton, Bedminster and Kingswood were attracting the heat back then. I think that Yate was viewed more like a place where you would go to watch a Stock, Aitken and Waterman Roadshow featuring Sinitta, Rick Astley and Sonia (email to author, 25 May 2017).

Cobra P.I. (Agent/Rapid Fire)'s framing of the relationship between the active nodes for hip hop in Bristol with his small home town of Yate, Gloucestershire, ten miles to the north-west, acted as a catalyst for a continued momentum through local practice. These other nodes, often diverting away from the power structures of universities to the neighbourhood, also induced excitement and empowerment in a similar way. These other spaces are also heterotopias of sorts; the sensations of excitement and empowerment linger within as return journeys home are made to country from city. It is both during the event and during the long head and tail of the hype and aftermath, I would argue, that regional hip hop gained its anchorage.

Chapter 6
The Identity of Hip Hop: Reality, Image and a State of Mind

It was a warm Saturday in Exeter during April 1989. Kilo had hired a camcorder for the week from Radio Rentals (or somewhere like that), and word had spread throughout the crew that filming would be taking place. There was no real strategy designed, but the loose plan was to meet at the bench in town and then walk down to The Wall of Fame[1] en masse—as one large posse—and just film our everyday hip hop activities. Even so, this prospect excited us all enormously; our collective crew SSA had gathered momentum over the previous few months, and as well as the core members located in neighbouring villages Whimple, Feniton, Sidford and Cowley Bridge, we had also accrued membership from neighbouring counties. We had also heard that some headz from Southampton were visiting Exeter for the weekend, as one of them had started seeing a local girl who had introduced him to our hip hop scene. My crew and I had driven into the city from Sidford, ecstatic about the day ahead. We excitedly talked about the possibility of filming a music video, the latest pieces we could capture down at The Wall,[2] and meeting hew headz; maybe Kilo would film some graffiti in production, and document the entire process. We always seemed to be running late, and as we approached the bench in the centre of the high street, a decent crowd had already gathered. I spied the usual suspects, clad in familiar checkered shirts (popularized in hip hop fashion by the film *Colors*), Nike Air Max and NY baseball hats, and headgear and footwear I did not recognize donned by our new extended family (I was awestruck as I clocked someone rocking Troop hi-tops).

As we joined the group, eyes flickered, scanning us as we did the same in return, clocking for jewelry, stopwatches, name-belt buckles and other hip hop accessories. Sporadic introductions were made and our swarm of Bboys headed west towards The Wall. We stopped at the historical underground passages, a small glimpse of Exeter's medieval past in the middle of the municipal modernism of Princesshay, reconstructed after the devastation of World War II, yet still reserved in its scale. The camera rolled as we ascended the dark tunnel into the open plaza, rapping and beatboxing as the occasional passerby glanced over. We were trying so much to "be urban"; we hung out here as the underground steps reminded us of the New York subway, but the real vibrancy of the day was captured at The Wall. With a 30-strong crew, the boombox blasting Chill Rob G's 'Court Is Now In Session', Bboys and writers running the disused weed-ridden tracks, tagging grey signal boxes, popping, locking, laughing and joking: the South Side Alliance had truly arrived. As the Penzance-bound train from London Paddington rushed by within metres of The Wall, I caught sight of passengers staring through the windows and down the grassy verge at such a hip hop spectacle. Had they seen anything like this outside the metropolis before? Right here, right now, in the middle of Devon, posse was in effect.

On Identity

Throughout the first decade of provincial British hip hop's life, radical transformations took place. Starting its journey as the latest craze imported from America, the first breakdancing explosion captivated thousands of young people. Hip hop died for many of the breakdancing tourists, but devotees soon realized that breakdancing was only the tip of the cultural iceberg. With the fading away of the voguing followers of fashion, the self-educating dived into the depths of hip hop to discover its past. The sonic, verbal and visual languages of American rap were developing at an exponential rate and overlapping with the first serious British hip hop records. By the close of the decade, distinguishing between American and British hip hop was effortless as the hip hop community of Britain arrived with its own identity. By 1989, British hip hop was beginning to own a sound, which by 1994 had become known as britcore. This was a sound of urgency, and while British artists acquired the rapid speed and intense sampling akin to such sounds by American artists such as Public Enemy, Big Daddy Kane and Kool G Rap, added layers of industrial noise were prevalent on countless recordings identifiable with British hip hop. Furthermore, the introduction of London vernacular language, colloquialisms and frantic scratch patterns solidified the British soundscape. Successful artists such as Hijack, Hardnoise and Katch

22 were among those mainly from London, so how did provincial British hip hop differ, if at all? What was the identity of hip hop in the non-urban, what were its images, its sounds, and what was its reality? Furthermore, this chapter asks, what was the state of mind of provincial British hip hop? These questions are addressed through further interview responses, and again I turn to the reifications of hip hop through product image as well as analysis of sound and lyrics. The critique offers a counterpoint and subaltern view of nationalism and Britishness and solidifies the notion of a critical regionalism in British hip hop.

In Chapter 2, I briefly introduced the idea of Britishness in relation to attitude through music movements and the spaces of nationhood, which are signified by various visual and sonic touchstones of identity. I discussed three scenarios, which, although pithy, relaunch the discussion here: "the Buffalo Gals Effect", "the London Posse Effect" and "the Street Sounds Effect" which are paramount to the structure of provincial British hip hop. Before returning to these three scenarios though, I want to explore further the context of Britishness in society. In simple terms, the structure of Great Britain comprises three countries: England, Scotland and Wales. The United Kingdom is a union of those same countries plus Northern Ireland (and several much smaller islands). Additionally, there are dependencies of the Crown (these being the Channel Islands and the Isle of Man), which are locally self-governed, and not actually part of the UK.[3] This may seem glaringly straightforward, but in fact this post-imperial geographic structure leads to enormous cultural identity confusion even within British society, where English people in particular often appear to stumble upon being asked their nationality. Exploring the period 1534–1707, Morrill states: "The English were the first to develop their name and identity, separating out their 'English' from their 'British' (= Celtic) origins, and clearing the confusion between their 'Angle' and 'Saxon' identity" (Morrill 1996: 6). However, in *The Making of English National Identity*, Kumar speaks of a "natural confusion" (Kumar 2003: 1) when discussing the locution "English – I mean British", which "alerts us to the enduring perplexities of English national identity" (Kumar 2003: 1). The separateness between English and British is a complex one, although the notion of Britishness appears to have more stability than Englishness. Kumar suggests that:

> Gone are the cosy assumptions of "Englishness", with its sleepy villages and ancestral piles. They have gone because the empire has gone, and so has British economic power... In whichever

direction they look, the English find themselves called upon to reflect upon their identity, and to rethink their position in the world (Kumar 2003: 16).

The idea of a new Britishness, however, surged through the noughties as both elite and populist multiculturalism grew, but during the mid-1980s to be British, and the notion of Britishness as a form of cultural identity, were constructed on less-trendy and more sinister grounds, at least for the youth, as Nat Drastic insists:

> I tended to develop disdain for "Britishness". To me, there's a lot of jingoism around "Britishness". That means as an identity it is often too enmeshed in colonialism and racism. All the "Britannia rules the waves" pomp and circumstance tend to be only a couple of steps away from Empire (email to author, 4 December 2017).

The narratives that construct nationality have variable effects on national identity, as Cook states: "The very idea of national identity seems to depend upon the stories a nation tells about itself to itself and others" (Cook 2004: 27). The idea that the nation tells its own story to itself is curious—in the case of Britain, the continuous affirmations it seeks about its national identity seem to unhinge its collective identity. These narratives are delivered to society (in Britain's case its subjects rather than citizens) through various agents: "Histories and novels, cinema, television and newspapers, banknotes and postage stamps, sport and ceremony can all become vehicles of national narrative, working on a major or minor scale, through the grandest gestures or the smallest hints" (Cook 2004: 27). The authority that controls these messages obviously varies, and the informal narratives or the provincial, rural or local stories do not necessarily carry the lowest impact. Growing up in south London, Remark describes a powerful sense of Britishness:

> More so in London than Brighton, because it being multicultural, the environment there is like a melting pot of people from around the world. I remember walking through Tooting market on the way to and from school with my class mates and smelling the aroma of stalls and cafes, the different kinds of music coming out of the record shop, the hustle and bustle of people who had all made Britain their home. We were all together in the community. That's the Britishness I know of and love and would call Great Britain (email to author, 24 April 2017).

Even though "it was the cold Thatcher years, when shops were closing due to the recession" (email to author, 24 April 2017), for Remark national identity existed through the narrative of the multicultural experience, a redemption of life that erases the historical canon "to demonstrate the prodigious, living principles of the people as contemporaneity" (Bhabha 2004: 208). Bhabha presents two ways in which the narratives of nationhood are brought into everyday life—the pedagogic and the performative, which create tension between them (Bhabha 2004: 209). The pedagogic canon delivers accounts of nationhood which are self-justifying and delivered as a singular truth or history, and once they penetrate the province their permanence is long and lasting, as change occurs gradually and slowly. The performative disrupts the rhythm of the pedagogic, as a "recursive strategy" (Bhabha 2004: 209). As a spatial and textual territory of identity, the performative blurs the boundaries between the start, middle and end of the pedagogic stories. Through both modes of national identity, Bhabha reiterates that the nation's people are crucial to the narratives, who make apparent a "contested conceptual territory where the nation's people must be thought in double-time" (Bhabha 2004: 209). People are both subject and object; they are the "'subjects' of a process of signification" and "the historical 'objects' of a nationalist pedagogy" (Bhabha 2004: 209). However, if the "continuist, accumulative, temporality of the pedagogical" (Bhabha 2004: 209) as conventional history is regurgitated within the province, then the pedagogic becomes acquired and practised—not as a performative, but as a spatio-local reiteration as in Scott Coombes' observations:

> Being a predominantly agricultural community, a large proportion of the local workforce would be destined to take jobs harvesting in the fields or working in vegetable "packhouses". These facts, coupled with Boston's relatively remote geographical location may have contributed to what I have always felt as being a particularly xenophobic, "hard man" attitude amongst many locals that unfortunately still appears prevalent to this day (email to author, 16 December 2017).

The narrative of Thatcherism "as a new ideological doctrine initially commanded most attention. But although there was some debate as to whether Thatcherism was or was not a Conservative doctrine, the real issue quickly became the relationship of this doctrine to the party's new statecraft" (Gamble 1994: 140). Thatcher's ideology became a personal regime, gaining both stronger support and fierce opposition in rural areas. In "New Ethnicities", Hall talks about:

> beginning to think about how to represent a non-coercive and a more diverse conception of ethnicity, to set against the embattled, hegemonic conception of "Englishness" which, under Thatcherism, stabilizes so much of the dominant political and cultural discourses, and which because it is hegemonic does not represent itself as an ethnicity at all (Hall 1992: 258).

Multiculturalism in Britain during the 1980s was still very much localized in the urban areas of the major cities. It was only here where the spatial, material and everyday practices which constructed representations of multiculturalism were beginning to transmit an alternative national identity, one that was not structured around the fallacies of imperialist ideology. However, it would take a long time before it began to counter the fixations of provincial narratives. Even within the more forward-thinking urban areas, the "largely successful creation of a British identity which linked the nations of Great Britain without submerging their distinctive identities" (Lynch 1999: 3), contained cultural identity crises. Mark Cowan explains the experience of living in Falkirk, Scotland during this time, and explicitly states he did not feel a sense of Britishness:

> That was the time of the Thatcher and Tory domination in politics. It was great for London and the south as many people prospered but it was very different at the other end of the UK. Pretty much everyone I knew felt they were treated as second class citizens and looked upon as a class below. Maybe worse when Scotland was used as guinea pigs for the dreaded poll tax a year before it was introduced down south. There were riots here and nothing happened, and not until the riots started in London was it finally scrapped (email to author, 30 April 2017).

The idea of Britishness is firmly linked to the pedagogic narrative, and as Thatcher built a pro-union approach to political rhetoric, the Tories were perceived by many as anti-Scottish. "Thatcherite authoritarian individualism was viewed as distinctly English in heritage and outlook" (Lynch 1999: 108). Yet within England many communities were equally as riled with Thatcher as in Scotland, with the miners' situation still remaining very vivid in people's histories: "the government's dismantling of the coalmining industry in the 1980s and 90s and putting nothing back in their place, essentially pulling the rug from underneath many working class communities" (Nat Drastic, email to author, 4 December 2017). Eraze alludes to the confusion that the Thatcher rhetoric brought to growing up in Devon: "It was quite a revolutionary time anyway, with Scargill and the political unrest of the Thatcher years, there was a lot of stuff going on. It was hard not to be affected by it, but it's also hard to pinpoint exactly why" (i/v, Exeter, 13 March 2017). Stepchild details the experience of these times:

> The "Salubritas Et Industria" (health and hard work) motto on the town's crest (and on my school tie) was sort of lost on us having come up in a pretty angry, lost world that had seemingly nothing to show for either. Divorce was epidemic both at home and in our headz, culturally the sense of "Britishness" had lost its wartime charm... all that was left of it was either on a tea towel or mug 'round your Nan's, it had come to represent all things rich, posh and distant that left—for the rest of us—a rather nasty after-taste of subservience, a sort of "us and them" division that had previously fuelled the solidarity of punk and two-tone and—for now—"England's dreaming"[4]... we had no choice but to look farther away for what was to be the sound of OUR generation (i/v, Swindon, 3 December 2017).

A core sector of British society was disenfranchised by the weight of Thatcherism, only exaggerated by further narratives masquerading as national identity. Discussing Scruton's "In Defence of the Nation", Lynch paraphrases and comments: "Allegiance to authority is a central feature of British nationhood but is undermined by multiculturalism as competing loyalties within the nation-state undermine obligation, shared loyalties and state authority" (Lynch 1999: 163). Writing in 1990, Scruton claims: "Over the last decade it has ceased to be either polite or politic for British subjects to defend the 'national idea' as the foundation of political order" (Scruton 1990: 53), in a bizarre defence of a national loyalty which fails to comprehend the evolving resistances and diversions to this nationhood. In many ways, Scruton's pedagogic narrative harks back to before the British State even existed, as in the early sixteenth century: "Policy aims were highly conservative—to maintain and strengthen control and only to extend it at the least possible cost" (Morgan 1996: 67).

For headz exploring hip hop in provincial Britain, the nation-state pedagogic idea of national identity was diverted by other versions of the performative, through representations of vinyl releases as alternative authoritative voices. This extends Bhabha's "space of cultural signification" (Bhabha 2004: 212), at which point I will return to my three scenarios. "The Buffalo Gals Effect" presents a pedagogic narrative for the identity of hip hop. Exported to Britain through the signifier of the music video and the song itself, it contains a reduced yet canonically acute representation of hip hop which is constructed in the performance of its narrative through the actions of the video and song's subjects. Malcolm McLaren consolidated and framed the pedagogic narrative, and by inclusion of Rock Steady Crew, the World's Famous Supreme Team and Dondi, the performative narratives of hip hop are replayed for the execution of the video. These narratives, originally given shape by their intentional diversion from the official pedagogic narrative of the United States of America, initially became some kind of official story of hip hop to its new audience. If at this point, it is possible to point to 'Buffalo Gals' and affirm "that is hip hop", then a double-edged formation of identity is revealed. "The Buffalo Gals Effect" provided many motifs and tropes of hip hop culture's identity and can be broadened to include those key representations through video, film and music discussed earlier in the book, which blurred the boundaries between definitions of unity and division in American national rhetoric. This obscuring and diverting of the American pedagogic through the representations of hip hop culture ultimately obscured and diverted the operations of the British pedagogic as hip hop's new followers in Britain began to consume, comprehend and practise an acquired performative narrative.

"The Street Sounds Effect" operates similarly to "the Buffalo Gals Effect", although a greater cultural distancing is apparent through the representations of the *Street Sounds Electro* series, not least due to the minimal visual information on the record sleeves. For dwellers in the provinces out of reach of other forms of hip hop presentation (such as Mike Allen's shows and Groove Records charts), there was much less material with which to gain knowledge and build up a narrative of the music contained on these records. Any other information, no matter how miniscule (such as the phrases and definitions on other record sleeves discussed in Chapter 2, and the tiny snippets one might stumble across in other media) was highly valuable to this ongoing quest to understand hip hop's identity. In the narrow window (just shy of two years) between hip hop's arrival and the broadcast of *Beat This! A Hip-Hop History*, there were many followers in the deepest provinces who were not yet even aware that hip hop was first a black culture, let alone rooted in African diaspora and the displacement and treatment of black and Hispanic communities in New York. During this period, followers of hip hop formed an imagined identity, fabricated from the actions of their own exploratory investigations and practices. This fact-finding and filling in of gaps intensified the imagination, and with each small discovery, a heightened desire to belong to something so beguiling yet enrapturing grew stronger, as Stepchild attests:

> Being so far in the outskirts came into its own where hip hop's concerned, it's like we were tuning in to a distant galaxy, odd fragments would crackle through in adverts, music videos, features, movies; we'd collect and add them to our shelf of understanding and interpret them our own way (i/v, Swindon, 3 December 2017).

To borrow a metaphor from Bhabha, the arrival of hip hop caused a "casting of shadows" across the provincial structures of national identity. The true power of hip hop's infiltration can be accounted for when one considers the phenomenon of practising hip hop without knowing it was hip hop, before it had a label. History was repeating itself; the American pioneers in the 1970s could not point to it and say: "that is hip hop", or "that is not hip hop"; hip hop just *was*. In provincial Britain, the signs of hip hop were slowly creeping in, but it was not yet objectified. Stepchild recounts the formative context: "Sugarhill Gang's hit wasn't that big a deal here, just part of the dying disco thing really, we didn't know there was this whole sub-culture attached, the concept of hip hop hadn't reached us yet, for now it was just electro funk" (i/v, Swindon, 3 December 2017). These provincial pioneers did not know it was hip hop, but they were practising hip hop.

"The London Posse Effect" turns to England's capital to unearth what was to become the outward-facing identity of British hip hop. Outward facing in what was to be exported to America, Australia and Europe, and outward facing to the home territories that lay outside the bounds of the M25. In terms of Britishness, this is where the narrative begins. It starts here as the British-made hip hop records before London Posse were arguably emulations of American rap—including the accent and dialect of the emcee. However, once British hip hop had framed its identity and was in control of its future, its journey to other countries became more robust, particularly other historic British colonies reaching those suffering apartheid, as Ariefdien and

Abrahams document in South Africa: "We grew up listening to both US and British hip hop. For many of us, DJ Pogo, MC Mello, and Hijack from the UK were as important as Public Enemy, N.W.A., and 2 Live Crew" (Ariefdien and Abrahams 2006: 264). With the arrival of London Posse in 1987 and the BBC's Open Space documentary *Bad Meaning Good* of the same year (shown in close proximity to Dick Fontaine's *Bombin'*), the hip hop identity that had been evolving in London radiated out into the suburbs, across the counties and into the far-flung depths of rurality. *Bad Meaning Good* was first shown at 7:30pm on Wednesday 5 August 1987 (triggering household arguments across the country as it clashed with ITV's *Coronation Street*).[5] Although hosted by British radio personality Tim Westwood, and with the aim of focus on the emergence of hip hop in London, LL Cool J's 'I'm Bad' is used as the opening theme, and Eric B and Rakim's 'I Know You Got Soul' as the closing theme, both American artists. It is not until almost six minutes into the 31-minute film that we see a hint of British hip hop practice, where the viewer spies DJ Fingers[6] in his bedroom mixing Isaac Hayes' 'Ike's Mood I', Gary Numan's 'Films', and Tom Jones' 'It's Not Unusual'; talking heads interviews are spliced into footage of live and studio performances courtesy of MC Crazy Noddy and DJ Fingers, Cookie Crew and Wee Papa Girl Rappers, Flyboy D and Daddy Speed, and a five-minute article on the London graffiti scene featuring Pride and Nicky covers the rich ground at the dawn of London's true hip hop identity. While it was mind-blowing to witness these homegrown artists performing and gaining an insight into the world of London hip hop, on reflection it is not until London Posse's appearance that London was on the cusp of a definitive shift from the emulation of New York hip hop to the neoteric voice of British hip hop.

With seven minutes to the close of the film, Westwood signs off his KISS-FM show, stating during the broadcast over Schoolly D's 'Saturday Night': "Right I'm outta here, gonna collect the London Posse. Strictly for my homie Bionic the supersonic with the gold in the mouth, going 'round the yard[7] to collect you…with the sound of music, the sound of soul; Bionic this one's for you, I'll be reaching your yard right now" (*Bad Meaning Good*, 1987). Upon collecting Bionic from his yard, Bionic rides in the back of Westwood's Ford Sierra Estate, and explains his approach to emceeing:

> Yeah well, number one, I do it in my own style like I was a reggae emcee before so, I still chat reggae lyrics and I do it in a rap style, but in a Yardie accent and I'd use my own Cockney accent.[8] I don't rap in an American accent or nuttin', like; that's what's

keeping English people back, rapping in their American accents instead of being in English accents (*Bad Meaning Good*, 1987).

To British headz, this was a revelation. Throughout the previous interviews, viewers had witnessed the first generation of British artists committed to vinyl talking naturally in their regional accents, while hearing their recordings and performances delivered in Americanized voices. Yet this was not perceived as problematic until London Posse's message. Brent Aquasky corroborates this view:

> *Bad Meaning Good* came out and then you saw Bionic and Rodney P and the way they added their flavour and I think that probably inspired a ton of others, the next swarm of rappers that came out in this country, that probably saw that at the time and thought, "we have got a scene and we don't need to follow the Americans. We can be influenced by Americans, but we don't need to follow them" (i/v, Bournemouth, 12 December 2017).

Shortly after this enlightenment, Westwood pulls over to collect Sipho, London Posse's human beatbox. Following a brief explanation of beatboxing, Bionic and Sipho launch into a rendition of 'My Beatbox Reggae Style' where Bionic incorporates Yardie and cockney dialect such as "spar, seckle, Jah know, bredrin, 'pon, gwarn" and "lads", and fluctuates between deep Jamaican Yardie and cockney accents. Before London Posse's self-titled debut EP and these moments in *Bad Meaning Good*, the only British reggae emcees that would have reached the provinces were Smiley Culture[9] and Pato Banton,[10] both of whom are of interest to the formative identity of British hip hop. Smiley Culture's singles 'Cockney Translation' and 'Police Officer' both offered cultural contextual narratives surrounding issues of identity. 'Cockney Translation' was presented as a guidebook for Jamaicans to the London East End speak, but was equally apt as a guide for non-Jamaicans to Yardie dialect through comedic comparative lyrics like: "Cockneys have names like Terry, Arfur and Del Boy / We have names like Winston, Lloyd and Leroy", and "You know dem have wedge while we have corn / Say cockney say be first, my son! We just say Gwan!" Pato Banton also bridges native British dialect with Yardie styles and exhibits an obvious relationship with hip hop through 1985's 'Hip Hop Lyrical Robot', where his substantial rap mutates between Yardie, British and American accents and dialects. His finest lyrics are on 'Gwarn!' (1985), where the narrative in the second verse recounts the stress of suffering a broken television and the widespread British culture of renting TV sets from Rediffusion:[11]

> Like a house is not a home without a television
> If you don't believe me ask my woman
> She will tell you when me mash up the telly
> When me mash up the telly
> When me mash up the television
> Is like the whole house was in contention
> The kids were giving me a lot of botheration
> Bawling "waah waah waah I wanna see Batman
> A-Team, Danger Mouse and He-Man"
> There was only one way I could solve the problem
> Which was to catch a taxi down to Rediffusion
> Rent a telly take it home and plug it in and turn it on
> When my woman see the telly she say "honey you fe
> Just just just just just just just Gwarn!"

Although these artists were active several years before London Posse and transcended some of the narratives of hip hop, aspects of Britishness and reggae music so beautifully, the major difference was not so much in the vocal disposition and delivery but rather the music itself, and moreover, the surge of hip hop culture in Britain. Reggae moved in waves through rural areas of Britain, and Junior Disprol from Bridgend, Wales explains the transition from reggae to hip hop:

> Brackla was farm land surrounded by trees and fields next to industrial estates, Bridgend town and other small villages. Coming from Cardiff it felt medieval. Alongside the Reggae they put us onto hip hop and dubbed us tapes of Doug E. Fresh and Slick Rick, Whistle and *Rap It Up* which was a compilation LP, I was hooked (email to author, 2 June 2017).

Writing in 1987 (the same year as London Posse's debut 12" and *Bad Meaning Good*), Hebdige recognizes the multiplicity of music culture in the mix, but particularly those overlaps with hip hop and reggae, and also acknowledges the part that Bristol played in this early scene: "In Bristol in South West England a hip hop DJ called Milo (the Bassmonger) is now scratching break-beats into reggae rhythms at clubs and parties… Yellowman makes a toast-rapping record with Afrika Bambaataa" (Hebdige 2000: 157). Of course, London Posse were not the first British hip hop artists: half a decade earlier the likes of Junior Gee, Dizzy Heights, and City Limits Crew were pioneering rap in London, but also rapped largely in American accents. So, on one hand existed the reggae/DJ crossover artists (Smiley Culture et al.) and on the other the hip hop/electro pioneers (Junior Gee et al.), yet while there was hip hop in Britain, there was no identifiable sense of Britishness in hip hop. I emphasize here that I am not dissing these artists who appropriate American phraseology, accents and dialect—they are the pioneers of British hip hop and for that they deserve utmost respect—but it was a pivotal moment for me when I first heard London Posse. The cultural fusion that they brought to hip hop grown from their own environments created a paradigm shift in the devolution of hip hop from a core American source, and subsequently launched the next stage of progression for hip hop in Britain. London Posse took a vocal and lyrical lead from the contextualization and ethos of the reggae emcees and a sonic approach from the sounds of American hip hop artists; and laden with cuts and samples from The Meters, tight beatboxing and Yardie-infused culturally relevant lyrics, an innate form of British hip hop arrived. However, London Posse were not the only crew developing a sense of Britishness in 1987, some of whom are discussed in the next section; but they were certainly the crew that had the most widespread impact in the provinces at this point. The narrative of the performative had begun to cast a shadow across the pedagogic thresholds of the countryside.

The three effects discussed in this section were paramount to the ways in which provincial headz identified with hip hop, and foundational in the building of an identifiable Britishness, a new heritage and a critical regionalism in hip hop. The next section, "Reality", challenges one of the most common phrases pronounced in hip hop: "keep it real", and here I interrogate this idea by asking what is it to be real in hip hop, and how can a realness manifest in the provinces? What is the identity of hip hop in the provinces, in a cultural arena that is staged as a strictly urban heterotopia? This is explored through a sonic and experiential reading of other formative British hip hop (produced at the same time as London Posse's debut). The section "Image" then draws upon a broader pool of British hip hop artefacts and events that epitomize the new Britishness and frames them within the provincial context. In the final section of this chapter, "A State of Mind" relates the local and the regional with the global issues in hip hop to solidify its critical regionalism and to present an alternative, rich education as counter to the pedagogic narrative of the nation-state.

Reality

To "keep it real" in hip hop culture, suggests that "it" (where the "it" refers to whatever element, practice, moment or event that requires the need for the statement) is in jeopardy of becoming unreal, or not real, or possibly surreal in any given situation demanding the use of the phrase. Simon Reynolds (1996) describes a two-fold sense of what is "real" in terms of hip hop, the most relevant here being: "First, it means authentic, uncompromised music that refuses to sell out to the music industry and soften its message for crossover".[12] Forman positions "the real" as a distinctive quality within hip hop culture:

> "The Real" has also emerged through the years as a uniquely resonant concept within hip hop culture and has accordingly been granted close attention here. In most cases it stands as an ill-defined expression referring to combined aspects of racial essentialism, spatial location, and a basic adherence to the principles and practices of the hip hop culture (Forman 2002: xviii).

Forman's description is rooted in the context of place, space and the 'hood, and its ethos and operations in relation to hip hop are undeniable. Ruzicka et al. observe that in Eastern and East-central Europe, the practices of hip hop are employed as a way to explore social vexation: "Rap is viewed by our informants as a tool for reflecting social reality, not fantasy or fictional stories" (2017: 220), and in exploring the authenticity in Czech rap, Oravcová outlines: "Whether they are rapping about materialism, flaunting their success, or claiming to be 'real' because they focus on the quality of expression and on a message with a substance, one thing all of these MCs have in common is the expression of their lived reality through rap" (Oravcová 2017: 272). Craig states: "In hip hop, there is an adage that has remained relevant as the language and rhetorical patterns of the culture have changed. That adage is 'keep it real'. The focus of this statement truly means to keep things brutally honest, truthful, raw, and uncut" (Craig 2017: 283). He continues to describe the tipping point between keeping it real and the pressures of broader cultural dynamics:

> Sometimes, to "keep it 100"[13] does not fall in line with popular sentiment, but requires one to completely go against the grain of what popular culture describes as "real", "authentic", and "true"

> ...to "keep it 100" means to stay true to oneself, regardless of what the outcome may be... The fact of the matter remains: to "keep it 100" is a straight hip hop paradigm...make NO mistake about it (Craig 2017: 283).

Elsewhere I suggest that realness links to identity through visual, sonic and spatial representations: "A broader sense of realness encompasses attitude, actions and the way in which one presents and displays oneself, often using material things as support mechanisms" (de Paor-Evans 2018a: 171). However, this is not without risk:

> In other words, a habitus is created based on the material culture of hip hop to reinforce one's realness and propagate what is deemed tasteful. Often though, this imagined realness is a constructed fabrication and not a contextual reality of one's self. Striving to be real, results in the unreal (de Paor-Evans 2018a: 171).

The things, objects, artefacts and spaces that one utilizes to frame one's realness require close attention, and an honest conversation with oneself. Mike Mac[14] endorses more of the self and less of the material:

> "Keep it real" couldn't be further from the truth in our ego massaging, cash driven society; but rap was always the truth I needed to hear and couldn't get anywhere else. This truth, although rarer to find, is "keeping it real" to me. That's why everyone should be themselves (i/v, Bristol, 20 April 2018).

Whirlwind D comments that the term "keeping it real" is "first and foremost a massive cliché", and continues to explain its empty existence due to overuse and misappropriation: "it's almost meaningless now because I guess at its root it's about being true to yourself but ultimately who can say what is real to someone else...'keeping it real' is doing what you want to do creatively, not being stifled by other people's vision of you" (i/v, Salisbury, 21 April 2018).

These considerations of "keeping it real" and "reality" fall quite distinctly into two halves of the same complex whole. If "keeping it real" is to stay true to one's self, one's belief and immersion in hip hop culture and the ethos of street, 'hood, city, or whatever other environment within which one dwells, then "reality" is the very essence of that environment. This environment is of course far from limited to the physical make-up of its built fabric but is constructed of the emotions and meanings of the environment with which one identifies. Furthermore, this environment fluctuates between the local, regional, national and international. Discussing authenticity, McLeod (2012) observes: "Invocations of authenticity are not used by all members of the hip hop community. Further, the use of keepin' it real and other such authenticity claims are openly contested by some" (McLeod 2012: 173). Keeping it real does risk self-parody, but in the British provincial the evolution of its own identity necessitated a reality. Pitcher's exploration in *Consuming Race* (2014) also touches upon this:

> Drawing implicitly on the familiar injunction in transnational hip hop culture against cultural betrayal (keeping it real, not selling out), the characteristics of "street" reference an unaffected connectedness to an idea of cultural origin, and are bolstered by older meanings in which the street is conceived as a place of ordinary or working-class identity (Pitcher 2014: 94).

This is especially true of London hip hop and the britcore sound: the working-class identity represented in the housing estates of Clapham, Streatham, Tottenham, Finsbury, Peckham, Stockwell, Brixton (and the list continues) was the absolute context for the birth of British underground hip hop. As Craig mentions, the adage "keep it real" feels as though it has always been attached to and continues to be central to the progress of hip hop, and this adage became more siloed with the creation of britcore, therefore it is important to explore britcore's origins through British hardcore hip hop to provide what I will call the "context of the real" in Britain. I should explain here that britcore was invented as a terminology to describe hardcore British rap music, but the term was invented somewhat retrospectively as well as outside Britain. Coined in 1994 in Europe (most headz will suggest Germany, but also Switzerland and Austria have been offered up as locations for the invention of the term), it is now used widely to identify the underground British sound of the first-generation hardcore artists from 1988 to 1993.[15] Additionally, the sub-genre of britcore has grown and still experiences buoyancy in Europe; furthermore there are European artists still working under this banner, as well as a new generation of British hip hop practitioners such as Planet of the Fakes and The Mantis Chapter. Interestingly, German labels such as Britcore Rawmance have also recently been issuing lost tapes and demos from the first generation of provincial artists that were lesser known than the original London crews such as Def Defiance and Krack Free Media.[16] Although a majority of headz are indifferent about the name "britcore", what the term has done for any form of reflective or historical analysis on the scene is not only provide the descriptive definition of the sound, but through close examination of britcore music aid an understanding of its context and what it was aiming to achieve. Furthermore, and of most importance to this book, the context of britcore furthers an understanding of the provincial context of the real.

Considering what britcore means, Specifik suggests:

> Hardcore UK rap or britcore as it's now known, is a reflection of gritty inner-city life and melancholic mind state, which I believe is a reflection of our climate and mood in the UK during the late 1980s and early 1990s. Hardcore to many is a mindset that helps people believe they are not selling out. It's anarchic and goes against the grain (p/c, Bournemouth, 21 April 2018).

Big Tunes D perceives britcore as:

> The sound of the ghetto in many ways. It's got that aggressive undertone, that reminds you of the punk scene back in the day… and hardcore, it's just got that raw essence…it just reminds me of when you get your early New York Bronx experience, hardcore graffiti…it's everything raw about hip hop, it's the rawest element of hip hop, I would say (i/v, Gloucester, 22 April 2018).

It is no surprise that the britcore sound retains a currency comparable with the DIY ethos and punk sound of underground Berlin. In the West Germany state of Schleswig-Holstein, the sounds of the British hip hop scene grew through sharing pirated tapes. Requiem89, from Itzehoe, recalls:

> Demon Boyz and Overlord X were other UK Rap acts I was digging back then; and later in 1991 a mixtape was handed around that had Gunshot's 'Battle Creek Brawl'; Blade's 'Forward' and Silver Bullet's '20 Seconds to Comply' on it. Gosh that tape was mind-blowing to me and my friends. The term britcore was not yet established at the time we first heard that stuff (email to author, 7 March 2017).

As the pivotal British hardcore records were released, they made their way to Germany via mixtapes and radio shows. Berlin's Rawman (and head of Britcore Rawmance, a niche contemporary independent label specializing in britcore) remembers:

> I found another show on East German radio, called *The YO Show*, hosted by Andre Langenfeld. So, I added this to my usual recording sessions, another source and better understanding of what was going on. Once there was a UK special, playing all the good stuff like Katch 22, Black Radical MKII, Cash Crew etc, and I got an idea about the British stuff. I was deep into Public Enemy, so that was the best thing I could have from there on (email to author, 9 February 2017).

Style Wars: The Evolution of Hardcore Hip-hop

Around the time of London Posse's debut, a very particular London-centric hardcore sound began to command British hip hop, which radiated from the capital across Britain. This was the cutting-edge sound of the capital, and it was music inspired as much by ska, reggae culture and the electro and jazz-funk movements as well as the effects of Thatcherism and the British reach of African and Jamaican-Caribbean diaspora. British headz were additionally enthused by this hardcore hip hop as it began to position itself as something counter to American rap. 1987 was a pivotal year in the canon of American hip hop music; it produced revolutionary debut albums *Paid In Full* by Eric B and Rakim, *Criminal Minded* by Boogie Down Productions, Public Enemy's *Yo! Bum Rush The Show* and MC Shan's Marley Marl produced *Down By Law*, as well as LL Cool J's kaleidoscopic *Bigger and Deffer*, the dense and original gangster sound of Schoolly D's *Saturday Night*, and T La Rock's old school reimagined *Lyrical King (From The Boogie Down Bronx)* largely produced by Mantronik. All of these American albums were received with love in Britain and remain stone-cold exemplars representing the dawn of what has become to be known as "hip hop's golden age", drawing upon a plethora of references and designing fresh styles which proved to critics and devotees that hip hop music had the flexibility to sustain itself. It was also entering a period of maturity and began to solidify the sound that would carry it through the next decade, aided by the sampler, Marley Marl's ground-breaking sample techniques and the montaging of full patterns of sampled music (*Yo! Bum Rush The Show* epitomizes this).[17]

Britain, however, was undergoing a transformation of its own. While British hip hop did exist on vinyl prior to 1987 with milestone records such as 'Style of The Street' (1984) by Broken Glass, The City Limits Crew's 'Fresher than Ever!' (1985), Grandmaster Richie Rich's 'Don't Be Flash' (1985), and 'Sleepwalking' by Family Quest (1986), the new sound of hardcore British hip hop can arguably be pinpointed to 'Here To Win' (1987) by London-based Faze One, which appeared on their only album *Heroes*. Produced by Dave Ogrin[18] and executively produced by Morgan Khan,[19] the song was the first by a British artist to sample James Brown's 'Funky Drummer' break through its entirety;[20] previously this had only been heard on American recordings such as Kool G Rap & DJ Polo's 'It's a Demo' (1986), 'Cars' by Afrika & the Zulu Kings (1986) and Easy Mike's 'The State We're In/It's Too Political' (1986). Whirlwind D[21] agrees: "The first real sound that I guess we now call britcore had to be Faze One's 'Here To Win', it kind of slipped under the radar I think but it definitely has that sound, it's a shame it didn't do better, it's a dope track" (i/v, Bournemouth, 8 December 2017). Ogrin clearly brought his understanding and experience in producing heavy drum and percussive patterns to Faze One's project. 'Here to Win' pioneers horror tropes in its lyrical content such as: "I'm back, evil and black", "low and behold, there is the evil", "roaring like a lion, devouring suckers", and "I'm heating up, the blood of kings flowing in one cup", aggrandized by reversed reverb on the vocal tracks, underlaid with dynamic and relentless cuts. The song's aggression plays out across just over four minutes, with emcees Stepski and Genio sparring over four verses, as even more echo-heavy samples, cow bells and sound effect drops litter the chorus sections. Sadly, this song was buried too deep among the rest of the album (much of which unfortunately is mediocre) and did not draw the attention it deserved but exemplifies the precursory attitude of britcore.

British hardcore hip hop embodies the attributes of its American predecessor through stripped-down instrumentation and favouring of heavy drum patterns (loud in the mix and particularly evident in Run-D.M.C.'s 'Sucker M.C.s' from 1983), minimal but powerful basslines, enraged lyrical content and delivery, and violent scratches and cuts. Hardcore hip hop has, over time, become incorrectly and disappointingly associated with the global reading of gangsta rap, which although fitting when other pioneers of hardcore hip hop such as Schoolly D and Too $hort enter the debate, the gangsta rap genre of the late 1980s triggered by the N.W.A. phenomenon swiftly became formulaic and, contrary to usual thought, quite safe in terms of corporate music production. The true course of hardcore hip hop follows Run-D.M.C. with songs such as Mantronix's 'Hardcore Hip Hop' (1985), 'That's Deep' by Doctor J.R. Kool (1986) and 'B-Boy Document' by Krown Rulers (1987), all of which carry the attitude towards hard, loud percussion and dark sample snippets. An unprecedented number of American hardcore hip hop records followed in 1988 largely due to the influence of Paul "C" McKasty's engineering skills, which set the benchmark for tough sounding hip hop. For many hardcore hip hop followers, 1988 arguably remains the most important year for the volume of quality American hip hop records produced. It is not unusual for provincial British hip hop headz to regard British output of the same era as comparable.

Run-D.M.C. were the primary crew that characterized the notion of hardcore, and donning matching black trilby hats, Adidas tracksuits and black leather jackets their image displayed a seriousness and the realness of the street that appeared to embody that of controlled fury. Their performances were bellicose, and both Run and D.M.C. would stomp up and down the stage, occupying its entirety and incorporating exaggerated and jagged physical gestures (particularly Run), enticing and antagonistic, much in discord with the more P-funk influenced visual representations carried by other hip hop artists of the time.[22] While much American hardcore hip hop's narrative is informed by street lifestyle, whose emcees acquire the role of hero-antihero-protagonist-antagonist, recounting stories related to battle, riches and pursuit,[23] British hardcore often contains themes connected to horror. Hijack's second release in 1988, a 12" EP for Music of Life, includes 'Hold No Hostage' and 'Doomsday Of Rap', and if London Posse's self-titled EP was a point of departure from the Americanized assemblages of the previous five years, Hijack's offering represents a definite point of arrival for British hardcore hip hop. While 'Style Wars' (Music of Life, 1988) delivered a powerful debut with intense, crisp raps loaded with 'Blow Your Head' samples,[24] the speed of both songs on 'Hold No Hostage' step up to a tremendous and unprecedented pace of 126bpm.[25] Kamanchi Sly delivers acutely accurate raps, expressing his dismay for commercial hip hop songs that sample predictable James Brown breaks: "The money maker hip-hop faker / Perpetrator and James Brown rhythm taker / For some monies raked in the sale / Now K. Sly must write true hate mail" ('Doomsday Of Rap', verse two), and concludes the song with:

> Styles Wars was the first to open eyes
> Flick with the wrist invent a stone tone twitch
> The group they grip and rip to evict

> It's the scratch that summons death
> Feel remorse in hell the last breath
> Those bells sounding the knell
> Summoning suckers to heaven or hell

Such was the reality of hip hop in the music industry in Britain, taking issue with the commercialized world was a common topic in the British underground, and to do so makes strong suggestions about one's awareness and "realness" in their practice; again, this was often illustrated through metaphors of horror. If what makes up the context of the real is most importantly to stay true to the essence of hip hop, one's self and one's environment, then Hijack fully achieved a state of realness. The environment in 'Hold No Hostage' is the false promises of industry and the misinterpretation of hip hop by sell-out artists, effectively a commentary on the incredible poor handling of hip hop culture in the British industry as major labels (and indeed, many independent labels too) had no idea how to work hip hop. The identity that was growing within the underground scene was not supported by industry, and artists rapidly understood that there coexisted an uneasy correlation between major labels and the socio-politics of Britishness, as the music industry hailed the arrival of acid and rave as if they were something Britain had created. This only served to drive British hip hop more underground, and more hardcore, and the DIY ethic (borrowed from punk) entered the context of the real.

Blade, who remains one of the most active and underground hip hop artists in Britain, practised the DIY ethic to the fullest. Rejecting offers of recording contracts (by Def Jam Recordings among others), he practised a version of realness where he consistently made hardcore underground records by embracing the DIY ethic and self-funded his own releases, firstly on his Raw Bass label and then subsequently on 691 Influential.[26] Blade's approach was so proudly underground that on his fourth release 'Rough It Up' (1991), the front cover adorned a hype label that read: "Pre-release product not for sale except on street corners and Groove", celebrating the fact he was without a distribution deal. Blade's previous EP releases 'Lyrical Maniac' (1989) and 'Mind Of An Ordinary Citizen/Forward' (1990) had positioned him as a strong artist in the field, and his tenacity was fuelled by his cultural context in the hip hop world and in his Armenian roots. 'Forward' is an intensely fast record, exacerbated by Blade's urgent delivery over the relentless samples of Bobby Byrd's 'I'm Coming' (Brownstone, 1971) and Baby Huey's 'Listen To Me' (Curtom, 1971), and hectic cuts by DJ Renegade.

The ethos of Leighton Buzzard's Silver Bullet draws heavily on the premise of horror. His debut release 'Bring Forth The Guillotine' (1989)[27] builds upon these themes; the sample-heavy song opens with the atmospherics of ESG's 'UFO' (99 Records, 1981) before launching into a 126bpm loop of James Brown's 'Super Bad' (King Records, 1971) laden with the sound effects of fired bullets, werewolves howling and stormscapes, and complex lyrics such as: "…ammo decks the bells / Seducing seductive coincide kill constructive / Sucker in the side so what destruct him / Detonation ammo decides when to slice and when his cuts perfect", and, "…can you feel death reapers interrogation / This ordeal to kill for real that's the deal / The debris will swill while the rhyme just bills". Further lyrical references to demons, snakes, exorcism, execution and requiem support the parallel themes of the metaphysical and consternation. The immediate sense of panic that this production induces upon listening leads not to anxiety, but to excitement. 'Untitled' by Hardnoise is arguably the finest moment in British hip hop on vinyl. 'Untitled' enthused the generation of its time to feel as though they could take full control of hip hop. Musically, the song comprises two percussion-heavy samples that form its structure: the intense drum breaks from 'Apache' by Michael Viner's Incredible Bongo Band (Pride, 1973) and 'Let A Woman Be A Woman, Let A Man Be A Man' by Dyke and the Blazers (Original Sound, 1969) underpin industrially oriented noise (largely from Marvin Gaye's '"T" Plays it Cool' of 1972) and hectic lyrical sparring between emcees TLP1 and Gemini. From the first brief verse by TLP1 commanding "…Hardnoise, start the panic!" to the final phrase by Gemini "…break it down suicidal!" the song exhaustively delivers such penetrating sound that challenges any suggestion of a more exemplary hardcore hip hop record. 'Untitled' is one of the most enigmatic of hardcore records, and with no clear theme or agenda delivers the power of British hip hop in an unprecedented way. Killa Instinct's 'The Bambi Murders' continues many of the ideas explored above, and further champions hardcore percussion in sampling the "Amen break",[28] frantic cuts and lyrics saturated with hostility and horror references: "…come on in a common kamikaze / Near machete ready, bad boy be the barrier / (the barrier!) / The living dead, me taking a shotgun with me / Running with the runner, run and gun down the enemy". A simple survey of British hip hop artists' names of the pioneering hardcore era of 1988–1992 reveals a clear message that aims to raise this sense of urgency. Gunshot, The Icepick, Huntkillbury Finn, Demon Boyz, Overlord X, First Frontal Assault, Point Blank, and Insane Macbeth, not to mention Hijack's tagline "The Terrorist Group", are all loaded with connotations to horror and terror.

The thematics discussed so far in this chapter begin to solidify the identity of the British underground. Thatcherism, horror, racism, commercialism and selling out coupled with overtly complex battle rhymes framed a distinct agenda for hardcore Britishness. However, keeping British hip hop real was not all about lyrical content, and cuts and scratches were crucial to underpin the soundtrack, to drop bombs, explosions, screams, sirens and horns, raising the alarm in the apocalyptic heat. Craig pleas for hip hop scholarship to 'Keep it 360' (Craig 2017: 283–96), a spin on "keep it real" and "keep it 100", to increase the presence of the DJ within scholarly discussion.[29] He argues quite eloquently that:

> The DJ—who utilizes the 360 degrees of circular vinyl and constantly connects elements of the past, present, and future though music. This idea moves the DJ full circle into hip hop historian, tastemaker, and trendsetter. Because, let's keep it 100: there would be no such thing as hip hop without the DJ (Craig 2017: 283–84).

Keeping it 100, I would support Craig's status of the hip hop DJ and its value in the British underground for two crucial reasons. Firstly, within the creation of British hip hop music, specifically during the era in question, to make music without a DJ would be absurd. Throughout every song by London Posse, Blade, Hardnoise (who along with Hijack included multiple DJs—more DJs than emcees, in fact), Gunshot, Demon Boyz, Caveman—almost without exception—the input of the DJ anchors everything. This was "keeping it 360". Cuts and scratches did much more than merely lace tracks; they balanced the emcee, provided ballast and brought harmony to the music, and emphasized the concept of songs. Providing intros, outros and linkages between emcees, the furious sounds of DJ Renegade, DJ Supreme, White Child Rix…and the list goes on, would be celebrated on record, not just at live performances: "Enter the scene DJ Supreme!… DJ Undercover, serves!" ('Doomsday Of Rap'), "Once again, Renegade, enter!" ('Forward'), and "White Child Rix!" ('Battle Creek Brawl').

In British hip hop, the DJ was the focal point of music production, and a key figure in its identity growth. With Manchester's Chad Jackson and London's Cutmaster Swift taking the crown at the 1987 and 1989 DMC World DJ Championships respectively, British DJs were gaining greater visibility, and this radiated out across the provinces. However, the DJ had been an anchor for lo-urban and rural crews since the mid-1980s, and the second point I want to make revolves around this anchorage. Craig mentions the DJ as one who "constantly connects elements of the past, present, and future though music" (Craig 2017: 283), and as well as illuminate these connections through their creative practice as in the case of DJ Renegade et al., there is also a much subtler and slower turning series of connections that occur—these connections are found in DJs' record collections. Returning for a moment to the notion of the bedroom discussed in Chapter 3, here DJs would collect and assemble, curating a vinyl archive to be explored, re-assembled and appropriated. I am not suggesting practitioners of other elements did not collect records, they did of course, but the DJ's collection is different: in appearance, organization, practicality, customization and use. Not only am I referring to a collection which acts as a library of sound, or a tactile history constructed of artefact, but a knowledge that knows each record intimately. Knowing exactly where the break is in that Bob James track, at what point the bells switch up, almost without a glance the DJ intimately knows the innermost secrets of 'Take Me To The Mardi Gras'.[30]

Thin strips of parcel tape, price stickers, sticky dots, arrows drawn in marker pens of assorted colours, and correction fluid, were used to demarcate the beginning and end of breaks, of words and phrases, noises and sound effects on vinyl that became the DJ's source material (see Figure 6.1). Scholars and practitioners have talked about the turntable as an instrument, most clearly Mark Katz who asserts defiantly: "The significance is easy to state, and I repeat: Grandmaster Flash and Grand Wizard Theodore transformed the turntable into a musical instrument" (Katz 2012: 61; see also Tanaka 2009, Webber 2003, Smith 2016). These records almost transformed into instruments themselves. As well as the customized visual cues, it was also possible to see where the groove had worn; upon close inspection, one could see the music. In each of these records was not only the story of the record and the music pressed into the vinyl, but the narratives ingrained and inscribed into it during its life in the hands of the DJ. This is more than an archive, this is vinyl as palimpsest, a rich history both personal and international. The importance of these records as active sources for hip hop's identity and realness was vital to lo-urban and rural headz; the major gateway to hip hop culture for those provincial DJs was through the artefacts, the reifications and the objects of hip hop, the things they could touch.

The Identity of Hip Hop 247

Figure 6.1: The visual clues of a typical marked-up record denoting start points for different scratch and cut bites. Photograph by author.

Image

So far in this chapter I have discussed the shift in Britishness as an alternate position to the pedagogic canon of the nation-state through the context of the real and the practices of British underground hip hop. This section explores the images of regionalism, and how the context of the real was represented and channelled between the polis, the rural and harder to reach provinces. This reach occurred through two main dynamics: live performances and record releases. Mainstream radio was still not playing much in the way of hip hop, and although some regional stations were latching onto rap music sporadically, there was little to no airplay given over to British hip hop, apart from commercial cross-over tunes. Bramwell states:

> In the late 1980s the Cookie Crew's singles 'Females' and 'Got To Keep On' as well as Monie Love's 'Monie In The Middle' and 'It's A Shame' adopted American hip hop styles. Rebel MC, whose single 'Street Tough' [Tuff, *sic*] reached number three in the UK charts, contributed to a distinctive reorientation in British music by combining US styles and techniques with his Caribbean cultural resources (Bramwell 2015b: 256).

The success of 'Got To Keep On' may also be attributed to the sample of Kraftwerk's 'Numbers' (1981) upon which the song is built, offering a clear nod to the electro sounds of the previous generation. While this may be the case, Cookie Crew experienced greater chart triumph on 'Rok Da House' by The Beatmasters (an electronic and house production crew)[31] which reached number five, and six months prior to 'Monie In The Middle' and 'It's A Shame', Monie Love's 'Grandpa's Party' reached number sixteen and enjoyed nine weeks in the Hit Parade.[32] Produced by Dancin' Danny D[33] (head A&R man at Chrysalis at this point), 'Grandpa's Party' capitalized on the fleeting hip-house scene. House music, the rave scene and Madchester were taking over mainstream media attention, largely due to the movements' associations with ecstasy, acid and other controlled substances, and illegal parties; it was really no surprise that the hip-house crossover tunes thrived. Manchester and London were the geographic focal points for the music industry and music media who sought to capitalize on this trend, yet bizarrely in the guts of the countryside where the illegal raves which were playing this music were happening, local rappers were sidelined.[34]

Whereas interesting and successful crossover transcended house and hip hop, and Monie Love, Susie Q and Remedee (Cookie Crew) were talented emcees, there was a frustration amongst the hip hop community as the message from thriving labels was that artists needed to "sound like…" (enter name of any charting artist of that week). Indeed, I experienced this when a temporary crew I was part of recorded a demo tape for BMG in 1989. BMG had approached DJ Hurry (from S.A.S., a well-regarded Plymouth DJ crew) as they were seeking to sign an artist with a hip-house sound (to compete with the artists aforementioned). Initially, Rola and I were slightly uncomfortable with the idea, but we did complete the project, and focusing on our vocals, we were content with the output. After several weeks of some tense and quite bizarre exchanges between BMG and our DJs, largely surrounding the issue of how the vocals sounded (most likely a euphemism for "we don't like your rural accents"), the project ceased. To move from a position where I strongly believed we would be signed, to one of outright rejection was puzzling, but a firm lesson in the actions of certain major labels and their approach. BMG envisioned what they wanted—and it was not us—but the relationships and jarring differences between how mass media was perceiving hip hop, the reality of underground hip hop, and provincial headz' acuity for hip hop was reinforced by image. As popular media continually misread or ignored the context of the real, a seismic change was underway with the rise of London-based indie labels (some owned by global parent labels, such as Mango Street/Mango Records/Island Records). This was a critical juncture between the urban underground and the far corners of the provinces.

One significant yet less celebrated 1987 British album is deserving of entering the conversation at this point. Before Mango Street and other sub-labels had become intrigued by British hip hop, *Known 2 Be Down* (Positive Beat Records) presented a snapshot of London underground hip hop. Produced by J. Woodburn (Zanga Zeb) and K.J. Plange (Skorpi Gad), the album is a collection of ten songs by various artists including The She Rockers Crew, Sir Drew, and Rapski. The sleeve features a portrait of all the artists as a collective, posing in front of a piece by No Limits Cru (with the title work based on an idea by Skam), reminiscent of Art Kane's exemplary 1958 photograph of jazz greats in "A Great Day in Harlem". Rola comments on the appearance of the record: "It was all about the cover for me, just to see a group of UK headz rockin' all that style. I'm sure a lot of peeps like us would have based the way they dressed on that cover" (email to author, 24 January 2018). To the provincial head, the front cover signposts everything desirable about a British context for hip hop. Rola's phrase "rockin' all that style" tunes into the underground habitus, and without a hint of turntables or microphones, this cover shouts "hip hop". Although the tropes used here are widely hip hop, the style that Rola refers to makes it discernibly British (Figure 6.2). From left to right 18 artists stand in Bboy stances and poses, all making direct eye contact with the viewer, donning a range of fresh gear. Sir Drew and Rapski pose in full tracksuits designed by Fila; others wear tracksuit bottoms by Adidas and a range of casual denim jeans by designers such as Chevignon and Chipie (with the random square and diamond-shaped patches). Fila, Nike and Adidas shelltoes can be spotted, as well as a splattering of black and brown casual shoes. Black leather caps, 8-Panel Newsboys and leather deerstalkers are worn by Papa Speng and DJ Dee; She Rockers are clad in denim, black MA-1 flight jackets and jumpers; and the Fly Girls are dressed chicly in trouser-suits and scarves. The wall behind—a backdrop drenched in vibrant graffiti—enveloped the artists and fully communicates graffiti's position in British hip hop. Although many of the designer clothes that are part of this image were also worn, and championed by, American hip hop artists,[35] it is the combination of style that generates a hip hop Britishness. By fusing Americanized and Italian sports brands with apparel donned by Britain's football casuals and British-Jamaican Yardies, an alternative wardrobe was created. Furthermore, the distinction is made clearer between British football hooligans and casuals with hip hop headz in the way in which they adorned themselves with their clothing and accessories. The distance between these looks increases as headz accessorize with name-belt buckles and other forms

Figure 6.2: *Known 2 Be Down*, 1987, front cover. Photograph by author.

The Identity of Hip Hop 251

of jewelry, adding fat laces to trainers and lifting the tongues out of the top of the shoe to ride high proud of the trouser leg. Some of these stylistic moves were seen before, of course (the Run-D.M.C. video for 'Walk This Way' from 1986 comes immediately to mind), but this was the first instance where the image of the British underground was portrayed with such gusto.

This imagery served as an inspiration and was empowering to those headz in far-flung rural areas who began to accessorize in similar ways, seeking appropriate alternatives where the objects of desire were not available. MC Flex wears a leather jacket with a fur-trimmed hood, slung low over the shoulders, reminiscent of the holy grail of jackets—the full leather double goose. Dressing in such a highly desirable jacket would grant immediate kudos, as DJ Format (then living in Chandler's Ford, Hampshire, a "boring place and not somewhere typically you'd find any hip hop or too many people into hip hop" [i/v, Brighton, 17 December 2017]), animates:

> I didn't even know about double goose back then, made with leather, I mean I'm talking about the Sunday market, you'd have a black bomber jacket, real cheap piece of crap, that had a horrible cheap white fur collar on it; and I wanted one of these like you wouldn't believe. I would've killed for one of those jackets, but I remember my mum and dad damn near crying with laughter when they saw them down the Sunday market—and I'm flipping out—and they're going, "that's the worst thing we've ever seen" and literally laughing! I'm like, "you don't understand, it's literally the coolest thing and I've got to have one" and they're laughing at me like, "no way are we buying one of those!" And I didn't have any money, what was I gonna do?! (i/v, Brighton, 17 December 2017).

Format's humorous recollection here points to an important image-shift from urban to provincial—another version of class-taste which is based on availability of apparel and accessories for provincial dwellers (refer also to the experience of Kilo and the Master Blast crew's matching tracksuits in Chapter 3). Junior Disprol's encounter is comparable with that of DJ Format's:

> I did identify myself as a hip hopper, but I didn't always have the funds for others to identify me as such, literally couldn't afford it. It was a change in circumstances when we moved to the sticks so those pre-disposable-cash-years I'd have to choose what I wanted

more for Christmas, records or daps [trainers]. It was a fucker because of the dress code, heh. I think it made me a bit more resilient though and less give a fuck. When I was old enough, I got a job after school at a Lo-Cost and used to save up and go to London to visit 4 Star General and Mash and kitted myself out in a Cabrini jacket, G-Force pants, Troop Cobra's and a faux Dapper Dan Louis Vuitton baseball cap. The epitome of fresh! (email to author, 2 June 2017).

DJ Format summarizes: "all we could do was do our best to try and imitate what we were seeing but without having the proper kit" (i/v, Brighton, 17 December 2017). My own encounter is somewhat similar. Since I first saw LL Cool J on the back cover of *Radio* (1985), I craved a Kangol hat, and this craving was enhanced by the back cover of MC Shan's *Down By Law* (1987). Kangols were evidently donned by many Bboys in *Wild Style* and *Style Wars*, but the permanence of the non-moving image of the record sleeve continually reinforced this desire. Eventually I discovered that a traditional gentleman's menswear shop in Exeter—Pinder and Tuckwell—had Kangol hats. One Saturday while browsing the Pringle and Lyle & Scott jumpers, a charcoal-grey chevron weave trilby caught my eye.[36] It was £14.99 and I bought it immediately (see Figure 2.4 in Chapter 2). Had there been the Bermuda-style Kangols that LL and Shan wore, naturally I would have leapt at the chance, but the model I purchased did not have any external sign it was manufactured by Kangol. Inside the hat was an angled series of white lines which repeatedly read "KANGOL KANGOL KANGOL", and on more than one occasion I showed my peers the inside of this hat, to justify its existence on top of my head. Through a lack of availability, it was not always possible to acquire the proper accessories, and by slightly altering one's wardrobe based on provincial availability, a strangely familiar image was formed.

It was not only the clothing itself on the cover of *Known 2 Be Down* that carries the motifs of hip hop; in the top right corner, the No Limits Cru's piece reads: "Know Why We're The Best", and in the far left "Wild Style", providing further linkages to the idea of style. Eraze highlights the value of the sleeve design:

Yeh, it was much more of a real immersion. The images of Supreme Team Show and Malcolm McLaren and things like that aren't moving ones in my memory, they're record covers, so they must've come out and been on sale, so that media train had already started... There was a record by Futura 2000 that was done with The Clash, 'The Escapades of Futura 2000', there must've been five releases and when you flipped them over and joined them all together it made this massive Futura piece...that was being into hip hop (i/v, Exeter, 13 March 2017).

Before *Known 2 Be Down*, any product-based representations of British hip hop that featured photographs of the artists were either commercially designed or far removed from the reality of hip hop. Examples such as The City Limits Crew's 'Fresher Than Ever!' (1985), Faze One's 'Layin' Down A Beat' (1986) and Private Party's 'Tennents/Puppet Capers' (1987)[37] conveyed a message of "hip hop as pop artist", designed in studios through photo shoots. In an analogous way to the paradigm shift Run-D.M.C. brought to the image of hip hop by dressing street (Adidas tracksuits, trainers and Kangol/trilby hats), the artists on *Known 2 Be Down* brought a closeness to their audience. Visually perceived as a true representation of the British underground scene, with songs such as Sir Drew and Rapski's 'Notting Hill', and Papa Speng's 'Hip Hop/Reggae Connection' and 'Operation Trident', this album delivered a draft strategy for British hip hop: it spoke image, identity, culture and politics. In 'Notting Hill', Rapski delivers a clear account of police harassment:

> Well I've been living in The Grove for such a long time
> And I can't even go on the front line
> 'Cause if I do I see the Babylon[38]
> They'll grab me by the hand and put me in the van
> And once in the van they'll hit me with a truncheon

The rap is delivered with absolute frankness, and over the sparse beats and funky serendipitous melodies locate everyday living in Ladbroke Grove, West London with experiences of racial tension from the authorities. The mesmerizing chorus "Notting Hill, we're talking about the bill", repeated four times after each verse, aids the switch-up of the lyrical content from the reality of authoritarianist racism to pure hip hop rap tropes, which increase as the song progresses: "I'm Rapski and I'm here to stay / At the top and there's no way that you're ever gonna stop me / If I try to go for my ambition / Don't try to stop me 'cause I'm a musician / And I've got to, got to, make you rock on / All night long until the break of dawn". Rapski builds on the use of the term "Babylon" and further contextualizes London's Jamaican influence on 'Hip Hop/Reggae Connection':

> 'Cause when I grab the microphone and you feel irie[39]
> Yeah, me and my posse gonna get funky
> Now—if you came down to an election
> I'm sure to be the people's selection
> 'Cause I'm always up to perfection
> This is called a hip hop–reggae connection

Fusing Jamaican terminologies with common hip hop tropes ("grabbing the microphone", "asserting his posse") and brag-rap metaphors ("he would gain the people's vote in an election contest due to his flawless rap skills"), Rapski's delivery is typical of hip hop flow over the archetypal electronic reggae rhythms that preceded the digital takeover.[40]

Papa Speng draws upon a range of global political issues in 'Operation Trident':

> Talking 'bout the state of South Africa today
> War in the ghetto what have you to say
> About the children getting shot on the way to school
> While the fascists sit back and relax by the pool
> If I was king then I would rule
> Not the king of the land or the king of the throne
> But the king that rocks the microphone[41]

Papa Speng's verses are epic in length, and his expressions transcend brag rhetoric and uncomplicated statements, "there's so much trouble in the world today…", the accessibility of which directly brings the signified to listening ears; the straightforwardness of his lyrics as rich and obvious as the culture on the sleeve. The following year, *Hard Core One* arrived, a lo-fi compilation album by label BPM, based in Camberwell, London. Largely a short-lived label releasing electronica, acid and breakbeat-esque house, BPM's *Hard Core One* captured the hardcore sonics of London hip hop, as *Known 2 Be Down* captured its visual. In talking about *Hard Core One*, Rola still holds this album in high regard: "I don't have one, but a mint copy is on my wish list, it was a dope, dope comp [compilation]; only had it on tape but I loved it" (email to author, 24 January 2018). Much like the formative years of American hip hop on vinyl, British crews were light on recordings, and did not have the depth of material to release albums straight away. The value of the compilation album was paramount to provincial hip hop once again, although unlike the Tommy Boy and Jive albums that helped relocate hip hop to Britain, this time it was the British compilation that was helping the London sound reach all corners of Britain.

The first compilation that comprised solely of British hip hop was *Street Sounds UK Electro* in 1984, and despite its collection of only seven tracks (with both Zer-O tracks being effectively the same in essence: 'Real Time' and 'Real Time (Retrospective Dub)'), its release divided the *Street Sounds Electro* fan base. Some loved and some loathed it, and its position in the release order of the series, sandwiched between *Crucial Electro 1* and *Crucial Electro 2* (which both included six tracks previously released on *Electro 1, 2* and *3*) had its audience worrying that electro had run out of steam. In a way they were right, but in the sense that the terminology and culture of hip hop was consuming electro as part of its multifaceted history. Interestingly, *UK Electro* is the only edition in the series that also gained releases in Germany on ZYX Records, Italy on Street Sounds/Panarecord, France on Streetwave, and Greece on Street Sounds/Virgin. Due to licensing agreements set up by Morgan Khan, unlike the other editions which all comprised American music, he held greater control over the tracks on *UK Electro*. However, this is also of cultural significance, and suggests that the desirability of British hip hop music in Europe shares a desirability that the British hip hop audience held to American hip hop.[42] In stark contrast to *Known 2 Be Down*, and much akin to the other *Electro* editions, this compilation gave no visual insight to its inherent culture (Figure 6.3). However, it shouted Britishness through its sleeve design: in place of a pale, pastel number was a pale, pastel Union Jack, and a smaller postage-stamp Union Jack top left under the Street Sounds logo. In the same font as "ELECTRO", a horizontal, thick black "U·K-" occupied the space top centre. The idea of the Union Jack in representations of British hip hop offers an alternative source of Britishness; how much this was intentional in the case of *UK Electro* is not clear, but nonetheless the message was crystal—British electro had arrived, not only in Britain, but also in mainland Europe.

Upon the subject of awareness of British hip hop outside one's immediate territory, again Chrome refers to the compilation albums by Music of Life that brought awareness of other British artists to the broader geography: "Not until *Def Beats* I suppose? I mean we knew the *UK Electro* LP back to front, and we had the Hardrock Soul Movement tracks, but we weren't aware of other artists on a national scale until around '89/90" (email to author, 8

Figure 6.3: *Street Sounds UK Electro*, 1984, front cover (French issue) and rear cover (UK issue). Photograph by author.

December 2017). Simon Harris's Music of Life label delivered three important compilations, which started as *Def Beats 1*, after which the series name was revised to *Hard As Hell*. Released in 1987, *Hard As Hell! Rap's Next Generation* reinforced what *Known 2 Be Down* was proving, a solid departure from relying on American hip hop to feed the culture. *Hard As Hell* broadened the diversity of British hip hop representing a wider catchment area of crews (although still with a south-east bias); however, the Music of Life album that firmly delivered the message was *1989 Hustlers Convention Live*, a kind of play on Bee-Bop's *Live Convention '81* (1981) and *Live Convention '82* (1982), and *Hustlers Convention* by Lightnin' Rod (1973), and claims to be "THE WORLD'S FIRST EVER LIVE RAP ALBUM". Recorded on 14 March 1989 live at Music of Life's second birthday at Café de Paris, London, the album showcases Asher D, Daddy Freddy, Demon Boyz, M.C. Duke, and

Merlin, all of whom were growing a substantial following in the provinces. American artists Queen Latifah, DJ Mark The 45 King and the pioneering Kool DJ Red Alert were also in the house that night. The 45 King as producer of The Flavor Unit and the tremendous earworm 'The 900 Number' the year before, and Queen Latifah working towards her debut LP *All Hail The Queen*, were highly regarded in contemporary American hip hop. What makes this album paramount when discussing the British hip hop position is not only the liquid, embryonic ragga-inspired flows tripling up on beats and syllables of Daddy Freddy and Mike J, nor is it the punchy freestyle battle exchanges of Merlin and MC Duke; it is the sheer honesty that exists in the live word. As MC Duke takes to the stage to perform his latest single, he preaches:

> Wait a minute, wait a minute, wait a minute...before I get involved in that I just wanna say big respect, massive respect to Cutmaster Swift 'cause he came through for England, you know what I mean? It's about time. And to all the English rappers, the posse out there, She Rockers, Dett, Mell "O", trouble, you know what I mean? We're all doing our thing, Funky Dope Maneuvers over there, you know what I mean? My posse in the corner there, you know what I'm saying? 'Cause it's about time we come forward, and '89 and '90 will be our year. Please. You know what I mean? Aiight,[43] yeah. We got London Rhyme Syndicate, we got a whole heap of superstars from over this side of the spit, you know what I'm saying? So, like, we're gonna do it as well. Please mister, come in (*Hustlers Convention*, 1989).

The instrumental of MC Duke's 'I'm Riffin (English Rasta)' is then dropped, with the introduction speech by Jesse Jackson: "All of us are one people, singing our music, popping our finger and doing our thing, let's give ourselves a big round of applause"[44] after which Duke sincerely endorses with "And you know that" before launching into a live rendition of 'Riffin''. Following 'Riffin'', Duke invites the "wizard" Merlin on stage, and at his first opportunity, Merlin harangues: "Here come the British! Cutmaster Swift—I salute you. Now I want y'all to know, the British will overtake the rap world as we know it." He reels off a list of artists and exclaims: "YES! The British are ready!" Later in the proceedings, Mike J from Demon Boyz again reiterates this position. At the outset of their show, Mike J requests DJ Devastate to cease the music as he vocalizes a similar attitude:

Now, London town, north south east and west, ya know say that the British talent's looking nuff recognition, seen? We want the USA to look at us and say "YES!" We can do it, seen? Haha, 'cause we rule, seen? Now recognition's what I'm looking, and I hope recognition's what you're looking, seen (*Hustlers Convention*, 1989).

These almost polemic expressions are fully charged, with the knowledge there are revered American artists in a full house oozing with some of the cream of British hip hop. Mike J, Merlin and Duke seize the opportunity to work up the crowd and deepen the belief that in hip hop Britain can supersede America. This is almost a battle cry, a war-like spirit, boosted by Cutmaster Swift's success and the breadth and depth of the Music of Life posse. The various enunciations of the power of the English/British are also fuelled by the previous seven years' toil, the experimentation and learning through the mimicking of American rap and the girth of the London reggae sound system. Daddy Freddy commands the ultimate "raggamuffin hip hop business", and poking fun at the cockney vernacular, exclaims "Come in 'Arry, know what I mean? Know what I mean, 'Arry?"[45] before launching into his Trenchtown rooted and unique dancehall DJ style and fashion with wingman Asher D. Daddy Freddy appears most often of all the vocalists on the album, and rocks a heavy ragga/dancehall performance with Mike J. The strength of the Jamaican influence is telling. Mike J's voice becomes more intense and Yardie sounding as he works with Freddy, and the performance morphs into an epic medley of raggamuffin splendour: part lament, part celebration.

When The 45 King rocks a short freestyle over 'The 900 Number' and 'Court Is Now In Session'—the traditional American call and response routines of "throw ya hands in the air"—the difference in style and approach is overwhelming; furthermore the crowd appear to sound much less engaged during The 45 King's slot. Hearing this for the first time through a bedroom turntable rig rather than being in the crowd, this difference was telling. The 45 King's piece sounded misplaced in its location almost halfway through side one, an uncomfortable old school swing in the midst of grimy, underground raggamuffin hip hop. This no uncertain power shift speaks of an intentional performativism acted out through the immediacy of the event, raising the temperature of Britishness in the venue, and through the reification of the album diffusing these spontaneous odes to British hip hop through the provinces. Neil Taylor proclaims his adoration of this album:

> I fucking LOVE the *Hustlers Convention* album. Coming from a reggae background before my hip hop passion formed, I always loved reggae and ragga influences in UK hip hop… I always knew we were emulating experiences we'd never have in Exeter. Admiring London, the US, Jamaica for "authenticity" and trying to stay true to the spirit of it while doing our white boy thing in Devon, proper rude bays! (p/c, 23 April 2018).

This album indeed acted as agent for provincial headz to emulate the intensity of the live jam, and while listening to, analysing and discussing albums draws one closer to the artist, the live recording enables one to reimagine the jam context by interpreting the incidentals, the spontaneous and the improvised. The rhetoric on *1989 Hustlers Convention Live* drew the provinces not only closer to British hip hop, but hip hop *in* Britain; and together with *Bad Meaning Good* and the recorded artefacts discussed above, a critical sense of Britishness was birthed. *1989 Hustlers Convention Live* was fundamental to an augmented understanding of the strength in the local vernacular and colloquialisms of London headz, which in turn strengthened the conviction that provincial practitioners could also trust in their own reality and realness to produce hip hop.

Identity in the Sticks

Two significant issues needed to be addressed in provincial rap: the accent and the content. Norfolk-based collective Products of The Entity were active in the late 1980s, and on 'Money In The Kitty', MC Squared rhymes: "Hokey cokey, pokey in and out like this / You got me vexed for making the money from selling out…". Over a chopped half-pattern of Melvin Bliss's 'Synthetic Substitution' (1973), and a hint of James Brown's 'Funky Drummer' (1970) overlaid with 'Dujii' (1971) by Kool and the Gang, the track keeps pace with the contemporary American sound of the time (à la Gang Starr and Naughty By Nature): "Living rough like Rab C. Nesbitt / You smile or frown I knock you down before you leg it / 'Cause it's like that I swing the argy-bargy anthem…", "Didn't get not money for my trouble / For the poison of pride I'm laying my coat in the puddle…", and "one hundred and eiiighty!". The lyrics draw upon popular British television and culture, phraseology and slang,[46] as well as link to American hip hop metaphors and phrases, "bringing the funk like Stezo…" and "In '88 I was fly…". On another track, Products of The Entity line-up four emcees rapping over an organic percussion assemblage with Funkadelic's 'Good Old Music' (1970) at its core, in a Leaders of the New School/Fu-Schnickens pass-the-mic style, delivering lyrics like "You got less wit than Jeremy Beadle", "Lend me an ear and I'll give it back / Entertain the people like *Crackerjack*", and "One a penny, two a penny hot cross buns",[47] and by doing so emphasize this relationship between British popular culture and American hip hop figures. The Products of The Entity example begins to demonstrate a crucial difference between London-centric and provincial rap which relates back to the origins of hip hop's transatlantic journey discussed in the first part of the book. In Chapter 2, I offered a model which illustrates the journey of hip hop as it infiltrated and morphed its way from America across Britain (Figure 2.1). This journey was the start of the cultural consumption/production of hip hop, and through its materialism and intangible cultural heritage led to a definite distinction in the style of hip hop music produced in London compared to less-urban areas. Where London artists could look towards Jamaican diaspora, family connections and urban issues, the provinces drew upon national tropes, identifiable cultural iconography and the shared experience of popular culture.

Some artists embraced their rural geography too, as in the case of Hidden Identity. Evil Ed has worked with a wide spectrum of emcees from the provinces and London, as he calls it: "from hood to meadow" (see Chapter 5),[48] and the quality of Evil Ed's contemporary productions retain strong linkages to the sounds and vibes of the provincial and rural. The "bumpkin", an abridged version of "country bumpkin", is a derogatory term for a rural dweller, suggesting an unsophisticated uneducated mindset. The bumpkin is an underground, countrified version of the urban marginal; mythically he is found stood in fields chewing blades of long grass, "drinking cider and discussing butter".[49] The comedic edge of Mistima's lyrics on the weed-fuelled 'Return Of Da Redeye' is a departure from the skull-snap vibe of House of Pain and Cypress Hill, and includes verbal references to K-Solo. Again, stylistic delivery is heavily influenced by American artists Leaders of the New School/Fu-Schnickens but also Funkdoobiest. The track is steeped in weed smoking, and celebrates the benefits of cannabis to creative practice: "So it's been a long time since I did this / So I rolled up a spliff and inflict lyrical fitness", located "in a deep dark cellar from the country". Mistima provides a clear position between the metropolis and rurality, and the separation of marijuana from other drugs, a common attitude in hip hop internationally at this time: "One member from my crew after partied and fled / Went to London took drugs and now he's fucked in the head…". Mistima's accent oozes flavour and morphs across southern British city to country twang to Yardie, the latter particularly evident in the line "When me tred me dance steps with me old spar seen Lionel Blair", where again a zany scene is imagined drawing on a British celebrity of the establishment.

On 'I Tink We're In Trubble' (named after the tight, sped-up cuts from Funkdoobiest's 'The Funkiest'), Mistima states Hidden Identity are "Droppin' science from the country / Crisp as Crunchie, smokin' on a spliff and gettin' funky". References to The Stone Age throughout the EP hint to K. Sly's rap style, and as Mistima namechecks the crew's families, friends and the small town north of Milton Keynes, this is especially reminiscent of 'Hold No Hostage': "all of the Wolverton crew, and all of the people that play our music... respect". 'Big Head 4 Da Dread' confirms the crew's relationship between the English rural and the blunted vibe of 1990s American hip hop, and opens with a soundbite from a regional news report:

> A typical English harvesting scene you might think, but this machine is gathering in Britain's first legal cannabis crop. Also known as hemp, these plants are being grown throughout Hertfordshire, Essex and Cambridgeshire for their fibre, the leaves will be dried and used by the paper industry and the stalks will be used for high quality bedding for horses (sampled on 'Big Head 4 Da Dread', 1994).

It was thought during the 1990s that the clement weather in East Anglia and the south-east of England would provide good growing conditions for hemp, and cultivation in the UK was re-legalized in 1993 and is a licensed activity.[50] This became a hot topic in the agricultural press, and increasingly of interest to the cannabis smoking community also associated with hip hop culture. Hidden Identity's intertextual play between the broader farming community and global hip hop maintains their playful approach to music and regional context, framed by references to the commercial cheese of popular satirical and post-new wave bans from their hometown: "Who, you, the hip hop guru / From the town that created The Barron Knights and Kajagoogoo / And the brother that took twenty seconds". The last reference relates to Silver Bullet and his second single '20 Seconds To Comply' (1989). These lyrics draw on American, British and local vernacular and colloquialisms in an effort to generate songs that triangulate international, national and regional influences. Within North American hip hop, Forman states that "space and place figure prominently as organizing concepts delineating a vast range of imaginary or actual social practices that are represented in narrative or lyric form and that display identifiable local, regional, and national aesthetic inflections" (Forman 2002: 3), and in rural Britain similar organization is present. Drawing upon references from television and figures from popular culture became commonplace in provincial hip hop music, more so than the work of artists from London. Through its presentation of hyperrealities, the television acts as a conduit for exaggerated, misrepresented and stereotypical themes and exaggerated tropes, signalling societal implosion (Baudrillard 1994: 79–86), and it is these themes and tropes that provincial hip hop artists reappropriate and expose. In his third hypothesis, Baudrillard suggests that: "Everywhere socialization is measured by the exposure to media messages. Whoever is under-exposed to the media is desocialized or virtually asocial" (Baudrillard 1994: 80). He continues to argue that media information does not produce meaning, and that: "Information devours its own content. It devours communication and the social" (Baudrillard 1994: 80). He talks about this as a myth, and that society are "all complicitous in this myth" (Baudrillard 1994: 80), and while he discusses counter-information in the form of pirate radio stations and antimedia, he does not account for a reframing and owning of these media myths. In the construct of provincial hip hop lyrics both simulacra and myth are used as a device with which to create a metaphor driven narrative, taken out of the zone of television's hyperreality and reframed, aiding the context of the real. Rather than the sign supplanting the real, the real is altered. The original perception of the simulacra disappears, and through reuse positions the imaginary against the everyday.

Four years prior to 'Blunted Bumpkin Buskers', Hidden Identity's demo *Greenbelt Chronicles* contains a mix of crunching, bass-heavy beats. 'Point Blank Range' includes a short verse of raggamuffin among angered battle rhymes, again centring on horror, terror and warfare tropes. 'Dead By Dawn' opens with more horror vibes, menacing basslines and crisp freestyle lyrics, plenty of "dead by dawn!!" haunting soundbites, and transformer cuts by Evil Ed. On '(The Real) Blaze Of Glory', the lines "Gone are the days of the patriotic", "The OG [original] rhyme emcee from the country", and chorus hollas of "we're the REALLL" followed by 'Blaze Of Glory' cuts from Jon Bon Jovi's soundtrack play on the sense of reality and country context, fading out to "You rode a 15 year old boy straight to his grave. And the rest of us, straight to hell" from *Young Guns II*. 'Slay Them' and 'Crucifix' continue these themes: "Kamikaze I'm making 'em nasty / Sure we're hot because we bake you like a pasty", "The depths of country mannerism exorcism not into racism", "Bass I'm in the place of the united colours race racism's…mmm a waste", "Yeah checkmate we're outta here like Maggie…"—recorded in

November 1990, the same month Thatcher resigned as prime minister and party leader following Michael Heseltine's campaign to challenge her leadership. The national political arena became subject matter for provincial as well as London-centric emcees, becoming another marker for the emerging synergy between urban and rural hip hop artists.

In the West Country, areas closer to London (such as Wiltshire) had experienced an influx of people leaving the capital, as Stepchild comments: "By the 1950s a swathe of Londoners had followed the industry there and by the end of the 1970s having deformed the accent into a sort of wurzel/mockney hybrid" (i/v, Swindon, 3 December 2017), although further west into Somerset, Devon and Cornwall, the local dialects were less diluted. The term "wurzel"[51] is used in place of bumpkin, popularized after the chart success of scrumpy and western band The Wurzels, whose hits 'The Combine Harvester' and 'I Am A Cider Drinker' (both 1976) are still played at festivals and weddings with a rural cultural history. A Somerset crew emerged at the turn of the millennium named Verbal Wurzels (although they rebranded themselves Lowercase in the early noughties), who had fully mastered the comedic, wurzel approach in their music. Much like Mistima and Products of The Entity, a liquid flow requiring the finest articulation was necessary to deliver their complex wordplay. Focusing on new school hip hop and grime, Bramwell comments: "The antiphony and humour exercised through rap are significant sources of pleasure. This pleasure is connected to confronting the challenges of dwelling in postcolonial London" (Bramwell 2015a: 30). However, humour and wit have been widely harnessed themes in provincial rap since the late 1980s for two reasons: first, due to the lack of "real hip hop" subject matter in spaces perceived as banal, and second, rural humour. It is only when one captures the humorous that the true real becomes apparent. I remember on several occasions at jams witnessing one of Roskoe Rockwell's sublime verses which opens: "The eloquent pelican with the sharpest beak in Wellington…", and from that point going forwards, he had the crowd hooked on every syllable. One comment from a member called "vikoi" on hijackbristol.co.uk in 2010, reads: "heehee I remember seeing Lowercase at Wellington Sports Centre when they were called the Verbal Wurzels about ten yrs ago. sick flow—BIG UP THE SOMERSET CHARM!"[52]

Positioning himself within a guise much like Shakespeare's recurring character of the politically incorrect and licensed fool, Samuel Otis pushes the social awkwardness of this trope to the sympathetic edge on 'Girly', with punchlines such as these: "Including the spark I'm confused for a start / Hey this girly hurts my heart / Alright I read *The Star* and I burp and fart /

I also appreciate walks in the park and certain works of art". This leads into a self-lamenting semi-boozy West Country twanged sung chorus by Otis himself. This character plays on the West Country accent in the sung hook "guuuuuurlleeeee", and the final section "It's not like I'm in love with you / I just wanna go to the pub with you / Or maybe a club or two / Luvver it's up to you". Tailed with Arthur Needlefluff's cuts of Guru's lyric "and I don't know when or if I'm gonna see her again…" the song fades out as if he is left alone in the pub at closing time. However, there is a class undertone here. The red-top tabloid *The Daily Star* is associated with the working classes; it is reactionist and hugely sensationalist with Tory tinges (published by Express Newspapers) and little intellectual content. Otis suggests this is his regular reading material while displaying other vulgarities yet also holds an appreciation of "certain works of art". His wordplay here, "certain" and "works of art" rather than merely "art", guides the listener to notions of stereotypical aspiring middle-class pursuits such as visiting galleries and discussing art.

The West Country identity grew tentatively from the late 1980s to the assertiveness shown in Verbal Wurzels/Lowercase's outputs, and although there was a caution in celebrating "West Countryness" in the formative years of provincial hip hop, there are evidences of its existence. Displays of West Countryness revealed themselves through graffiti and rap. In 1989, weeks before the Operation Anderson bust, Eraze bombed every brick and concrete surface throughout Princesshay, Exeter with his recognizable "ERAZE" tag, but also with the huge words "YER BAY!" (written approximately two feet high) underneath and alongside his name. "Bay", or "Bey" (depending on which part of Devon from which one hails) is an informal local colloquialism for males, or a term of endearment, usually used in place of more national terms such as "bloke" or "mate" (and has an equal female counterpart in "maid"). In addition to the colloquial reference, this wordage is a play on Flavor Flav's hype catchphrase "Yeah Boyyeee!", apparent on a myriad of Public Enemy records between 1987 and 1989. Public Enemy's albums *Yo! Bum Rush The Show* and *It Takes A Nation Of Millions To Hold Us Back* had enormous impact on the hip hop community in Britain, and Flavor Flav's mischievous, enduring, and also political antagonistic position resonated among the youth and offered an alternative entrance to Chuck D's partisan assertiveness. Jamrozik (2015) discusses forms of hip hop location, suggesting that: "Hip hop culture acknowledges a paternal continuity between the space and the person" (Jamrozik 2015: 229). Eraze's bombing of the town centre's municipal modernist façades at once place his practice as one of affirmation. "YER BAY!" affirms his "Devon-ness" and his ownership of hip hop language through a regional reiteration of Flav's phrase reclaiming the street "which inherently embodies hybridity" (Yamakoshi and Sekine 2016: 354); and *because* of his bombing of Princesshay, his love for his hip hop locale.

In the same year as Exeter was drenched in Devonian shouts of "YER BAY!", Plymouth produced MC Mad Cow, whose name was taken from the BSE[53] pandemic in Britain, triggering the ban on sales of organ-based meat for human consumption, despite the Conservative government insisting that BSE posed no threat to humans.[54] In October 2000, *The Guardian* ran a story about Devon dairy farmers, the Palmers, who ran an "80 strong herd of Friesians on 87 acres of farmland owned by Devon County Council" in Diptford.[55] They experienced 14 cases of BSE leading to profit losses of over £13,000 per year. Stories like this were common across the region. At "Dance Raw 3" during March 1990, MC Mad Cow was introduced by his crew, and took to the stage snorting and wobbling like a deranged bovine, much to the amusement of the crowd. In response, and due to the beef (no pun intended) my crew had with Mad Cow's, during our show I rapped "I'm the freshest emcee in the county of Devon / And how do I rock it? Twenty-four seven / So back to yer farm as I gots the mic now / Better and faster than a mad cow know how", which induced approving cheers from those representing Exeter and East Devon, and jeers from those that had travelled across the moorland from the west. Rural rap drew upon its socio-political context as it gained confidence in its identity over a comparatively brief period. I would attribute this confidence building to the consolidation of the provincial hip hop community which was strongly underpinned by accepting it was not London. Taking part in the regular jams also bred a self-assurance in one's own use of accent and vernacular styles, as Slicerman states:

> Our events were more jams until the late 80's early 90's, we'd hook up with peeps, The Bont [Pontarddulais, small town further into Wales] boys, Jay, Dee Rock, Demomix [Dwain] etc. and have party jams. This is what inevitably led us to find our own style using our own accents, deejaying and producing style fully (email to author, 12 April 2017).

Concurrent to the enlightenment of the regional accent was the relationship with British identity and a peer group mentality, as Junior Disprol frames:

"First time seeing and hearing other Welsh crews especially made things seem real British too… when you heard British emcees there was no reason not to get on it, they were the same as us" (email to author, 2 June 2017).

As emcees developed their vocal styles through their native accents, it became commonplace to diss those that persisted to rap in a fake accent, as Rola demonstrates on 'Perpetrating Frauds': "You gotta make it without being a fake / One minute you're a ragga next you're an American / Puffing and panting when you're British you'd better diminish / Finish and come across your own way…". 1989 was an important turning point for regional rap, and although regional accents and topics were clearly emerging, the stigma attached to ruralism still meddled with provincial confidence. Regarding how country folk are audibly perceived by others, Dren suggests "most people hear your accent and assume that you're slightly dim witted" (email to author, 20 June 2017), while Ricky Also observes the visual perception by others within the province but outside the hip hop community, interestingly referring to hillbillies: "we probably looked like a bunch of crazy hillbillies to everyone else" (email to author, 21 January 2018). Deed discusses the broader cultural implications of drawing on rural life in hip hop: "trouble is …what are you gonna rap about, 'yeah the price of hot cross buns has gone up', yeah I'm gonna go out militant style, you know, make a load of hardcore rap about the state of council drains and that".[56] In discussing Shakespeare, Ricœur (1986) suggests the metaphor as something outside the bounds of suspension of the real:

> …we must reserve the possibility that metaphor is not limited to suspending natural reality, but that in opening meaning up on the imaginative side it also opens it towards a dimension of reality that does not coincide with what ordinary language envisages under the name of natural reality (Ricœur 1986: 211).

The tropes and iconography used in metaphors within provincial lyrics needed to include an element of quirkiness, and by doing so acknowledged its own unconventional origins and the canon of American and London hip hop, yet forged sympathetic and respectful relationships to hip hop of the polis. This approach aided its affirming position, its sense of realism and its state of mind.

A State of Mind

The hip hop state of mind is the trickiest component of hip hop to quantify. On one hand it is intangible, flexible and malleable, in its invisible existence and continual reframing and contextual dialectic. At the same time, the hip hop state of mind is a constant, with the key agenda to challenge oppression, and formulaic and conventional life. The notion of the hip hop state of mind was enforced in Rakim's lyric in 'Mahogany' (1990): "She asked how come I don't smile I said / 'Everything's fine, but I'm in a New York state of mind'" and reinforced by Nas on 'N.Y. State of Mind' (1994), which samples Rakim's lyric in the chorus (and signposts Billy Joel's 1976 song 'New York State of Mind'). The New York state of mind is a social, political and highly contextual, consciously constructed mental position which began to form during the 1970s in the neglected and forsaken toxic environments of New York City, but is strongly rooted in black diaspora and steeped in cultural history. During this embryonic era, those champions of knowledge (Bambaataa, et al.), provided insights and clues to cultural heritages outside of the immediacy of America, embedded within Afrofuturist thought (de Paor-Evans 2018b). These history lessons provided significant prompts for the clear emergence of black consciousness in hip hop. Triggered largely by Public Enemy and Boogie Down Productions,[57] crews such as X-Clan, Positively Black, Poor Righteous Teachers, Brand Nubian, A Tribe Called Quest, and Jungle Brothers, and individuals such as Queen Mother Rage, Tragedy Khadafi the Intelligent Hoodlum and Ice Cube, brought bespoke versions of consciousness to hip hop. Following the previous discussion on keeping it real, the state of mind of hip hop is a slightly different animal, yet there are also overlaps. Where one's level of engagement with the real is exposed through actions, reifications, how one presents oneself in relation to a set of social and political constructs and the development of one's institutional, objectified and embodied cultural capital, the state of mind is the positional outcome of the habitus driven by the assembly of cultural capital. So how does the hip hop state of mind relate to the provinces of Britain?

Hip hop's black consciousness movement and Afrocentric thought[58] rapidly evolved during the emergence of the British underground and America's hip hop golden era. By this point, American hip hop music had become easier to discover in the provinces thanks to a much greater number of retailers stocking it (although much still got missed, the most essential conscious rap was available), and due to the network of sharing tapes formed from crews and jams as British hip hop grew. As London artists performed around the provinces, these jams provided opportunities for further sharing of conscious hip hop, informing the state of mind of the provincial. Some backed away from the culture as it grew politically but for others it added a depth and importance that enriched their engagement, and brought visibility to minority groups in white dominant areas. Hip hop had become a truly worldwide culture, with emerging regionalist styles and directions. Again, Neil Taylor describes these points of arrival as direct factors that helped align the provincial position within the greater hip hop discourse:

> Putting the pieces together, and comprehending that there was a unifying culture, being interpreted differentially by geographic location, was another way in which I felt connected even though I was separated by distance and circumstances from the core of hip hop. Regional representation and participation under the umbrella of worldwide culture has always been important and understanding how local pressures shaped output was an early lesson I learned (email to author, 2 March 2017).

Focusing on his own self-discovery of hip hop knowledge, Evil Ed strengthens this point:

> I was learning about black history, the issues affecting people in inner cities and all the time this positive message of self-improvement and making something out of nothing. It wasn't aimed at me directly, I know that, but as a kid I didn't think that intensely about it, I just soaked it all in (email to author, 14 June 2017).

Vincent states that: "By 1989 a number of essential connections were being made between the richness of African history and culture, the creative strength of seventies funk and soul, and the positive potential of hip hop" (Vincent 1996: 311). For the first time, the hidden black histories of America, Africa and the Caribbean were being revealed to a largely non-black audience, and through facts and narratives delivered through hip hop records, provincial headz were learning about the black diaspora, slavery and oppression as well as Africa's original wealth, culture and lifestyles. Hip hop offered a two-tiered way into gaining knowledge about black culture. There was the direct fundamental knowledge relating to names, dates, events and facts, and the signposting to further reading, concepts, ideas and the histories that provincial British schools chose to ignore. Mark Cowan corroborates this education: "I learned a lot about black culture and history through books about slavery, the black panthers, the civil rights movement. I had learned a lot about music too, from jazz, to funk, soul, rock'n'roll" (email to author, 30 April 2017). Not only was hip hop signposting and delivering an education outside the remit of the institution, it was encouraging its audience to explore their own cultural circumstances. He continues:

> Through listening to rap music, I kept hearing these names being mentioned by the artists, people that I had never heard of. So, I began to research a lot of these people. I took a keen interest in the black power movement, reading books about Huey P. Newton, Marcus Garvey, Malcolm X and the Civil rights movements. I think feeling so detached and unable to do anything no matter how I voted, paired with events throughout Scotland's past—highland clearances, selling off large parts of land, oil revenues going to Westminster—I felt there was some similarities to the Civil rights movement and what its objectives were. Not necessarily comparing the events that happened in America during the movement, but the overall aim to be treated fairly and equally in society, was one that I, and many others in the UK could identify with (email to author, 30 April 2017).

Cowan's reflections illustrate how learning from hip hop enabled him to frame his own context, and similarly Neil Taylor remarks that education through hip hop did not stop at gaining knowledge, but furthered his political position and social engagement:

> It helped me critically engage social issues by providing me with perspectives normally elided from the dominant narrative. It also gave me greater empathy for diverse cultural groups, again through getting to hear others' perspectives and living conditions that were so utterly different to my own. It fueled my passion for justice and gave me courage to speak up and out because I was informed. It made me a champion of the dispossessed, supporter of the independent, and someone determined to not sell out (email to author, 2 March 2017).

Teachings about black culture also began to be delivered through British artists, most discernibly Katch 22 and Black Radical MKII. Albums such as Katch 22's *Diary Of A Blackman Living In The Land Of The Lost* and Black Radical Mk II's *The Undiluted Truth (A Blackman's Leviathan)* (both 1991) respectively used the narratives of black history previously hidden from mainstream British education as vehicles for organizing a mind state of black culture with intonations of identifiable local, regional and national themes. Records such as these further supported the need for provincial headz to examine the British context in finer detail. Both "state of mind" and "keeping it real" are deeply intertwined and exemplify the importance of hip hop's fifth element. "I think that there are far more than [the four elements]", Herc maintained in 2005, "the way you walk, the way you talk, the way you look, the way you communicate" (quoted in Chang 2007: xi); and these representations, I would argue, are the results of knowledge.

I would like to conclude this chapter by returning to the idea of critical regionalism. By the late 1980s, the britcore sound, the use of natural accents and contextual lyrical content, helped solidify a national British hip hop identity; it became its own urban, critical regionalism which radiated across the land from London, but it was not until the early 1990s when hip hop practitioners in the provinces became critically regionalist, which I would argue was the result of a seven-year process. From hip hop's first British provincial permeation during 1983 and the subsequent progression of consumption and production of its practices, critical observations and education, and as importantly its distancing from both America and London, this offered the provinces the space to evolve its own form of hip hop. In this sense, to keep it real means to be regionally critical, and the state of mind is one's approach to critical regionalism. Furthermore, this is not exclusive to hip hop, but rather the critical regionalism of hip hop supports one's approach to life in a much broader sense, as Specifik states: "a hip hop mentality is a way that you would tackle everything" (i/v, Bournemouth, 27 October 2017).

To "tackle everything" in this way, one's sense of reality must be grounded in the realities of one's context and sense of the everyday. Kit (YML) spoke of the slow revolution he experienced from his early perception of hip hop's urban fallacies to comprehension of how he saw his position within the culture:

> Initially my rural upbringing held me back as I thought I could only be relevant in hip hop if I had a gnarly urban upbringing filled with pain and hardship, but as time went on, I started to

understand the whole "keep it real" ethos. It then became quite an important thing for me to tell my side of the story, how hip hop looked from my perspective (email to author, 24 April 2017).

Stepchild corroborates such an approach, and eloquently represents the true essence of a hip hop state of mind:

> If I learned that it wasn't about how I fitted into hip hop it was about how hip hop fitted into me, once you nail that equation it becomes an honest conversation and you start to produce the best of both. I became "Stepchild" because I was, both domestically and in my adopted culture, both had been a negative that deserved a positive spin but it was gradual, identity took a while. Apart from a few crews a lot of us were still a bit American with it so there's a lot of early stuff I cringe at, but it wasn't long before I was comfortable with my own tone and that's when the fun really begins, you've sort of got to get over it before you can get truly comfortable. Where I used to obsess over the competition I now know there is no competition because no one can beat me at being me (i/v, Swindon, 3 December 2017).

To this end, the state of mind of provincial British hip hop is a continual critique of one's knowledge-of-self within a critically regionalist frame. What is paramount to the critical position of the provincial head returns somewhat to Griswold's provincial positivism (1990: 1582), where questions are posited within a localized narrative in order to progress discourse. For woke headz in provincial Britain, hip hop became a palimpsest of learning, where the various sites of hip hop raise issues of oppression, confrontation, racism, and where socio-political identities are affirmed with "unretractable embodied consciousness" (Ashlee, Zamora and Karikari 2017: 90). This palimpsest continues to gather layers, and also draws on notions of experience, the sensory experiences that fulfil the love for hip hop music, and the awareness of self and other individual and collective experiences, both negative and positive.

Conclusions: Critical De-regionalism, Dispelling the Myth and Revealing the Invisible

Hip hop culture in the British provinces runs deep; and the perspectives of those headz that dwelled outside of major cities have helped shape this book. As I suggested at the outset, three key questions needed to be addressed: first, the urban fallacy that British hip hop is solely a city-centric culture located in areas of high urban density; second, to evidence and attest that hip hop developed in British provinces as a critically regional and de-regional hybrid culture; and third, that the practices of hip hop developed in the provinces provided a structure for greater critical engagement within hip hop and broader society—which here is discussed in the section "Revealing the Invisible". The cultural acquisition, cultural evolution, production and ultimately the identity of provincial British hip hop have been evidenced through the investigations in each chapter, and as I have shown, the presence of hip hop outside of London, Nottingham, Manchester, Bristol and other major cities throughout its formative decade in Britain existed, thrived and grew as a hybrid culture. This hybridity developed through the consumption of four major mechanisms: the broadcast audio/visual, the recorded product/artefact, the spatiality of country/city, and the local/national narratives of Britishness. As critical consumption contested moments of these phenomena, processes of production engaged in a dialectic, pushing back on certain industry-led reifications, assumptions and positions—both authoritative (industry and establishment) and autonomous (individual and crew). These processes of production informed the methods of practice which would in turn establish a hybrid culture that located itself between the canon of British and American hip hop of the time. British hip hop from the provincial perspective became critically de-regional as much as regional, framing itself within narratives that question its very existence in the provinces. British hip hop is not something trapped in urbanism, nor is it purely consumed by the provinces. The roots of its cultural production in the landscape of the country are now over 37 years old, and its pioneering practitioners are in the middle of their lives, some with families, children and grandchildren. Many of these practitioners are still active in hip hop, and armed with the hip hop state of mind, knowledge, skills and approach to the everyday learned through hip hop culture have enriched their experiences in life. As well as closing this study through its three main conclusions, the sections that follow also offer some propositions for the future of hip hop studies.

Hybrid Culture and Critical De-regionalism

By the time breakdancing and graffiti were being practised across the nation, hip hop had already become a culture of some hybridity. By the close of 1983, Nottingham's Rock City Crew, Manchester's Broken Glass and Wolverhampton's Bboys were regularly performing. In the provinces Bboying and writing was also well underway, and as attested in Chapters 1 and 2, these early practices and experimentation in the provinces paved the way for DJing and emceeing and an appetite for gaining hip hop knowledge. I would argue that the quest for knowledge was largely driven by engagement in practice—the diverse and inclusive way in which hip hop music originated substantially informed how it was received and acquired. When the provincial British youth were offered the cultural tamping embodied in film and sonic reifications, the practices of graffiti and Bboying were so explicit that it was almost as if the music was incidental, simply a vehicle to empower the creativity of breaking or a backdrop to throwing up tags. In their chapter in *Global Noise: Rap and Hip Hop Outside the USA* (2001), Hesmondhalgh and Melville make a claim that "the most significant passages of hip hop from the United States to the United Kingdom should not be understood as localization" (Hesmondhalgh and Melville 2001: 86). They then pursue this line of thought averring that the music culture they wish to explore "represent[s] such a transformation of these origins that the term localization, with its connotations of local adjustment to a still-intact form, hardly seems valid" (Hesmondhalgh and Melville 2001: 86). While their chapter then progresses into an investigation of breakbeat, drum 'n' bass and trip hop, I find it peculiar to draw a line under regional hip hop in pursuit of the obvious. What I hope I have achieved in this book is the opposite of Hesmondhalgh and

Melville's claim, that actually the nuances and "local adjustment" in regional and provincial British hip hop run deeper than they may appear.

The hip hop habitus in the provinces is constructed from the assemblages of regionalism, de-regionalism, globalization and post-globalization. The regional assemblages are those that contain local vernacular language: colloquialisms, quips, phrases and terminologies which only make sense in the space of that region. To again take a departure from DeLanda, the assemblage of the region may be the material culture, sonic and spatial context which determines the subject of its region, where people of such regions become part of that assemblage. That assemblage is constructed of reifications and representations that present what it is to be a Devonian, a Dorsetter, a Cornwallian, or a Geordie, for example. These regions primarily exist at odds with the cultural capital of the hip hop habitus (Bourdieu 2010: 74–75) that I discussed in Chapters 4 and 5 and acted as the foremost obstacle to the formative development of provincial hip hop; one is reminded again of Deed's (see Chapter 6) sardonic yet almost surrendering comment about the mundanity of real material to draw from. However, from studying high quality American and London-centric hip hop culture, headz recognized both the absurdities and values in their provincial assemblages.

Of paramount significance in the evolution of provincial hybrid hip hop culture was the recorded artefact, and its value cannot be underestimated in what it taught young non-urban headz. One of the major lessons here was in recognizing what dwelling as an urban inhabitant meant, and while the urbanism portrayed by many provincial headz may appear bizarre, these portrayals were part of the process of cultural hybridity. These representational practices which mimicked those of original practices of hip hop—birthed within an urban locale in a globalized world on the brink of post-globalization—were in fact practices of de-regionalism, cultural practices which in part rejected the conventional praxis contained within the routines of regional assemblage. When graffiti writers began to write on barns, farmer's trailers and flood drains; when DJs created mixes with local news reports and emcees inaugurated the regional dialect and local accent, hybridity had arrived. In *Performing Identity/Performing Culture*, Dimitriadis (2009) discusses the resurrection of the regional with particular reference to the 1990s and 2000s. He observes that this pronounced regionalism was "a regionalism that went hand-in-hand with the 'crew' ethic" (Dimitriadis 2009: 38). Talking about America, he continues to explain that: "As hip hop circulated nationally and internationally, communities around the country reclaimed it in particular ways" (Dimitriadis 2009: 38). The globalization of hip hop forced the underground to become more regional, more off-radar and more local, producing hip hop that sought affirmation of its local identity. British provincial hip hop was seeking the very same—although not necessarily as a reaction to the closing of the loop of globalization, but that it emerged *as* hip hop was turning global, and was forced to develop its character. Rather than seeking reinvention, it was seeking invention.

The relationship between American records, British compilations and regional consumer terrain provides an opportunity to investigate an assemblage and habitus of some difference to the urban canon of hip hop. DeLanda states that in order to explore social assemblage: "All that is needed is a plausible model of the subject which meets the constraints of assemblage theory, that is, a model in which the subject emerges as relations of exteriority are established among the contents of experience" (DeLanda 2013: 47). The epistemologies of hip hop culture are born through a collection of experiences, fostered through the assemblage process. This process of assemblage was, on one hand, carried out at a distance from the apparent heart of the culture, yet on the other hand—and of paramount importance to provincial hip hop culture—the framing of an emotional centre, constructed through the habitus of the non-urban. Yet again, Neil Taylor's discussion of the emotional sense of centre is significant:

> Putting the pieces together, and comprehending that there was a unifying culture, being interpreted differentially by geographic location, was another way in which I felt connected even though I was separated by distance and circumstances from the core of hip hop (email to author, 3 October 2017).

Those in more rural areas had to work differently at hip hop in a sense, as Brent Aquasky remembers: "we had to work harder in a way, from the country, really work to connect in", and use spatial and geographic limitations as an advantage. Again, one is reminded of Brent's tagging of the tree stumps:

> I remember the storm of 1987 and all the trees that came down, and we lost power for a couple of weeks, we had no electricity and no phone, and we were stuck in the village for days on end, because we had Forestry Commission enclosures on either side of our village and we just couldn't get out and when all the trees were chopped back I just thought it was a good idea to tag. We had nowhere to tag, I lived in the middle of a forest, so I just went

and tagged all the tree stumps that had fallen down across the road (i/v, Bournemouth, 12 December 2017).

As a teenager who was relocated from South London to Devon in 1983, Kilo missed the "original boom of hip hop" in London, so he took inspiration from Bboys in the media such as Rock Steady Crew, New York City Breakers, Dynamic Rockers, and:

> all the usual sorts of things, but in addition, it was anything that we could get hold of via the media. For example, when *Bad Meaning Good* dropped, that was something that really captivated me. Because being from London but not living in London, it kind of made me feel, you know, that urge to be back involved with everything.[1]

Kilo continues to comment that he could relate to the key figures in *Bad Meaning Good* "more so than the Americans", and that in terms of the film's impact, it "knocked us into check".[2] This self-checking that Kilo references is an example of one pivotal moment for the start of critical regionalism. It is impossible to pinpoint an exact period of enlightenment; however as I have demonstrated through the book much provincial illumination was charged by film and non-moving image representations. The impact of these moments lies in the response of the recipient-practitioner to his or her own practice and cultural context. Where Powell talks about critical regionalism and the university, he argues for the importance of a pedagogic project where there exist regional connections between campus and the wider landscape. He states that: "Indeed, it may be equally important to pursue this pedagogical project at institutions that have even less of a sense of mission to their surroundings because their students come from elsewhere…" (2007: 215). The teaching and learning in provincial British hip hop's former years was without strategy; it was autonomous and by osmosis, and indeed both the provincial adopters of hip hop and hip hop's sources were from "elsewhere". Powell continues to suggest "universities that, by virtue of their status as 'research' institutions, have even stronger allegiances to a geographically decontextualized model of the circulation of knowledge" (2007: 215). The idea that a critically informed discussion takes place within a decontextualization of location is central to the evolution of critical regionalist hip hop. Until the first reifications of local and regional hip hop were produced the level of regional criticality was intangible, and any analysis was based on skill and technique, hence critiquing the practices of hip hop through form and without context. Very swiftly however, skill, technique and an improving level of practice coupled with what they were learning from hip hop artefacts equipped early practitioners with an embodied knowledge to challenge their context. As I explored in Chapter 3, these appropriated spaces and territories were paramount to critically regional hip hop, not least for the circulation of knowledge within provincial settings, but for the execution of a shared and contextualized knowledge evidenced through practice within such locations; the case of Barclays exemplifies this. Although these early forms of critical regionalism in the provinces share some experiences with hip hop's emergence in London, the provincial demographics, lack of black and ethnic minority culture and much reduced access to contemporary American hip hop production augured in a hybrid culture rooted in elsewhere but grown in the province.

Proximity and distancing between rural corners and urban centres aided this evolution of critical regionalism through reflection. As I demonstrated through much of the book, the journeys that provincial headz undertook—from visiting local and regional capitals (such as Exeter, Bristol, Glasgow and Nottingham) and England's capital offered a space-time realm which was neither rural nor urban. As one traversed through rural to urban/urban to rural, one could anticipate, predict and reflect—in a zone where the province and the capital were melded by time. On another occasion, the provincial head might be classed as the somewhat derogatory "visitor", one who filches and exploits cultural capital for personal gain (usually with little return to the culture in question). However, as I attest in Chapters 4 and 5, the experiences of these regional journeys and reframing techniques fuelled a development of practice which positively contributed to the broader national growth of hip hop. This growth manifest particularly through music, but also through Bboying and graffiti, for example Swindon's Bboy crew, Scarecrows (UK Breakdance Championship Finalists 1999) and Bournemouth's Second To None. Musically, Hidden Identity, Def Defiance, and Krack Free Media demonstrated variable relationships between local/regional and national cultural contexts in their lyrics, while primarily drawing sonic influences from America and the emergent britcore sound. Of course, there were an array of crews across the British Isles in a similar position. A very local/regional sound, bespoke to each region, picked up on colloquialisms and vernacular phraseology, tropes and semantics, but always reframed them within the bounds of 1980s hip hop practice. Each region's outputs and productions were serving a purpose, serving the locale, and serving their crews and listeners. Although most provincial crews tried to land a recording contract with a London label, these efforts were largely cursory and apathetic; what counted was regional success.

These formative productions anchored the regional position of British hip hop for the nineties and noughties, and a swathe of acutely regionalist artists followed with independent, local or self-released recordings such as Bristol's Numskullz ('Enough Of That', 1996), Turroe (*The Shit Starter*, 2001), South Wales' Fleapit (*Music From The Ditch*, 2002), and Chattabox from South Shields in the north-east of England (who also teamed up with Somerset's Samuel Otis on the *Hard Graft* mixtape from 2011). More recently artists such as Jackie Chat present a confidence in their regional identity, such as in the song 'My Land' (2017), which opens with the rural parodic trope "get off my land" (a common jibe aimed at rural folk), before Jackie launches into an incensed chorus: "This is my land", where verse one poses the rhetoric: "How come half these rappers have to rap in different languages?", and further chorus chants of "'ere bey, get off 'er my land" which, following eight patterns of slick scratching, launches the outro: "Pasties, cider, tractors and tiddies / You're listening to the bey reppin' Exeter City / This is Jack Chat / This is Jack Chat", mischievously playing on Johnny Dynell and New York 88's 1983 rap on 'Jam Hot' (famously borrowed by Norman Cook for Beats International). However, unlike Verbal Wurzels, Jackie Chat does not play the eloquent fool, but rather offers straight-up hip hop with a seriousness in his West Country identity, a central theme in his songs. 'My Land' acts as a sequel to his 2014 song 'This Is Your Land', which opens with a wide horn stab, and Jackie's salutation "Alright, beys?" builds around the hook and riffs of Sharon Jones and the Dap-Kings' version of Woody Guthrie's protest song 'This Land Is Your Land' (2004). In Jackie's alternative version, the politics of territoriality relate to the cultural realities of the West Country, while taking issue with fraudulent dialect. Through snippets of narration in between verses, Jackie relentlessly exposes local rappers attempting to sound like London artists: "Where you from?... So why the fuck are you talking like that, then?", "I'm proud to come from here, that's why I sound like I'm from here...", "listen blud...", "shud up!", "no, but fam...", "shud up, bey!", and "why you talking like a Yardie mate, ain't you from Tiverton?" observe truisms in the post-global hip hop world. Meanwhile, his wordplay contextualizes and challenges: "You need to slow down rep you with your own sound / Run that shit that really truly goes down in your own town / Eight out of ten guns 'round here belong to farmers / When mad people are being bad you're home in your pajamas", addressing the issue of faux-gangsterism and false representation in music.

On one hand, it is curious that rap in the sticks still requires songs like this as the post-global/de-regional culture of hip hop continually develops, yet on the other hand, it remains very much needed as music corporations persistently flog the long-dead horse of a universal urban rap culture. Far from novelty, Jackie Chat represents the veritable voice of serious provincial hip hop, some thirty years after its inception. More recent celebratory practice of critically regional hip hop such as Jackie Chat's productions provokes questions about how far and diverse regionalism in British hip hop has developed and invites an exploration of its future. Furthermore, I am sanguine about the prospect of further academic and practice-based research which positions detailed interrogations of closely regionalist hip hop in the post-global and de-regional contours of the future. For me, studies of this nature will not only fill in significant gaps of hip hop knowledge in regions other than those already examined, but will expand knowledge of critical regionalism in cultural studies and ethnomusicology. Further still, the learning gained by engagement in regional hip hop practices contributes to a deeper understanding of regional contexts, as I have demonstrated in this book. I hope that the work presented here in relation to critical regionalism underpins some of these future anticipated studies.

Dispelling the Myth

The urban status in hip hop ran so deep that although the culture had spread across the breadth of North America by the time it reached Britain, it was still all about the New York narrative. The graffiti phenomenon aided this communication and provided a visual to the sonic story, but again, reinforced the urban. The mythology instilled during the formative years of hip hop in Britain can in some respects be forgiven, as its representations, spanning across the social spheres of media from news reports to hip hop records, contained solely references to urbanism. This is hardly surprising: hip hop was birthed in the most urban of sites, and its primary transatlantic journeys carried the allegories of the city. Through the pop-cultural crossovers of McLaren's reifications, to the scenes of *Style Wars*, *Beat Street* and *Wild Style*, the Street Sounds label, albums like *Street Beats*, and songs like 'Street Justice', signifiers to all things street, strongly connotated with all that is "urban", were ingrained in all things hip hop. A combination of urban density, history of soul and reggae, black diaspora and a precedent in transcultural music, dance, multiculturalist environment and sense of community led to Britain's first crews in London, Manchester, Birmingham, Bristol, Nottingham, Coventry and Wolverhampton being formed.

When it dawned on the media that the youth in Britain were not just consuming American hip hop but adopting it—and producing it themselves—commissioned reports such as DJ Steve Devonne's on breakdancing (Channel 4) from Covent Garden hit the airwaves. "From the ancient tribal drums, to the sounds of the city streets",[3] all the signs of this new culture pointed to the urban. However, as I have shown throughout the book, provincial and rural hip hop practice began only a mere fraction after its urban arrival. Yet, the excitement of the city sells, so even though breakdancing and graffiti were being practised widely and regularly across the provinces by late 1983, the commercial music industry continued to push urban symbolism to sell their compilation albums. In turn, the occupation of WHSmith and Woolworths' record racks countrywide by British releases such as 1984's *Breakdance Fever*, and even still in 1988 with Stylus Music's budget compilation *Hip Hop and Rapping in the House* whose sleeve depicts a generic skyscraper-esque city profile, the continual message to mainstream society was that hip hop equals urban, rap equals city. Terms like "urban music" (championed by New York DJ Frankie Crocker in the 1970s) which embody hip hop and rap as much as soul, rhythm and blues, reggae, dancehall, jungle, drum 'n' bass, house, garage, and more recently dubstep and grime, continually reinforce the status of the city.

Since the renaissance of record buying and the invention of the 7" 45rpm record at the end of the 1940s, the urban experience has been represented, celebrated and vilified through songs such as Petula Clark's 'Downtown' (1965), and Martha and the Vandellas' 'Dancing in the Street' (1964). In reference to 'Downtown', Adam Krims writes: "The downtown district is cathected as a locus of excitement, adventure, and even cheerful escape" (Krims 2007: 2), and 'Dancing in the Street' expounds the idea of excitement, as everyday people are offered an: "…invitation across the nation / A chance for folks to meet", where, we are promised, "There'll be laughing, singing, and music swinging / Dancing in the street". Krims talks about an "urban ethos" (2007: 1–25), which he surmises as a relationship between urban environments, the quotidian and "those who create and shape media culture" (2007: 25). I would amplify that those who shape the media culture that surrounds us are fostered by the relationship between artist and industry (in the case of DIY production, this is one and the same thing). For me, the cheerful escape that Petula Clark sings about celebrates the spectacle of the urban, represented in the practices of shopping and consuming, and the motifs and tropes of hip hop enabled the music industry to easily design and present compilation albums as a locus of excitement. As consumers consumed these albums by breakdancing and rapping along to them, and used them to develop their own practice, they became validated as an inherent component in the praxis of provincial British hip hop.

It is only when distancing occurs (as discussed in much of the book) that the space and time are provided to reflect on the representations of urbanism in hip hop, and only during that reflective process can the British hip hop head begin to comprehend the differences between metropolis and provincial forms of hip hop. The distancing through the dromosphere fuels a sense of apprehension and anticipation as provincial headz arrive, engage and depart from scenarios in the polis. Then, when compared with the context outside the dromospheric experience, the nuances between hip hop practice are noticed. Furthermore, the concept of the myth, which, combined with the signified, results in inferior quality reifications of hip hop such as the representations in *Breakdance Fever*. Within the myth of urban hip hop there are further complexities in that the signification presented in the example of *Breakdance Fever* is also based on an already loaded urban myth. Elsewhere I solidified my position on these visual approaches:

> ...the artwork sleeves sold a myth of the urban, displaying staged scenarios and cultural tokens of boomboxes, barbed wire, corrugated fencing and mock-graffiti painted in studios, captivating an audience disconnected from the reality of the metropolis. The dynamism of the urban sells; it is cool, fast and exhilarating, but these processes of production resulted in unsatisfactory reifications that did not solidify much of the genuine processes and intangibility of hip hop culture, but rather enticed consumers to buy into an urban fallacy (de Paor-Evans 2018c: 192).

In 'Flashback', Arsonists observe "Graffiti and breaking took a back seat / 'Cuz the A&R's couldn't figure how to make they ends meet..." (Fondle 'Em Records, 1997), yet what was happening through record sleeve design was that the elements of graffiti and breaking were exploited to sell the other elements of hip hop music, boosting the urban myth. By the time industry and consumer tourists abandoned graffiti and breaking, hip hop was already siloed as urban phenomena.

The dispelling of hip hop's urban myth in this book works both ways, and the rural does not function in isolation. As Lefebvre illustrates succinctly in *The Urban Revolution*, the relationship between rural and city operates as "the society that results from industrialisation, which is a process of domination that absorbs agricultural production" (Lefebvre 2003: 2). Woods (2011) also indicates similar thinking and engages with the rural in a global manner, and when discussing the British colonies and crops such as maize and potatoes attests that "the transportation of 'rural' objects and diffusion of rural ideas was not all one-way, but also flowed back from the colonies to Europe" (Woods 2011: 26). Similar cultural conduits are found in hip hop. As much as the work in this book attests to British hip hop's parallel evolution outside major cities and conurbations, it also gives rise to the hypothesis that rural and natural elements existed within urban hip hop's realm. When provincial headz talk about the city, one also thinks about the parks in New York, of 'South Bronx' by Boogie Down Productions, where KRS-One narrates: "They tried again outside in Cedar Park / Power from a street light made the place dark", and of MC Shan's testament that "They used to do it out in the park" from the song of the same name, and the socio-politics in 'The Message': "Can't walk through the park, 'cause it's crazy after dark". In addition to these literal moments are the plethora of rural metaphors in New York hip hop, most obviously in crew names such as Jungle Brothers which contains a multiplicity of meaning: not least giving visibility to the Motherland. In this book I have explored the blurred boundaries between the urban within rural British hip hop and previously (albeit briefly) outlined the rural in New York hip hop in my article 'Soft Tension: Reimagining Urbanism and Rurality through the Spatio-cultural Practices of Hip Hop' (2018), but how does the rural realm manifest itself in urban hip hop, and how does rural hip hop manifest itself in the urban realm? There is much work to do here, and I am optimistic that the study presented in this book might act as a platform for such future projects. I look forward to scholarship that presents a more comprehensive exploration, particularly in Britain and the wider geographies of Europe. I am further optimistic that this book can be used as a foundation for multispatial and transcultural explorations into reggae, drum 'n' bass, UK garage and grime; to not only understand the transience, displacements and placements of these music cultures but also challenge the conventions of spatial materiality they inhabit.

Revealing the Invisible

In *Identities and Social Change in Britain since 1940* (2010), Mike Savage explores in detail the personal languages of social history, and by "avoiding the grand functionalist theorizing of American sociology, the focus was on eliciting accounts from which sociologists could unravel how people's ordinary situations shaped their lives, actions, thoughts, and endeavors" (Savage 2010: 237). Savage presents a clear contextual value in the research material gained from autobiographical and personal accounts, a method that has been fundamental to my work in this book. Its value feels most apparent here, as the interviewees reflect on their lives and the impact of hip hop culture. Rollefson concludes that "hip hop is a remarkably historicizing form of popular culture" (Rollefson 2017: 226), and "is a cultural practice through which European youth both perform their resistance from and relation to their respective nations" (Rollefson 2017: 227). Indeed, the hip hop headz of provincial Britain performed forms of resistance to their local and regional and national socio-political climate, historicizing the evolution of regional hip hop while critiquing London-centric and American rap. But, in the longer term they created a life-structure which although has gradually become invisible for some, remains critical to their considerations in everyday life. These non-obvious, invisible attributes of provincial British hybrid hip hop culture are the most significant and impactful parts of the culture I have attempted to define throughout this book. Hip hop has shaped provincial headz' families, DJ Krash Slaughta attests:

> I met my wife through hip hop as she used to DJ also in a duo as a female DJ duo called Cuts D-fined. We both have very loyal and great friends for life through hip hop. You just can't buy that kind of thing, can you? I'm sure people in other scenes feel the same about their music or friends & experience/experiences through music but for me, hip hop has been a big part of life and always will be. I still DJ today, playing all kinds of music learned through crate digging, which as you know is another form of the hip hop art, and now enjoy collecting music or learning about music from others. I will never stop learning through this music and thank god for hip hop. It's paved the way for a better way of life and without it, I would be lost (email to author, 6 April 2017).

ShellToeMel also explains the depth of the hip hop family:

> Hip hop has affected my life without a doubt. I danced for the love of the music at the beginning of my journey in the eighties. I went on to teach and perform throughout the community. I got to train and learn from artists such as Mr. Wiggles and Ken Swift from the Rocksteady crew who first played a part in my introduction to hip hop. I met up with some guys who formed a crew named Flyin' Jalapenos and I became a member of the crew and we are now celebrating our fifteen-year anniversary this year. My kids are children of hip hop. Their fathers are a DJ and a graff artist and I would not have met them without hip hop (email to author, 23 April 2017).

The power of hip hop on headz' personal journeys through life is also paramount to personal development and reflection, as Rola states:

> Every choice I've made in my life that's led me right up to the situation that I'm in now is all because of hip hop. It changed everything. I wouldn't be who I am now. All my friends, family and loved ones that I have is all because of hip hop. There's no doubt my life would have gone down a completely different path (email to author, 25 March 2017).

DJ Format's response raises similar life-changing points:

> I like to think that hip hop somehow, I just found this culture that somehow just spoke to me and it just somehow laid the foundation for how I was going to live the rest of my life. I don't really know why it spoke to me so much, but somehow the idea of being creative but with very little resources and just kind of, just having a lot of energy and fun and just doing something for the hell of it, I try to keep the mentality to this day. Whether I do or not is questionable at 44 years old but yeah, definitely (i/v, Brighton, 17 December 2017).

Nat Drastic also holds dear the personal values: "It's given me a sense of belief in myself. It will always be there. Like I'll always be in Pontefract" (email to author, 25 February 2017), which DJ Bex also commented upon:

"I think hip hop gave me the courage to have a little swagger, I am only 5'7", but seriously it has taught me to see past the front, it has given me peace of mind at times of difficulty" (email to author, 27 March 2017). Chrome's testament reinforces the convictions of Rola, Nat, and DJ Bex:

> Hip hop gave me confidence to be more sociable and extrovert. I was a very timid boy and so it was really hard for me to step on stage in front of people… I feel I've gained a wealth of knowledge from hip hop. From not only listening to the music but from learning the dance, the geography, the books and gaining so many friends worldwide. I don't believe I would have got this from any other culture (email to author, 25 February 2018).

And for GeeSwift, hip hop was a link to outside rurality: "I lived in Whimple in Devon. It was very rural. The main employment was the local cider factory", so discovering hip hop culture offered a richer focus for life:

> I saw hip hop music as a way to express myself. It made me more of an individual. Hip hop has been part of my life for 29 years. It gave me the confidence to start rapping, producing. It gave me a focus for so long, this will never change (email to author, 20 June 2017).

Cobra P.I. (Agent/Rapid Fire) also talks about the broader holistic and lasting impact of hip hop culture:

> Well it's now in my DNA so there's no choice at this point. Whether it's hearing the banging drums of a break by THE METERS, reminiscing about a killer verse by KANE, looking mesmerized by QBERT'S perfection of his craft or seeing a freshly painted burner by CHEO, I will never get bored of the art form that has provided the backdrop to my life so far (email to author, 25 May 2017).

Finally, on the personal aspect, Junior Disprol affirms:

> It's been a massive driving factor in my life. It's made me work hard on my craft, given me the stamina to keep going through hard times, been a massive source of fun and enjoyment, made

me friends and relationships, instilled an independent attitude and work ethic, taken me to other countries, put me on stage with people I grew up listening to and put me on wax which is a biggie still (email to author, 2 June 2017).

Dr. Syntax claims the value of hip hop as a professional practising artist:

I'm a full-time B boy making noise! I'm an MC by profession, I don't do anything else. It's undoubtedly shaped my world view. It's taken me around the world. Pretty much all the close friends I have are through making music. Complete strangers come up to me and compliment me. That's insane. So yeah, I owe rather a lot to hip hop (email to author, 1 May 2017).

A similar impact was experienced by Tom Dartnell whose career path was formed by hip hop:

It did shape my life in terms of the friends I have and the direction my career often took. As I said earlier, when I was at school I made a fanzine about British hip-hop and that satisfied two things: my passion for UK rap and my desire to work in magazines. Then this was repeated when I got to write for *HHC (Hip Hop Connection)*. Later on, I worked for *Graphotism* for a while because I had magazine experience and a background in graf. Then a fellow *HHC* journalist hooked me up with a job at the magazine company he worked for. So, what I'm basically saying is that my involvement in hip-hop led to all these career breaks (email to author, 12 June 2017).

Graffiti writer and artist Ricky Also emphasizes the worthiness of a hip hop career:

It has given me a sense of anything is achievable, you just need to put the work in. Hip hop was originally about a do-it-yourself attitude, you don't need much to create something that you and mates buzz off and then fuck everyone else. It's also an amazing scene when you can meet/work with/or paint with your heroes, people who have influenced your life. And they are proper heroes, people who have earned it, and not just famous because they look good or from a privileged background or have just gained a massive Instagram following. It's taught me originality is essential, to be genuine and to work hard at what you love (email to author, 21 January 2018).

Evil Ed acknowledges the broader education that hip hop has given him:

It taught me so much about life I wouldn't have learned from school or my parents. It led to me meeting so many people from different places and different walks of life and it gave me a purpose, a goal to work towards, to make records. It gave me my identity completely. I've been living hip hop for over three quarters of my life, listening to the music, going to the jams, making records, connecting with other hip hop people (email to author, 14 June 2017).

Sleician Cullen summarizes:

Hip hop, music, most definitely has saved my life, I had many encounters with the dark side this world has to offer and hip hop at that time had a huge part in keeping me grounded, don't get me wrong, I love all music and making various forms of it being a published musician, but if it boils down to it, if I had never got into hip hop culture, I feel I would [n]ever have made music…it saved me. I create and listen to all forms nowadays, but I still love hip hop like I did when I first got into the culture, being a father of three, two dogs, beautiful woman in my life, own business and still making music and creating art, I couldn't be more grateful (email to author, 12 April 2017).

I will conclude this part with a word from Craig Leckie: "Hip hop supplied the soundtrack for my life. And in its purest sense hip hop was human. Hip hop was life itself" (email to author, 29 April 2017). There is one final point I would like to make: while the conclusions above follow the body of work in this book and are based upon a set of reflective interviews, artefact, visual and sonic analysis, literature review, a range of ethnographies, and are anchored in certain historic parameters, these stories deserve to be taken into the future of hip hop research, education and practice. The work here has proven the value of provincial hip hop practice as critical to a way of life: offering an education, encouraging questioning and building confidence in pushing life's multiplicity for many. I call to my hip hop scholars, practitioners, educators, participants, consumers, producers and peers to shape, take responsibility for and to support provincial hip hop's scholarly future—not only for the future generations of hip hop headz, but the older ones, and the members of society outside the realm of hip hop: potential funders, stakeholders and other beneficiaries of this great field of hip hop scholarship. Let us work together to build the future of regional-rural hip hop; let us show them what it can do, and let them show us what they can do.

Postscript

The day I was completing this monograph, I was scrolling through Instagram (I am a self-confessed addict of posting a record each day and following thousands of folks involved in hip hop culture across the globe), and one particular post caught my eye. Wiltshire's DJ Baila posted a photograph of himself crouched in a country lane posing with a bunch of 7" singles and a portable turntable (serious diggers' equipment for record hunting—and in fact the one pictured with DJ Baila was found in the field, excuse the pun), by a signpost that read "Digging Lane" (Figure 7.1). He was returning from a rural record fair near Oxford and took the opportunity for a photographic quip. This affirmed for me not only the acceptance of hip hop in rural areas, but the embracing of ruralness *and* hip hop, and the richness of this combination. As I continued to scroll through my Instagram feed I noticed more than ever posts from the many forty-somethings I follow and their daily celebrations as teachers, parents, professional designers, artists and DJs, social workers and authors—all of whom have been championed by a subaltern vocational and/or academic education in hip hop. And those headz whose hip hop influence is less obvious in their everyday careers display their love for and impact of the culture through their actions as friends and colleagues. With cuts in arts education and the need to raise awareness of wellbeing across the UK, maybe the future of provincial hip hop is to channel its practice into teaching those outside its bounds. Perhaps this is the next journey of research into British hip hop from the provincial perspective.

Now, what we really need are critical studies on the formative years of hip hop in the cities of London, Birmingham, Bristol, Manchester, Nottingham, Cardiff, Belfast, Glasgow and Wolverhampton. This historical analysis of the urban evolution of British hip hop is essential to challenge and progress the

Figure 7.1: Swindon's DJ Baila in Digging Lane. Photograph by Harrison Ford.

discussions initiated in *Provincial Headz*, which we owe to hip hop. I await those monographs with great anticipation.

Notes

Preface

1 Refer to Glossary for a definition of *hip hop headz*, or *headz*.
2 Although one could argue that the science fiction and futuristic tropes and effigies that abstractly adorned the sleeves of the *Electro* series linked in some way to the concept of Afrofuturism.
3 Rooted in electro, Man Parrish's seminal anthem 'Hip Hop, Be Bop (Don't Stop)' from 1982 was a club crossover success, and apart from this record there was minimal visibility of the phrase "hip hop" in the British context until mid-1984.

Introduction

1 Hip hop consists of four core physical elements (which I prefer to call practices), and these consist of *DJing*, *rapping/emceeing*, *Bboying* and *graffiti writing*, which evolved at various points during the 1970s. Subsequently, the mental and metaphysical element of *knowledge* was created during the early 1980s, with *human beatbox* (early 1980s) and *production* (late 1980s) also factoring in as hip hop's sixth and seventh elements. While there are other elements discussed within hip hop such as fashion and language (see Chang 2007), I would position language within the element of knowledge, and place fashion within the realm of hip hop's reifications and representations rather than its practices.
2 It is essential to the scholarship of hip hop studies that a future academic study be produced which specifically brings visibility to the experiences of provincial headz of Black and Minority Ethnic (BAME) origin.
3 Self-release cassettes were rarely stocked in record shops, and were usually sold at school, college or on the street or at jams. Occasionally a local independent shop may have taken a small number of these to sell on a "sale or return" basis.
4 The Oxford English Dictionary (OED) added "woke" in June 2017, and define woke adjectively meaning: "woke, adj.2 figurative and in figurative contexts.

Originally: well-informed, up-to-date. Now chiefly: alert to racial or social discrimination and injustice; frequently in *stay woke*." *Oxford English Dictionary*, http://www.oed.com/view/Entry/58068747?rskey=6YMygL& (accessed 11 October 2017). Merriam-Webster (2017) note that the term became more widely used after the police shooting of Michael Brown in 2014 (https://www.merriam-webster.com/words-at-play/woke-meaning-origin, accessed 10 May 2019). For me, the definition of woke which resonates the strongest is by Ashlee, Zamora and Karikari (2017): "We define wokeness as critical consciousness to intersecting systems of oppression. Specifically, to be a woke person is to hold an unretractable embodied consciousness and political identity acknowledging the oppression that exists in individual and collective experiences" (2017: 90).
5 DeLanda's theory of assemblage in *A New Philosophy of Society* (2013) takes assemblage theory as presented by Deleuze and Guattari in *A Thousand Plateaus* (1980) as its point of departure.
6 Refer to Glossary for a description and definition of *dig* and *digging*.
7 The term *britcore* is a post-rationalization, and was invented by the European fan base, at some point circa 1994. Refer to Glossary and p. 238 for further information.

Chapter 1

1 1520 Sedgwick Avenue, The Bronx, New York City is commonly accepted as the birth of hip hop, and the first "block party", where DJ Kool Herc threw a party in the communal room for his sister's birthday (see Chang 2007).
2 'Everything Is Everything', Lauryn Hill, Ruffhouse Records, 1998.
3 "'TAKI 183' spawns pen pals" was the headline and this story is extensively referred to in much documentation about the origins of graffiti including *Style Wars* (1983), *Subway Art* (1984), *The History of American Graffiti* (2011), and *Getting Up* (1984).
4 Refer to Glossary for definition of *DJing* and *Bboying*.
5 For a detailed description of conurbation, see Geddes, *Cities in Evolution* (1949).
6 Refer to Glossary for cultural definition of *boombox*, also known as a *ghetto blaster*.
7 *Tagging* is the act of writing one's tag, or graffiti name; refer to Glossary for more detail.
8 Refer to Glossary for *graffiti writer/writing*. The term *writing* is used throughout this book.
9 Lee Quinones during interview for *Style Wars: Revisited*, one of the extras on the 2006 DVD edition of *Style Wars* (1983), dir. Silver and Chalfant.
10 KRS-One and Rakim are generally considered two of the most revered emcees worldwide, with both often considered as the GOAT (greatest of all time). Kool

G Rap, Big Daddy Kane, Melle Mel and Nas are also often discussed as worthy of this title.
11 In *Style Wars* (1983) Noc 167 states "everybody's got their own arrow... I like that though". (This quote is often incorrectly referenced as by Zephyr or Dondi White.)
12 These works of graffiti became known as *masterpieces*, or simply *pieces*. Refer to Glossary for definition and description.
13 See Toop (1985) and Chang (2007), *Wild Style* (1983), *Style Wars* (1983) and *Graffiti Rock* (1984) for further evidence of this phenomenon.
14 Records now considered as exemplary and timeless hip hop breakbeats include 'Funky Drummer' by James Brown (1970), 'Apache' by Incredible Bongo Band (1973) and 'Ashley's Roachclip' by The Soul Searchers (1974) and have been sampled numerous times in rap records.
15 See *Hip Hop Evolution*—episode 1 (2016), Netflix (accessed 4 November 2017).
16 Refer to Glossary for definitions and variations of *battling*.
17 Refer to Glossary for definition of *crews*.
18 The actions of headz initially operated in a reactionary way before they developed into a set of spatial and material counter-tactics based on close reflection of their experiences. This developed rapidly over a period of only seven years.
19 Refer to Glossary for *emcee*. *Emcees* are distinguished from *rappers* as the vocalists who rap, host, interact and support the DJ during live performances; in effect, they are masters of ceremony, whereas rappers simply rap. To be an emcee is perceived as being superior to a rapper.
20 Common tropes include: "who's in the house?", "if you're from the Bronx make some noise", and so on. Cowboy (Furious Five) is credited as championing this method of crowd interaction (Flash in Toop 1985: 72).
21 Funk, soul, breaks, reggae, rock, electro and rap music are the terms used in this book to describe genre-specific hip hop music.
22 Coke La Rock states himself that he was really "just shouting out people's names", although there was a clear intention to interact with the crowd, use the microphone at particular points during DJ Kool Herc's show, and add a layer to the already dynamic music collage presented by Kool Herc. See *Hip Hop Evolution*—episode 1 (2016), Netflix (accessed 3 November 2017).
23 Although Cowboy (Furious Five) invented the phrase "hip hop", Lovebug Starski is credited as the champion of the phrase which he would chant during his residency at the Disco Fever (Bambaataa in Toop 1985: 56). Crash Crew were one of the first crews to obtain a recording contract, and Kurtis Blow was the first artist to sign to a major label (Mercury Records).
24 In 2017, American acts like Lil Yachty, Young Thug and Rich The Kid are classed as rap artists, but hip hop's elder statemen (such as Pete Rock) argue they contribute precious little to hip hop culture.
25 By employing a similar method, the rhythms of these disco-rap records covered or borrowed from well-known disco records, most notably 'Feel The

Heartbeat' (1981) by The Treacherous Three, T-Ski Valley's 'Catch The Beat' (1981), 'A Heartbeat Rap' (1981) by Sweet G (covering Taana Gardner's 1981 record 'Heartbeat'), 'It's Nasty (Genius of Love)' (1981) by Grandmaster Flash & Furious Five, 'Genius Rap' (1981) by Dr. Jeckyll and Mr. Hyde (covering Tom Tom Club's 1981 release 'Genius of Love'), and 'Rap, Bounce, Rockskate' (1980) by Trickeration (covering Vaughan Mason and Crew's 'Bounce, Rock, Skate, Roll' from 1979). These examples echo the respective original versions and display a clear intention to enter the commercial dance record market, which at the time was swamped with the tail-end of disco music.

26 Refer to Glossary for *bitten*, or to *bite*, which in basic terms means to copy disrespectfully.

27 Disco Mix Club (DMC) is a worldwide organization advocating the role of the DJ in the world of music. Since DMC's focus on the annual world mixing championships, the organization gained close alignment with hip hop artists, and this relationship peaked between 1986 and 1988 when winners DJ Cheese (US) and Cash Money (US) respectively were working closely with emcees Word Of Mouth and Marvelous. *DMC World DJ Championships*, http://www.dmcdjchamps.com/about.php (accessed 22 February 2018).

28 See Smith 2016 for an extensive study on the turntable as musical instrument.

29 Refer to Glossary for definition of *deck*.

30 Although the original SL-1200 and SL-1210 are discontinued, Panasonic launched a new model in 2016 at an outrageously overpriced figure, and most DJs prefer to seek out second-hand models Mk1–Mk5.

Chapter 2

1 On 3 January 1980 Kurtis Blow performed 'Christmas Rappin'' on *Top Of The Pops*, and was the first hip hop artist to sign to a major label (Mercury Records), and was also the first to achieve gold status for his 1980 single 'The Breaks'.

2 'The Message' was also appropriated for a Green Cross Code road safety advertisement in the UK during 1983, which had an impact on the broader recognition of the song, although sadly dumbing down the "don't push me 'cause I'm close to the edge" metaphorical hook line into a literal translation not to step out into the road without looking.

3 See "Politics, Class and Ideology" (208–241) in Andrew Gamble's insightful political history text *The Free Economy and The Strong State: The Politics of Thatcherism* (1994).

4 Coventry's The Specials and Woking's The Jam respectively constructed strong socio-political narratives through much of their work, notably The Specials' 'Ghost Town', 'Man At C&A' and 'Why?', and The Jam's 'Eton Rifles', 'In The City' and 'Time For Truth', the latter of which embodied suggestions of the ideology of the British Empire and criticizing Prime Minister James Callaghan:

"Whatever happened to the great Empire? / I think it's time for truth, and the truth is you lost, Uncle Jimmy" (1977).
5 *Blue Peter* often broadcast "show and tell" stories about how to make something for the garden (which viewers would then see placed in the Blue Peter garden by the in-house gardener), or shown how to craft a sledge, or a bird-table—perfect aspirations of a middle-class lifestyle.
6 Growing up in Lancashire, *Grange Hill*'s creator Phil Redmond was exposed to Marxist-based philosophies in "the great socialist Jerusalem of the North-West" (Wintle 2016).
7 Often hip hop shows were broadcast from pirate stations, many of them part of the tower block pirate radio movement, named after their locations. Much akin to the pirate stations of the 1960s that broadcast from the sea, the 1980s pirate stations broadcast from tower blocks and were more difficult to trace to any particular flat, and radio equipment could be relocated to a different apartment with an early enough warning before authorities arrived at the flat in question. The influence of national radio shows is discussed in detail in Chapter 4.
8 It is important to note that at this point Groove Records were promoting an electro/funk chart, and not a hip hop chart. The early incarnation of hip hop in Britain was commonly called electro, largely due to the weight of the *Street Sounds* series, but equally because the very notion of hip hop as a cultural phenomenon had not yet become tangible in Britain. This is an interesting point which arose during several of the interviews I conducted, most notably with Darren Norris aka Big Tunes D, which is discussed later.
9 It should be noted that wartime immigration also accounted for many immigrants in Britain, who were mainly located in Liverpool and London, although a very small number of people of West Indian origin were the descendants of ex-slaves from the 1800s. It should further be noted that: "Black people—by whom I mean Africans and Asians and their descendants—have been living in Britain for close on 500 years. They have been born in Britain since about the year 1505. In the seventeenth and eighteenth centuries thousands of black youngsters were brought to this country against their will as domestic slaves" (Fryer 2010: xiii).
10 Tom Dartnell was one half of 1990s British rap crew Metaphorce, editor of *Behind Enemy Lines* fanzine, and a writer for *Hip Hop Connection* magazine between 1996 and 2008.
11 *2001 Census Briefing, Six: Ethnicity and Religion*. The Research and Consultation Unit, Brighton and Hove City Council. http://www.brighton-hove.gov.uk/sites/brighton-hove.gov.uk/files/downloads/citystats/6_Ethnicity_Religion.pdf (accessed 24 June 2018).
12 The Wild Bunch were originally a sound system before they released any records. Initiated in the early 1980s and based in the St Paul's, Montpellier and Bishopston districts of Bristol, they battled in soundclashes with other Bristol sound systems inspired by the reggae sound system movement. For an in-depth discussion on

the formative years of Massive Attack, see Melissa Chemam's *Massive Attack: Out of the Comfort Zone* (2019).
13 This perception surrounds the idea of relative distancing, a recurring theme throughout the book.
14 Other British labels that specialized in hip hop were Champion, Cooltempo and FFRR, although these labels favoured issuing US artists' music under licence.
15 'My Fair Lady/London Bridge Is Falling Down' possibly dates back to the late Middle Ages, although the words were first published in 1744. See Fuld (2000).
16 In many published works on the subject, the term *Britishness* is used interchangeably with *Englishness*. While "Britishness" is favoured in this book, certain references contain the word "Englishness", which illustrates one of the facets of confusion faced within British identity.
17 It also needs to be stated that there is an inherent problem within the concepts of Britishness and Englishness, in that the two terms are used interchangeably by much of broader society, both informally and formally. There is not the space in this work to fully discuss the differences between Great Britain, the United Kingdom, England, Scotland, Wales, Northern Ireland, the Republic of Ireland (Eire), and the six thousand smaller islands that comprise the British Isles. This is far more than semantics; misjudgements and confusion regarding cultural identity in Britain have been rife since its inception, and at the time of writing, these issues are being exacerbated by Brexit.
18 *Beat This!: A Hip Hop History*, dir. Dick Fontaine, 1984.
19 Planet Patrol's 'Play At Your Own Risk' (1982) was edited with sections of 'Planet Rock' from the same 24-track tape that did not make the final 'Planet Rock' single cut.
20 https://www.discogs.com/master/view/19152 (accessed 10 January 2018).
21 Afrika Bambaataa was accused in 2014 of a series of sexual abuse allegations, the first of which was alleged by Ronald Savage, a member of the Zulu Nation during the 1980s. This has been a shock for hip hop culture, and particularly the Zulu Nation; however no single person runs a culture, and hip hop is regrouping and recovering from this. The fact remains that 'Planet Rock' was paramount to hip hop's development, and to avoid discussing the value and importance of the record due to these recent events would be to avoid history.
22 The popularization and impact of the megamix is discussed in more depth within Chapter 5, 'On Production'.
23 'Cheap Thrills' (1983) was Planet Patrol's second single following 'Play At Your Own Risk'.
24 'Looking for the Perfect Beat' (1983) followed the enormous success of 'Planet Rock' as Afrika Bambaataa's follow-up single.
25 From the film *808* about the Roland TR-808. Los Angeles/London: You Know Ltd, 2015.

26 'Looking for the Perfect Beat' (1983), 'Renegades of Funk' (1983), and 'Frantic Situation' (1984), all produced by Arthur Baker and released on Tommy Boy Records.
27 All lyrics contained in this paragraph from 'Planet Rock' by Afrika Bambaataa & the Soul Sonic Force (1982).
28 Deliverance were founded by Audio J, Ryman, Survive, Remark, Rage, Fatal, Forge & Kid Blast, releasing four hip hop 12"s in the mid-1990s on European Rhyme-Records and subsequently Nutcracker Records (1994–96).
29 Refer to Glossary for definition of *boombox*.
30 Only one of the five songs was not produced by Arthur Baker, this being 'Pack Jam', by Jonzun Crew, produced by the Maurice Starr/Michael Jonzun production partnership.
31 Refer to Glossary for *pop/poppin'* and *lock/lockin'*.
32 These were the principles of hip hop culture according to the Universal Zulu Nation, exemplified in 'Unity' by Afrika Bambaataa and James Brown (1984). This record is crucially important to hip hop culture of this time, not only for its promotion of the Zulu Nation manifesto, it was also the first collaboration between James Brown and a hip hop artist, James Brown's funk music being a cornerstone of hip hop culture.
33 Mark Dery first used the term "Afrofuturism" in 1992, affirmed in Nelson (2000).
34 *Kicks* is a hip hop terminology for trainers or sneakers, now in common usage worldwide.
35 *Breakdance: The Movie* was explicitly renamed for the European audience, amid concerns that viewers outside the United States would not grasp its original US title of *Breakin'*.
36 Rola, a formidable emcee from Sidford, Devon was one-third of Numskullz who signed to Bristol-based Hombré Recordings during the 1990s and were formed following the split of Def Defiance in 1993. Rola continues to produce and engineer hip hop and has engineered over 500 songs for artists across the breadth of Britain since 2013.
37 Richard "Rumage" Cowling, another member of Numskullz, was living in Broadclyst at this time, a small satellite village a few miles outside Exeter, Devon. He later relocated to the seaside town of Exmouth, Devon.
38 'Reckless' was the only rap song that appeared on the *Breakdance: The Movie* soundtrack album, which illustrates well the softer approach to the totality of the project. Ice-T's emerging profile as an emcee was undoubtedly strengthened due to his appearance in both the film and on Chris "The Glove" Taylor and Dave Storr's 'Reckless', having released only one single prior to this, the 1983 record 'Cold Wind-Madness/The Coldest Rap' (Saturn Records), where in fact the raps only appear on the B-side.
39 Refer to Glossary for the definition of *uprock*.

40 This was the new line-up of Grandmaster Melle Mel and the Furious Five—Scorpio, Cowboy, King Louie, Kama Kaze Kid and Tommy Gunn, reconfigured after the original members of Grandmaster Flash & The Furious Five.
41 The Radway Cinema remains the only cinema in the coastal town of Sidmouth, Devon. In the 1980s it often screened films a week or more after the nearest larger towns, and also missed many releases due to the fact it only has a single screen, so I was only delighted when the Radway showed *Beat Street*.
42 In *Non-places: Introduction to an Anthropology of Supermodernity*, Marc Augé discusses spaces such as transit hubs, routes, hotel chains, and retail outlets as non-place, places without specific identities. The subway scene in *Beat Street* typifies this notion, and this non-place, juxtaposed with the Bboys striving for identity and hierarchy, presents an opportunity for inquiry into the relationship between individual and collective identity versus identity of place. The nature of the space alters during the battle, and a distinction could be drawn between "geometric space" and "anthropological space" (Merleau-Ponty 2013).
43 Fab 5 Freddy and Beside are responsible for the most cut-up soundbite of all time, the "Ahhhhh this stuff is really fresh" from the close of 'Change The Beat' (1982).
44 Grand Wizard Theodore is widely credited with inventing the scratch. For a more detailed description of scratching see Katz (2012) which covers the evolution of DJing from hip hop's early inception.
45 It is crucially important here to stress two things:
(1) Whether graffiti is an element of hip hop culture or not has been an ongoing debate within graffiti culture since the 1970s, and this study does not seek to dismiss the view that graffiti is disconnected from hip hop. However, this work does support the synergy between graffiti, Bboying, DJing and rap, and their shared (to a certain degree) state of mind, counter-cultural evolution and social commentary as introduced under "Locating the Spatial" in Chapter 1 (and at points throughout the remainder of the book), and;
(2) All four practices existed before these films were produced, including in provincial Britain, but the release of these films into society and their subsequent impact anchored these practices as the elements of hip hop due to the compressing of culture (cultural tamping, discussed in the final section of this chapter)—the film took the place of a lack of contextual history and experience.
46 Gary Byrd was a radio jock, artist and personality, and released a spate of funk and rap records between 1970 and 1986, mainly under the name Gary Byrd and The G.B. Experience. His biggest commercial success was with 'The Crown', the only release on Stevie Wonder's WonDirection Records, which benefited from distribution and worldwide release through Motown Records.
47 Mel Brooks recorded a spurious rap song titled 'To Be or Not to Be (The Hitler Rap)', in which he took on the persona of Adolf Hitler. The record was produced by Pete Wingfield of Olympic Runners, whose 1974 song 'Grab It' remains a breakbeat staple of hip hop music.

48 Taken from Kilo's interview in the UltraCab by All City Steve on the *Allcity TaxiTalk Show*, 2 June 2018, https://www.youtube.com/watch?v=zZ6tUGWUySA&t=2948s (accessed 4 June 2018).
49 The song itself is a designed piece of hip hop engineering, as McLaren approached Trevor Horn, renowned for his electronic sound engineering and production skills which were at the time gathering momentum with his work on Frankie Goes to Hollywood's releases. This is important here as the scratching and drum programming that emulated an authentic hip hop sound was manufactured by Trevor Horn, and it is unclear how much of an input, if any, the World's Famous Supreme Team had, but they were achieving radio success on New Jersey station WHBI which raised the kudos of 'Buffalo Gals' within existing hip hop circles.
50 It is interesting to note that in response to Rodney P's statement, DJ Premier raises his eyebrows in surprise that such a song could signal hip hop's starting point, which suggests that this song on either side of the Atlantic holds very different values.
51 *Bredrin* is a Rastafarian subdialect word for brethren, commonly used in London hip hop/reggae culture.
52 See Glossary for definition of *jam*.
53 However, during the following year the releases of 'Hey You (The Rock Steady Crew)' by the Rock Steady Crew, 'Rockit' by Herbie Hancock and 'Street Dance' by Break Machine caught my attention again, through the video representations as much as the exciting synthesized sounds. Another record that was pivotal for many in 1983 was 'White Lines (Don't Don't Do It)' by Grandmaster & Melle Mel, and while I did not fully understand the socio-political message embodied within Melle Mel's lyrics or the interpolated melody and rhythm from experimental band Liquid Liquid's 'Cavern', the punch of the rap and the mesmerizing music fascinated me. The films *Breakdance* (1984), *Beat Street* (1984) and *Wild Style* (1983) were pivotal, and the availability of their associated soundtrack LPs led to school lunchtime discussions about the best songs, rappers, cuts and sounds.
54 Nick Egan was McLaren's conceptual partner (or critical friend) and responsible for the art direction for *Duck Rock* and the development of the *Duck Rock* boombox. Additionally, he directed the artwork for Bow Wow Wow.
55 Donnay were a sports brand of choice during the 1980s, and were in abundant supply in the provinces, where there was equally a shortfall of Fila gear (which would have been the brand of choice, had the football hooligans not consumed the very small amount of Fila offerings).
56 https://albumcoverhalloffame.wordpress.com/2013/08/16/interview-with-nick-egan-the-making-of-the-album-cover-for-duck-rock/ (accessed 2 January 2018).
57 Ibid.
58 This film was a reincarnation of earlier ideas by Julian Temple and McLaren during their time at art school (where McLaren spent almost a decade).

59 Arguably *Duck Rock* was a form of radical post-modernism, some 29 years before the term was first used by Charles Jencks to describe a new form of architecture that revisited contextual counterpoints and embraced the "hybrid trope" (Jencks 2011: 62).
60 Livingstone was designated a new town under the New Towns Act of 1946 and was one of five new towns to ease overcrowding in Glasgow. The first occupants moved into the new town four years after the shale mining ceased in 1962. The new town was only 16 years old when 'Buffalo Gals' was released.
61 "Graf" is a colloquialism for *graffiti*, often used in conversation within the British hip hop community. See Glossary.
62 https://www.nrscotland.gov.uk/statistics-and-data/statistics/statistics-by-theme/population/population-estimates (accessed 29 May 2017).
63 UK Data Census, 1981, https://census.ukdataservice.ac.uk/get-data/aggregate-data (accessed 29 May 2017).
64 Heanor is a small historic parish, documented in the Domesday Book of 1086 as Hainoure; 30% of the area is currently within a green belt.
65 Compassion in World Farming, https://www.ciwf.org.uk/media/5235182/Statistics-Dairy-cows.pdf (accessed 6 April 2018).
66 Chrome, from hip hop crews Def Tex and Chrome and Ill Inspired, has been highly active in British hip hop culture since the 1980s, his vinyl debut album with Def Tex being *Tutorial Sessions II*, on the independent Norwich-based label Soundclash Records in 1994. Chrome was living in the small town of Stone, Staffordshire when he discovered hip hop, and later moved to Norwich, Norfolk in the late 1980s. His lyric "spray up my ghetto giving that *Duck Rock* feel" appears on his 2013 song 'I Remember When', an ode to the touchstones and artefacts of 1980s hip hop.
67 The element that was by far the most widely practised during hip hop's "craze" period was breakdancing due to there being no prerequisite for equipment, tools or skills—it was much more immediate.
68 Big Tunes D is one of Gloucester's staple DJs, playing regularly for SGVC (Stroud and Gloucester Vinyl Connection) and hosting his hip hop show on Gloucester FM 96.6.
69 These moments of mimicry are crucial to the progression of provincial hip hop praxis and are discussed in depth throughout Chapter 5 on the processes of production.

Chapter 3

1 At that point, we had no idea that the origins of Bboying lay in the break. Hip hop had been delivered to us through electro music, and that is what we breakdanced to.

2. The Nike two-tone windcheater was the Bboy's jacket of choice and was originally issued in a limited colour scheme with the two-tone grey and the blue-grey being the most common. The jacket was light and forgiving with a smooth finish which made it the perfect garment for Bboying. The availability of Nike products was rare in Devon at this time, which increased the status of these objects of desire.
3. Puma were the trainer of choice; with a lack of availability of Puma States (as worn by Rock Steady Crew and almost every other Bboy seen on the big screen by that point), these models were the next best thing.
4. The *top hat* is a breakdance move which requires two people, one taller/heavier person and one smaller/shorter person. The larger of the two dancers lifts the smaller dancer by his/her hips and places them horizontally atop his/her head at the belly. The heavier dancer, then providing anchorage and a central pivot point, starts to spin on the spot increasing speed and momentum to the point where centrifugal force takes over, then both dancers spread their arms (and the top dancer their legs too) giving the appearance of a gravity-defying dance move.
5. I must confess a personal loathing for the terminology "street art", and what it represents. The graffiti of hip hop operates within three aesthetic and practice-defined acts: tagging, bombing, and piecing. Graffiti is first and foremost a political act, and an art form second. This is not to do disservice to the creative endeavours of graffiti writers or those who mastered the practices of graffiti and who now may practise street art, nor is the same intended for those practitioners that have only ever made street art and call themselves street artists (or indeed those academics who study the field), but a distinction must be made between the two. Graffiti practice *is* the hip hop state of mind, street art is not, and to discuss them casually or as synonymous is problematic.
6. Graffiti Research Lab: Dedicated to outfitting graffiti artists with open source technologies for urban communication. http://www.graffitiresearchlab.com/blog/ (accessed 3 April 2018).
7. See MacDowall (2017: 231–49) for an in-depth qualitative and quantitative analysis of the production and consumption of digital graffiti.
8. See Martin H. Krieger's *Urban Tomographies* (2018) for visual projects and detailed investigations into urban tomography. Krieger positions this in the urban realm, and speaking on his urban tomographies project: "You bring curiosity and knowledge about urban processes, or of physiology, to these imaging modalities, whether as an expert or as a layperson…their value lies in what they allow you to imagine about what is going on…allowing the viewer to imagine a whole, a notion of what is being displayed, a process or an institution that would produce these aspects" (2).
9. *Blackbook* is writers' terminology for graffiti sketchbook, containing densely packed outlines, tags and process sketches and, at times, other writers' tags.
10. *The Independent*, 12 October to 18 October 1989.

11 Dave Brinkworth went on to work with Mark Pritchard as downtempo electronic duo Harmonic 33 as well as one half of drum 'n' bass artist Use Of Weapons and one third of breakbeat group Capio.
12 Here I use the word "dwelling" to mean the everyday rituals of living, and "working" to mean engagement with the practices of hip hop.
13 Due to its regulation by the Gulf Stream, Cornwall's climate and sub-tropical summer conditions well support the growth of palm trees.
14 https://www.margaretthatcher.org/document/106689 (accessed 1 August 2019). Original article dated 23 September 1987, Margaret Thatcher, Interview for *Woman's Own* ("no such thing as society") (interviewed by Douglas Keay).
15 Artists in the wider national British hip hop frame addressed some of the issues embedded in Thatcherism's anti-societal tactics with a fierce dialectic at the tail end of the 1980s and early 1990s (Black Radical Mk II, London Posse, Katch 22, Ruthless Rap Assassins, for example). However, the counter-attacks within such narratives were also built on a deeper history of British oppression and structural racism.
16 Refer to Glossary for *emcee* and *DJing*.
17 "Barclays—A Quick History", https://www.archive.barclays.com/items/show/5419 (accessed 22 January 2018).
18 *Electro On The Street (Mixed By Herbz) 80's*. Mel Kent "Herbie". https://www.mixcloud.com/Herbz/electro-on-the-street-mixed-by-herbz-80s/ (accessed 16 May 2018).
19 BHS (British Home Stores) was a British department store founded by three US entrepreneurs in 1928. A staple of homewares to British citizens, BHS slid from success in the FTSE 100 Index to final administration in 2016 after it failed to secure a buyer. One of the main reasons for provincial crews wearing less designer sportswear during this time was due to lack of availability and funds. Kilo recalls the visual impressiveness of the crew's matching kit: "Also we went to, in either '84 or '85, we went to see Kurtis Blow at the Town & Country Club in Kentish Town, and that was quite significant because we were stood outside in the queue and there was a few of us there, I think Spider might've been there, we went as a crew…and we had those blue and yellow tops on. We all had those on and no word of a lie, Kurtis Blow arrived (the queue was already outside) and singled us out. He came over and said, 'you guys look dope', 'cause we all had matching tops. We got into a battle inside…'cause we looked like a decent proper crew, we ended up battling someone like Live To Break I think, inside the venue, 'cause we were these outsiders who looked really cool" (i/v, Cambridge, 23 May 2017).
20 'It's Time to Rock' by Great Peso and Mr. Nasty was the opening track to edition 5, the most electrifying *Street Sounds Electro* album.
21 Sidmouthian is the demonym for a person from Sidmouth or Sidford, Devon.
22 There was always more chance of occupying Barclays for a longer period if Exeter City FC were playing at home as these were the days of football hooliganism and

the police were preoccupied at St James Park. The hooligan contingent at Exeter City FC was called the "Sly Crew", with whom various negotiations took place during the 1980s and early 1990s.
23 *Graffing* is slang for writing graffiti. Refer to Glossary for a broader definition.
24 'Triple Threat' by Z-3 MCs was the only one of the eight Beauty and the Beat Records releases that was distributed to record shops outside the major cities.
25 https://www.redrow.co.uk/ (accessed 23 January 2018).
26 Certainly, in Devon, it was not uncommon in the 1980s for teenagers to catch the bus an hour into Exeter purely for the gimmick of visiting Kentucky Fried Chicken or Wimpy (there was no McDonald's or Burger King).
27 "We did have a train line that ran through the New Forest, through Brockenhurst, and Brockenhurst became like a writer's bench for me, cos there'd be trains coming in through Portsmouth, trains coming down from Weymouth, from Waterloo, so you'd just sit there and start benching and checking out what went past. It was always in the toilets as well, 6.57 [a football hooligan firm linked to Portsmouth F.C.] everywhere, and in the seats, yeah, that was a big influence on me as well. Cos I just thought it was one person, I had no idea it was like a thousand-strong football hooligan firm or something" (Brent Aquasky, i/v, Bournemouth, 17 December 2017). This evidences my point that spatial and material territories of hip hop such as the writer's bench are a mentality rather than purely a physical structure. Hegemonic labels of space and place are reimagined and appropriated within the emerging construct of the (rural) hip hop state of mind.
28 In de Paor-Evans (2018c), I discuss the blurred boundaries between what is considered urban and what is considered rural in the hip hop contexts of New York and Devon. The chapter proposes that: (1) hip hop studies enrichens through the rural/urban debate, (2) new imaginings of what is rural, what is urban and what is hip hop become possible, thus leading to potential new networks, and (3) the results of such networks "become a critically regional form of hybrid practice, working with other spatial, material, rural, and urban cultural practices" (2018c: 193). In many ways, the work in *Rurality Re-imagined* acted as a point of departure for the study in this book.

Chapter 4

1 Analysis derived from data sourced from https://www.discogs.com/search/?limit=250&q=White+Lines+grandmaster&format_exact=Compilation&type=all&country_exact=UK&page=1 (accessed 30 April 2018).
2 Commercial hip hop compilation albums during this era include *Break Dancing* (1984, Columbia/CBS) issued in the US and across Europe, the sleeve design incorporating two breakdancers and the words "BREAK DANCING" painted in poorly executed graffiti; *Scratch & Break* (EMI, 1983), which again features poorly painted graffiti characters and the graffiti lettering "Scratch & Break"

painted on a dilapidated brick wall; and *Breakdance* featuring audio breakdancing lessons on side two by Alex and The City Crew (1984, K-Tel). Interestingly, the other issues from Mexico, Panama, Brazil, Columbia, Venezuela, Australia, New Zealand, Portugal, Canada, and the UK, all feature the same audio guidance on side two, but have very different track listings for side one which can be attributed to song licensing and availability in each respective country. Furthermore, there are three different cover designs—the Canada, Australia, New Zealand and UK issues display photographs of members of Alex and The City Crew in staged breakdance moves, while the US and Latin American issues depict the breakers in a silhouetted illustration in front of a brick wall adorning graffiti with a night-time city skyline in the distance.

3 "The Famous Charisma Label" was formed by Tony Stratton-Smith in 1969 and was subsequently acquired by Virgin Records Ltd, the year prior to the majority of their commercial hip hop releases.

4 'Hey DJ' was produced by Stephen Hague who also produced the two Rock Steady Crew songs on the album, and had previously worked on pop-punk, rock and new wave music, producing for The Zippers, Jules and the Polar Bears, Slow Children, and Gleaming Spires, before his brief flirt with commercial hip hop, after which he had major success with Orchestral Manoeuvres in the Dark, Pet Shop Boys and New Order. Like Trevor Horn, he was a producer of some magnitude within the broader synth-pop genre.

5 Refer to Glossary for definition of *uprock* and *uprockin'*.

6 *Number One* was a teen pop magazine, similar to *Smash Hits*, although it had the advantage in terms of chart news that it was published weekly, unlike its rival which was fortnightly. It enjoyed ridiculing *Smash Hits*, often referring to it as "Sm*shed Tw*ts". *Number One* also ran features on Malcolm McLaren, Break Machine and *Breakdance: The Movie*. Circulation peaked at around 178,000 before its termination in early 1992.

7 It is also worth noting that during the same time mini-albums of (re)mixes became popularized such as Howard Jones' *The 12" Album* and Tina Turner's *Private Dance Mixes*, and the fashionability of the 12" single gave these mini-albums greater currency.

8 http://www.officialcharts.com/artist/40398/world-famous-supreme-team/ (accessed 30 April 2018).

9 http://www.officialcharts.com/artist/20155/malcolm-mclaren/ (accessed 30 April 2018).

10 1980s headz and casuals shared many representations of clothing, and during this period the pastel hues of yellow, pink and pale blue were a firm statement of taste and cultural materialism as both appropriated the established styles of Scottish brands Pringle and Lyle & Scott as well as the French Lacoste brand.

11 Dolby Dee recalls the photo shoot was a "good earner" and helped him to get to know Killian, and attempt to attract him to the Sidewalk crew.

12 Like the *Street Sounds Electro* series, the sleeve was conceived and designed by Carver's, yet seemed to lack the impact of the pathbreaking *Electro* design.
13 Laswell's extensive and unique production and writing style throughout the 1980s included a majority of the celluloid releases, plus production on Herbie Hancock's genre-shifting electro-future-jazz albums *Perfect Machine*, *Sound-System*, and *Future Shock*: "In a sense they were the test runs for the massively successful Herbie Hancock recordings. The influences are all there: heavy metal, punk, computer games, cartoons, European minimalism—tied together by the march of the digital drummer and the myths, legends and style of Bboy culture" (*Rap Graffiti*: liner notes).
14 American 12"s were pressed at 33.3rpm, and UK pressings at 45rpm (however this has much changed since the late 1990s, with UK 12"s now pressed at 33.3rpm as standard). So, to have the "Ahhhhh this stuff is really fresh" soundbite on an album at 33.3rpm, provincial British DJs had an identical space/time experience as those using the American 12", fostering greater closeness with their city counterparts.
15 Morgan Khan had previously launched the label Streetwave in 1981, releasing singles under licence from the US, and Street Sounds was to become the album counterpart and sublabel to Streetwave.
16 18 May 1985, http://www.officialcharts.com/search/albums/street-sounds-electro-7/ (accessed 29 January 2018).
17 Frick 'N' Frack's 'Go Southside' and 'Who's On Mine' were two such songs from edition 18 that were never released elsewhere and believed to be mixed from an acetate especially cut for this purpose.
18 Johnny F.'s Liberty Grooves record shop was a crucial hip hop hub in Tooting, South London during the 1990s which also, as a label, released Solid 'n' Mind's (Whirlwind D and Johnny F.) debut single 'An Original Break' (1990).
19 'Just Having Fun (Do The Beat Box)' and 'The Original Human Beat Box' were blended together by DJ Maurice assisted by DJ Noel for *Street Sounds Electro 6*, resulting in a sublime and epic beatbox journey of over ten minutes in length.
20 It should also be noted that in the same year as *Street Sounds Electro 1* was released, an uncannily similar concept album was released in the Netherlands. *Scratch Tracks* (High Fashion Music, 1983) was also a mixed album, blended by Ben Liebrand and also featured 'The Return Of Captain Rock' although other songs are more aligned to the Euro-house genre. Furthermore, the graphic was designed with a comparable ethos to that of Carver's work, but its execution was much less successful (additional note: there also exists a UK sequed compilation album entitled *Designed for Dancing (Volume One)*, released in 1983. Although it includes a breakdancer on the sleeve design, the music is largely synth-pop. This does, however, illustrate the broad impact of Bboying on the commercialization of popular music product).
21 Side two, *Street Sounds Electro 1*, mixed by Mastermind.

22 Side two, *Street Sounds Electro 5*, mixed by Bunny Rock Inc. featuring DJ Maurice and DJ Noel.
23 This enabled an analytical comparison to take place between the full version played on John Peel and the Electro mixes. This provided essential learning for how mixes and blending were procured.
24 Including *New York Vs. LA Beats* (1985), and *Best of the West Coast* (1988).
25 At the same point, Carver's sleeve design (which had morphed slightly over four years) was replaced by a full graffiti design by ACE.
26 Although the series was renamed and rebranded, the catalogue identifier prefix "ELCST" (Electro Street Sounds) remained.
27 Cooltempo was owned by Chrysalis Records Ltd. as a sub-label specializing in dance and black music. The label began to take an economic and cultural interest in hip hop in 1984, releasing songs such as Cutty's 'Naughty Times' (1984). Their most successful hip hop release was arguably Doug E. Fresh & The Get Fresh Crew's 'The Show' (1985).
28 Champion was similar to Cooltempo, and covered a broad spectrum of black music, with their biggest commercial hip hop release being Whistle's '(Nothing Serious) Just Buggin'' (1985). While their main focus became dance and house orientated, they were responsible for bringing the sounds of Sugar Bear, Chubb Rock and True Mathematics to non-urban Britain.
29 Streetwave was the earliest label to press UK issues of stateside records, although mainly released tracks that also appeared on the *Electro* series by artists such as Just-Ice, U.T.F.O., The Bboys and 12:41.
30 http://www.mikeallencapitalradio.com/home/interviews/mike-allen-interview (accessed 15 February 2018).
31 http://www.djfood.org/rip-mike-allen/ (accessed 1 November 2017).
32 Maurice Vass, managing director, speaking in December 1981 on the mission of DevonAir, an independent radio station launched on 7 November 1980. http://www.devonairfm.com/history.htm (accessed 15 February 2018).
33 An interesting cultural shift occurred in mid-February 1986 when the Groove Electro Funk Chart changed its name to the Groove Hip Hop Sales Chart. This moment is pivotal in the development of hip hop: electro as a genre was fading and hip hop as a cultural phenomenon had become more established, apparent in the acceptance and use of "hip hop" as the chosen terminology. The much-increased usage of the term "hip hop" can also be attributed to the key arrival of a particular hip hop sound and song structure. I would argue that 1986 is the year that the true genre of hip hop music landed.
34 Masquerade was a London-based crew including label owner Morgan Khan, who had partial success with crossover hip hop/dance records 'One Nation' (1985) and 'Set It Off' (1985) and, in 1986, 'Solution (To The Problem)'.
35 The Groove charts have been inspected between 28 January 1984 and 25 June 1988, and despite a slight improvement in the ratio of records available/heard in areas with no pirate radio or National Fresh (reaching a minimum of five

unheard records from the final chart analysed), the average remained at almost half (9/20). Three sources were triangulated to reach this conclusion: cassettes of Mike Allen's shows, the Groove charts as published in *Echoes* magazine, and http://www.mikeallencapitalradio.com/home/groovecharts/ (accessed 16 February 2018).

36 As I was musing over the exemplars of Peel's hip hop selection, I posted the YouTube link to High Potent's 'H.P. Gets Busy' on Facebook, and within three minutes Parker commented in the thread: "Love this track, taped it off John Peel" (Facebook comment, accessed 16 February 2018), presenting instant closure on the reach and impact of Peel's non-obvious playlist.

37 'H.P. Gets Busy' was Jay-Z's first appearance on vinyl in 1986, and his reference to "doing work" here is almost predictive of the business and economically focused future he was to undertake.

38 The import record carried a weightier cultural capital the further away one moved from a large city due to its scarcity. While breakdancing in a local park in 1985, Evil Ed says: "It was on this day at the park that I saw my first ever import 12″. An older kid we knew had a copy of 'The Show' by Doug E. Fresh and I remember seeing it and then being hooked on import vinyl from then on" (email to author, 14 June 2017).

39 'Cracked Out' by Masters of Ceremony, 'Jane Stop This Crazy Thing' by MC Shan, and 'Monster Crack' by Kool Moe Dee were all released in 1986 and illustrate the social pressures of crack during the mid-1980s in New York.

40 The (R) was a restricted rating and used prior to the introduction of the standard PARENTAL ADVISORY label (PAL) in the US in 1990 (UK 2011).

41 Digging in the crates is the practice of searching for records, often with the intensity of a forensic examination or archaeological dig. To be a professional digger requires time and devotion, and dedicated diggers will widen the sites of their digs to include any possible location where there might be records, such as junk shops, charity shops, flea-markets, jumble sales, car-boot sales, tips, and conventional record fairs and shops. There is potential for digging to be framed as an element of hip hop in its own right, as, first and foremost, hip hop centred on playing records.

Chapter 5

1 Within this work, the theory of "thirdspace" as developed by Homi Bhabha (*The Location of Culture*, 2004) also relates to the work of Edward Soja (*Thirdspace*, 1996) and Henri Lefebvre's "spatial triad" (*The Production of Space*, 1991).

2 Records like Sugar Bear's 'Don't Scandalize Mine', Rob Base and DJ E-Z Rock's 'It Takes Two', and 'King of the Beats' by Mantronix were popular in raves. The impact of hip hop within rave culture has been discussed by the author

in "From Broken Glass to Ruf Diamonds: Manchester Hip Hop", in Mazierska 2018, although a full study is very much needed to fill this gap in knowledge.
3 What is also fascinating is that similar techniques were invented concurrently across the country during the same period, and none of the interviewees mentioned being taught pause-button mixing outside of their locale, but rather alluded to discovery first-hand.
4 An *edit* and a *megamix* both used analogue cut 'n' paste and splicing techniques similar to the methods pioneered by dub producers. The differences between the two is that the edit is a spliced and often shorter version of a single longer song, often made for radio play but also including a key element of creativity (such as the many edits by The Latin Rascals), whereas the megamix is also edited, but generates a new jam from editing and mixing a multitude of existing songs. These were commonplace on compilation albums, championed by Tommy Boy on *Greatest Beats*, but gained momentum in Britain through the UK-only compilations *Upfront* and *Serious Beats* (Serious Records) and *Ultimate Trax* (Champion). This is important as these compilations were freely available in provincial Britain.
5 Although not a pause-button mix, 'The Adventures Of Grandmaster Flash On The Wheels Of Steel' was arguably the first cut-up and spliced record and remains hugely influential and widely cited by DJs. Released in 1981 on Sugar Hill Records it was three years ahead of other prominent cut-up records, most notably 'Mastermixes' (1984), and 'Lessons 1, 2 & 3' (1985) by Double Dee & Steinski.
6 It is interesting to note that within Leckie's correspondence, he states "I still have the original broadcasts on a grip of TDK SA90s. Thankfully, they are still in top shape, and a perfect snap-shot of my youth". This demonstrates the archival nature of the self-manufactured, culturally contextual hip hop artefact.
7 The physical length of tape in a standard D90 cassette would be 128.5875 metres with the tape running at 1.875 inches per second, and most commercial D90 cassettes have a total running time of around 94 minutes.
8 See Virilio 2008: 7–8, 141; and Virilio 1993: 243–69.
9 See also Virilio 2006, for a detailed presentation of dromology.
10 See de Paor-Evans 2018c.
11 This is the same village bus shelter as described in Chapter 3 and Figure 3.18.
12 Marley Marl, Ced Gee, Q-Tip and DJ Premier were highly influential producers who during the late 1980s all championed sampling in unique ways stateside, while in Britain the harder and more industrial productions of Hardnoise, Hijack and Gunshot were beginning to take hold, although Silver Bullet's 'Bring Forth The Guillotine' (1989) produced by Ben Chapman exemplified how a hip hop record could pack in a number of well-known sampled funk patterns to compose a song.
13 These compilations were created and edited by Luis Flores aka "BreakBeat Lou" and Leonard "BreakBeat Lenny" Roberts.

14 It was also possible that the breakbeat on a *UBB* album reached the British provinces before the hip hop track that sampled it. These glitches in space-time potentially told a different chronological story to actual sequences of sampling events, particularly to those outside the New York hip hop habitus.

15 A clever tactic on the part of *UBB* was not to publish the artist's name on the sleeve. Song information is present in terms of title, publisher and writer credits, although the omission of the artist name made for more challenging digging as headz strived to track down the original issues.

16 The extended breaks were helpful to DJs for blending and mixing; there was more time to cue up the second copy as the first break was playing, so if the first pattern drop was missed there was another opportunity.

17 "I'm a kilo" is a Big Daddy Kane vocal drop from 'Raw' (1988). Both 'Raw' and 'Long Live The Kane' were highly influential to 'Music Fusion' with their lack of melody and tough drum samples, and the use of "I'm a kilo" was a nod to South Side Alliance creator, Kilo.

18 A diss track or diss song is intended to disrespect people (hence, 'diss'). Diss tracks became common during the 1980s and were popularized by the myriad of diss records surrounding the "Roxanne Wars", which spun out of the U.T.F.O. Versus The Real Roxanne war; and although staged, Roxanne Shante's entering into the frame triggered a host of other diss records.

19 'Street Level' was the only regional radio show that played any form of hip hop music regularly, and although DevonAir was very late to the party, the area at last had a regional show playing rap music despite starting five years after Mike Allen's show on Capital Radio. However, it was a show lacking in longevity, and after a relatively short period DevonAir reverted to playing no rap music, continuing the mission of Maurice Vass.

20 The *super-crew* is a term I introduce to define a crew constructed of several other crews, each of whom holds a specific agenda or practice specialization. These crews collaborate on larger projects which demand the multifarious nature of hip hop practice, while also producing a holistic layer of identity for the super-crew's members.

21 Whereas no false representations of people were used, sleeves were usually designed incorporating fashionable graphics with tenuous links to the records' subject matter—it was rare to see photographs of the real artists on British and European releases, which only succeeded in concealing their histories and presence.

22 It is worth noting that the 1982 UK 12" Sugar Hill issue of 'The Message' by Grandmaster Flash & The Furious Five comprises a solid black background with the title and artist name in white typewriter font. Also included in white text are the song lyrics, which upon such an intense visual ground amplify the gravity of the song. In many ways, 'Untitled' was as much a seismic shift in hip hop music as 'The Message'.

23 The first three Public Enemy albums feature the statements which run repeatedly along the bottom edge like a scrolling newsflash: "…THE GOVERNMENT'S RESPONSIBLE…" (1987), "FREEDOM IS A ROAD SELDOM TRAVELED BY THE MULTITUDE…" (1988), and "THE COUNTER ATTACK ON WORLD SUPREMACY…" (1990). Blade was heavily influenced by P.E.; I recall him animatedly telling me how he could not stop playing 'Rebel Without A Pause' for days when it first dropped and was captivated by the way they had sampled James Brown's 'The Grunt'.
24 p/c, Minneapolis, 18 April 2018.
25 p/c, Westbury, 26 April 2018.
26 Evil Ed, personal correspondence, 17 April 2017.
27 This also addressed a public complaint that had arisen from the previous Dance Raw where Soul II Soul DJs were billed. An arguably misleading advertisement on the part of the promoter suggested it was Soul II Soul the band—but naturally none of the "famous" members of the band performed Soul II Soul's hit songs, rather it was a DJ set.
28 I would add that the technical control of the space is handled by the sound engineers; however, I remain firm in the position that the performer controls the space as: (1) rehearsed: the performer liaises with the engineer before the performance for briefing, and (2) improvised: the engineer reacts to the proceedings unfolding on stage.

Chapter 6

1 The Wall of Fame, or simply The Wall, was an illegal gallery space and the most significant location for graffiti practice in Exeter, and existed on the long elevation of a redundant building, trackside of the mainline to London. The Wall of Fame was not an exclusive to Exeter: wherever there were writers in operation, there would be a wall of fame, often in close proximity to transport infrastructure.
2 The pieces at The Wall usually ran for about a month before they were painted over, but sometimes longer. The advantage of having a wall of fame in a sparsely populated area meant for fewer writers, resulting in reduced competition for wall space. As such, the finest pieces ran for almost a year.
3 *The Commonwealth: United Kingdom.* http://thecommonwealth.org/our-member-countries/united-kingdom (accessed 3 January 2018).
4 The phrase "England's dreaming" from Sex Pistol's 'God Save The Queen' (1977) echoed the sentiment through the intentionally dreary chant "no future", as the pedagogic sense of national Britishness had all but collapsed in the young generation.
5 The lowest number of households in the UK watching *Coronation Street* in 1987 was 11.9 million (4 May), while its peak viewing figure that year was 26.65 million on Christmas Day. Source: Broadcasters' Audience Research Board,

http://www.barb.co.uk/resources/tv-facts/tv-since-1981/1987/top10/ (accessed 20 April 2018).
6. DJ Fingers aka Karl Gibson was the DJ for London-based crew Sindecut, and also the author of *The Misappropriation of Hip Hop* (2010) which focuses on the crisis of hip hop's direction in the noughties.
7. The term *yard* is derived from the Jamaican vernacular for home, and shares a relationship with *Yardie*, a term used largely within the Caribbean and Jamaican expatriate and diaspora communities in Britain.
8. *Cockney* is a name given to a native of East London, traditionally one born within earshot of Bow Bells, but has come to mean anyone from London with an East End or Cockney twang.
9. British-born singer and DJ, Smiley Culture, was close to a household name during the mid-1980s. After performing with Saxon Sound System, he had two hits, 'Police Officer' being the more successful peaking at number 12 in the UK Official Singles Charts after which he hosted the Channel 4 show *Club Mix* during 1986–87.
10. Pato Banton is a British-born reggae singer and DJ who was most famously linked with UB40, but his finest work was through his partnership with dub maestro Mad Professor.
11. Rediffusion Limited also had strong links with the former British colonies, with over 90 per cent of all Rediffusion broadcasters in the Caribbean islands being of West Indian nationality (Lent 1976).
12. Originally published as "Slipping into Darkness", *The Wire* 148, June 1996, https://www.thewire.co.uk/in-writing/essays/the-wire-300_simon-reynolds-on-the-hardcore-continuum_4_hardstep_jump-up_techstep_1996_ (accessed 7 January 2017).
13. "Keep it 100" is an extension of "keep it real".
14. Mike Mac, emcee from Jedi Mics, grew up on a farm in the village of Buckland Monachorum, Devon. Jedi Mics released three 12″ singles between 2002 and 2004.
15. See, for example, the German-based site, https://www.undergroundunited.de/.
16. In Germany a buoyant underground britcore scene is still maintained, thriving on both the releases and previously unreleased material of its heyday, and newly produced music.
17. For a detailed discussion, analysis and critique on sampling in hip hop, see Williams 2013.
18. Dave Ogrin was an established producer renowned for his tough approach to digital percussion in the mid-1980s, producing and programming on many successful hip hop records for Fresh 3 M.C.s, The Real Roxanne, Fat Boys and Grandmaster Flash, and also engineered the pioneering drum-heavy 'Here Comes That Beat!' by Pumpkin and the Profile All-Stars (1984).
19. Morgan Khan's labels Street Sounds and Streetwave released a significant number of hip hop records through the 1980s and, following the partial success of

his own band Masquerade, he executive-produced Faze One, one of the earliest UK hip hop crews to release a full-length album. By recruiting the experience of Dave Ogrin to produce 10 of the 12 tracks, the album carried the fat, percussive sound that Khan was aiming for.

20. Clyde Stubblefield's drum break on 'Funky Drummer' (1970) is arguably the most sampled drum break in hip hop history. Although originally released on a 45 in 1970 (King Records), this break was largely discovered by UK hip hop DJs and producers in 1986 when Polydor released *In the Jungle Groove*, a double album containing previously unreleased songs and extended versions, and unofficially the same year on *Ultimate Breaks & Beats* (SBR512, Street Beat Records, 1986). It should also be noted that the first hip hop record to sample 'Funky Drummer' with clarity was 'The Classy M.C.s' by Quick Quintin & M.C. Mello J. (Barnes Records, 1985), using the original 45 as their sample source.

21. Whirlwind D was the emcee in Solid 'n' Mind, who released two 12"s in 1990 and 1991. Growing up on the borders of Surrey and South London, he and Johnny F ran the Liberty Grooves record shop and label based in Tooting (South London).

22. Kool Moe Dee, Fearless Four, Melle Mel and the Furious Five were still donning flamboyant, post-modern and colourful clothing inspired by the funk styles of Parliament and Funkadelic when Run-D.M.C. arrived in 1983 with their pared-down, seriously street appearance.

23. One particularly is drawn to Nas here: his debut album *Illmatic* is drenched in personal, observational and highly contextual narrative.

24. 'Blow Your Head' by Fred Wesley & The J.B.s was sampled the previous year by The Bomb Squad on Public Enemy's 'Public Enemy No. 1', a record that had a monumental impact globally and served as a keen point of reference for Hijack's debut.

25. Previously, most British hip hop records peaked at approximately 100bpm.

26. Blade named his label 691 Influential after the telephone dial code "691" for Deptford, South London.

27. While 'Bring Forth the Guillotine' was Silver Bullet's debut release as a solo artist, he was previously part of Triple Element (also signed to Tam Tam Records), a crew who released only one 12", 'What's Dat Sound' (1988), although there are clear hints even here to what would become the themes of horror associated with britcore including a melody akin to *The Twilight Zone* and heated vocal delivery.

28. The "Amen break" is a hip hop colloquialism for The Winstons' 'Amen, Brother' (Metromedia Records, 1969) which became the backbone percussion break for many britcore, jungle, and drum 'n' bass records of the 1990s.

29. Echoing Todd Craig, I would also make a plea to practitioners to resurrect the status of the DJ. For approximately the past 15 years or more, there has been an uncountable number of records from almost every country that produces hip hop music that omits the skills of the DJ. This is hugely problematic, and a result of the formulaic "guest artist-producer syndrome" popularized by Kanye West;

however, the origin of this shift in structure sits with Nas' 1994 debut album *Illmatic*.

30 'Take Me To The Mardi Gras' (1975) is an exemplary break by Bob James, used famously in Run-D.M.C.'s 'Peter Piper' (1986), which, in turn, was cut, mixed and scratched to within an inch of its life in Cutmaster Swift's winning 1989 DMC World DJ Championships routine.

31 The Beatmasters also worked with British emcee Merlin, on 'Who's In The House?' which reached number 8 in the Official UK Singles Chart, http://www.officialcharts.com/artist/26807/beatmasters/ (accessed 22 April 2018).

32 http://www.officialcharts.com/artist/25262/monie-love/ (accessed 22 April 2018).

33 Dancin' Danny D of D-Mob fame was largely responsible for bringing acid house to mainstream attention. Through his hit 'We Call It Acieeed', he was also responsible for a swathe of young people shrieking "ACIEEEEEEEEEDDD!!!" repetitively at schools, on buses, in youth centres, or at the kitchen table.

34 For a critical discussion on the relationship between the baggy scene, Madchester and hip hop, see de Paor-Evans (2018a). It should also be noted that not all hip-house/house records released by British artists who made their start in hip hop were fronted by corporate labels; Joi Bangla Sound, Mel-O-Dee and Skorpi Gad experienced independent success in other genres of dance music.

35 Most notably artists that championed sports gear were influenced to made records about them. Fila undoubtedly came out on top in terms of volume, with songs like: 'Put Ya Filas On' by Schoolly D (1985), 'Do The Fila And The Peewee Dance' by MC Boob AKA Steady B (1986), and many references to Fila in Roxanne Shanté's 1986 record 'The Def Fresh Crew' ("bumped into Biz he had a Fila too / I said 'Yo, Biz Markie what you wanna do?'"), as well as artists naming themselves after the brand (Fila Phil, and Fila Fresh Crew). KRS-One: "I only wear Nikes not Adidas or Reeboks" (Word From Our Sponsor, 1987) brought a status comparison to the conversation, but the most wide-reaching was Run-D.M.C.'s 'My Adidas' (1986), which famously resulted in the first musicians to land a sponsorship deal with a sportswear brand.

36 We would be constantly followed around every gentleman's outfitters as these were targets for shoplifters from both football and hip hop culture. Tactics involved taking two jumpers into the changing room and emerging with one (the other either still worn under your own top or stuffed down your trouser leg) and snipping the labels out of the back of designer clothing in order to stitch over the labels of cheaper brands.

37 London Posse's 1987 self-titled EP and Three Wize Men's 'Urban Hell' 12" single from 1986 could be regarded as exceptions here; the former presents a photograph of London Posse ascending an escalator, and the latter features a dark urban street, black and white scene montaged with graffiti in the British style of the time, although neither covers blatantly illustrate the visual identity of hip hop to the extent of *Known 2 Be Down*.

38 Chiefly among Rastafarians, a contemptuous or dismissive term for aspects of white culture seen as degenerate or oppressive, especially the police.
39 Irie (chiefly in Jamaican English) means nice, good or pleasing (used as a general term of approval).
40 The arrival of The RX-5, Yamaha's flagship sample-based drum machine in 1986, became the drum machine and sequencer of choice for many dancehall and ragga producers such as Steely & Clevie, Prince Jammy and Mr. Doo by the close of the 1980s.
41 "Not the king of the land or the king of the throne, But the king that rocks the microphone" duplicates part of the chorus from American rapper M.C. Chill's 'MC Story' (1986). Although this would be traditionally labelled biting (see Glossary), Papa Speng's delivery owns this line.
42 Syncbeat, Broken Glass and Forevereaction's contributions were also released on parent label Streetwave, and Zer-O's tracks were not released elsewhere, leaving only Rapologists' track, signed to London-based Billy Boy/Bluebird.
43 "Aiight" is a contraction of "alright", used throughout the UK hip hop community during the late 1980s. Interestingly, the term is historically used in the same way in parts of rural Britain, particularly Devon.
44 Sampled from 'Introduction' by Reverend Jesse Jackson, the opening track on the album *The Living Word—Wattstax 2* (1973).
45 "Know what I mean, 'Arry?" became British boxing heavyweight Frank Bruno's catchphrase, which emerged from his verbal sparring with sports commentator and interviewer Harry Carpenter during the 1980s and 1990s. These moments of television became regarded as quintessentially British.
46 Gregor Fisher (as Rab C. Nesbitt) and Jeremy Beadle were regular comedy stars of British television during this era. Argy-bargy is a late nineteenth-century revision of a Scottish phrase, first used earlier in the 1800s in the form "argle-bargle". Robert Louis Stevenson used the former version in *Kidnapped*: "Last night ye haggled and argle-bargled like an apple-wife" (originally published 1886). "I'm laying my coat in the puddle" is a reference to the sixteenth-century anecdotal myth of Sir Walter Raleigh doffing his cloak and covering over a muddy puddle to protect Queen Elizabeth as she walked. "One hundred and eiiighty!" is the top score in darts, the British game popularized in the twentieth century in pubs, and furthermore by the British television quiz show *Bullseye* of the 1980s.
47 From the English nursery rhyme first published in the late eighteenth century. However, this theme also appeared much earlier in the satirical *Poor Robin's Almanack*, 1733, noting: "Good Friday comes this month, the old woman runs, With one or two a penny hot cross buns".
48 Evil Ed, personal correspondence, 17 April 2017.
49 This mythical view of the bumpkin held by urbanites is recreated brilliantly in Bruce Robinson's film *Withnail and I*, as Marwood reflects upon an H.E. Bates novel; see *Withnail and I*, original screenplay, Bloomsbury Film Classics Series (Bloomsbury, 1998), p. 51.

50 https://www.gov.uk/hemp-growing-licence (accessed 24 April 2018).
51 *Wurzel* is derived from the German word *mangelwurzel*, a fodder crop developed and grown to feed livestock dating back to the eighteenth century in Britain and Ireland. In Somerset, "Punkie Night" is celebrated on the last Thursday of October, and in tune with Hallowe'en rituals, children carve out mangelwurzel and fashion jack o' lanterns.
52 http://www.hijackbristol.co.uk/board/the-forum/lowercase-and-chattabox-vid/ (accessed 14 April 2018).
53 *BSE*—Bovine Spongiform Encephalopathy, which aggressively attacks the nervous system of cattle.
54 By March 1996, "10 cases of CJD in people aged under 42" resulted in their deaths, which led to the destruction of 4.5 million cattle. This was when the government first acknowledged that BSE could be transferred from cattle to humans. The disease and the controversy surrounding this situation had a disastrous effect on farmers across the UK, as well as many rural roads and routes being shut to the public. https://www.centerforfoodsafety.org/issues/1040/mad-cow-disease/timeline-mad-cow-disease-outbreaks (accessed 25 April 2018).
55 https://www.theguardian.com/uk/2000/oct/27/bse.geoffreygibbs (accessed 25 April 2018).
56 Interview with Deed, *The Pioneers: The British Hip Hop Documentary* (2000).
57 See earlier records such as Brother D with Collective Effort's 'How We Gonna Make The Black Nation Rise?' (Clappers records, 1980), which also received a UK release in 1982 and 1985 on Island Records/4th and Broadway.
58 See Asante (2016: 1–6) for a detailed discussion of the terminologies associated with Afrocentric studies. Asante offers a critical bibliography including details of Afrocentric, Afrocentricity, and Afrocentrism. Rollefson (2008) also presents a key Afrofuturist hip hop position; see also de Paor-Evans 2018b.

Chapter 7

1 Taken from Kilo's interview in the UltraCab by All City Steve on the *Allcity TaxiTalk Show*, 2 June 2018, https://www.youtube.com/watch?v=zZ6tUGWUySA&t=2948s (accessed 4 June 2018).
2 Ibid.
3 'The Prophecy, Part 1 (In The Beginning)', from M.C. Chill, *M.C. Chill*. 1986. Fever Records SFS 001. Vinyl album.

Bibliography

Ariefdien, Shaheen, and Nazli Abrahams. 2006. "Cape Flats Alchemy: Hip Hop Arts in South Africa". In *Total Chaos: The Art and Aesthetics of Hip Hop*, edited by Jeff Chang, 262–70. New York: BasicCivitas.
Asante, Molefi Kete. 2016. "Afrocentricity". In *The International Encyclopedia of Communication Theory and Philosophy*, 1–6. New Jersey: Wiley-Blackwell. https://doi.org/10.1002/9781118766804.wbiect128
Ashlee, Aeriel A., Bianca Zamora, and Shamika N. Karikari. 2017. "We Are Woke: A Collaborative Critical Autoethnography of Three 'Womxn' of Color Graduate Students in Higher Education". *International Journal of Multicultural Education* 19.1: 9–104. https://doi.org/10.18251/ijme.v19i1.1259
Augé, Marc. 1995. *Non-Places: Introduction to an Anthropology of Supermodernity*. London: Verso.
Austin, Joe. 2001. *Taking the Train: How Graffiti Art Became an Urban Crisis in New York City*. New York: Columbia University Press. https://doi.org/10.7312/aust11142
Avramidis, Konstantinos, and Myrto Tsilimpounidi, eds. 2017. *Graffiti and Street Art: Reading, Writing and Representing the City*. Oxon: Routledge. https://doi.org/10.4324/9781315585765
Ballon, Hilary, and Kenneth T. Jackson. 2007. *Robert Moses and the Transformation of New York*. New York: W.W. Norton.
Barthes, Roland. 1970. *Writing Degree Zero and Elements of Semiology*. Boston, MA: Beacon Press.
—1977. "The Grain of the Voice". In *Image, Music, Text*, 179–89. London: Fontana.
—2009. *Mythologies*. London: Random House Vintage Classics.
Baudrillard, Jean. 1994. *Simulcara and Simulation*. Ann Arbor, MI: University of Michigan Press.
Berman, Marshall. 1983. *All That Is Solid Melts into the Air: The Experience of Modernity*. London: Penguin Books.
Berman, Marshall, and Brian Berger, eds. 2007. *New York Calling: From Blackout to Bloomberg*. London: Reaktion Books.

Berry, Wendell. 2007. "The Regional Motive". In *Architectural Regionalism: Collected Writings on Place, Identity, Modernity, and Tradition*, edited by Vincent B. Canizaro, 36–41. New York: Princeton Architectural Press.
Bhabha, Homi K. 2004. *The Location of Culture*. Oxon: Routledge.
Borden, Iain. 2013. *Drive: Journeys through Film, Cities and Landscapes*. London: Reaktion Books.
Bourdieu, Pierre. 1993. *The Field of Cultural Production*. Cambridge: Polity Press.
—2010. *Distinction: A Social Critique of the Judgement of Taste*. London: Routledge.
Bramwell, Richard. 2015a. *UK Hip Hop, Grime and the City*. Oxon: Routledge. https://doi.org/10.4324/9780203069271
Bramwell, Richard. 2015b. "Council Estate of Mind: The British Rap Tradition and London's Hip Hop Scene". In *The Cambridge Companion to Hip Hop*, edited by Justin A. Williams. Cambridge: Cambridge University Press.
Bromberg, Craig. 1991. *The Wicked Ways of Malcolm McLaren*. London: Omnibus Press.
Buttel, Frederick H., and Howard Newby. 1980. *Rural Sociology of the Advanced Societies*. Lanham, MD: Allanheld, Osmun.
Butler, Judith, and Gayatri Chakravorty Spivak. 2007. *Who Sings the Nation-State?* London: Seagull Books.
Castleman, Craig. 1982. *Getting Up: Subway Graffiti in New York*. Cambridge, MA: MIT Press.
Chalfant, Henry, and Martha Cooper. 1984. *Subway Art*. London: Thames and Hudson.
Chalfant, Henry, and James Prigoff. 1987. *Spraycan Art*. London: Thames and Hudson.
Chang, Jeff. 2007. *Can't Stop Won't Stop*. London: Ebury Press.
Chemam, Melissa. 2019. *Massive Attack: Out of the Comfort Zone*. Bristol: Tangent Books.
Cook, Jon. 2004. "Relocating Britishness and the Break Up of Britain". In *Relocating Britishness*, edited by Ewa Mazierska et al., 17–38. Manchester: Manchester University Press.
Craig, Todd. 2017. "Keep It 360". In *Hip Hop at Europe's Edge: Music, Agency, and Social Change*, edited by Milosz Miszczynski and Adriana Helbig, 283–96. Bloomington: Indiana University Press. https://doi.org/10.2307/j.ctt2005sm8.20
Crewe, Louise, and Nicky Gregson. 1997. "Tales of the Unexpected: Exploring Car Boot Sales as Marginal Spaces of Contemporary Consumption". *Transactions of the Institute of British Geographers* 23.1: 39–53. https://doi.org/10.1111/j.0020-2754.1998.00039.x
Daniels, Stephen. 1989. "Marxism, Culture and the Duplicity of Landscape". *New Models in Geography* 2: 196–220.
Davies, Nick. 1983. "The Anatomy of a Soccer Slaying". *The Sydney Morning Herald*, 9 August.

Davies, Hannah, and Peter Kelley. 1999. *Children's Television in Britain: History, Discourse and Policy*. London: British Film Institute.

de Certeau, Michel. 2002. *The Practice of Everyday Life*. Berkeley: University of California Press.

de Paor-Evans, Adam. 2018a. "From Broken Glass to Ruf Diamonds: Manchester Hip Hop". In *Sounds Northern*, edited by Ewa Mazierska, 155–73. Sheffield: Equinox Publishing.

—2018b. "The Futurism of Hip Hop: Space, Electro and Science Fiction in Rap". *Open Cultural Studies* 2.1: 122–35. https://doi.org/10.1515/culture-2018-0012

—2018c. "Soft Tension: Reimagining Urbanism and Rurality through the Spatio-cultural Practices of Hip Hop". In *Rurality Re-imagined: Villagers, Farmers, Wanderers and Wild Things*, edited by Ben Stringer, 186–93. Novato, CA: ORO Editions.

—2018d. "The Intertextuality and Translations of Fine Art and Class in Hip Hop Culture". *Arts* 7: 80. https://doi.org/10.3390/arts7040080

Dehaene, Michiel, and Lieven De Cauter. 2008. "The Space of Play: Towards a General Theory of Heterotopia". In *Heterotopia and the City: Public Space in a Postcivil Society*, edited by Michiel Dehaene and Lieven De Cauter, 87–102. London: Routledge. https://doi.org/10.4324/9780203089415

DeLanda, Manuel. 2013. *A New Philosophy of Society*. London: Bloomsbury Academic.

Deleuze, Gilles, and Félix Guattari. 2016. *A Thousand Plateaus*. London: Bloomsbury Revelations.

Dennis, James M. 1998. *Renegade Regionalists: The Modern Independence of Grant Wood, Thomas Hart Benton, and John Steuart Curry*. Madison, WI: University of Wisconsin Press.

Dickson, Andrew. 2015. "Phil Redmond and Susan Tully: How We Made *Grange Hill*". *The Guardian*, 23 February 2015. https://www.theguardian.com/culture/2015/feb/23/phil-redmond-susan-tully-how-we-made-grange-hill (accessed 5 May 2017).

Dimitriadis, Greg. 2009. *Performing Identity/Performing Culture: Hip Hop as Text, Pedagogy, and Lived Practice*. New York: Peter Lang.

D'Souza, Miguel, and Kurt Iveson. 1999. "Homies and Homebrewz: Hip Hop in Sydney". In *Australian Youth Subcultures: On the Margins and in the Mainstream*, edited by Rob White, 55–64. Hobart: Australian Clearinghouse for Youth Studies.

DuBose-Simons, Carla J. 2014. "Movin' On Up: African Americans in the South Bronx in the 1940s". *New York History* 95.4 (Fall): 543–57. https://doi.org/10.1353/nyh.2014.0001

Emery, Andrew. 2017. *Wiggaz with Attitude: My Life as a Failed White Rapper*. n.p.: Fat Lace Publishing.

Evans, Adam. 2014. "On the Origins of Hip Hop: Appropriation and Territorial Control of Urban Space". In *Consuming Architecture*, edited by Daniel Maudlin and Marcel Vellinga, 185–201. London: Routledge.

Ferrell, Jeff. 1993. *Crimes of Style: Urban Graffiti and the Politics of Criminality*. New York: Garland.
Flint, Anthony. 2011. *Wrestling with Moses: How Jane Jacobs Took on New York's Master Builder and Transformed the American City*. New York: Random House.
Forman, Murray. 2002. *The 'Hood Comes First: Race, Space, and Place in Rap and Hip-Hop*. Middletown, CT: Wesleyan University Press.
Foucault, Michel. 1978. *The History of Sexuality – Volume 1: An Introduction*. New York: Random House.
—1986. "Of Other Spaces: Utopias and Heterotopias" (trans. Jay Miskowiec). *Diacritics* 16.1: 22–27. JSTOR, www.jstor.org/stable/464648. https://doi.org/10.2307/464648
Fowler, David. 2008. *Youth Culture in Modern Britain, c. 1920–c. 1970*. New York: Palgrave Macmillan. https://doi.org/10.1007/978-1-137-04570-6
Frampton, Kenneth. 1993. "Toward a Critical Regionalism: Six Points for an Architecture of Resistance". In *Postmodernism: A Reader*, edited by Thomas Docherty, 268–80. Oxon: Routledge.
Fryer, Peter. 2010. *Staying Power: The History of Black People in Britain*. London: Pluto Press.
Fuld, J. J. 2000. *The Book of World-famous Music: Classical, Popular, and Folk*. Massachusetts: Courier Corporation.
Gadamer, Hans-Georg, Joel Weinsheimer, and Donald G. Marshall. 2004. *EPZ Truth and Method*. New York: Bloomsbury.
Gamble, Andrew. 1994. *The Free Economy and the Strong State: The Politics of Thatcherism*. London: Macmillan. https://doi.org/10.1007/978-1-349-23387-8
Gastman, Roger, and Caleb Neelon. 2010. *The History of American Graffiti*. New York: HarperCollins.
Geddes, Patrick. 1949. *Cities in Evolution*. London: William and Norgate.
George, Nelson. 1985. *Fresh, Hip Hop Don't Stop*. New York: Random House Inc.
Gibson, Karl. 2010. *The Misappropriation of Hip Hop: Resurrecting the Eternal Principle of Hip Hop's Spiritual Significance*. n.p.: The Tree of Life Books.
Greenberg, Clement. 1961. "Modernist Painting". In Gregory Battcock, *The New Art: A Critical Anthology*. New York: E P Dutton.
Griswold, Wendy. 1990. "Provisional, Provincial Positivism: Reply to Denzin". *American Journal of Sociology* 95.6: 1580–83. https://doi.org/10.1086/229465
Halfacree, K. 2006. "Rural Space: Constructing a Three-fold Architecture". In *The Handbook of Rural Studies*, edited by P. Cloke, T. Marsden and P. Mooney, 44–62. London: SAGE Publications. https://doi.org/10.4135/9781848608016.n4
Hall, Stuart. 1992. "New Ethnicities". In *"Race", Culture and Difference*, edited by James Donald and Ali Rattansi, 252–59. London: Sage Publications.
Haraway, Donna. 1991. "Situated Knowledges: The Science Question in Feminism and the Privilege of Partial Knowledge". In *Human Geography: An Essential Anthology*, edited by J. Agnew, D. N. Livingstone and A. Rodgers, 108–128. Malden, MA: Blackwell.

Harvey, David. 2000. *Spaces of Hope*, vol. 7. Oakland, CA: University of California Press.
—2006. *Spaces of Global Capitalism*. London: Verso.
Haslam, Nick. 2012. *Psychology in the Bathroom*. London: Palgrave Macmillan. https://doi.org/10.1057/9780230367555
Hebdige, Dick. 1988. *Hiding in the Light*. London: Routledge.
—2000. *Cut 'n' Mix*. London: Routledge.
—2003. *Subculture: The Meaning of Style*. London: Routledge.
Heidegger, Martin. 1971. "Building Dwelling Thinking". In *Poetry, Language, Thought*, edited by Martin Heidegger, 145–61. Translation and introduction: Albert Hofstadter. New York: Harper & Row.
—1993. *Basic Writings*. London: Routledge.
Hegel, Georg. 1993. *Introductory Lectures on Aesthetics*. London: Penguin.
Hesmondhalgh, David and Caspar Melville. 2001. "Urban Breakbeat Culture: Repercussions of Hip Hop in the United Kingdom". In *Global Noise: Rap and Hip Hop Outside the USA*, edited by Tony Mitchell, 86–110. Middletown, CT: Wesleyan University Press.
Huet, A., et al. 1977. *La Marchandise Culturelle*. Paris: CNRS.
Huxley, David. 2002. "'Ever get the feeling you've been cheated?': Anarchy and Control in the Great Rock'n'Roll Swindle". In *Punk Rock: So What?*, edited by Roger Sabin, 81–99. London: Routledge.
Iveson, Kurt. 2017. "Graffiti, Street Art, and the Democratic City". In *Graffiti and Street Art: Reading, Writing and Representing the City*, edited by Konstantinos Avramidis and Myrto Tsilimpounidi, 89–99. Oxon: Routledge. https://doi.org/10.4324/9781315585765
Jamrozik, Zaneta. 2015. "Beauty is Not the World: Relocation Detroit in Eminem's Video *Beautiful*". In *Relocating Popular Music*, edited by Ewa Mazierska and Georgina Gregory, 225–44. London: Palgrave Macmillan. https://doi.org/10.1057/9781137463388_12
Jencks, Charles. 2011. "Contextual Counterpoint". In Special Issue: "Radical Post-Modernism". *Architectural Design* 81.5. Ed. Charles Jencks et al., 62–67. https://doi.org/10.1002/ad.1295
Katz, Mark. 2012. *Groove Music: The Art and Culture of the Hip Hop DJ*. New York: Oxford University Press.
Kim, Jongchul. 2011. "How Modern Banking Originated: The London Goldsmith-Bankers' Institutionalization of Trust". *Business History* 53.6: 939–59. https://doi.org/10.1080/00076791.2011.578132
Krieger, Martin H. 2011. *Urban Tomographies*. Pennsylvania: University of Pennsylvania Press. https://doi.org/10.9783/9780812204940
Krims, Adam. 2007. *Music and Urban Geography*. London: Routledge.
Kumar, Krishan. 2003. *The Making of English National Identity*. Cambridge: Cambridge University Press. https://doi.org/10.1017/CBO9780511550058
Lefebvre, Henri. 1991. *The Production of Space*. Oxford: Blackwell.

—2003. *The Urban Revolution*. Minneapolis, MN: University of Minnesota Press.
—2004. *Rhythmanalysis: Space, Time and Everyday Life*. London: Continuum.
—2014a. *Toward an Architecture of Enjoyment*. Minneapolis: University of Minnesota Press.
—2014b. "From the City to Urban Society". In *Implosions/Explosions: Towards a Study of Planetary Urbanization*, edited by Neil Brenner, 36–51. Berlin: Jovis.
Lent, John A. 1976. "Caribbean Mass Communications: Selected Information Sources". *Journal of Broadcasting & Electronic Media* 20.1: 111–25. https://doi.org/10.1080/08838157609386380
Levy, Shawn. 2003. *Ready, Steady, Go!: The Smashing Rise and Giddy Fall of Swinging London*. London: Broadway Books.
Lipsitz, George. 1994. *Dangerous Crossroads: Popular Music, Postmodernism and the Poetics of Place*. London: Verso.
Lynch, Philip. 1999. *The Politics of Nationhood: Sovereignty, Britishness and Conservative Politics*. Hampshire: Macmillan Press.
Macdonald, Nancy. 2001. *The Graffiti Subculture: Youth, Masculinity and Identity in London and New York*. New York: Springer.
MacDowall, Lachlan. 2017. "# Instafame: Aesthetics, Audiences, Data". In *Graffiti and Street Art: Reading, Writing and Representing the City*, edited by Konstantinos Avramidis and Myrto Tsilimpounidi, 231–49. Oxon: Routledge. https://doi.org/10.4324/9781315585765
Mailer, Norman, and Jon Naar. 1974. *The Faith of Graffiti*. New York: HarperCollins.
Martin, Peter. 2004. "Culture, Subculture and Social Organization". In *After Subculture: Critical Studies in Contemporary Youth Culture*, edited by Andy Bennett and Keith Kahn-Harris, 21–25. Basingstoke: Palgrave Macmillan. https://doi.org/10.1007/978-0-230-21467-5_2
Massey, Doreen. 2014. *For Space*. London: Sage Publications.
Mazierska, Ewa, ed. 2018. *Sounds Northern*. Sheffield: Equinox Publishing.
McLaren, Malcolm. 1981. Interview in *New York Rocker*, December.
McLeod, Kembrew. 2012. "Authenticity within Hip Hop and Other Cultures Threatened with Assimilation". In *That's the Joint! The Hip Hop Studies Reader*, edited by Murray Forman and Mark Anthony Neal, 164–78. Oxon: Routledge.
Merleau-Ponty, Maurice. 2013. *Phenomenology of Perception*. London: Routledge. https://doi.org/10.4324/9780203720714
Miller, Daniel. 2014. *Stuff*. Cambridge: Polity Press.
Miller, Ivor. 2015. "Hip-Hop Visual Arts". In *The Cambridge Companion to Hip-Hop*, edited by Justin A. Williams, 32–41. Cambridge: Cambridge University Press. https://doi.org/10.1017/CCO9781139775298.005
Monteyne, Kimberley. 2013. *Hip Hop on Film: Performance Culture, Urban Space, and Genre Transformation in the 1980s*. Jackson, MI: University Press of Mississippi. https://doi.org/10.14325/mississippi/9781617039225.001.0001
Morgan, Hiram. 1996. "British Policies before the British State". In *The British Problem c. 1534–1707: State Formation in the Atlantic Archipelago*, edited

by Brendan Bradshaw and John Stephen Morrill, 66–88. London: Macmillan. https://doi.org/10.1007/978-1-349-24731-8_3

Morra, Irene. 2014. *Britishness, Popular Music, and National Identity: The Making of Modern Britain*. London: Routledge.

Morrill, John. 1966. "The British Problem, *c.* 1534–1707". In *The British Problem, c. 1534–1707: State Formation in the Atlantic Archipelago*, edited by Brendan Bradshaw and John Morrill, 1–38. New York: Palgrave Macmillan. https://doi.org/10.1007/978-1-349-24731-8_1

Natter, Wolfgang, and John Paul Jones III. 1993. "Signposts towards a Post-structuralist Geography". In *Postmodern Contentions: Epochs, Politics, Space*, edited by J. P. Jones, Wolfgang Natter, John Paul Jones III and T. R. Schatzky, 165–203. New York: Guildford Press.

Nelson, Alondra. 2000. "Afrofuturism: Past-Future Visions". *Color Lines* (Spring): 34–37.

Nuttall, Jeff. 1970. *Bomb Culture*. London: Paladin.

Oravcová, Anna. 2017. "The Power of the Words: Discourses of Authenticity in Czech". In *Hip Hop at Europe's Edge: Music, Agency, and Social Change*, edited by Milosz Miszcynski and Adriana Helbig, 267–82. Bloomington, IN: Indiana University Press. https://doi.org/10.2307/j.ctt2005sm8.19

Pahl, R. E. 1968. "The Rural-Urban Continuum". In *Readings in Urban Sociology*, edited by R. E. Pahl, 263–305. Oxford: Pergamon Press. https://doi.org/10.1016/B978-0-08-013293-8.50017-8

Peel, John, and Sheila Ravenscroft. 2005. *John Peel: Margrave of the Marshes*. London: Bantam Press.

Philips, David, and Allan Williams. 1985. *Rural Britain: A Social Geography*. Oxford: Blackwell.

Piper, Adrian. 2008. "Political Art and the Paradigm of Innovation". In *The Life and Death of Images: Ethics and Aesthetics*, edited by Diarmuid Costello and Dominic Willsdon, 111–33. London: Tate Publishing.

Pitcher, Ben. 2009. *The Politics of Multiculturalism: Race and Racism in Contemporary Britain*. Hampshire: Palgrave Macmillan.

—2014. *Consuming Race*. Oxon: Routledge.

Plunz, Robert. 1990. *A History of Housing in New York City*. New York: Columbia University Press.

Powell, Douglas Reichert. 2007. *Critical Regionalism: Connecting Politics and Culture in the American Landscape*. Chapel Hill, NC: University of North Carolina Press.

Powers, Stephen. 1999. *The Art of Getting Over: Graffiti at the Millennium*. London: Macmillan.

Raunig, Gerald. 2007. *Art and Revolution: Transversal Activism in the Long Twentieth Century*. Los Angeles: Semiotext(e) Active Agents.

Reynolds, Simon. 1996. "Slipping into Darkness". *The Wire* 148. http://www.thewire.co.uk/in-writing/essays/the-wire-300_simon-reynolds-on-the-hardcore-continuum_4_hardstep_jump-up_techstep_1996_ (accessed 7 January 2017).

Ricœur, Paul. 1986. *The Rule of Metaphor: Multi-disciplinary Studies of the Creation of Meaning in Language*. London: Routledge & Kegan Paul.

Robinson, Bruce. 1998. *Withnail and I. Bloomsbury Film Classics Series Original Screenplay*. London: Bloomsbury.

Rodriquez, Jason. 2006. "Color-blind Ideology and the Cultural Appropriation of Hip Hop". *Journal of Contemporary Ethnography* 35.6: 645–68. https://doi.org/10.1177/0891241606286997

Rollefson, J. Griffith. 2008. "The 'Robot Voodoo Power' Thesis: Afrofuturism and Anti-anti-essentialism from Sun Ra to Kool Keith". *Black Music Research Journal* 28.1: 83–109.

—2017. *Flip the Script: European Hip Hop and the Politics of Postcoloniality*. Chicago: University of Chicago Press. https://doi.org/10.7208/chicago/9780226496351.001.0001

Rose, Tricia. 1994. *Black Noise: Rap Music and Black Culture in Contemporary America*. Middletown, CT: Wesleyan University Press.

Ruzicka, Michal, et al. 2017. "Hip Hop as a Means of Flight from the 'Gypsy Ghetto' in Eastern Europe". In *Hip Hop at Europe's Edge: Music, Agency, and Social Change*, edited by Milosz Miszcynski and Adriana Helbig, 212–27. Bloomington, IN: Indiana University Press. https://doi.org/10.2307/j.ctt2005sm8.16

Said, Edward. 1978. *Orientalism*. New York: Pantheon Books.

Savage, Mike. 2010. *Identities and Social Change in Britain since 1940: The Politics of Method*. Oxford: Oxford University Press. https://doi.org/10.1093/acprof:oso/9780199587650.001.0001

Schloss, Joseph G. 2014. *Making Beats: The Art of Sample-based Hip Hop*. Middletown, CT: Wesleyan University Press.

Scruton, Roger. 1990. "In Defence of the Nation". In *Ideas and Politics in Modern Britain*, edited by Jonathan Clark, 53–86. London: Palgrave Macmillan. https://doi.org/10.1007/978-1-349-20686-5_4

Sinker, Mark. 1992. "Loving the Alien in Advance of the Landing: Black Science Fiction". *The Wire* 96. http://web.archive.org/web/20060209100352/http://www.thewire.co.uk/archive/essays/black_science_fiction.html (accessed 25 June 2017).

Smith, Sophy. 2016. *Hip Hop Turntablism, Creativity and Collaboration*. Oxford: Routledge.

Snyder, Gregory J. 2009. *Graffiti Lives: Beyond the Tag in New York's Urban Underground*. New York: NYU Press.

—2017. "Long Live the Tag: Representing the Foundations of Graffiti". In *Graffiti and Street Art: Reading, Writing and Representing the City*, edited by Konstantinos Avramidis and Myrto Tsilimpounidi, 264–73. Oxon: Routledge. https://doi.org/10.4324/9781315585765

Söderbaum, Fredrik. 2016. *Rethinking Regionalism (Rethinking World Politics)*. London: Palgrave Macmillan. https://doi.org/10.1057/978-1-137-57303-2
Soja, Edward W. 1996. *Thirdspace: Journeys to Los Angeles and Other Real-and-Imagined Places*. Oxford: Blackwell.
Speers, Laura. 2017. *Hip Hop Authenticity and the London Scene*. Oxon: Routledge. https://doi.org/10.4324/9781315661049
Stringer, Ben. 2018. *Rurality Re-imagined: Villagers, Farmers, Wanderers and Wild Things*. Novato, CA: ORO Editions.
Tanaka, Atau. 2009. "Sensor-based Musical Instruments and Interactive Music". In *The Oxford Handbook of Computer Music*, edited by Roger T. Dean, 233–57. Oxford Handbooks. Oxford: Oxford University Press.
Thornton, Sarah. 1996. *Club Cultures: Music, Media, and Subcultural Capital*. Middletown, CT: Wesleyan University Press.
Toop, David. 1985. *The Rap Attack: African Jive to New York Hip Hop*. London: Pluto Press.
van Veen, Tobias C. 2016. "The Armageddon Effect". In *Afrofuturism 2.0: The Rise of Astro-Blackness*, edited by Reynaldo Anderson and Charles E. Jones, 63–90. Lanham, MD: Lexington Books.
van der Velden, Jacobus Hermanus Antonius. 2007. *Strikes Around the World, 1968–2005: Case-studies of 15 Countries*. Amsterdam: Amsterdam University Press.
Vincent, Rickey. 1996. *Funk: The Music, the People, and the Rhythm of the One*. New York: St. Martin's Griffin.
Virilio, Paul. 1993. *L'insécurité du Territoire*. Paris: Galilée.
—2006. *Speed and Politics*. South Pasadena, CA: Semiotext(e).
—2008. *Negative Horizon*. London: Continuum.
Webber, Stephen W. 2003. *Turntable Technique: The Art of the DJ*. Boston, MA: Berklee Media/Berklee Press.
Weight, Richard. 2013. *Mod: A Very British Style*. London: Bodley Head.
Wikström, Patrik, and Robert Burnett. 2009. "Same Songs, Different Wrapping: The Rise of the Compilation Album". *Popular Music and Society* 32.4: 507–22. https://doi.org/10.1080/03007760802327599
Williams, Justin A. 2013. *Rhymin' and Stealin': Musical Borrowing in Hip-Hop*. Ann Arbor, MI: University of Michigan Press. https://doi.org/10.3998/mpub.3480627
Williams, Patrick J. 2011. *Subcultural Theory*. Cambridge: Polity Press.
Williams, Raymond. 2014. *Keywords: A Vocabulary of Culture and Society*. Oxford: Oxford University Press.
Wintle, Angela. 2016. "Phil Redmond: 'I was a Marxist—strongly opposed to inheritance tax'". *The Telegraph*, 7 February 2016. http://www.telegraph.co.uk/finance/personalfinance/fameandfortune/12140684/Phil-Redmond-I-was-a-Marxist-strongly-opposed-to-inheritance-tax.html (accessed 5 May 2017).
Wood, Andy. 2009. "'Original London Style': London Posse and the Birth of British Hip Hop". *Atlantic Studies* 6.2: 175–90. https://doi.org/10.1080/14788810902981050

Woods, Michael. 2011. *Rural*. Oxon: Routledge.
 https://doi.org/10.4324/9780203844304
Wylie, John. 2007. *Landscape*. London: Routledge.
Yamakoshi, Hidetsugu, and Yasumasa Sekine. 2016. "Graffiti/Street Art in Tokyo and Surrounding Districts". In *Routledge Handbook of Graffiti and Street Art*, edited by Jeffrey Ian Ross, 345–56. Oxon: Routledge.
Young, Robert J. C. 2008. *The Idea of English Ethnicity*. Oxford: Blackwell.
Youngquist, Paul. 2016. *A Pure Solar World: Sun Ra and the Birth of Afrofuturism*. Texas: University of Texas Press.

Filmography

Ahearn, Charlie. 2000. *Wild Style*. London: VCI. VHS.
Bertoglio, Edo. 2000. *Downtown 81*. London: ILC Prime. DVD.
Davidson, Sue. 1987. *Open Space, Bad Meaning Good*. London: BBC2.
D'Cruz, Jaimie. 2016. *The Hip Hop World News*. London: BBC4.
Derby-Cooper, Sam, and Claude Knight. 2016. *NG83 When We Were Bboys*. Nottingham: NG83 Productions. DVD.
Dunn, Alexander. 2015. *808*. Los Angeles: You Know Films. Amazon Prime Video.
Fontaine, Dick. 1984. *Beat This! A Hip Hop History*. BBC. VHS.
Holman, Michael. 2002. *Graffti Rock*. New York: MTH Productions. DVD.
Silver, Tony, and Henry Chalfant. 2006. *Style Wars: Revisited*. Pennsylvania: MDV Visual. DVD.

Discography

Afrika Bambaataa & the Soul Sonic Force. 1982. 'Planet Rock'. New York: Tommy Boy. Vinyl 12".
Broken Glass. 1984. 'Style of the Street'. London: Streetwave. Vinyl 12".
Def Defiance. 1990. *Music Fusion!* Exeter: DD Shack Productions. Cassette tape.
Def Defiance. 1992. *Hazardous*. Exeter: DD Shack Productions. Cassette tape.
Def Defiance. 2016. *Hazardous*. Berlin: DD Britcore Rawmance. Vinyl album.
Def Defiance. 2016. *Music Fusion!* Berlin: DD Britcore Rawmance. Vinyl EP.
D.J. Scott La Rock, Blastmaster KRS-One & D-Nice. 1986. 'South Bronx/The "P" Is Free'. New York: B-Boy Records. Vinyl 12".
Funkmaster Wizard Wiz. 1986. 'Crack It Up'. Tuff City. Vinyl 12".
Hijack. 1988. 'Hold No Hostage/Doomsday Of Rap'. London: Music of Life. Vinyl 12".
London Posse. 1987. 'London Posse'. London: Big Life. Vinyl 12".

Mad Professor & Pato Banton. 1985. *Mad Professor Captures Pato Banton*. London: Ariwa. Vinyl album.
The Organization. 1985. 'The Big Beat'. LA: Techno Hop Records. Vinyl 12".
Rammellzee vs. K-Rob. 1983. 'Beat Bop'. New York: Profile Records. Vinyl 12".
Various Artists. 1983. *Street Sounds Electro 1*. London: Street Sounds. Vinyl album.
Various Artists. 1983. *The Perfect Beat*. London: 21 Records. Vinyl album.
Various Artists. 1984. *Beat Street (Original Motion Picture Soundtrack)—Vol. 2*. New York: Atlantic. Vinyl album.
Various Artists. 1984. *Breakdance Fever*. Köln: Jive. Vinyl album.
Various Artists. 1984. *Hip Hop—the Original and Best*. London: Charisma Records. Vinyl album.
Various Artists. 1984. *Street Sounds Crucial Electro 2*. London: Street Sounds. Vinyl album.
Various Artists. 1984. *Street Sounds UK Electro*. London: Street Sounds. Vinyl album.
Various Artists. 1985. *Rap Graffiti*. London: Charly Records. Vinyl album.
Various Artists. 1987. *Known 2 Be Down*. London: Positive Beat Records. Vinyl album.
Various Artists. 1989. *1989 Hustlers Convention Live*. London: Music of Life. Vinyl album.

Glossary of Terms

battle, battling

A battle can arise between crews or individuals to deal with a disagreement. Battling takes place within all hip hop practices, and a key component of hip hop knowledge and the hip hop state of mind is understanding and practising battle skills and techniques. Battle tactics include but are not limited to: intimidation, exercising strength, power, skills and knowledge greater than that of one's opponent; and dissing, ridiculing, and generally flexing with more style, creativity and artistry than one's opponent and in more exacting synergy with the music. Battles are often peer-reviewed or judged by audiences or peer-practitioners with specialisms in the practice in question.

Bboy, Bgirl

Those that practise the art of Bboying.

Bboying

The practice of breakdancing, popping, locking, often executed within peer group, recreation, practice, performance or battle scenarios. The earliest forms of Bboying appeared during the mid-1970s, although closely related dance moves have been evidenced in Kaduna, Nigeria, as early as 1950.

beatbox (human), beatboxing

The act of emulating a breakbeat, beat or rhythm by using one's vocal chords, mouth and other body parts (hands, face and throat). Popularized by Doug E. Fresh, The Human Beat Box (Fat Boys), and Biz Markie, beatboxing, similar to *turntablism*, has become a practice that also exists outside the conventional parameters of hip hop culture.

bite, biter

To *bite* is to copy and is seen as the lowest form of practice. A *biter* is one who bites and will not easily reclaim any credibility once the *bite* has been proved or demonstrated, as biting is seen as the opposite to originality, which all practising headz strive for.

boombox

The name given to an upright, portable cassette player. When evaluating the boombox its presence is as important as its sound. Size, output and frequency range are contributing factors to the appeal of the boombox. Three of the most desirable boomboxes linked to hip hop culture are the Sharp GF-777, the JVC RC-M90 and the Lasonic TRC-931. *Boombox* has thankfully replaced the derogatory term, ghetto blaster.

britcore

A term popularized by German audiences in the mid-1990s to describe hardcore British hip hop by crews such as Hardnoise, Killa Instinct, and Gunshot. Britcore is typified by fast-paced beats accompanied by industrial and aggressive noise samples, furious cuts and scratches, and quick-fire lyrical delivery. It should be noted that britcore is a reflective and post-rationalized term in that it was invented much later than the style of music it describes. There remains a core audience in Germany and surrounding European countries that continue to champion the britcore sound, with many artists continuing to make music that aspires to the britcore sound of the late 1980s and early 1990s.

crews

A group of *headz*, also known as a posse, clique or troop; music groups and label mates are often referred to as *crews*, although the term originated through graffiti crews and Bboy crews.

cutting

A development of scratching; cutting employs a slide, rotary, or cross-fader to cut undesirable sounds (usually those sounds on pull-back) from certain moments during the record's movement resulting in greater clarity of edit in the resulting sound.

deck

Alternative word for a turntable or record player.

dig, digging

The act of searching for records either to collect, sample, or draw inspiration from. The deeper one digs increases one's knowledge and chance of finding new beats previously undiscovered and is part of the strive for originality.

DJing

The umbrella term for the practice of mixing, cutting and/or scratching; the practice of performing with or without an emcee. First popularized in hip hop by DJ Kool Herc in the early to mid-1970s.

emcee (MC)

One who practises the art of rap within the broader context of hip hop performance and culture. Emcee is the true term for a rapper who also commands a live show, can freestyle and perform in a cypher, and has a broader palette of skills than simply an ability to rap. The term derives from "Master of Ceremony" (and alternatively "Microphone Controller").

graff, graf

An abbreviation of graffiti.

graffiti writer/writing

Graffiti existed before the other elements of hip hop culture, and was, in many ways, absorbed by the development of hip hop as a visual, contextual and spatial anchorage which helped bring visibility to hip hop culture. Graffiti in terms of hip hop's forefather, can be evidenced during the mid-1960s. I intentionally avoid the term graffiti artist, arguing that graffiti is first and foremost a socio- and spatio-political act.

hip hop headz/headz

Often used in place of "folks", or "people", a hip hop head or simply a head is a person who is submerged in hip hop culture, and who embraces hip hop culture fully, more so than just consuming hip hop music or listening to hip hop. A head holds hip hop knowledge and will be well versed in hip hop history and its practices.

jam

Jam has three distinct meanings: firstly, a *jam* is an event, a party, or a concert; secondly, a *jam* is a record, a track or a song; and thirdly, it is also used in the conventional form of an abbreviation of the jamboree.

knowledge

Hip hop knowledge envelops hip hop history, musicology, contextual positioning, Afrofuturism, African American histories, social histories, politics, humanities, knowledge of self and one's state of mind, and other fields of study connected with the development, improvement and contribution of new teaching and learning within hip hop culture. Brought into hip hop's cultural arena by Brother D, Rammellzee and K-Rob, and Afrika Bambaataa & Soulsonic Force during the early 1980s, and expanded by artists such as Public Enemy, X-Clan, Poor Righteous Teachers, and KRS-One.

lock/lockin'

Similar to *poppin'*, but with more jolts and freezes.

masterpiece/piece

Fully executed graffiti works which will often display a wide range of colour, technique, letters, characters and backgrounds. It is usual practice for a piece to occupy the entirety of its site.

mixing

The practice of blending one record with another, often with the aim to achieve new syncopated beats/rhythms and/or smooth transition from one beat/rhythm to another. The origin of this practice lies in extending the breakdown part of records to extend the percussion break to infuse the dynamism of Bboying. Originally attributed to Francis Grasso, mixing was practised by DJ Kool Herc and later perfected by Grandmaster Flash.

pop/poppin'

A dance move or series of moves where dancers tense and jolt their muscles and joints in a short spasm to create movement.

rapper

One who practises the art of rap (not necessarily within hip hop culture).

rapping and emceeing (MCing)

The practice of reciting poetry, lyrics, spoken word narratives in rhyme and rhythm, often accompanied by a beat, but also practised a capella. Emceeing differs from rapping in that emceeing also encompasses hosting a situation, building an atmosphere and overseeing a performance, as opposed to the purely technical practice of rapping which is fundamental to delivering raps.

As a result of these differing practices, there is also a marked difference between a rapper and an emcee (MC).

sampler/sampling

During the late 1980s the sampler became a critical component in the making of hip hop music. Pioneered by producers such as Marley Marl and Mantronik, and developed by artists such as Large Professor, Pete Rock, J Dilla and Q-Tip, sampled-based hip hop has become the cornerstone of hip hop construction.

scratching

The practice of creating new sounds by engaging one's hand with a playing record, and rhythmically pulling and pushing the record back and forth while the needle sits within the groove at particular and identified points. Early experimentation soon discovered that direct drive turntables are best equipped for this practice. Grand Wizard Theodore is commonly credited with inventing the scratch in 1975.

turntablism

A later derivative of DJing developed in the 1990s, turntablism stretches the traditional boundaries of hip hop culture. Turntablism performances are often delivered with two or more DJs working simultaneously and create the entire sound purely with turntables.

uprock/uprockin'

Uprockin' is a style of Bboying where the dancers remain on their feet and emulate combat moves.

Index

1989 Hustlers Convention Live (album) 256–8
808 49, 141
    '808 Beats' (song) 125
    808 (film) 295*n*25
    Roland TR-808 47, 184

Adams, Ross 56, 74–6, 122, 157
Adidas 32, 173, 242, 249, 253, 312*n*35
Afrika Bambaataa 2, 26–7, 29, 46–9, 51, 53, 57, 60, 69, 165, 235, 295*n*21, 295*n*24, 296*n*27, 296*n*32, 329
Afrocentric 267, 314*n*58
Afrofuturism 51, 290, 296, 329
    Afrofuturist 2, 35, 51, 147, 267, 314*n*58
"Ahhhhh this stuff is really fresh" 136, 297*n*43, 304*n*14
AJ (Hardnoise) 201–2, 204–5
Allen, Mike 42, 155–6, 160–2, 175, 230, 305*n*30, 306*n*35 *see also* Capital Rap Show
alternative 138, 149, 179, 213, 228, 230, 250, 255, 264, 278
    education xvi, 235
    experience 179
    location 115
    records 155
    territory 104

architecture xii, 18–19, 81, 83–4, 105, 166, 218, 299*n*59
Arsonists 281
authentic 236, 298*n*49
    authenticity 149, 152–3, 236, 238, 259
authority 8–9, 33, 73, 81, 108, 151, 191, 199, 211, 215, 226
    cultural 197, 199
    local 185, 214
    state 229

Bad Meaning Good (film) 232–4, 259, 276
Baker, Arthur 36, 46–7, 49, 296*n*26, 296*n*30
Barthes, Roland 138–40, 146–7, 150–1
'Battle Cry' (song) 49, 57–8
battles 17, 29, 57, 81, 113, 174, 326
'Beat Bop' (song) 166
beatbox 124–5, 152, 233, 290*n*1, 304*n*19, 326
'Beatbox' (song) 57
Beat Street (film) 55–60, 74–5, 86, 90, 116, 126, 129, 279, 297*n*41–2, 298*n*53
Beat This!: A Hip Hop History (film) xiii, 51, 60–1, 69, 130, 149, 230, 295*n*18

Bhabha, Homi xii, 7, 9, 19, 72–3, 76, 82, 227, 230–1
'The Big Beat' (song) 159
Bionic 62–3, 71, 232–3 *see also* London Posse
black
 culture xiii–iv, 3, 231, 268, 269–70
 history 60, 202
 histories 3, 268
blackbooks 99
Blade (emcee) 11, 205–7, 211, 220, 239, 243, 245, 260, 309n23, 311n26
Blade (graffiti writer) 75
block party 24, 147–8, 291n1 *see also* block parties 14, 24, 44
Boogie Down Productions 24, 240, 267, 282
Bourdieu, Pierre xii, 7, 10, 149–51, 156, 159–60, 163–4, 169, 197, 199, 274
'Breaker's Revenge' (song) 49, 57, 80 *see also* Baker, Arthur
Break Machine xi, 116, 132, 298, 303
Breakdance Fever (album) 125, 131, 133, 139–40, 176, 280–1
Breakdance: The Movie (film) 55–60, 74, 116, 126, 296n35, 296n38
breaks xv, 23, 25, 110, 121, 169, 187, 189, 242, 244, 246, 286, 292n21, 293n1, 308n16, 311n20
Brent Aquasky 87–8, 97–8, 119, 122, 164, 233, 275, 302n27
'Bring Forth The Guillotine' (song) 244, 307n12, 311n27
Bristol xi, xv, 43, 99, 116, 163, 167, 192, 221, 234, 272, 280
britcore 11, 224, 238–41, 270, 277, 291n7, 310n15, 311n27, 311n28, 327 *see also* British hardcore
Britcore Rawmance 238, 240
British hardcore 200, 238, 240–2 *see also* britcore

Britishness 1, 8, 10, 37–8, 43–6, 172, 202, 225–6, 228–9, 231, 234–5, 243–5, 247, 250, 255, 258–9, 272, 295n16, 295n17, 309n4 *see also* Englishness
'Broadway' (song) 15, 166 *see also* Duke Bootee
Bronx, The xv, 13, 16, 28, 57, 61, 108, 128, 137, 291n1, 292n20 *see also* South Bronx
bus shelter 17, 41, 119, 180, 185, 307n11 *see also* shelter
Byrd, Gary 60–1, 77, 297n46

capitalism 16, 123, 177
 consumer-capitalism 16, 27
 industrial 16
Capital Rap Show 155–6, 160 *see also* Allen, Mike
Captain Rock 35, 51, 304n20
cassettes 5, 104, 114, 143, 160, 163, 174, 190, 290n3, 306n35, 307n7
Chad Jackson 130, 175, 245
Chris "The Glove" Taylor xii, 56–7, 296
Chrome 74, 255, 285, 299n66
Clash, The 134, 136, 253
Cobra P.I. (Agent/Rapid Fire) 221, 285
'Cockney Translation' (song) 233
Coke La Rock 25, 292n22
colonial 72–3 *see also* postcolonial
colonialism 37, 46, 226
colloquialism 224, 259, 261, 264, 274, 277, 299n61, 311n28
communities
 farming 39, 261
 hip hop 3 *see also* hip hop community
 mining 39
conflict 15, 37, 59, 69, 81, 96, 114, 123, 177, 212
conservatism 39–40

Coombes, Scott 42, 115, 137, 162, 227
Covent Garden 62–3, 280
Cowan, Mark 37, 103, 183, 228, 269
'Crack It Up' (song) 166–7
Craig Ellis Leckie 157, 163, 173, 177
Craig, Todd 236–8, 245–6
creative practice 1, 54, 125, 152, 178, 246, 260
Cullen, Sleician 287
cultural
    acquisition 7–8, 34, 72, 77, 272
    bricolage 40, 63, 66
    capital 149–54, 159, 267, 274, 277, 306n38
    context xii, 8, 10, 25, 29, 35, 50, 233, 243, 276–7
    distancing 20, 39–40, 161, 189, 230
    dynamics 12, 236
    exclusion 21
    heritage 3–4, 7, 9, 19, 38, 42, 60, 72, 75, 77, 83, 197, 260, 267
    hybridity 9–10, 274
    identity 44, 225–6, 228 *see also* local identity
    positioning 8, 11, 20
    practice 3, 33, 76, 123, 151, 274, 283, 302n28
    production 11, 29, 82, 104, 149, 168, 193, 196–9, 217, 273
    shift 77, 305n33
    triad 35, 40, 72
Cutmaster Swift 245, 257–8, 312n30

Daddy Freddy 256–8
Dana Dane 15
Darren Norris aka Big Tunes D 75, 77, 104, 239, 294n8, 299n68
Dartnell, Tom 92, 129, 162, 286, 294n10
Davy DMX 169–70
de Certeau, Michel 125
De Stijl 34, 145

decoding 118, 123, 176 *see also* recoding
Def Defiance xii, 186, 189–90, 192, 210–12, 220, 239, 277, 296
DeLanda, Manuel xii, 7, 10, 176, 182, 274–5, 291
Demon Boyz 43, 192, 198, 220, 239, 244–5, 256 *see also* Mike J
Denny, Simon 42
de-regionalism 12, 126, 274 *see also* regionalism
DevonAir 155–6, 189, 305n32, 308n19
diaspora 11, 42, 49, 51, 61, 267, 268, 280
    African 231
    Jamaican 260
    Jamaican-Caribbean 240
dig (for records) 10, 50, 61, 160, 165, 168–9, 291n6, 306n4, 328
    diggers 168–9, 180, 288, 306n41
    digging 11, 75, 165, 168–70, 184, 239, 283, 291n6, 306n41, 308n15, 328
distinction 6–7, 10, 29, 42, 44, 125, 149, 153, 165, 197–8, 250, 260, 297n42, 300n5
distribution 134, 143, 145, 149, 153–4, 243, 297n46
DIY (production) 126, 186, 188, 190–1, 200, 202, 239, 243, 280 *see also* do-it-yourself
DJ Baila 288–9
DJ Bex 115, 173, 217, 284–5
DJ Cheese 161, 175, 293n27
DJ Format 211, 251–2, 284
DJ Jamez Gant 168
DJ Kool Herc 13–14, 25–6, 57, 61, 77, 291n1, 292n22, 328–9
DJ Krash Slaughta 71, 103, 173, 175, 183, 221, 283
DJing 14, 26, 31, 59, 74, 76, 109–10, 183, 273, 290n1, 291n4, 297n44, 297n45, 328

DMC (Disco Mix Club) 30, 175, 245, 293n27, 312n30
do-it-yourself 45, 286 *see also* DIY (production)
Dolby Dee 131, 139, 303n11
domestic 5, 7, 9, 30, 94–5, 105, 113, 119, 150–1, 178, 185, 196, 217
    slaves 294n9
    space 93, 96–7, 106, 108
    rituals 96, 106
domesticity 9, 39, 80, 94, 97, 99, 109, 116
Dondi (White) 66–7, 70, 75, 86, 230, 292n11
'Doomsday Of Rap' (song) 200–1, 242, 245 *see also* Hijack
Doug E. Fresh 57, 143, 234, 306n38, 342
    and The Get Fresh Crew 136, 305n27
Dr Syntax 286
Dren Throwdown 105–8, 111, 143, 148, 157, 266
dromology 11, 172, 180, 182 *see also* Virilio, Paul
    dromosphere 7, 172, 180–2 *see also* Virilio, Paul
drum 'n' bass 31, 273, 280, 282, 301n11, 311n28
Duck Rock (album) 9, 62–7, 69, 128, 157, 298n54, 299n59, 299n66
"Duck Rocker" 66–8, 131
Duke Bootee 15, 116, 166

emceeing 6, 25, 56, 109, 149, 232, 273, 290n1
England 44, 93, 225, 228, 234, 257, 261, 278
Englishness 45, 225, 228, 295n16, 295n17 *see also* Britishness
environment 84, 96, 183, 185–6, 226, 237–8, 243, 280
    built 15–17, 21, 24, 39, 58, 71, 78, 96
    emulated 38
    graffiti 21
    music 15, 27
    natural 16–17
    rural 91, 145
    urban 85, 97, 123
Eraze 38, 52, 67, 98–9, 102, 110, 189, 229, 252, 264
ethnomusicology xii, 279
Europe xv, 11, 25, 36, 47, 58, 140, 202, 231, 236, 238, 255, 282, 302n2
Evil Ed 48, 76, 121, 142, 148, 162, 174–5, 185, 208–9, 260, 262, 268, 287, 306n38

Fab 5 Freddy 59, 134, 297n43
Fat Boys xii, xiv, 310, 326
Faze One 241, 253, 311n19
Fila 99, 249–50, 298n55, 312n35
flyers 5, 99, 104, 212
football
    casuals 250
    hooliganism 10, 37, 298n55, 301n22, 302n27, 312n36
    rivalry 194
Forman, Murray xii, 2, 15, 44, 81, 96, 108, 236, 261–2
Foucault, Michel xii, 7–8, 84, 91, 172, 214–16, 218–19
Frampton, Kenneth 19
funk 14, 23, 25, 29, 42, 47, 51, 57, 90, 134, 141, 165, 187, 189, 259, 268–9, 292n21, 296n26, 296n32, 297n46, 307n12, 311n22
    electro funk 42, 77, 231, 294n8, 305n33
    P-funk 242
Futura 2000 134, 136–8, 253

Gadamer, Hans-Georg 9, 54, 69

GeeSwift 285
globalization 31, 274 *see also*
  post-globalization
Grand Wizard Theodore 59, 246,
  297*n*44
Grandmaster Caz 28
Grandmaster Flash xi, 23, 30, 36,
  59, 63, 177, 246, 293*n*25, 297*n*40,
  307*n*5, 308*n*22, 310*n*18, 329
Groove Records 42, 153, 155–6, 160,
  163, 193–4, 294*n*8
    Groove Records charts 230

Hancock, Herbie 176, 298*n*53, 304*n*13
Hardnoise 43, 200–4, 210, 224, 244–5,
  307, 327
Hardrock Soul Movement xiv, 255
Haring, Keith 66, 88
Harlem 3, 8, 15, 24–5, 69, 84, 282
Harris, Simon 43, 148, 256 *see also*
  Music of Life
Hebdige, Dick 8, 11, 68, 147, 149, 196,
  234–5
Heidegger, Martin 105–8
Herbie (Exeter) 112–4, 301*n*18
hermeneutic 9, 69
heterotopia 8, 10, 25, 123, 172,
  214–19, 221–2, 235
Hidden Identity 208–11, 260–2, 277
hierarchy 152, 197, 212–14, 219
Hijack 11, 43, 45, 190, 192, 200–1,
  203, 207, 210, 224, 232, 242–5, 263,
  307*n*12, 311*n*24
hip hop
  artefacts 104, 151, 235, 277
  community 224, 238, 248, 264–6,
    299*n*61, 313*n*43
  education xvi, 40, 51, 53, 61,
    137, 179, 235, 269–70, 287–8
  grime 263, 280, 282
  habitus 41, 149, 153, 155,
    158–60, 163–4, 170, 274

practice xii–xiii, 1, 9, 11–12, 57,
    59–60, 66, 83, 104, 108, 123,
    140, 149, 164–5, 219, 232, 277,
    279–81, 287, 308*n*20, 326
  praxis 7, 13, 75, 83, 299*n*69
  regional xiii, 12, 113, 163, 178,
    220–2, 273, 276–7, 279
  rural 41, 121, 263, 280, 282,
    302*n*27
Hip Hop—the Original and Best
  (album) 125, 127–8, 130–2, 149
'Hip Hop/Reggae Connection' (song)
  253–4
Hip Hop World News (film) 62–3
HMV 34, 141, 144, 153, 167–8, 189
horror 241–5, 262

Ice Cream Promotions 212–13, 215
Ice-T xii, 57, 296
ideology 4–6, 18, 39, 227–8, 293*n*4
Independent (newspaper) 100
intertextual 261

Jackie Chat 278–9
James Brown 134, 168, 241–2, 244,
  259, 292*n*14, 296*n*32, 309*n*23
Jeffrey Daniel 63
Junior Disprol 152, 234, 251, 265, 285

Kangol 32–3, 252
Khan, Morgan 34, 36, 117, 125, 140,
  241, 255, 304–5, 310 *see also*
  Streetwave
Killa Instinct 221, 244, 327
Kilo xv, 47, 61, 86, 89–90, 98, 101–2,
  104, 110, 113–14, 190–1, 193–6,
  209, 223, 251, 276, 298*n*48, 301*n*19,
  308*n*17, 314*n*1
KISS FM 167, 232
Kit (YML) 270
Known 2 Be Down (album) 249–50,
  252–6, 312*n*37

Krack Free Media 239, 277
Kraftwerk xi, 47, 56, 248
Kurtis Blow xii, 26–7, 36, 292–3, 301

Laidley, Herbie (Mastermind) 147–8, 176, 304*n*21
Laswell, Bill 134, 138, 304*n*13
Lefebvre, Henri xii, 7, 9, 16, 19, 24, 39, 82–3, 109, 117–18, 282, 306, 319*n*
Lemon Grove, The 198, 213–14, 216–18, 220
liminal space 17, 81–2, 221
LL Cool J xiv, 32, 232, 240, 252
local identity 10, 45, 275
localism 11, 15
lo-fi 5, 10–11, 125, 172, 254
London Posse 43, 45–6, 62, 190, 208, 231, 232–5, 240, 242, 245, 301*n*15, 312*n*37
'Looking For The Perfect Beat' (song) 47–9, 295*n*24, 296*n*26

Mantronik 240, 330
    Mantronix xiv, 187, 242, 306
Massey, Doreen 19
materialism 92, 236, 260, 303*n*10
MC Duke 43, 198, 215–19, 257
MC Shan 32, 240, 252, 282
MC Squared 259
McLaren, Malcolm xi, xiii, 36, 46, 60, 62, 68, 70–1, 74, 88–9, 127–8, 131, 179, 230, 252, 303
megamix 47, 136, 174–6, 295*n*22, 307*n*4
Melle Mel 57, 132, 174, 176, 292*n*10, 297*n*40, 298*n*53, 311*n*22
Merlin 257–8
metalanguage 139–40
metropolis 7, 14, 17, 20, 34–5, 38–40, 85, 97, 117, 155, 167, 224, 260, 281
    metropolises 4, 14, 85

Michael "Spider" Hooper 55, 301*n*19
microcosm 109, 186, 199
Mike J 257–8 *see also* Demon Boyz
Mike Mac 157, 207, 237, 310*n*14
Miller, Daniel 151
mimicry 7, 9, 72–6, 82–3, 149, 299*n*69
mixing 23, 69, 111, 113, 131, 147–8, 174–5, 194, 232, 293*n*27, 307*n*4, 308*n*16, 328 *see also* pause-button
Moses, Robert 16, 21, 84
multicultural 4, 38, 43, 226–7
    multiculturalism xi, xv, 4, 45–6, 226, 228–9
Music of Life 43, 190, 198, 200, 208, 242, 255–6, 258

Nat Drastic 57, 178, 226, 229, 284
National Fresh 155, 305*n*35 *see also* Capital Rap Show
nationhood 225, 227, 229
nation-state xv, 45, 52, 81, 214, 229–30, 235, 247
neoliberalization 123
Newcleus xiv, 34, 42, 51, 147, 202
Nice One 71
non-place 58, 297*n*42
Northern Ireland xiii, 93–4, 157, 225, 295*n*17
Numskullz 278, 296*n*36, 296*n*37 *see also* Def Defiance

Operation Anderson 99–100, 192, 198, 264
'Operation Trident' (song) 253–4
Otis, Samuel 263–4, 278
Our Price 34, 141, 144, 163

Packman, The 34–5, 147
Papa Speng 253–4, 313*n*41
Parker 60, 76, 306*n*36
pastiche 17, 112
Pato Banton 233, 310*n*10

pause-button 124, 175, 177–9, 183
  mix(es) 148, 172, 174–5, 177, 179, 182, 184, 307n3
  mixing 177, 307n3
Peel, John 17, 121, 124–5, 148, 156–9, 163, 167, 180–1, 185, 305n23, 306n36
Perfect Beat (album) 47–8, 52–3, 55
'Perpetrating Frauds' (song) 190, 266 *see also* Def Defiance
pioneers 3, 21, 33, 57, 59–60, 62, 74, 110, 187, 231, 235, 241
'Planet Rock' (song) 27, 36, 46–8, 51, 61, 295n19, 295n21, 295n24
police 58, 99, 115, 197–9, 206, 291n4, 302n22, 313n38
  British Transport Police 198
  harassment 36, 253
  'Police Officer' (song) 233, 310n9
postcolonial 7, 70, 263
post-globalization 45, 274 *see also* globalization
productivity 139–40, 149
provincial positivism 14, 271
Public Enemy 165, 193, 200, 206, 224, 232, 240, 264, 267, 309n23, 311n24, 329
punk 44–5, 65, 68–9, 134, 190, 229, 239, 243
  pop-punk 68, 303n4, 304n13
  post-punk 38, 68, 134, 136
  punk rock 44, 62

Queensbridge 15

racism 61, 226, 245, 253, 262, 271
  structural and structured xv, 36, 301n15
ragga 257–9, 266, 313n40
  raggamuffin 258, 262
Rakim 12, 20–1, 240

Rap Graffiti (album) 125, 132, 134–8, 304n13
'Rapper's Delight' (song) 15, 27–9, 36
Rapski 249, 253
Rawman 240
(re)appropriation 13, 24, 30, 67, 70
recoding 92, 109, 118, 123, 176 *see also* decoding
reggae 25, 29, 46, 232–5, 240, 253–4, 258–9, 280, 282, 292n21, 294n12, 298n51, 310n10
regionalism 8–9, 11–12, 18–19, 75, 78, 109, 121, 126, 225, 235, 247, 270, 274, 276–7, 279 *see also* de-regionalism
reifications xiv, 36, 42, 55, 74, 77, 90, 109, 164, 177, 225, 246, 267, 272–4, 276, 279, 281
Remark 38, 226–7, 296n28
Remer 100, 198
Requiem89 239
Richard "Rumage" Cowling 56, 296n37
Richie B 122
Ricky Also 87, 161, 266, 286
robotics 23, 56, 74–5, 104
Rock Steady Crew 52–3, 57, 69–71, 85, 128–9, 131, 230, 276, 298n53, 300n3, 303n4
Rodney P 62, 71, 233, 298n50 *see also* London Posse
Rola xii, 58, 67, 103, 110, 113, 116, 171, 187, 189–90, 193–5, 198, 210, 214, 248–9, 254, 266, 284–5, 296n36 *see also* Def Defiance
Rollefson, J. Griffith xv, 36, 283, 314n58
Rose, Tricia xii, 2
Run-D.M.C. xiv, 32, 130, 241–2, 251, 253, 311n22, 312n30
rural graffiti 91
rurality 17, 91–2, 119, 123, 161, 232, 260, 282, 285, 302n28

sample 65, 136, 169, 178, 187, 240–2, 244, 248, 311n20, 313*n*40
   sampler 179, 187, 240, 330
   sampling 107, 149, 168–9, 187, 224, 244, 307*n*12, 308*n*14, 310*n*17
Scarse 92, 101–2, 210, 213–14
Scotland xiii, 37, 50, 103, 129, 225, 228, 295*n*17
semantics 117–18, 138, 200, 277, 295*n*17
semiotics 117–18, 138–9
Serious Records 141, 307*n*4
ShellToeMel 129, 284
shelter 119–22, 189 *see also* bus shelter
Shure SM-58 32, 110, 218
sign 131, 138–40, 162, 248, 252, 262
   signifier 139–40, 230
Silver Bullet 239, 244, 261, 307, 311
Sir Drew 249, 253
Si Spex 55, 75, 111, 143, 158, 168
sleeve design (record) xiv, 11, 52, 90, 118, 129, 131, 145, 176, 181, 200, 208, 252, 255, 281, 302*n*2, 304*n*20
Smiley Culture 233, 235, 310*n*9
social
   cohesion 45
   engagement 269
   histories 283, 329
   practice 45, 261
   status 13, 219
   structures 39, 84, 150, 196
socialism 39–40
   socialist 294*n*6
sociolinguistics 7
socio-political 51, 61, 73, 165, 170, 206, 265, 271, 283, 293*n*4
Soja, Edward 9, 19, 82–3, 109
soul (music) 23, 25, 29, 42, 132, 134, 141, 187, 189, 232, 268–9, 280, 292n21
Soulsonic Force/Soul Sonic Force 26–7, 46, 48–51, 57, 60, 165, 296*n*27

South Bronx 3, 8, 15, 24–5, 69, 84, 282
   see also Bronx, The
sovereignty 18
spatial *see also* spatio-cultural
   engagement 7, 24, 82
   process 7
   production 7, 9, 24, 80, 82–3, 219
spatio-cultural 1, 9, 15, 17–18, 29, 40, 84, 123, 282
Specifik xv, 129, 141, 168, 175, 202, 239, 270
status 4, 7, 30, 40, 44, 72, 132, 152–3, 185, 212, 215, 245, 276, 279–80, 293*n*1, 300*n*2, 311*n*29
   class 33
   commercial 27
   social 13, 219
Stepchild 47, 152, 161, 208, 229, 231, 263, 271
Street Sounds Electro (album series) xii–xiii, 36, 42, 116, 125, 130, 140–1, 143, 145–6, 156, 175, 187, 230, 255, 301*n*20, 304*n*12
   Street Sounds Electro 1 (album) xii–xiii, 34, 140, 142–3, 304n20, 304n21
   Street Sounds Electro 5 (album) 74, 112, 305*n*22
   Street Sounds Electro 6 (album) 304*n*19
   Street Sounds Crucial Electro 1 (album) 143, 176
   Street Sounds Crucial Electro 2 (album) 47
   Street Sounds UK Electro (album) 255–6
Streetwave 117, 140, 144–5, 156, 255, 304*n*15, 305*n*29, 310*n*19, 313*n*42
   see also Khan, Morgan
Style Wars (film) 36, 55, 59, 74, 86, 95, 116, 129, 252, 279, 291*n*3, 291*n*9, 292*n*11, 292*n*13
suburbs 16, 155, 232

Such 91–3
Sugar Hill Records xiv, 28, 116, 141, 154–5, 176, 307n5
Sugarhill Gang 27–8, 36, 231
Swindon 163 *see also* Stepchild
synth 47, 105, 107, 127, 129, 188
    synth-pop 303n4, 304n20

tags 95, 97, 99, 119, 129, 137, 163, 273, 300n9
Taki 183 14, 137, 291n3
Taylor, Neil 164, 207, 213, 258, 268–9, 275
Thatcherism 10, 109, 227–9, 240, 245, 293n3, 301n15
Third Space (Bhabha) 7, 9, 82
Thirdspace (Soja) 9, 82–3, 109
Thornton, Sarah 151–2
T La Rock 32, 240
Tommy Boy Records xii, 46–8, 154–5, 176, 255, 296, 307
Toop, David xii, 2, 26, 134, 136–8, 292n13, 292n20, 292n23
Top Of The Pops (television show) 36, 63, 74, 293n1
transatlantic xii, 3, 7–8, 36, 90, 145, 166, 260, 279
transformer (scratch) 183, 262
transmission 39, 118, 123, 151
    radio 126
turntable(s) 9, 30–2, 52, 57, 62, 104–5, 131, 137, 169, 175, 179, 183, 211, 246, 249, 258, 288, 293n28, 327, 330
    SL-1200 (Technics) 30–2, 293n30
    SL-1210 (Technics) 30, 293n30

Ultimate Breaks & Beats (album series) 187, 308n14, 308n15, 311n20
Uncle Colin 143, 163
Union Jack 255
Unknown DJ 124–5, 141
urban myth 125, 138, 281–2

vandalism 4, 30, 83, 100
Verbal Wurzels 263–4, 278
vernacular 9, 18, 28–9, 66, 81, 96, 105, 277, 310n6 *see also* colloquialism
    cockney 258
    language 224, 274
    local 209, 259, 261
    London 224
    styles 265
Virilio, Paul xii, 7, 11, 172, 180, 307 *see also* dromosphere

Wales xiii, 37, 225, 234, 265, 278, 295n17
Wall of Fame 102, 223, 309n1, 309n2
West Street Mob xii, 147
Whirlwind D xv, 141, 146, 237, 241, 304n18, 311n21
'White Lines (Don't Don't Do It)' (song) 126, 132, 174, 176–7, 252, 298n53
white majority space xv, 83
WHSmith 34, 141, 280
Wild Bunch, The 43, 294
Wild Style (film) 36, 55, 58–9, 86, 95–7, 129, 137, 157, 252, 279, 292n13, 298n53
Williams, Justin A. xv, 310n17
Woods, Michael 16, 91, 282
Woolworths 141, 280
World's Famous Supreme Team xi, 62–3, 68–71, 88–9, 127–9, 131, 230, 298n49
"writer's bench" 119, 302n27

Yardie 232–3, 235, 250, 258, 260, 278, 310n7

Z-3 MCs 117, 153, 302n24
Zulu Nation (Universal) 26, 49, 89–90, 165, 295n21, 296n32

www.ingramcontent.com/pod-product-compliance
Lightning Source LLC
Chambersburg PA
CBHW050846240426
43667CB00022B/2934